Say I Love You.

4

by
Kanae Hazuki

Kanae Hazuki
presents

Chapter 13

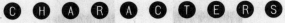

CHARACTERS

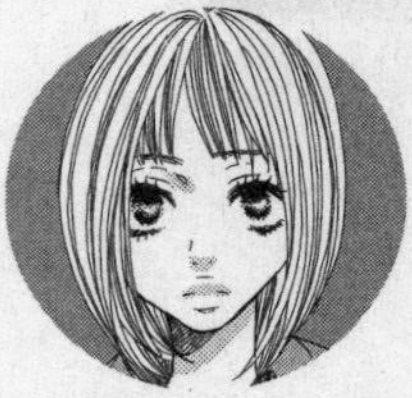

Mei Tachibana

A girl who hasn't had a single friend, let alone a boyfriend, in sixteen years, and has lived her life trusting no one. She finds herself attracted to Yamato, who, for some reason, just won't leave her alone, and they start dating.

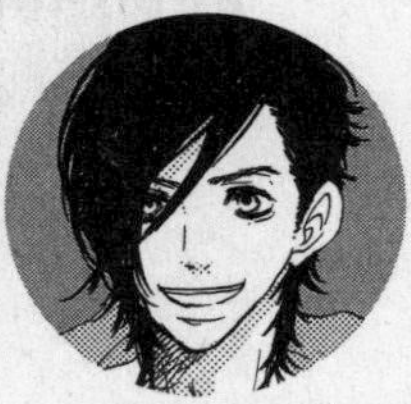

Yamato Kurosawa

The most popular boy at Mei's school. He has the love of many girls, yet for some reason, he is obsessed with Mei, the brooding weirdo girl from another class.

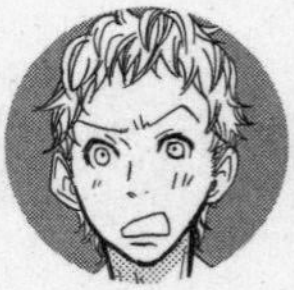

Yamato's friend and Mei's classmate. He used to harass Mei, which is how Mei and Yamato met.

Nakanishi

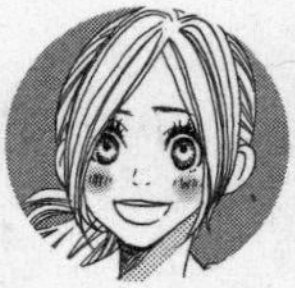

A girl in Mei's class who admires Yamato. Unlike her other classmates, she interacts with Mei just as she interacts with everyone else. She has started dating Yamato's friend Nakanishi.

Asami

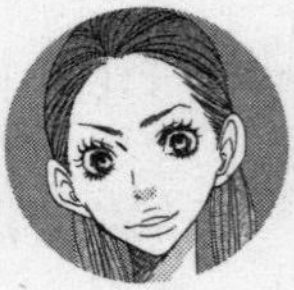

She likes Yamato and was jealous of Mei, but now that she has seen Mei trying so hard to confront her own insecurities, it seems she has acknowledged Mei's efforts...?

Aiko

An amateur model who has her sights set on Yamato. She has transferred to Mei and Yamato's school and is in Yamato's class. She learned that Mei is his girlfriend and apologized for her behavior, but then she invited Yamato to model for her magazine.

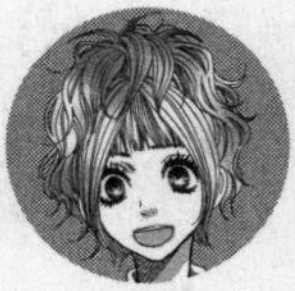

Megumi

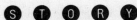

STORY

Mei Tachibana spent sixteen years without a single friend or boyfriend. One day she accidentally injured Yamato Kurosawa, the most popular boy in her school. Ironically, that made him like her, and he unilaterally decided that they were friends. He even kissed her like he meant it. Mei had a very difficult time opening her heart, but she was gradually drawn in by Yamato's kindness and sincerity, and they started dating. Mei realized that she was in love, and she began to awaken to her femininity, but then Megumi, an amateur model who had her eyes on Yamato, transferred to their school and invited Yamato to model with her. For the first time, Mei feels distanced from Yamato...

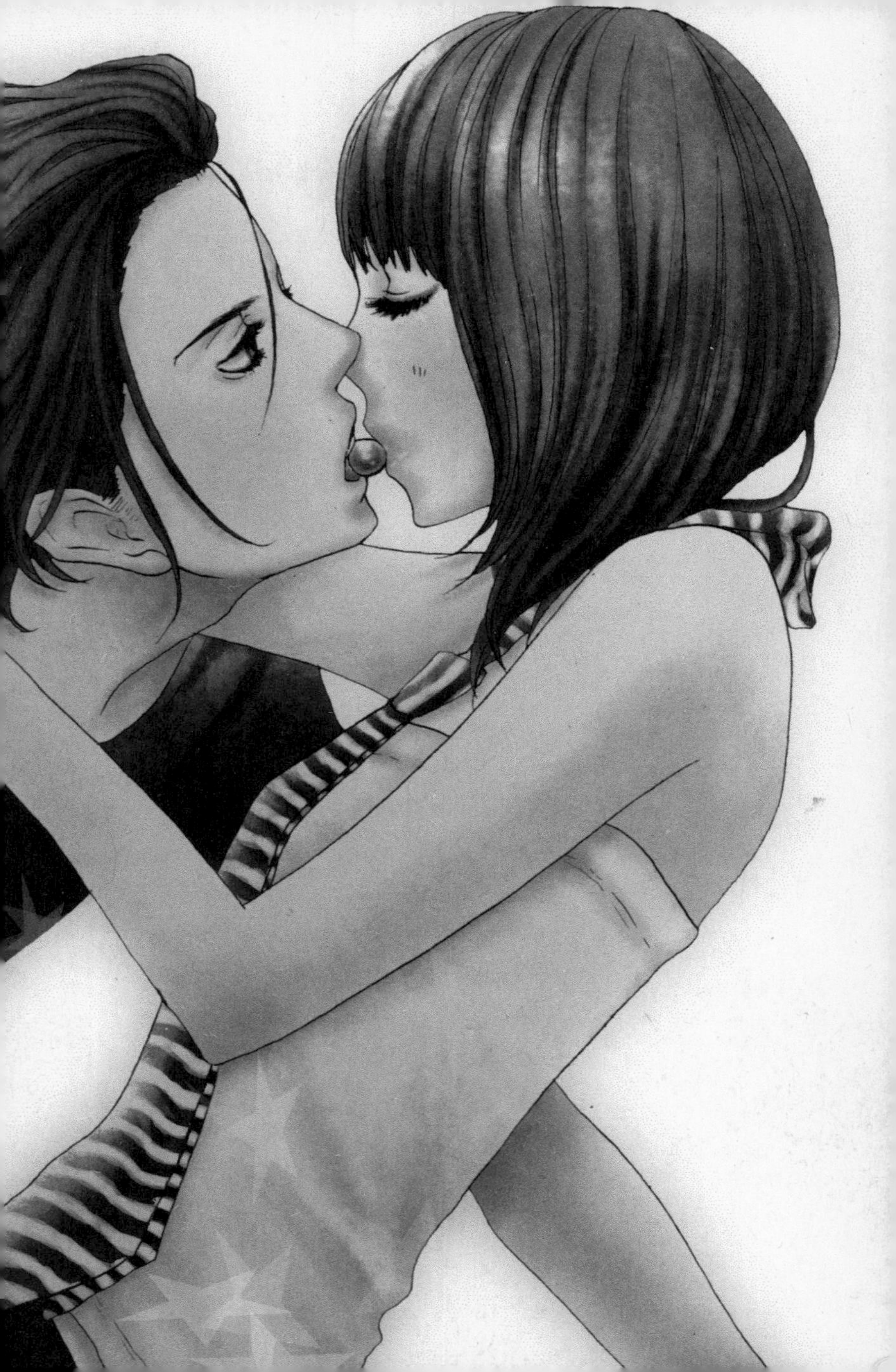

Chapter 13

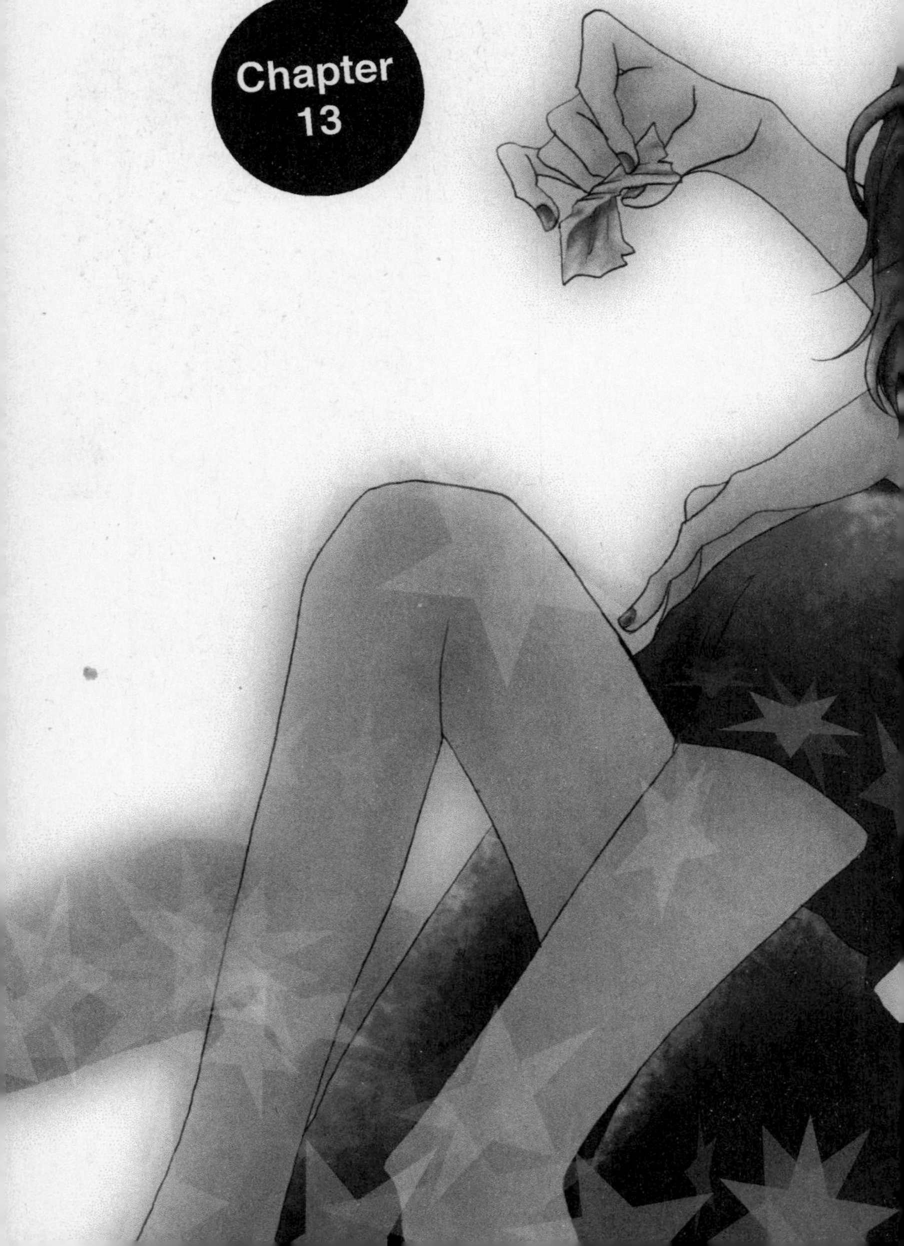

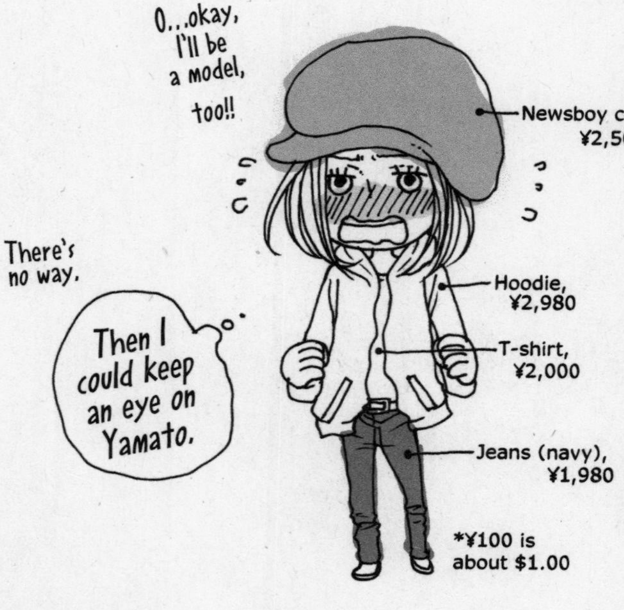
O...okay, I'll be a model, too!!
Newsboy cap, ¥2,500 *
There's no way.
Then I could keep an eye on Yamato.
Hoodie, ¥2,980
T-shirt, ¥2,000
Jeans (navy), ¥1,980
*¥100 is about $1.00

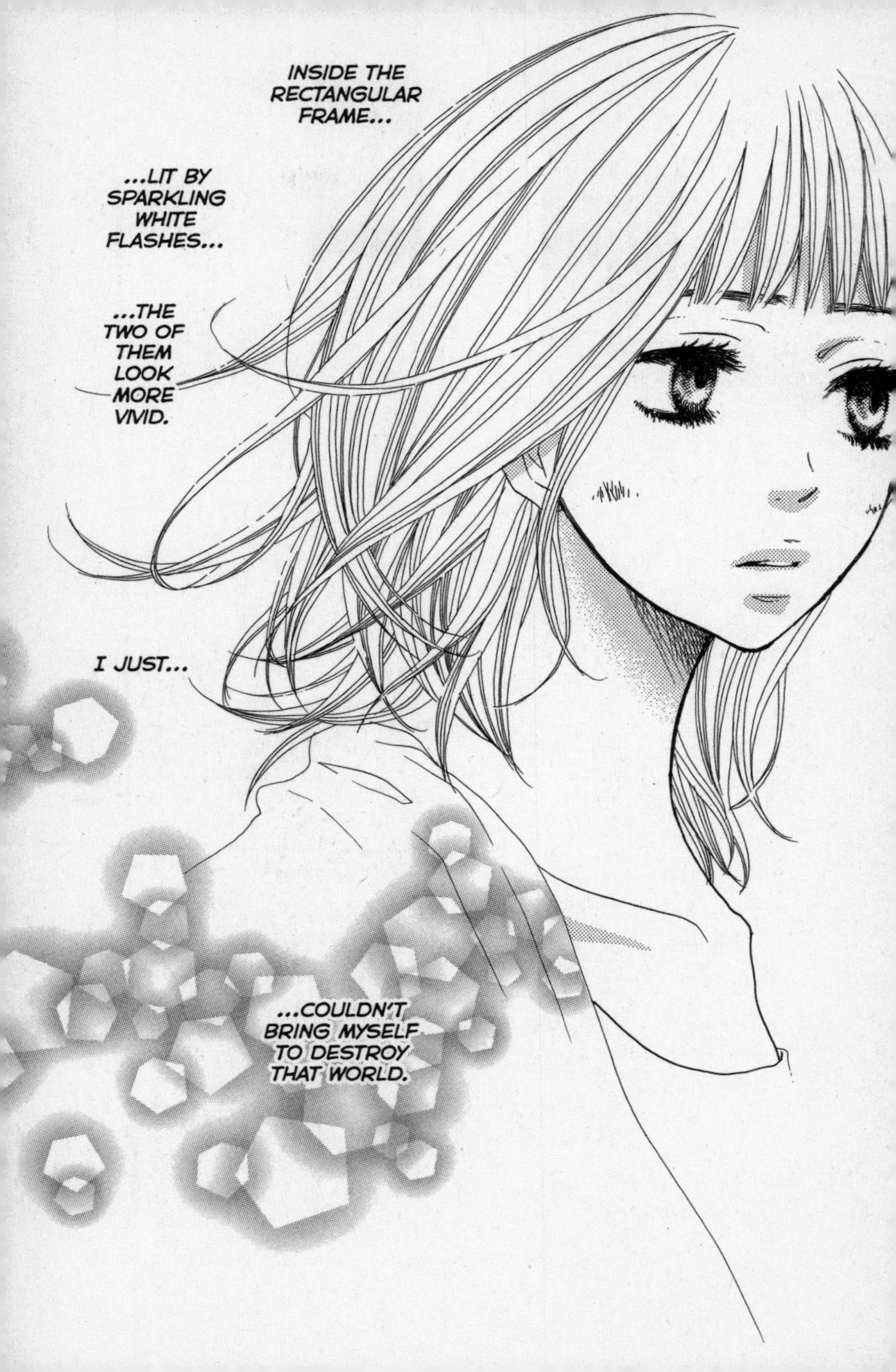
INSIDE THE RECTANGULAR FRAME...
...LIT BY SPARKLING WHITE FLASHES...
...THE TWO OF THEM LOOK MORE VIVID.
I JUST...
...COULDN'T BRING MYSELF TO DESTROY THAT WORLD.

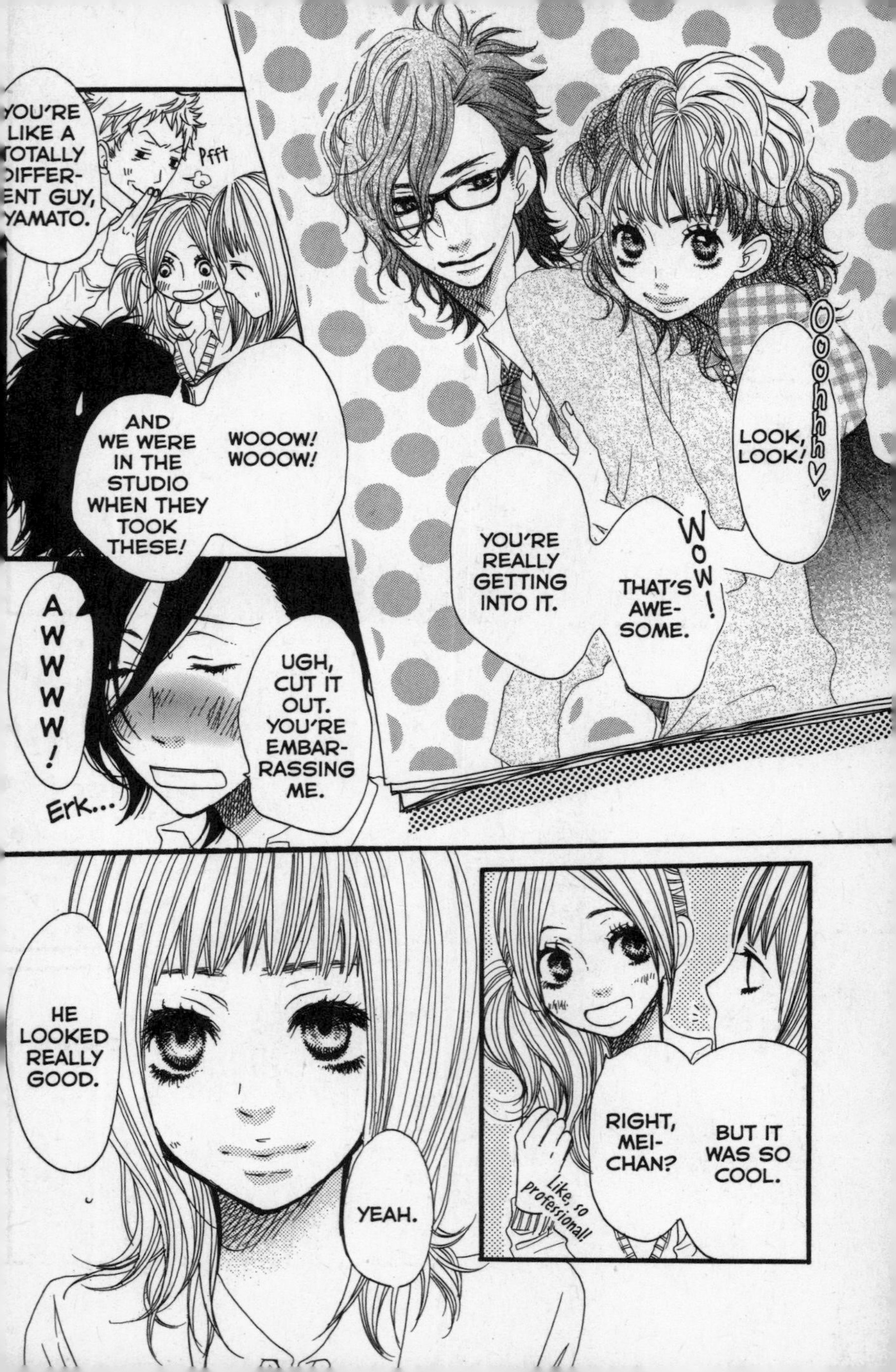

Ooohhh♡
LOOK, LOOK!
WOW!
THAT'S AWESOME.
YOU'RE REALLY GETTING INTO IT.
YOU'RE LIKE A TOTALLY DIFFERENT GUY, YAMATO.
Pfft
WOOOW! WOOOW!
AND WE WERE IN THE STUDIO WHEN THEY TOOK THESE!
UGH, CUT IT OUT. YOU'RE EMBARRASSING ME.
AWWWWW!
Erk...
BUT IT WAS SO COOL.
RIGHT, MEI-CHAN?
Like, so professional!
YEAH.
HE LOOKED REALLY GOOD.

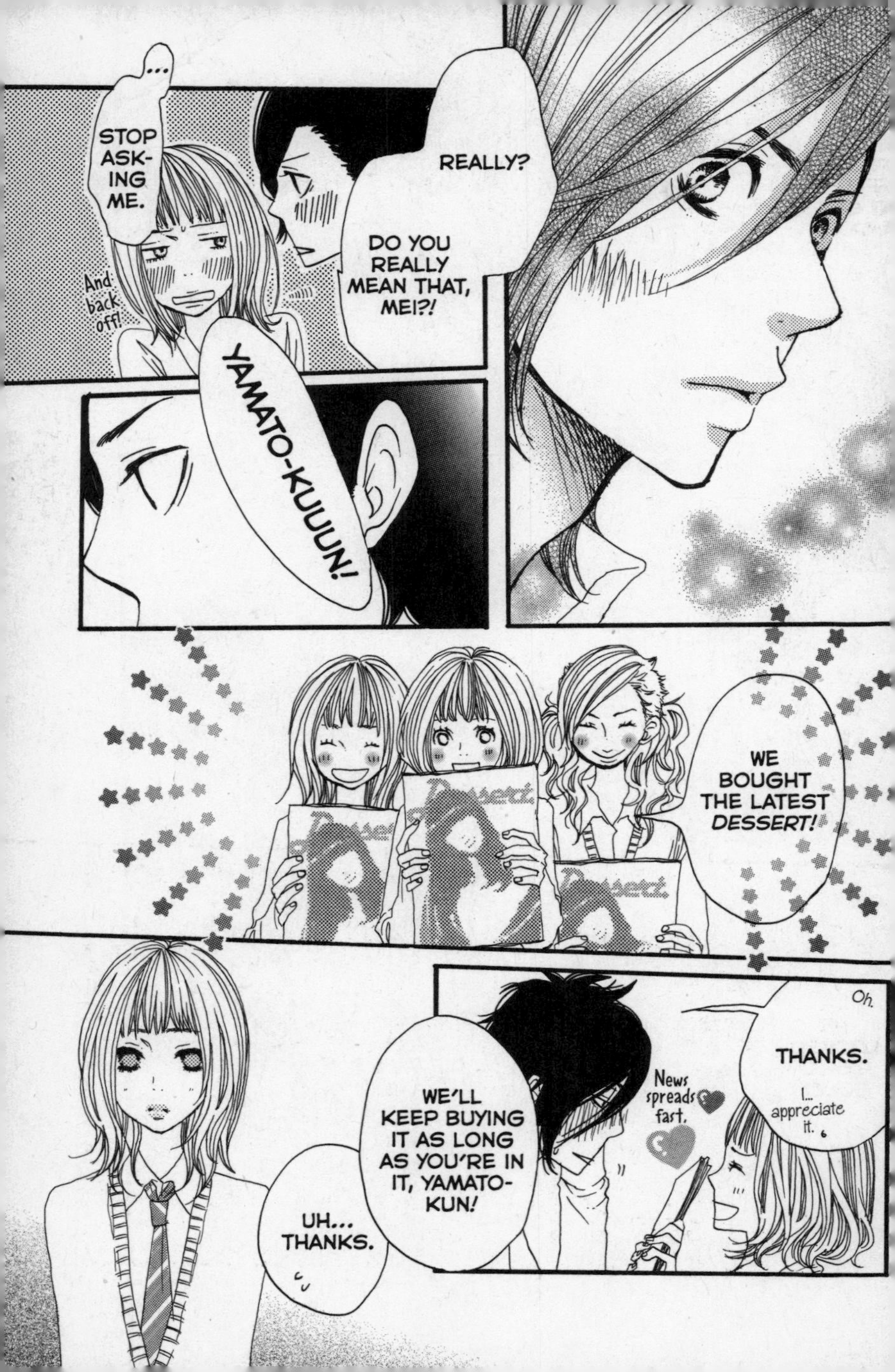
REALLY?
DO YOU REALLY MEAN THAT, MEI?!
...
STOP ASKING ME.
And back off!
YAMATO-KUUUN!
WE BOUGHT THE LATEST DESSERT!
Oh.
THANKS.
I... appreciate it.
News spreads fast.
WE'LL KEEP BUYING IT AS LONG AS YOU'RE IN IT, YAMATO-KUN!
UH... THANKS.

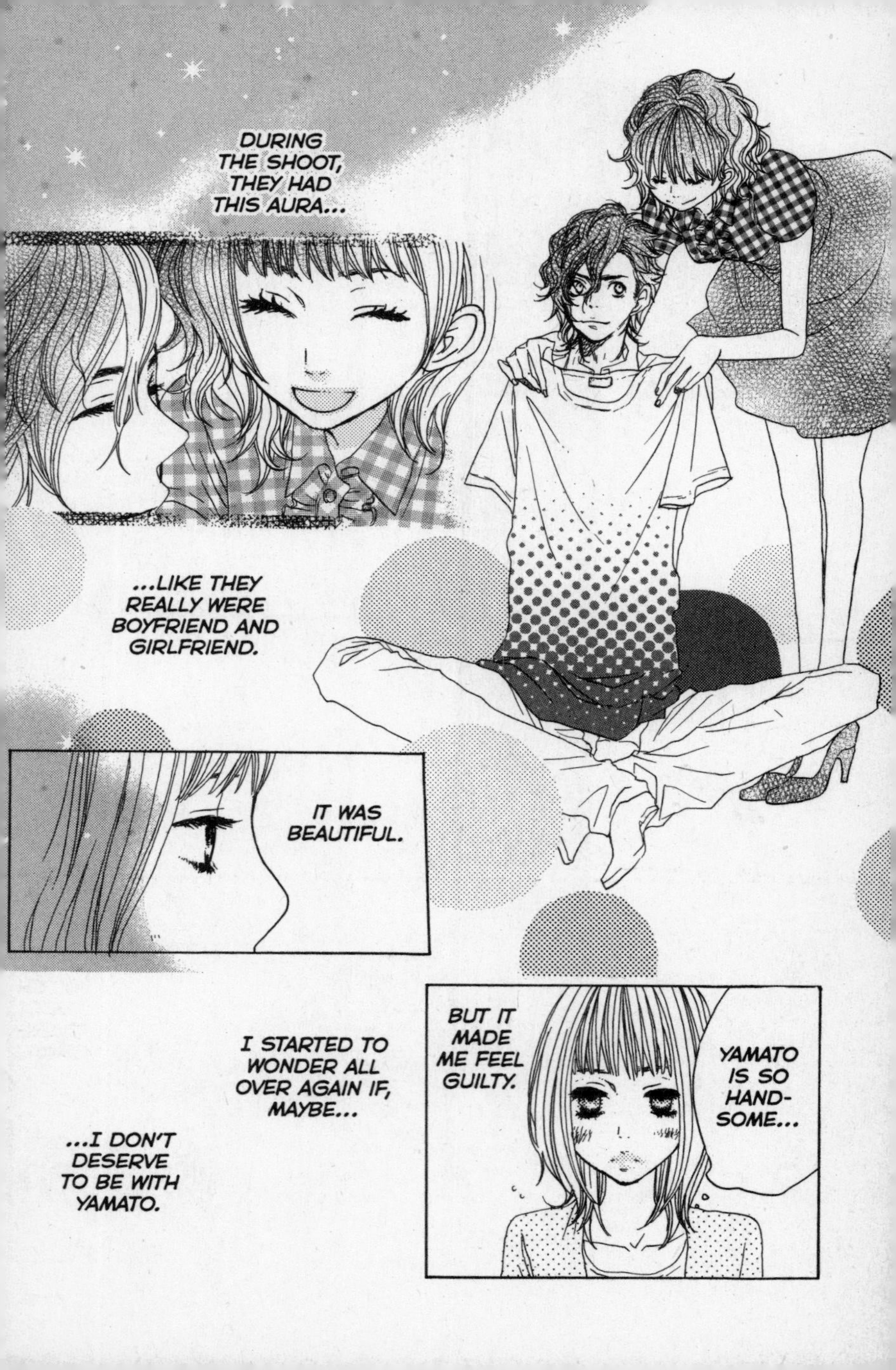
DURING THE SHOOT, THEY HAD THIS AURA...
...LIKE THEY REALLY WERE BOYFRIEND AND GIRLFRIEND.
IT WAS BEAUTIFUL.
YAMATO IS SO HAND-SOME...
BUT IT MADE ME FEEL GUILTY.
I STARTED TO WONDER ALL OVER AGAIN IF, MAYBE...
...I DON'T DESERVE TO BE WITH YAMATO.

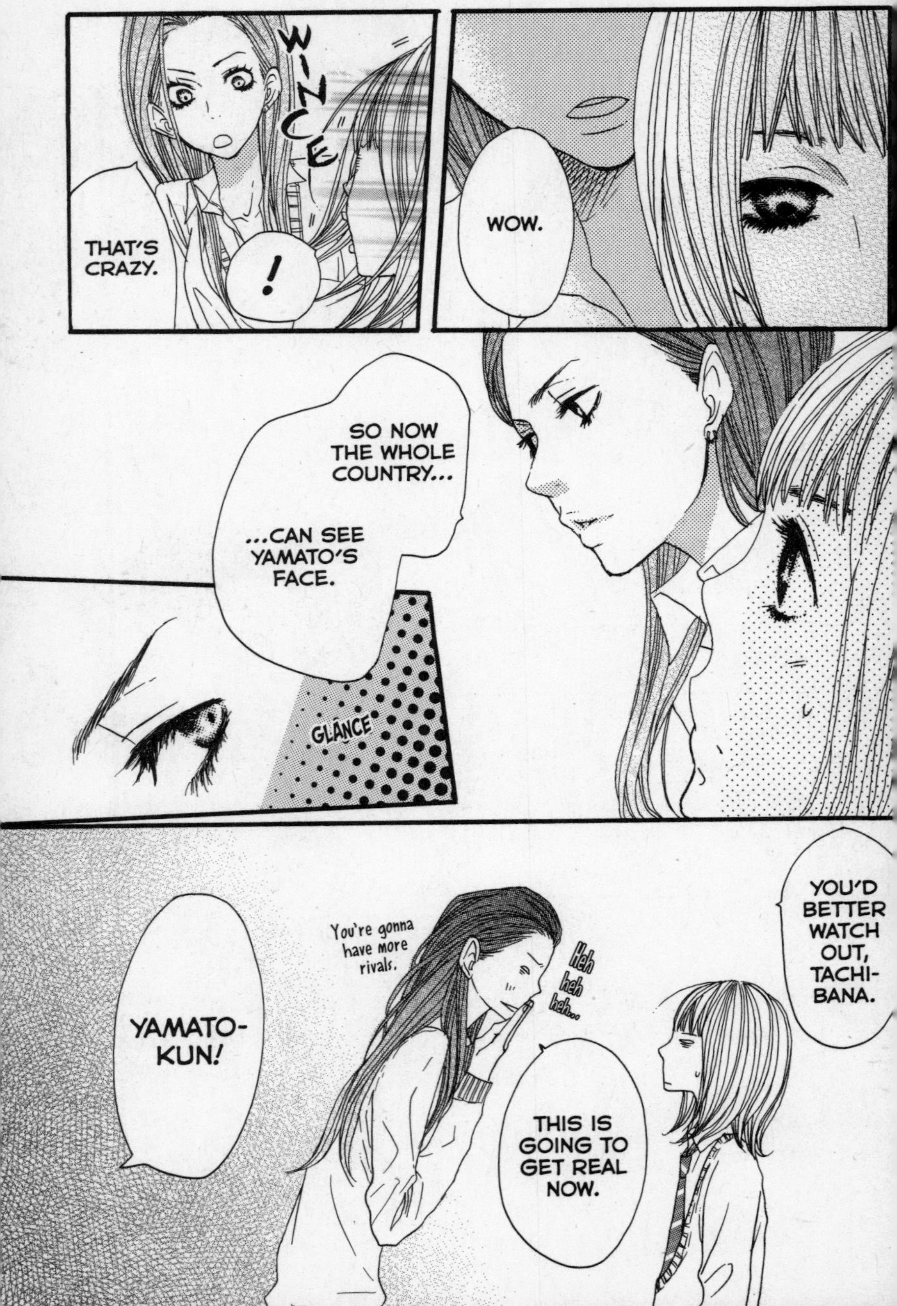
WOW.
WINCE
!
THAT'S CRAZY.
SO NOW THE WHOLE COUNTRY...
...CAN SEE YAMATO'S FACE.
GLANCE
YOU'D BETTER WATCH OUT, TACHIBANA.
Heh heh heh...
You're gonna have more rivals.
THIS IS GOING TO GET REAL NOW.
YAMATO-KUN!

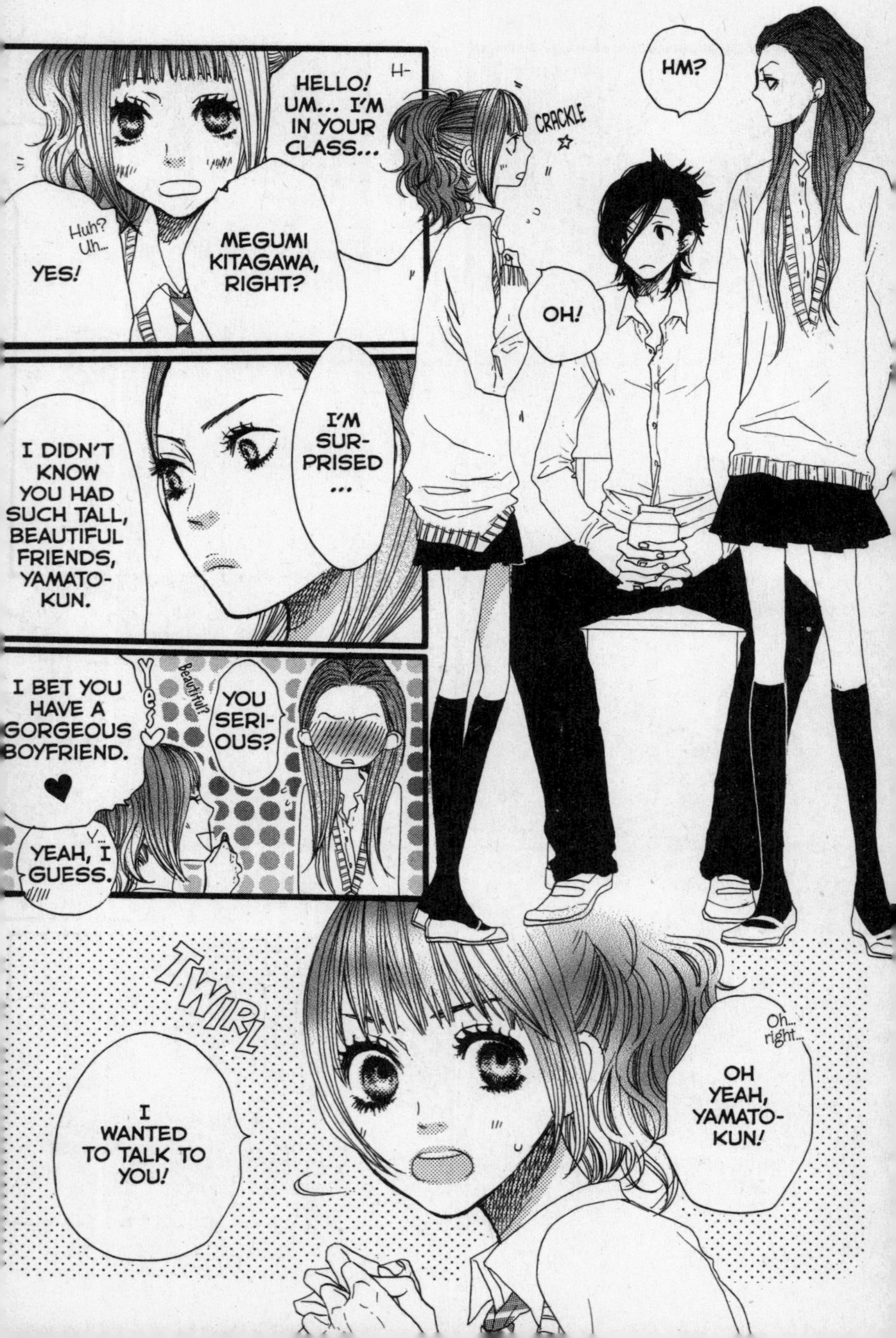
HM?
CRACKLE ☆
OH!
H-
HELLO! UM... I'M IN YOUR CLASS...
MEGUMI KITAGAWA, RIGHT?
Huh? Uh...
YES!
I'M SURPRISED...
I DIDN'T KNOW YOU HAD SUCH TALL, BEAUTIFUL FRIENDS, YAMATO-KUN.
YOU SERIOUS?
Beautiful?
Yes♥
I BET YOU HAVE A GORGEOUS BOYFRIEND. ♥
Y... YEAH, I GUESS.
TWIRL
Oh... right...
OH YEAH, YAMATO-KUN!
I WANTED TO TALK TO YOU!

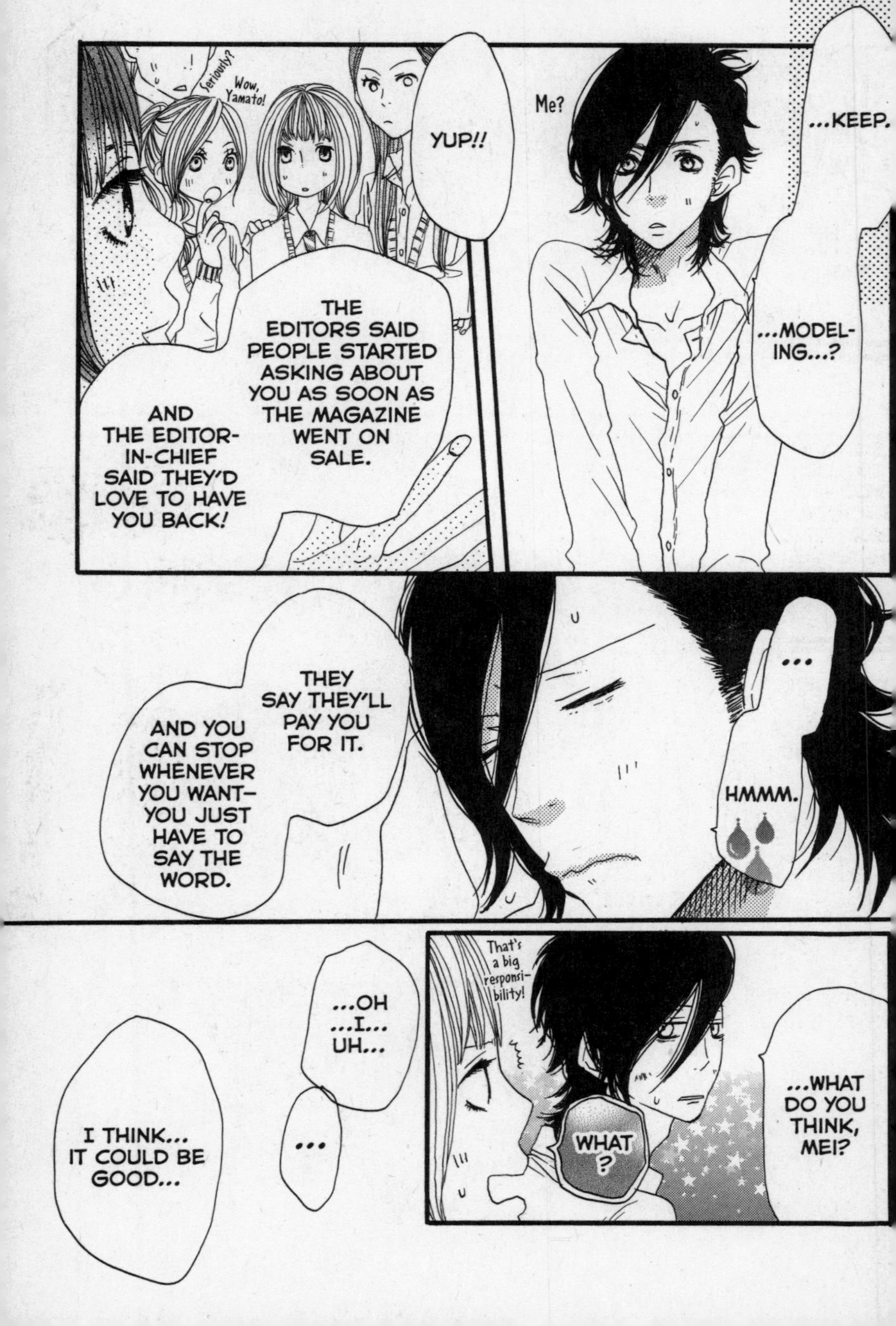
...KEEP.
...MODEL-ING...?
Me?
YUP!!
Wow, Yamato!
Seriously?
THE EDITORS SAID PEOPLE STARTED ASKING ABOUT YOU AS SOON AS THE MAGAZINE WENT ON SALE.
AND THE EDITOR-IN-CHIEF SAID THEY'D LOVE TO HAVE YOU BACK!
...
HMMM.
THEY SAY THEY'LL PAY YOU FOR IT.
AND YOU CAN STOP WHENEVER YOU WANT—YOU JUST HAVE TO SAY THE WORD.
...WHAT DO YOU THINK, MEI?
WHAT ?
That's a big responsibility!
...OH ...I... UH...
...
I THINK... IT COULD BE GOOD...

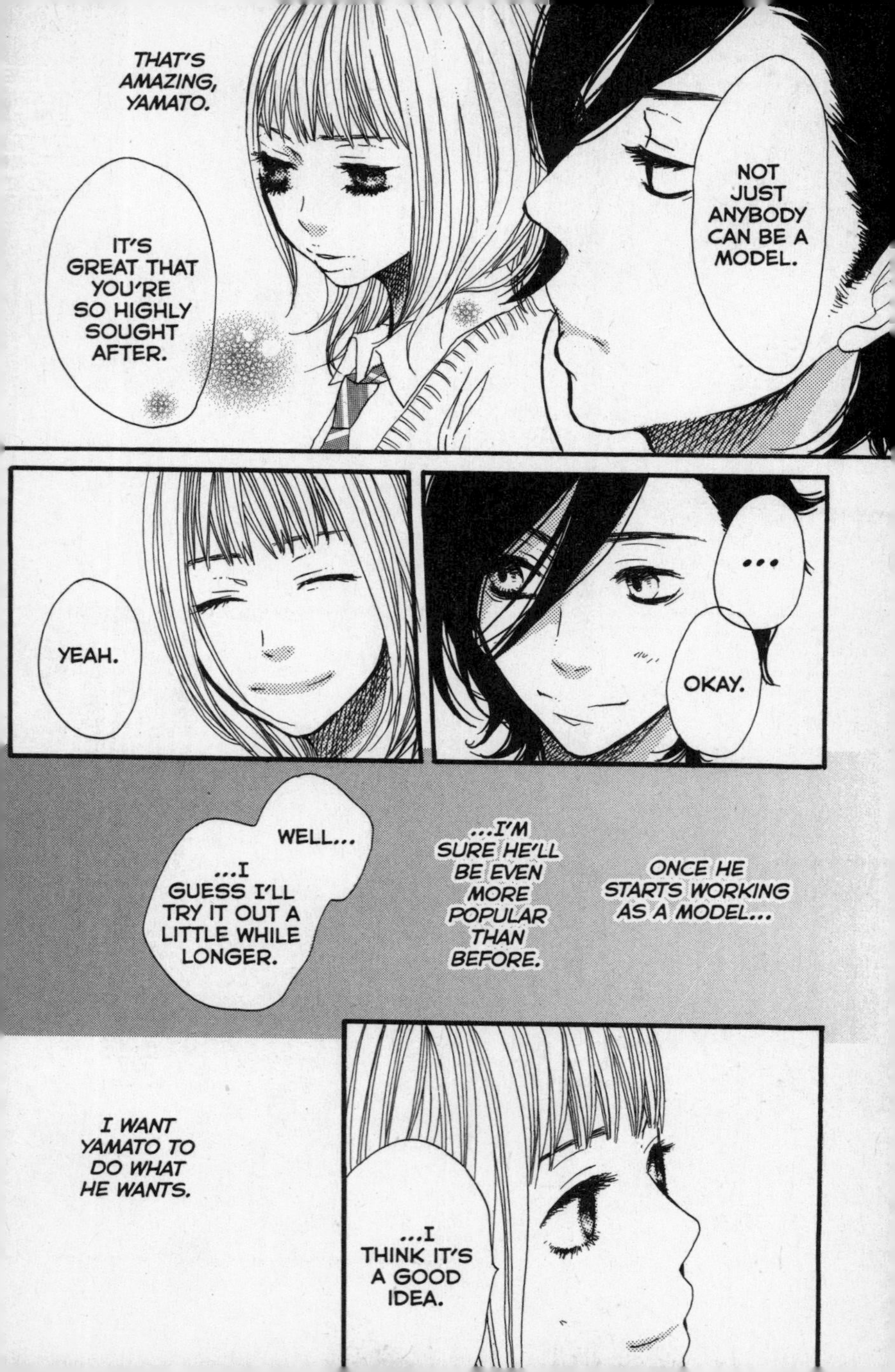
NOT JUST ANYBODY CAN BE A MODEL.
THAT'S AMAZING, YAMATO.
IT'S GREAT THAT YOU'RE SO HIGHLY SOUGHT AFTER.
...
OKAY.
YEAH.
ONCE HE STARTS WORKING AS A MODEL...
...I'M SURE HE'LL BE EVEN MORE POPULAR THAN BEFORE.
WELL...
...I GUESS I'LL TRY IT OUT A LITTLE WHILE LONGER.
...I THINK IT'S A GOOD IDEA.
I WANT YAMATO TO DO WHAT HE WANTS.

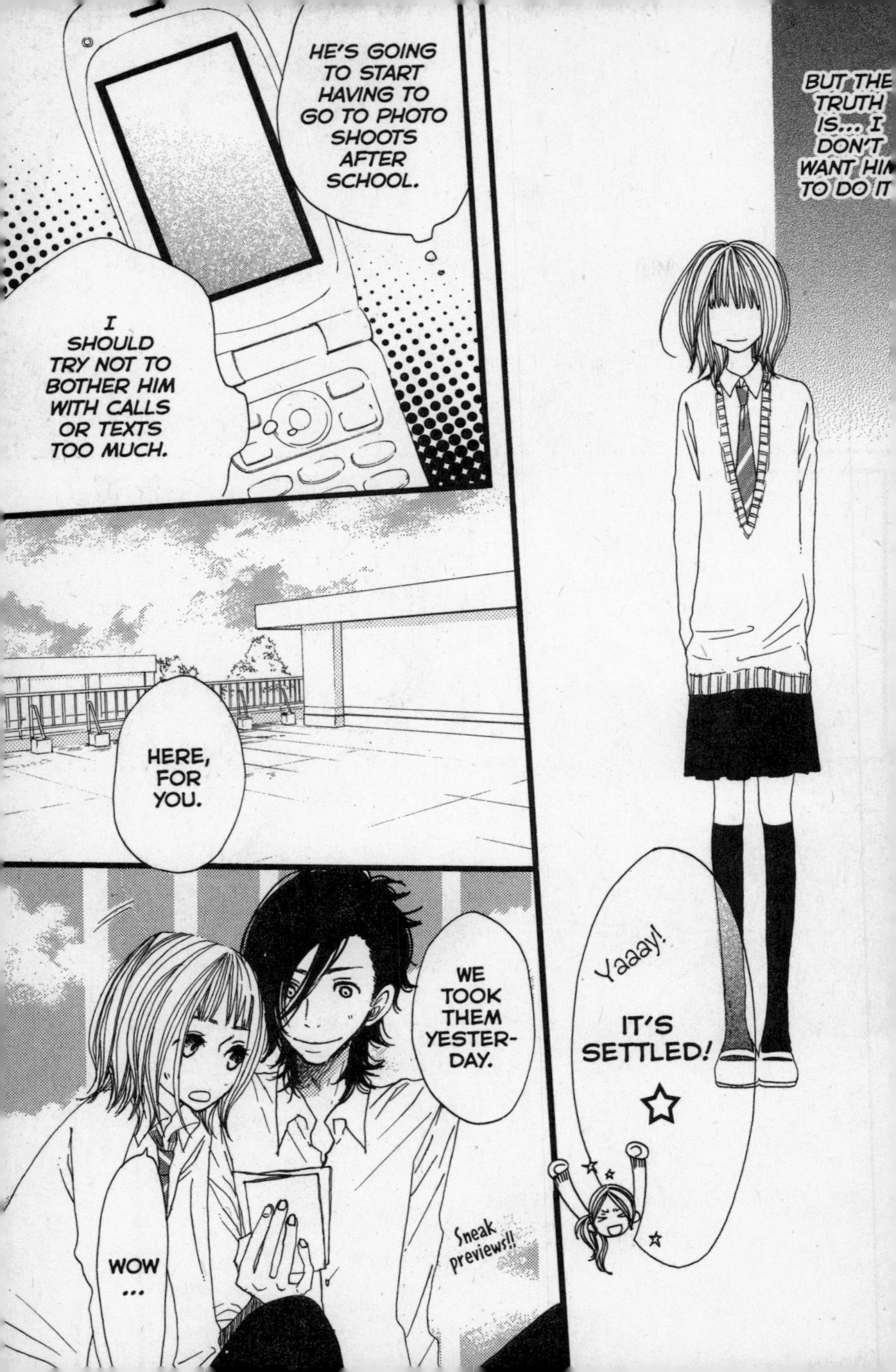
BUT THE TRUTH IS... I DON'T WANT HIM TO DO IT
Yaaay!
IT'S SETTLED! ☆
HE'S GOING TO START HAVING TO GO TO PHOTO SHOOTS AFTER SCHOOL.
I SHOULD TRY NOT TO BOTHER HIM WITH CALLS OR TEXTS TOO MUCH.
HERE, FOR YOU.
WE TOOK THEM YESTER-DAY.
Sneak previews!!
WOW ...

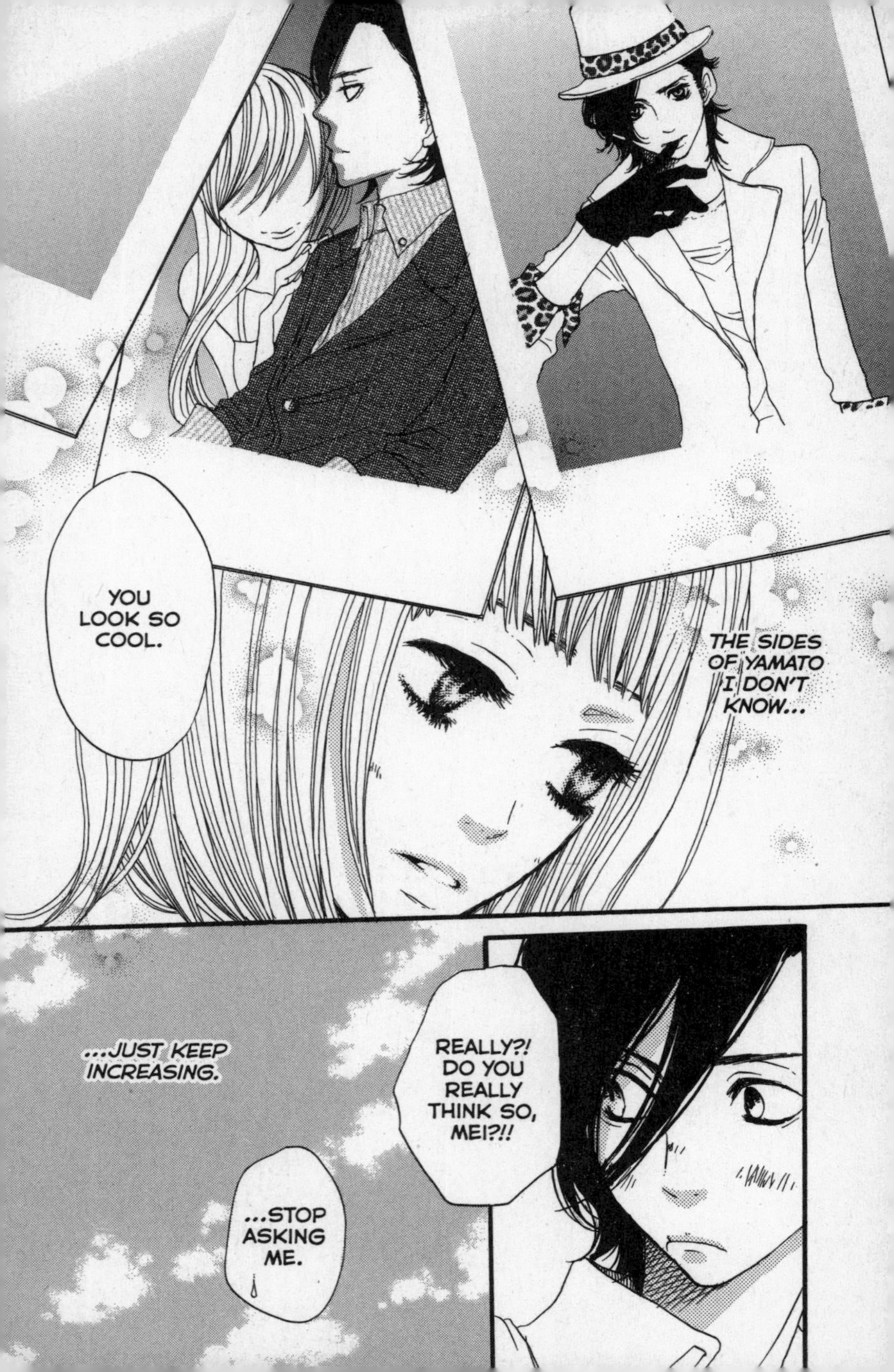
THE SIDES OF YAMATO I DON'T KNOW...
YOU LOOK SO COOL.
REALLY?! DO YOU REALLY THINK SO, MEI?!!
...JUST KEEP INCREASING.
...STOP ASKING ME.

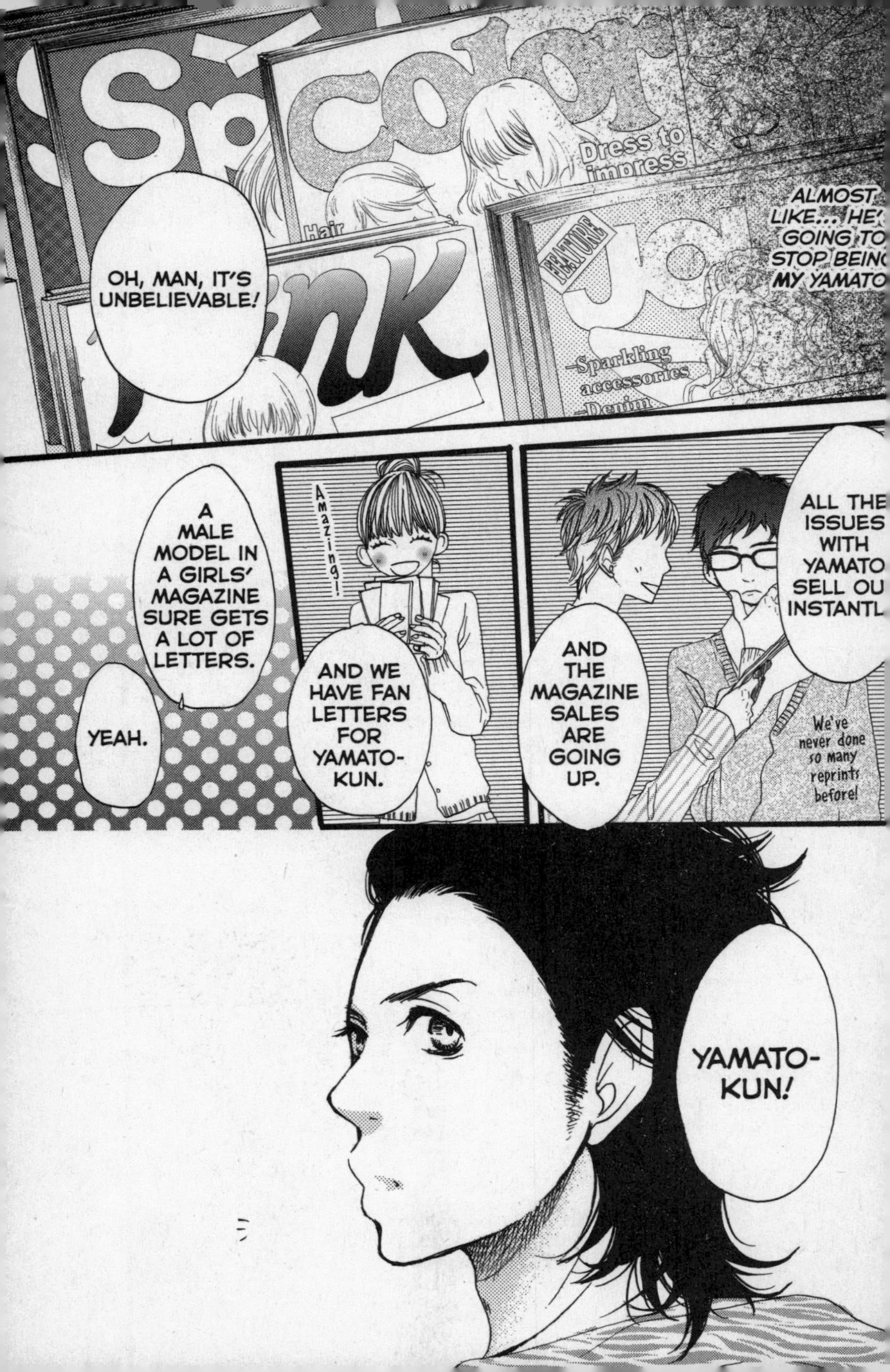
ALMOST LIKE... HE' GOING TO STOP BEINC MY YAMATO
Dress to impress
Hair
FEATURE
Sparkling accessories
Denim
OH, MAN, IT'S UNBELIEVABLE!
ALL THE ISSUES WITH YAMATO SELL OU INSTANTL
We've never done so many reprints before!
AND THE MAGAZINE SALES ARE GOING UP.
Amazing!
AND WE HAVE FAN LETTERS FOR YAMATO-KUN.
A MALE MODEL IN A GIRLS' MAGAZINE SURE GETS A LOT OF LETTERS.
YEAH.
YAMATO-KUN!

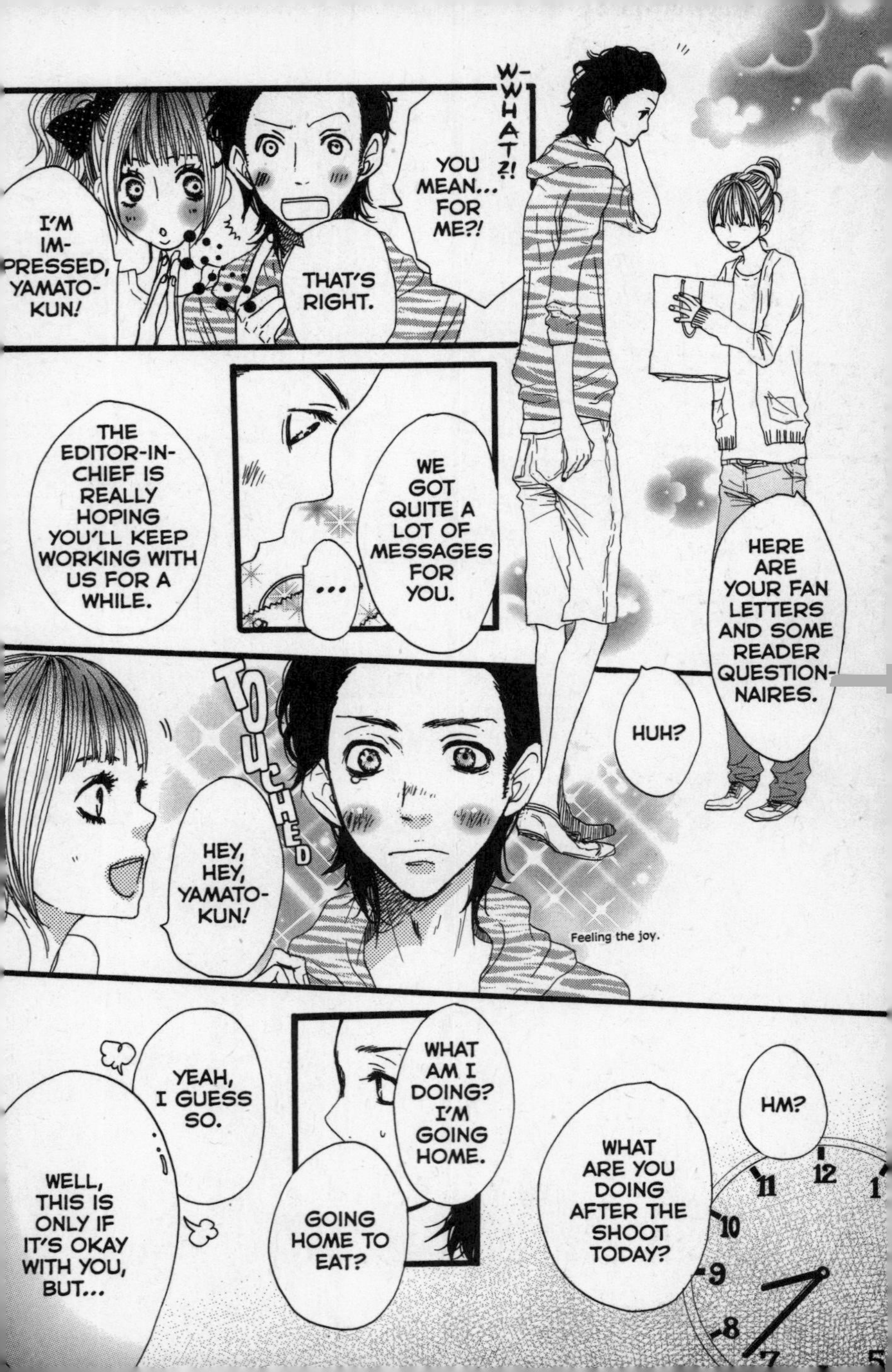
HERE ARE YOUR FAN LETTERS AND SOME READER QUESTIONNAIRES.
HUH?
W-WHAT?!
YOU MEAN... FOR ME?!
THAT'S RIGHT.
I'M IMPRESSED, YAMATO-KUN!
WE GOT QUITE A LOT OF MESSAGES FOR YOU.
...
THE EDITOR-IN-CHIEF IS REALLY HOPING YOU'LL KEEP WORKING WITH US FOR A WHILE.
TOUCHED
Feeling the joy.
HEY, HEY, YAMATO-KUN!
HM?
WHAT ARE YOU DOING AFTER THE SHOOT TODAY?
WHAT AM I DOING? I'M GOING HOME.
GOING HOME TO EAT?
YEAH, I GUESS SO.
WELL, THIS IS ONLY IF IT'S OKAY WITH YOU, BUT...

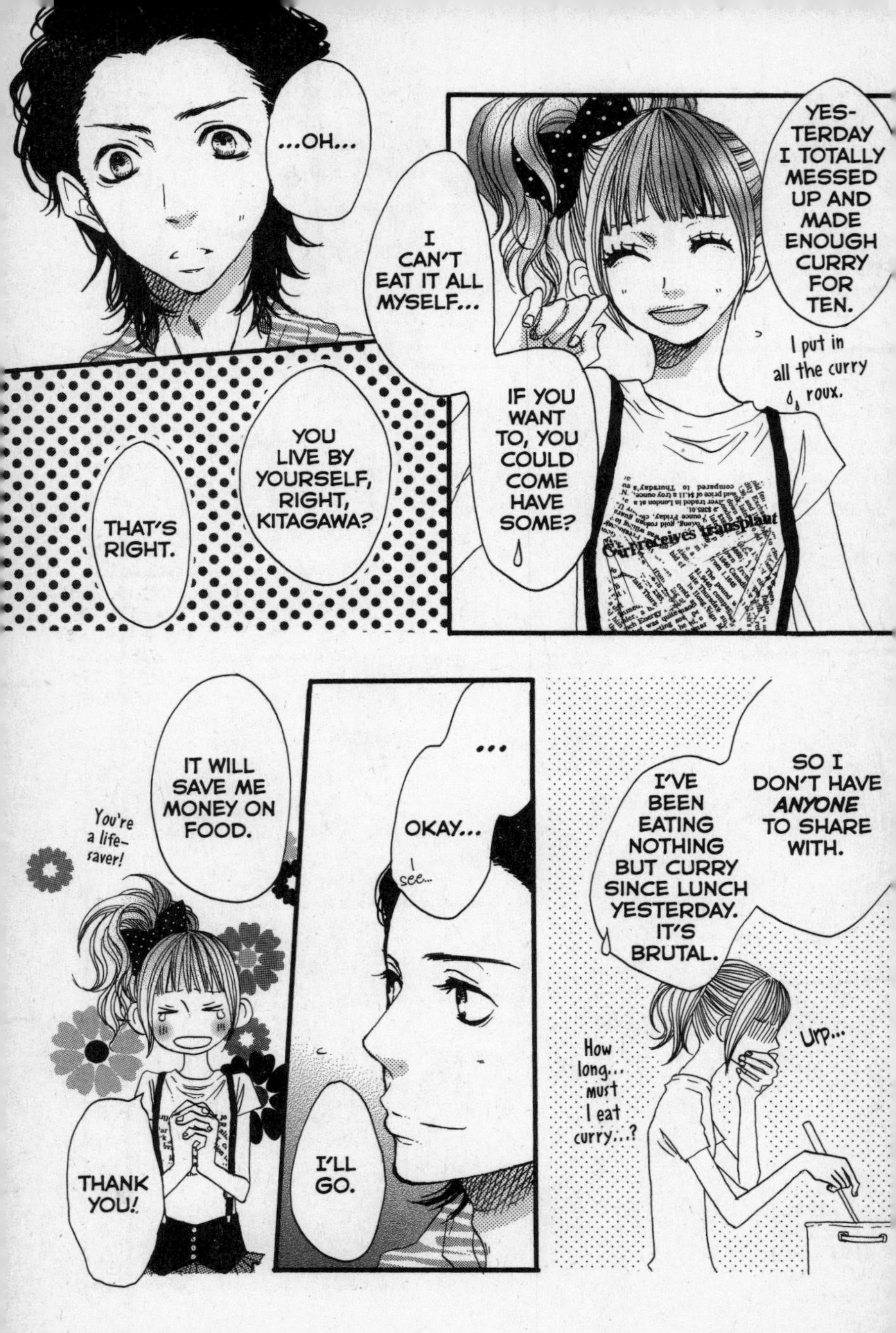
YES-TERDAY I TOTALLY MESSED UP AND MADE ENOUGH CURRY FOR TEN.
I put in all the curry roux.
I CAN'T EAT IT ALL MYSELF...
IF YOU WANT TO, YOU COULD COME HAVE SOME?
...OH...
YOU LIVE BY YOURSELF, RIGHT, KITAGAWA?
THAT'S RIGHT.
SO I DON'T HAVE *ANYONE* TO SHARE WITH.
I'VE BEEN EATING NOTHING BUT CURRY SINCE LUNCH YESTERDAY. IT'S BRUTAL.
Urp...
How long... must I eat curry...?
...
OKAY...
I see...
I'LL GO.
IT WILL SAVE ME MONEY ON FOOD.
You're a life-saver!
THANK YOU!

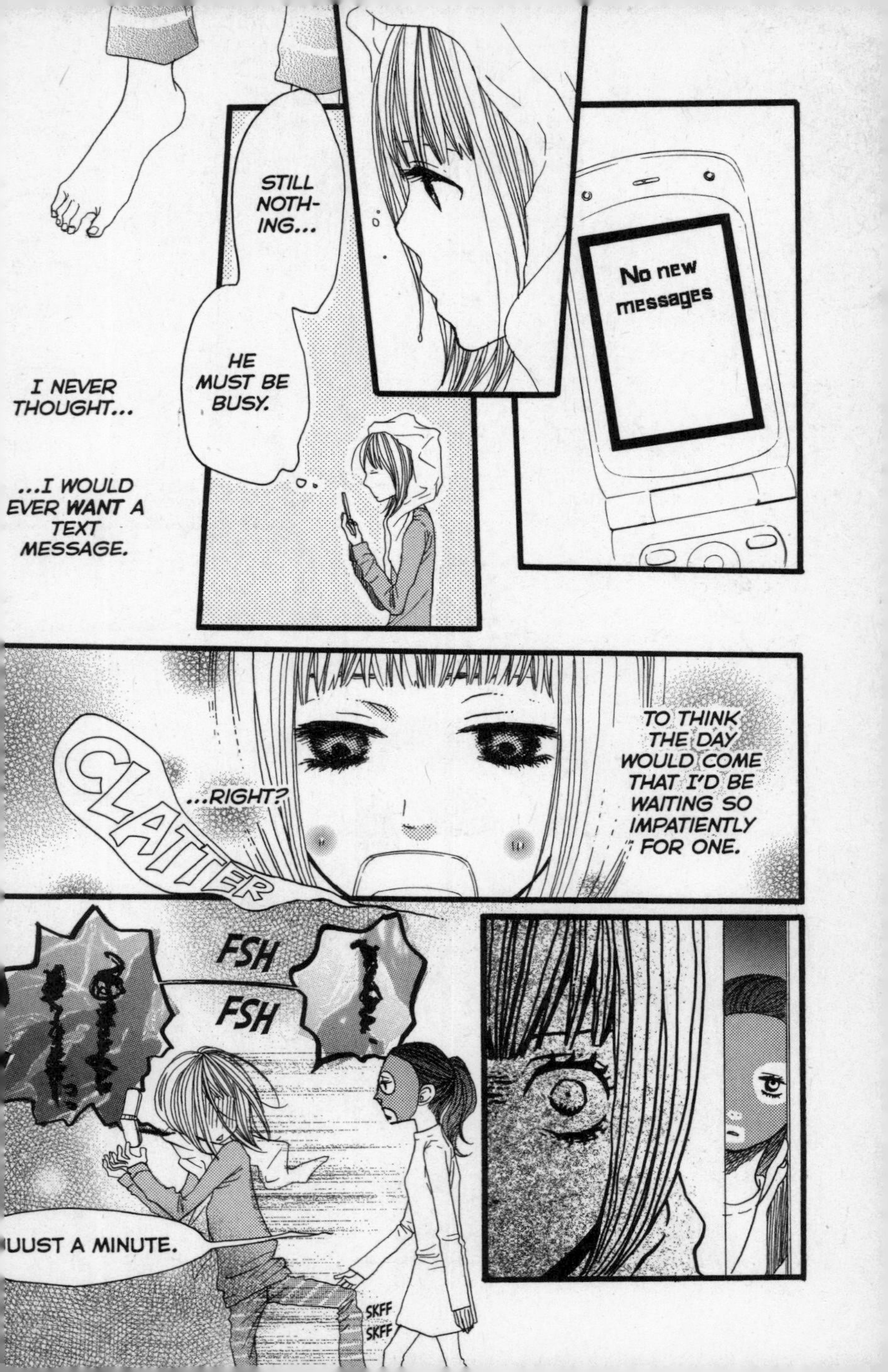
No new messages
STILL NOTHING-ING...
HE MUST BE BUSY.
I NEVER THOUGHT...
...I WOULD EVER WANT A TEXT MESSAGE.
TO THINK THE DAY WOULD COME THAT I'D BE WAITING SO IMPATIENTLY FOR ONE.
...RIGHT?
CLATTER
FSH FSH
UUST A MINUTE.
SKFF SKFF

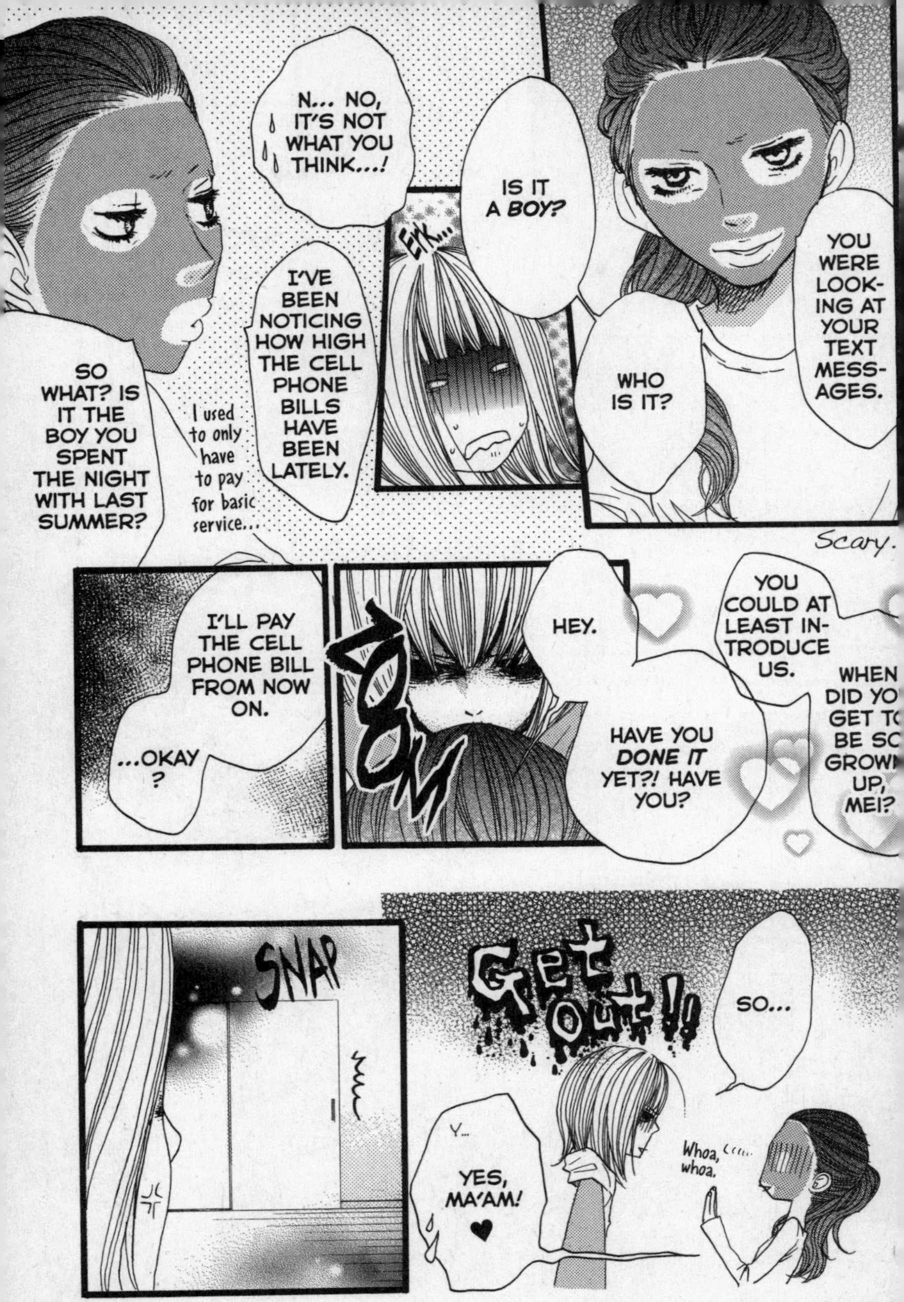
YOU WERE LOOKING AT YOUR TEXT MESSAGES.
WHO IS IT?
IS IT A *BOY?*
EEK...
N... NO, IT'S NOT WHAT YOU THINK...!
I'VE BEEN NOTICING HOW HIGH THE CELL PHONE BILLS HAVE BEEN LATELY.
I used to only have to pay for basic service...
SO WHAT? IS IT THE BOY YOU SPENT THE NIGHT WITH LAST SUMMER?
Scary.
WHEN DID YO GET TO BE SO GROWN UP, MEI?
YOU COULD AT LEAST INTRODUCE US.
HEY.
HAVE YOU *DONE IT* YET?! HAVE YOU?
DOOM
I'LL PAY THE CELL PHONE BILL FROM NOW ON.
...OKAY?
SO...
Get out!!
Whoa, whoa.
Y...
YES, MA'AM!
SNAP

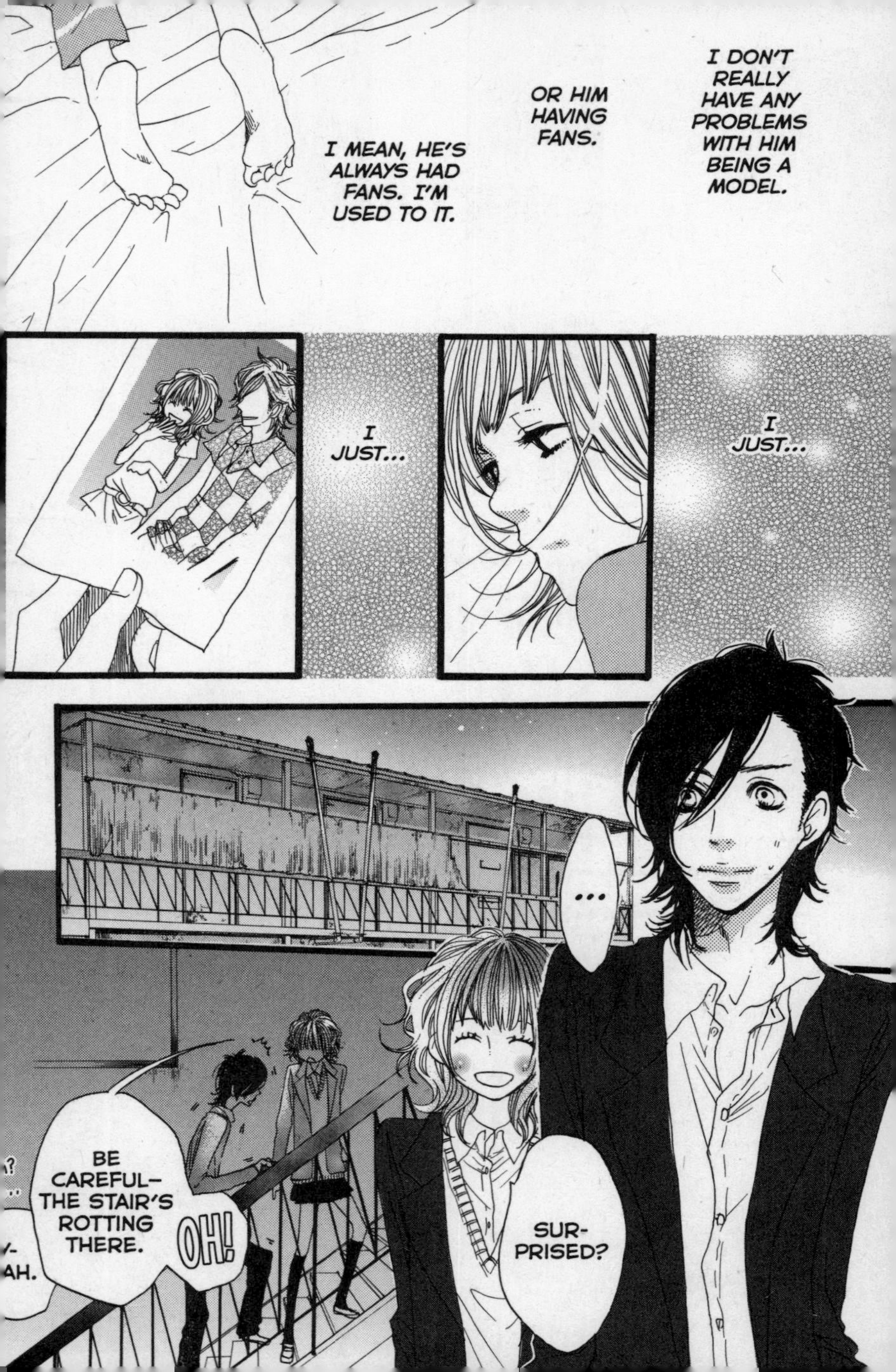
I DON'T REALLY HAVE ANY PROBLEMS WITH HIM BEING A MODEL.
OR HIM HAVING FANS.
I MEAN, HE'S ALWAYS HAD FANS. I'M USED TO IT.
I JUST...
I JUST...
...
SUR-PRISED?
OH!
BE CAREFUL—THE STAIR'S ROTTING THERE.

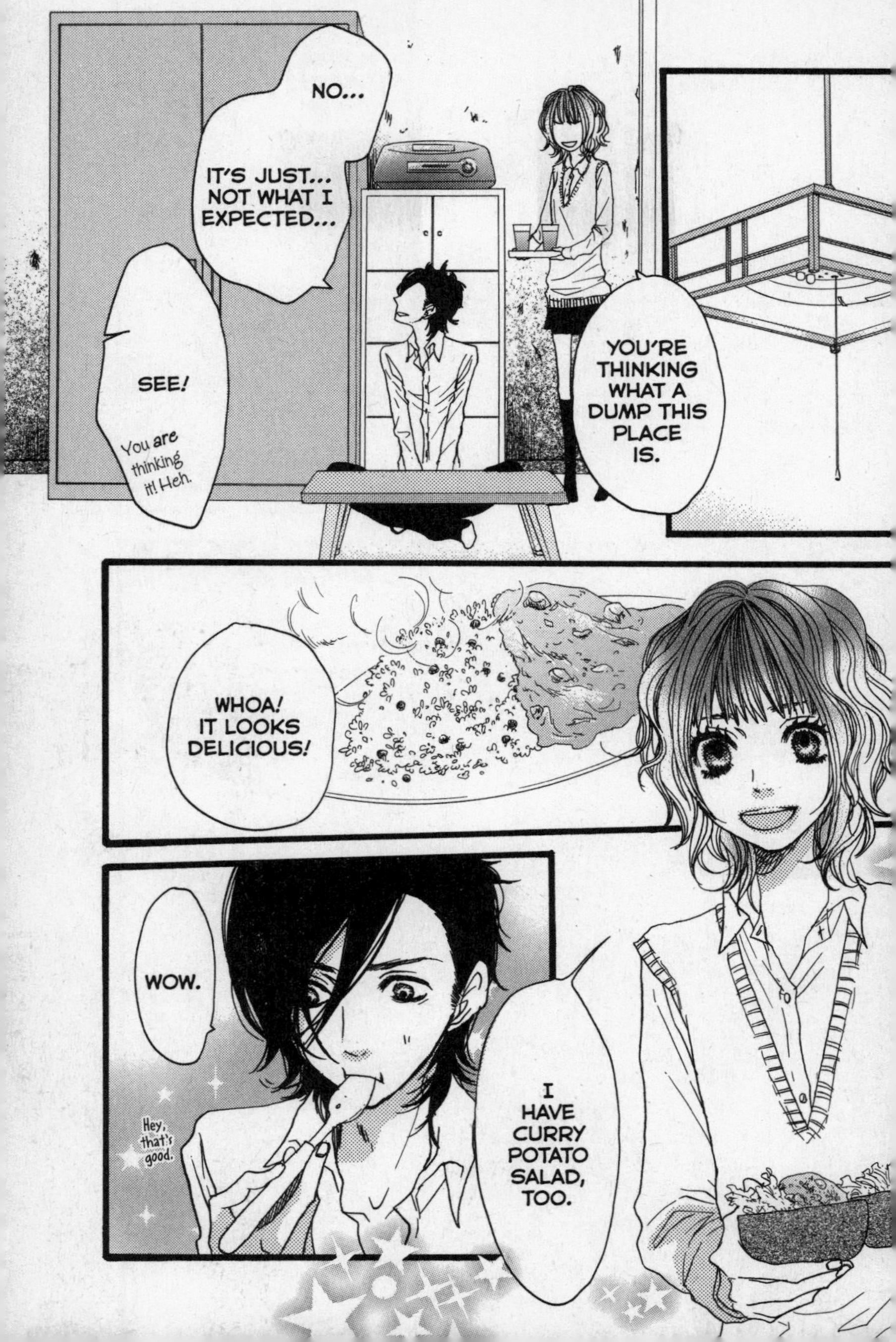

YOU'RE THINKING WHAT A DUMP THIS PLACE IS.
NO...
IT'S JUST... NOT WHAT I EXPECTED...
SEE!
You are thinking it! Heh.
WHOA! IT LOOKS DELICIOUS!
I HAVE CURRY POTATO SALAD, TOO.
WOW.
Hey, that's good.

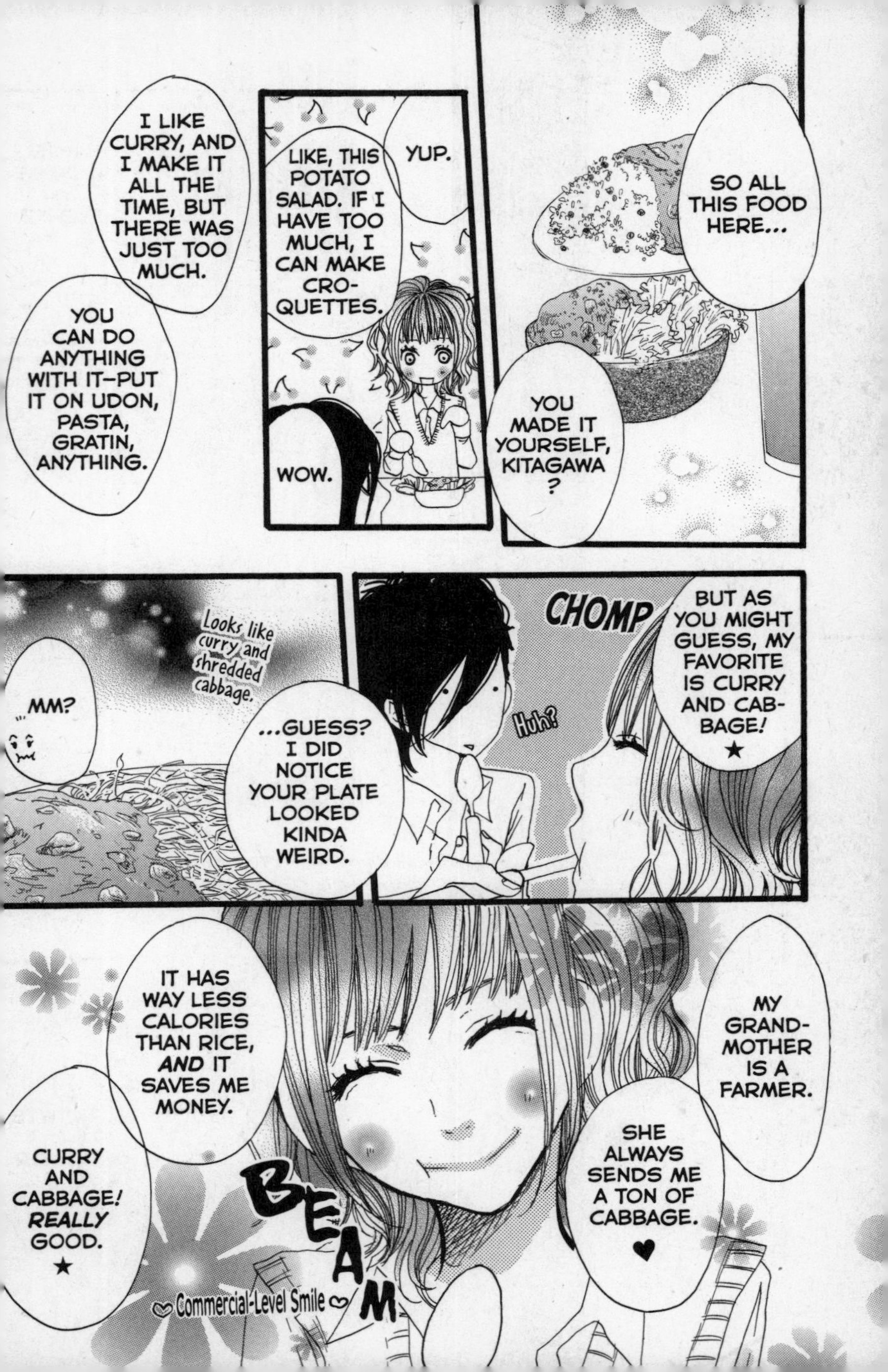
SO ALL THIS FOOD HERE...
YOU MADE IT YOURSELF, KITAGAWA?
YUP.
LIKE, THIS POTATO SALAD. IF I HAVE TOO MUCH, I CAN MAKE CRO-QUETTES.
WOW.
I LIKE CURRY, AND I MAKE IT ALL THE TIME, BUT THERE WAS JUST TOO MUCH.
YOU CAN DO ANYTHING WITH IT—PUT IT ON UDON, PASTA, GRATIN, ANYTHING.
BUT AS YOU MIGHT GUESS, MY FAVORITE IS CURRY AND CAB-BAGE! ★
CHOMP
Huh?
...GUESS? I DID NOTICE YOUR PLATE LOOKED KINDA WEIRD.
Looks like curry and shredded cabbage.
MM?
MY GRAND-MOTHER IS A FARMER.
SHE ALWAYS SENDS ME A TON OF CABBAGE. ♥
IT HAS WAY LESS CALORIES THAN RICE, AND IT SAVES ME MONEY.
BEAM
CURRY AND CABBAGE! REALLY GOOD. ★
Commercial-Level Smile

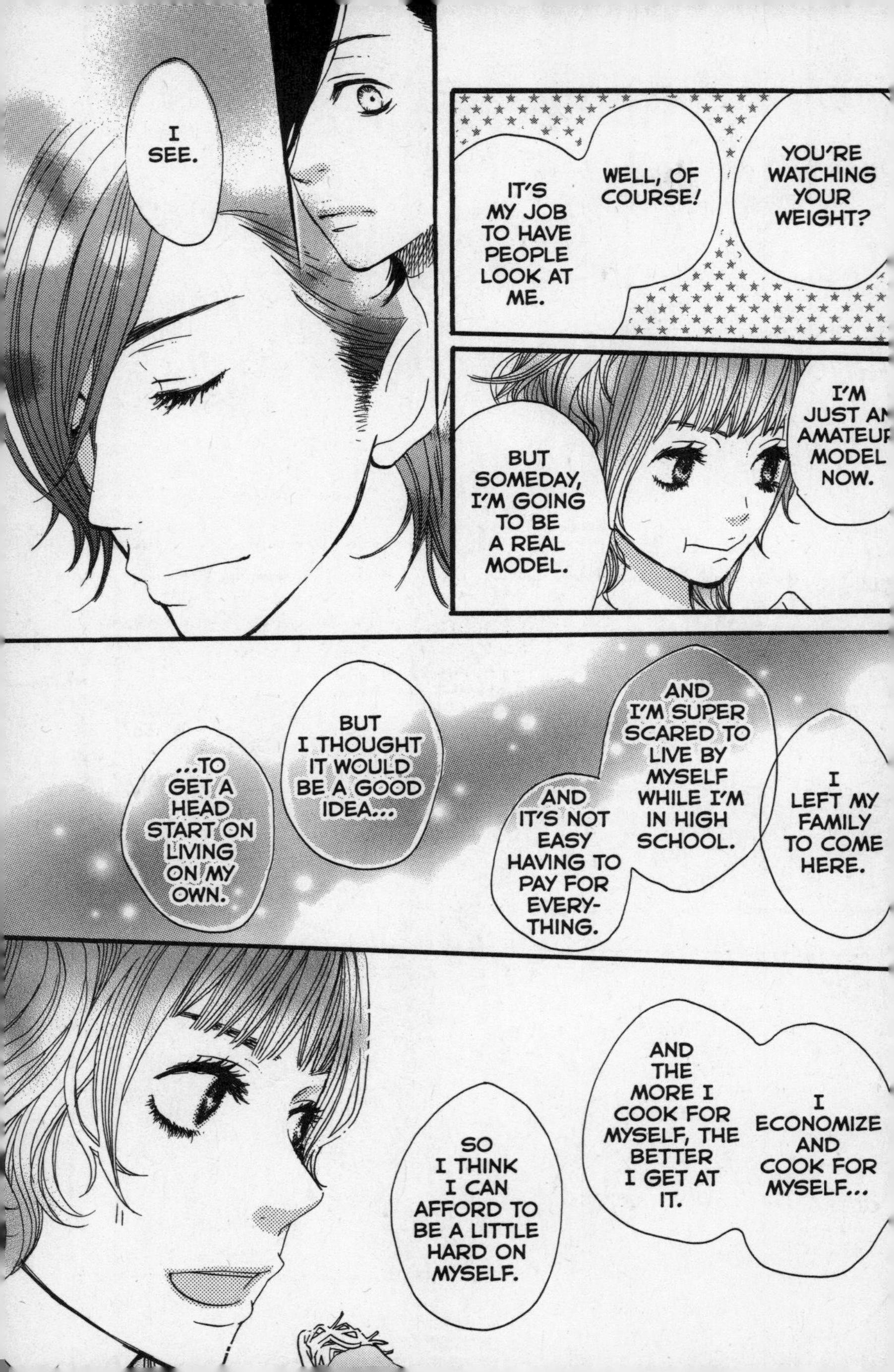
YOU'RE WATCHING YOUR WEIGHT?
WELL, OF COURSE!
IT'S MY JOB TO HAVE PEOPLE LOOK AT ME.
I'M JUST AN AMATEUR MODEL NOW.
BUT SOMEDAY, I'M GOING TO BE A REAL MODEL.
I SEE.
I LEFT MY FAMILY TO COME HERE.
AND I'M SUPER SCARED TO LIVE BY MYSELF WHILE I'M IN HIGH SCHOOL.
AND IT'S NOT EASY HAVING TO PAY FOR EVERY-THING.
BUT I THOUGHT IT WOULD BE A GOOD IDEA...
...TO GET A HEAD START ON LIVING ON MY OWN.
I ECONOMIZE AND COOK FOR MYSELF...
AND THE MORE I COOK FOR MYSELF, THE BETTER I GET AT IT.
SO I THINK I CAN AFFORD TO BE A LITTLE HARD ON MYSELF.

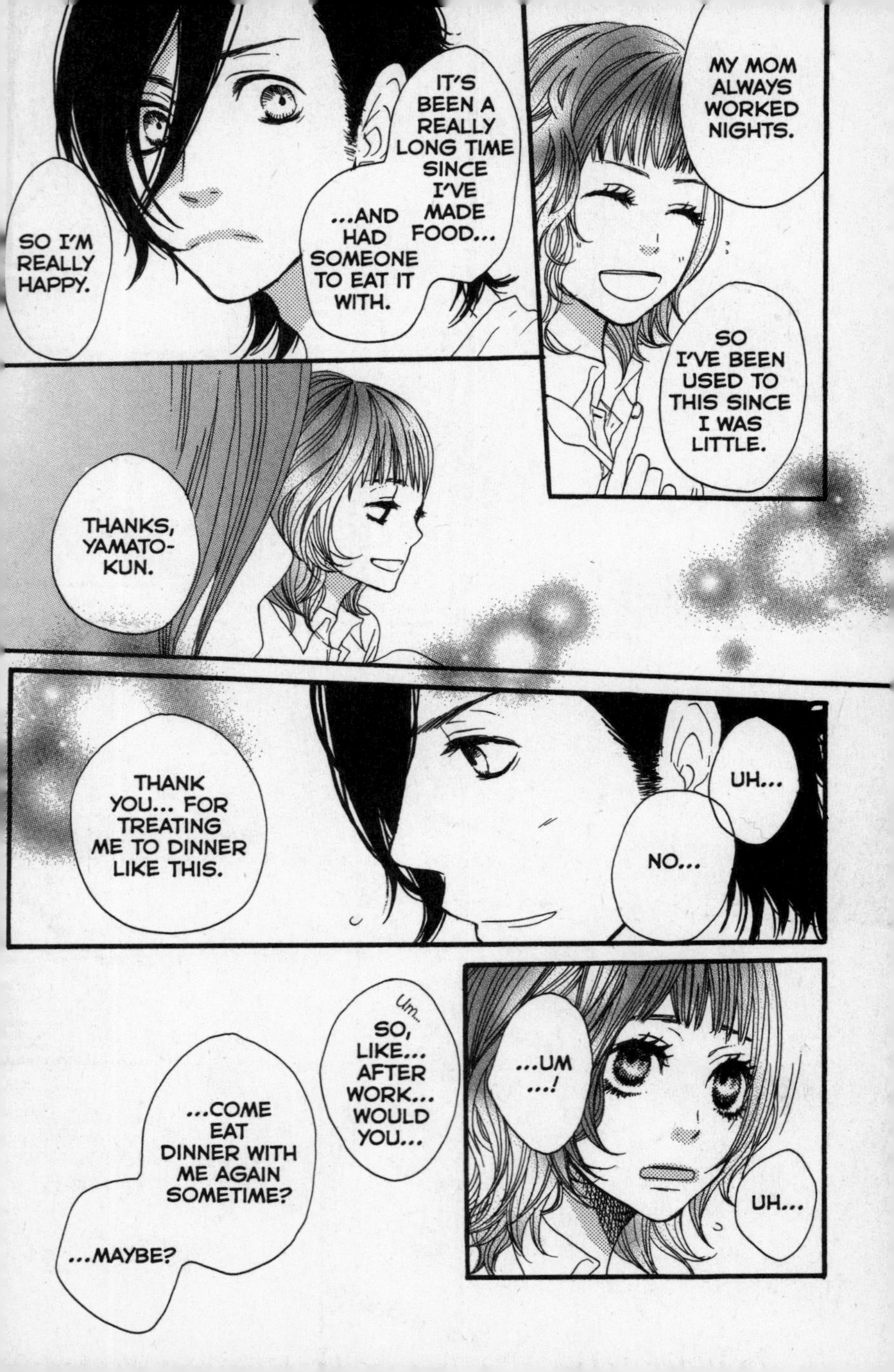
MY MOM ALWAYS WORKED NIGHTS.
SO I'VE BEEN USED TO THIS SINCE I WAS LITTLE.
IT'S BEEN A REALLY LONG TIME SINCE I'VE MADE FOOD...
...AND HAD SOMEONE TO EAT IT WITH.
SO I'M REALLY HAPPY.
THANKS, YAMATO-KUN.
UH...
NO...
THANK YOU... FOR TREATING ME TO DINNER LIKE THIS.
UH...
...UM ...!
Um...
SO, LIKE... AFTER WORK... WOULD YOU...
...COME EAT DINNER WITH ME AGAIN SOMETIME?
...MAYBE?

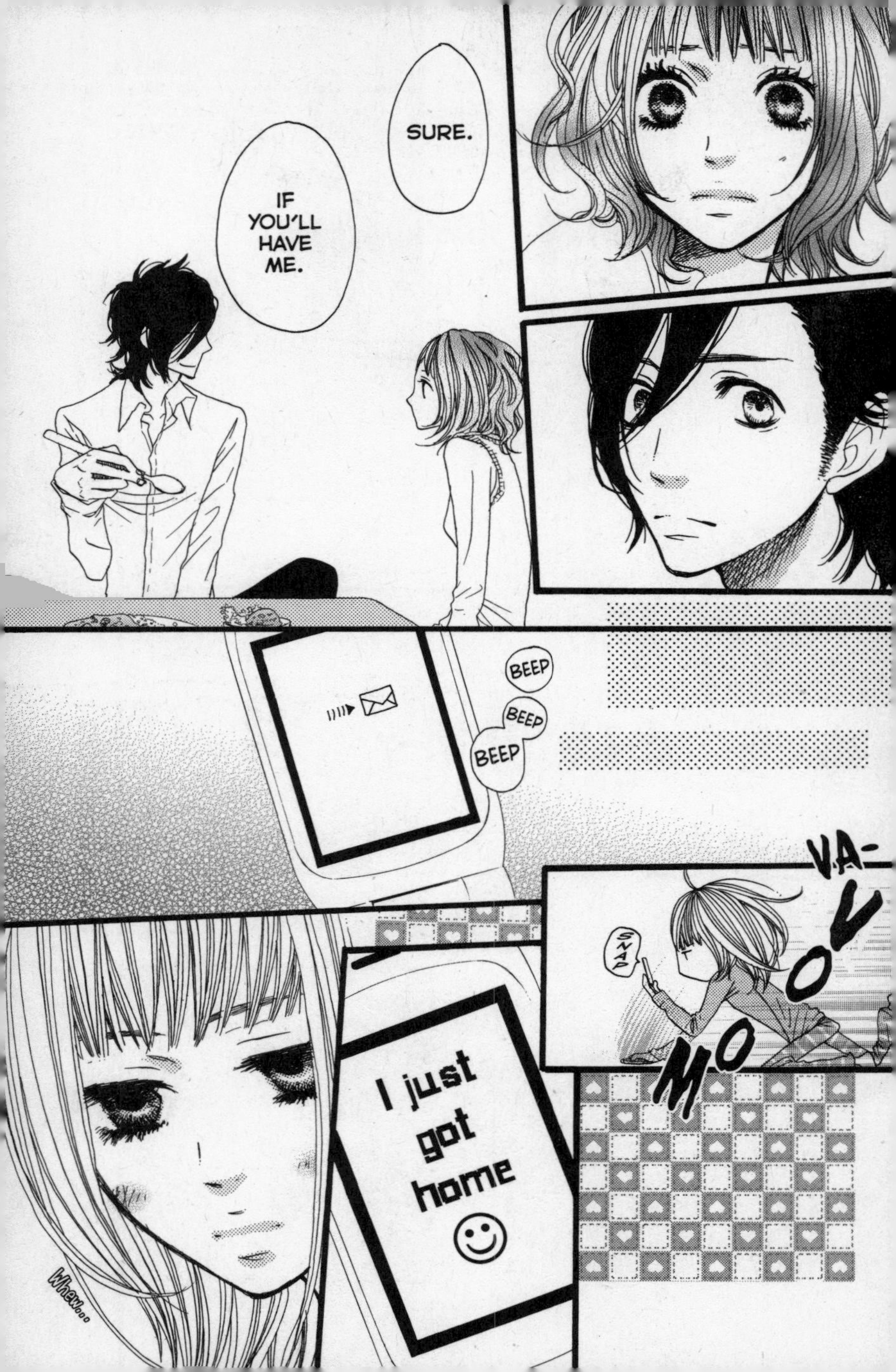
SURE.
IF YOU'LL HAVE ME.
BEEP
BEEP
BEEP
V.A-VOOOM
SNAP
I just got home
Whew...

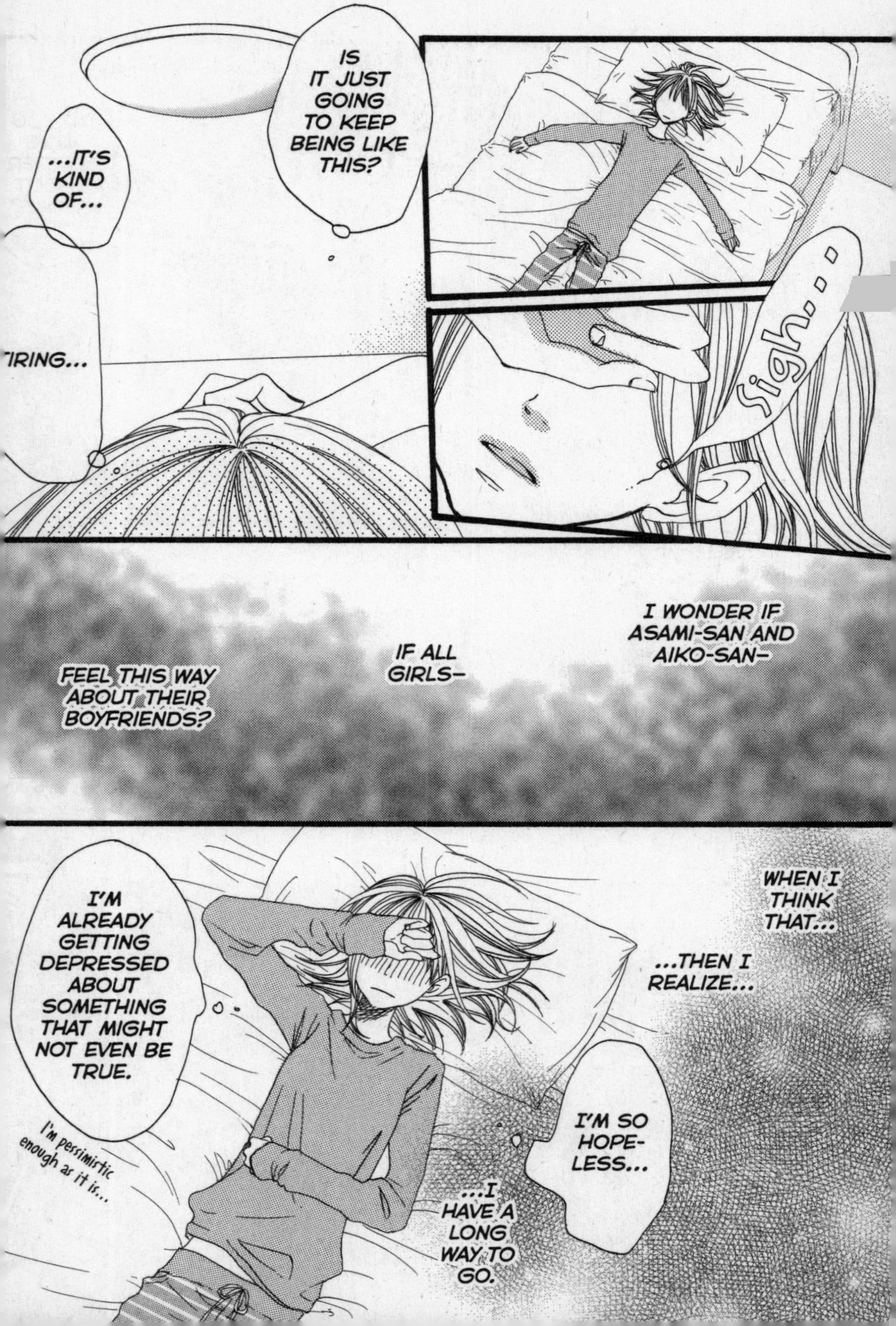

Sigh...
IS IT JUST GOING TO KEEP BEING LIKE THIS?
...IT'S KIND OF...
TIRING...
I WONDER IF ASAMI-SAN AND AIKO-SAN–
IF ALL GIRLS–
FEEL THIS WAY ABOUT THEIR BOYFRIENDS?
WHEN I THINK THAT...
...THEN I REALIZE...
I'M ALREADY GETTING DEPRESSED ABOUT SOMETHING THAT MIGHT NOT EVEN BE TRUE.
I'M SO HOPE-LESS...
...I HAVE A LONG WAY TO GO.
I'm pessimistic enough as it is...

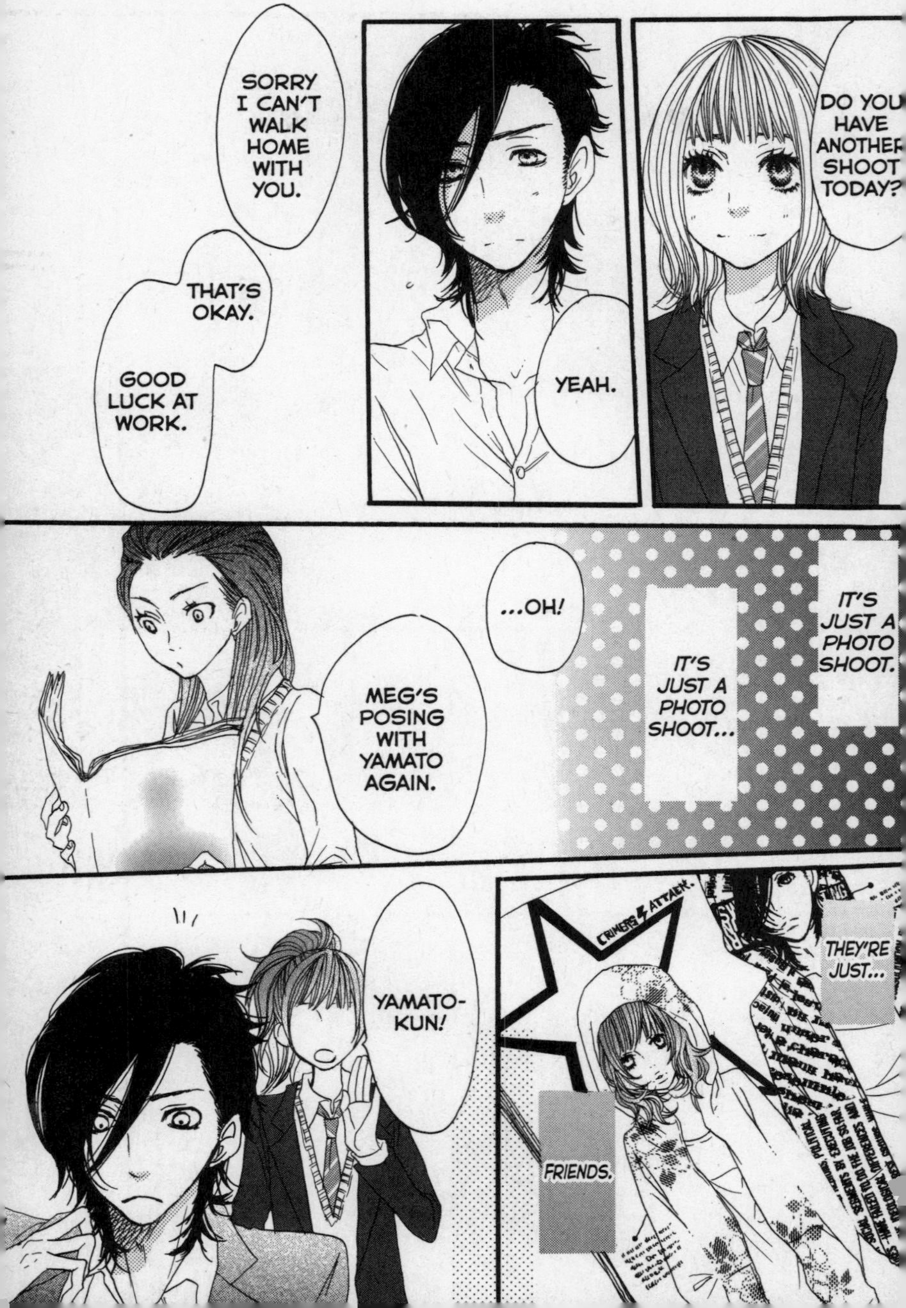
DO YOU HAVE ANOTHER SHOOT TODAY?
YEAH.
SORRY I CAN'T WALK HOME WITH YOU.
THAT'S OKAY.
GOOD LUCK AT WORK.
IT'S JUST A PHOTO SHOOT.
IT'S JUST A PHOTO SHOOT...
...OH!
MEG'S POSING WITH YAMATO AGAIN.
THEY'RE JUST...
FRIENDS.
YAMATO-KUN!

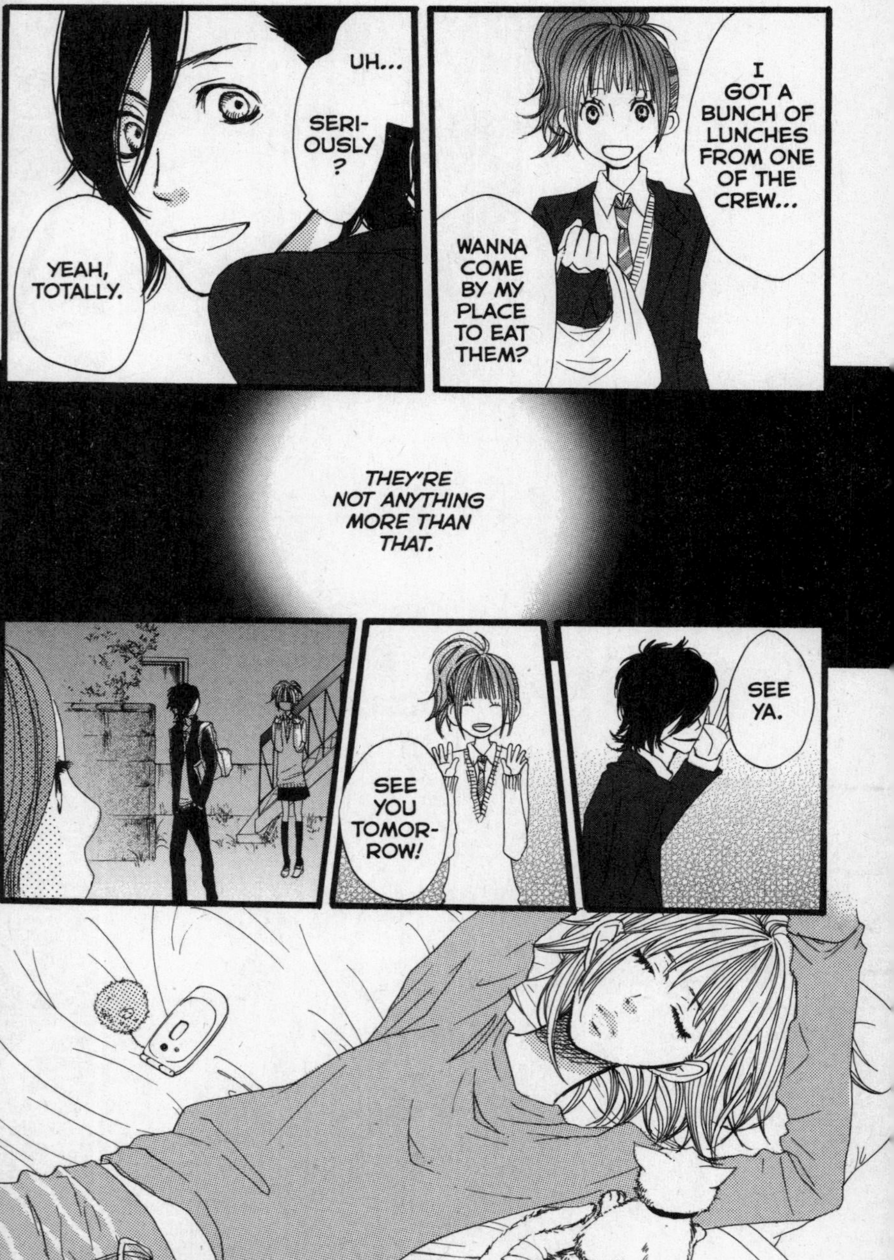
I GOT A BUNCH OF LUNCHES FROM ONE OF THE CREW...
WANNA COME BY MY PLACE TO EAT THEM?
UH...
SERIOUSLY?
YEAH, TOTALLY.
THEY'RE NOT ANYTHING MORE THAN THAT.
SEE YA.
SEE YOU TOMORROW!

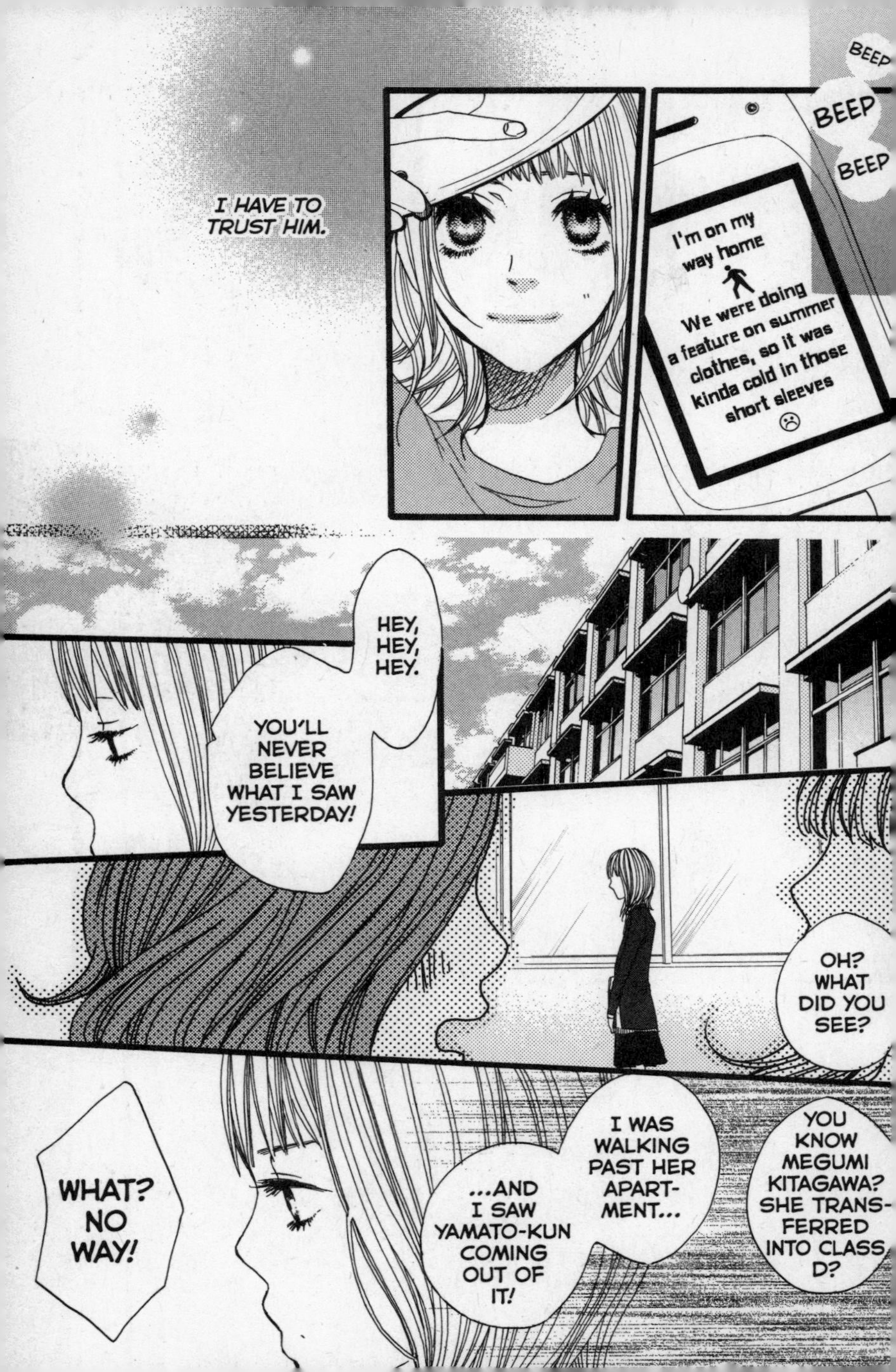
BEEP
BEEP
BEEP
I'm on my way home
We were doing a feature on summer clothes, so it was kinda cold in those short sleeves
I HAVE TO TRUST HIM.
HEY, HEY, HEY.
YOU'LL NEVER BELIEVE WHAT I SAW YESTERDAY!
OH? WHAT DID YOU SEE?
YOU KNOW MEGUMI KITAGAWA? SHE TRANS-FERRED INTO CLASS D?
I WAS WALKING PAST HER APART-MENT...
...AND I SAW YAMATO-KUN COMING OUT OF IT!
WHAT? NO WAY!

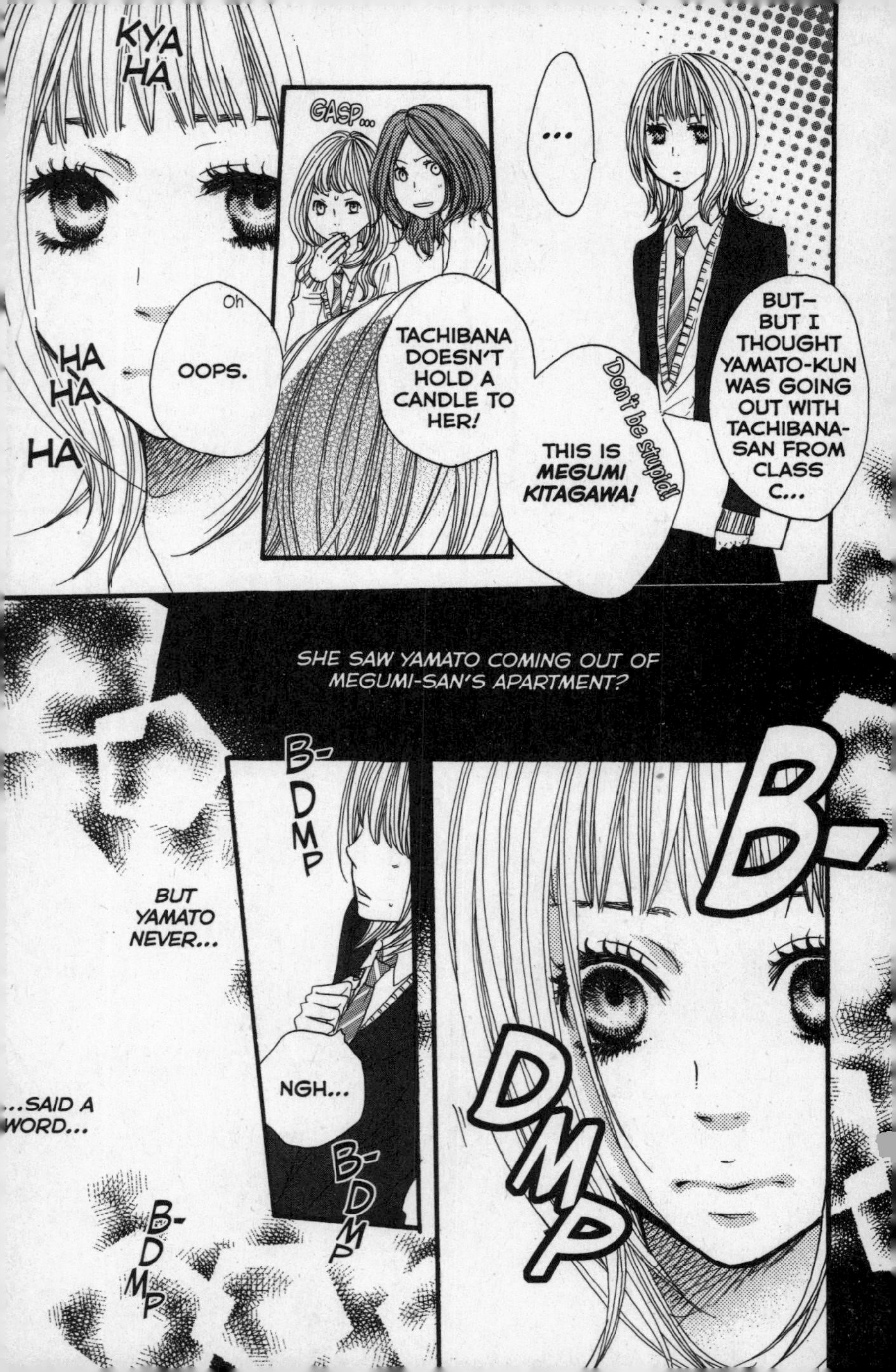

...
BUT— BUT I THOUGHT YAMATO-KUN WAS GOING OUT WITH TACHIBANA-SAN FROM CLASS C...
Don't be stupid!
THIS IS MEGUMI KITAGAWA!
TACHIBANA DOESN'T HOLD A CANDLE TO HER!
GASP...
KYA HA
Oh
OOPS.
HA HA HA
SHE SAW YAMATO COMING OUT OF MEGUMI-SAN'S APARTMENT?
B-DMP
B-DMP
B-DMP
NGH...
B-DMP
BUT YAMATO NEVER...
...SAID A WORD...
B-DMP

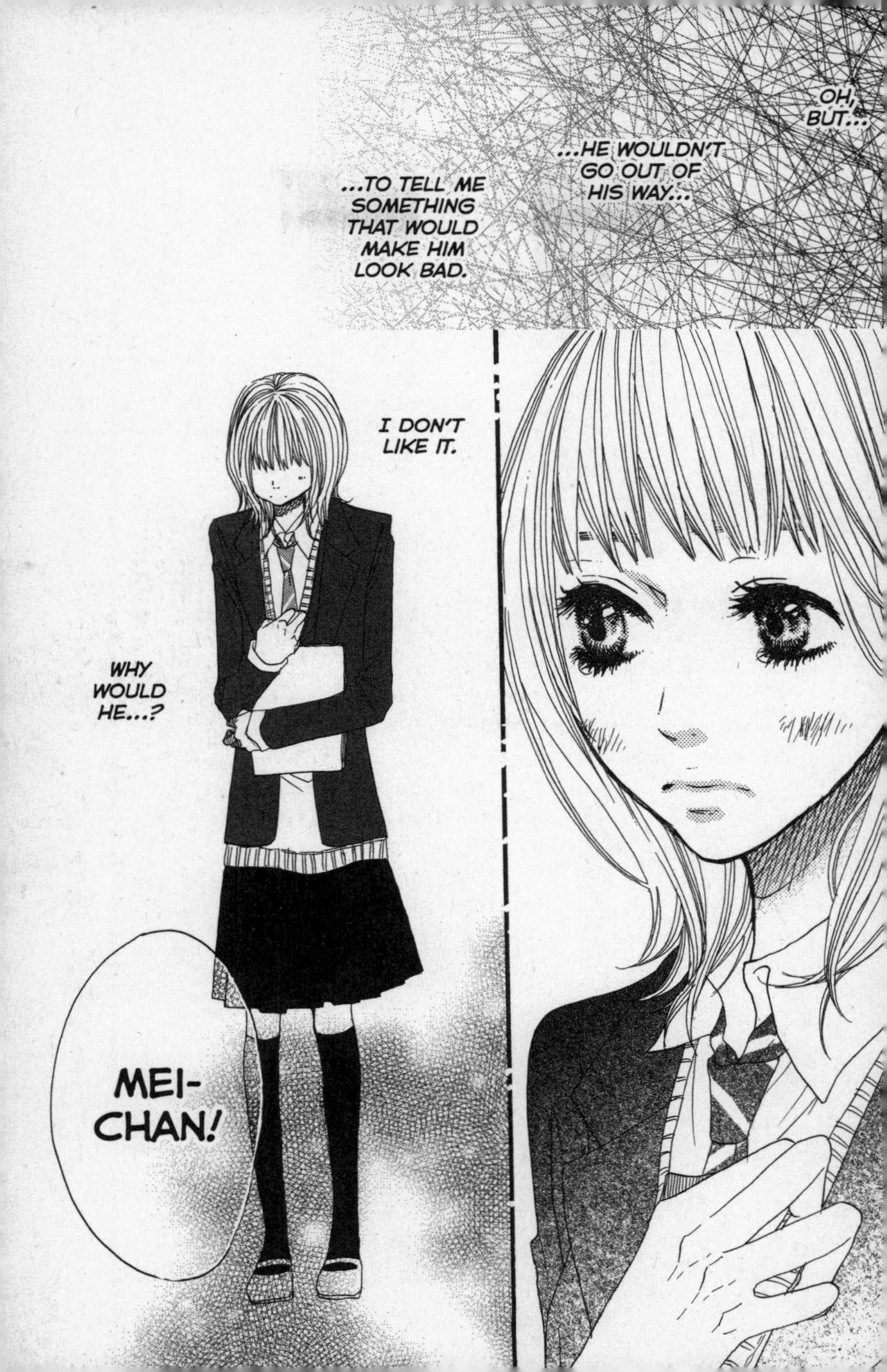
OH, BUT...
...HE WOULDN'T GO OUT OF HIS WAY...
...TO TELL ME SOMETHING THAT WOULD MAKE HIM LOOK BAD.
I DON'T LIKE IT.
WHY WOULD HE...?
MEI-CHAN!

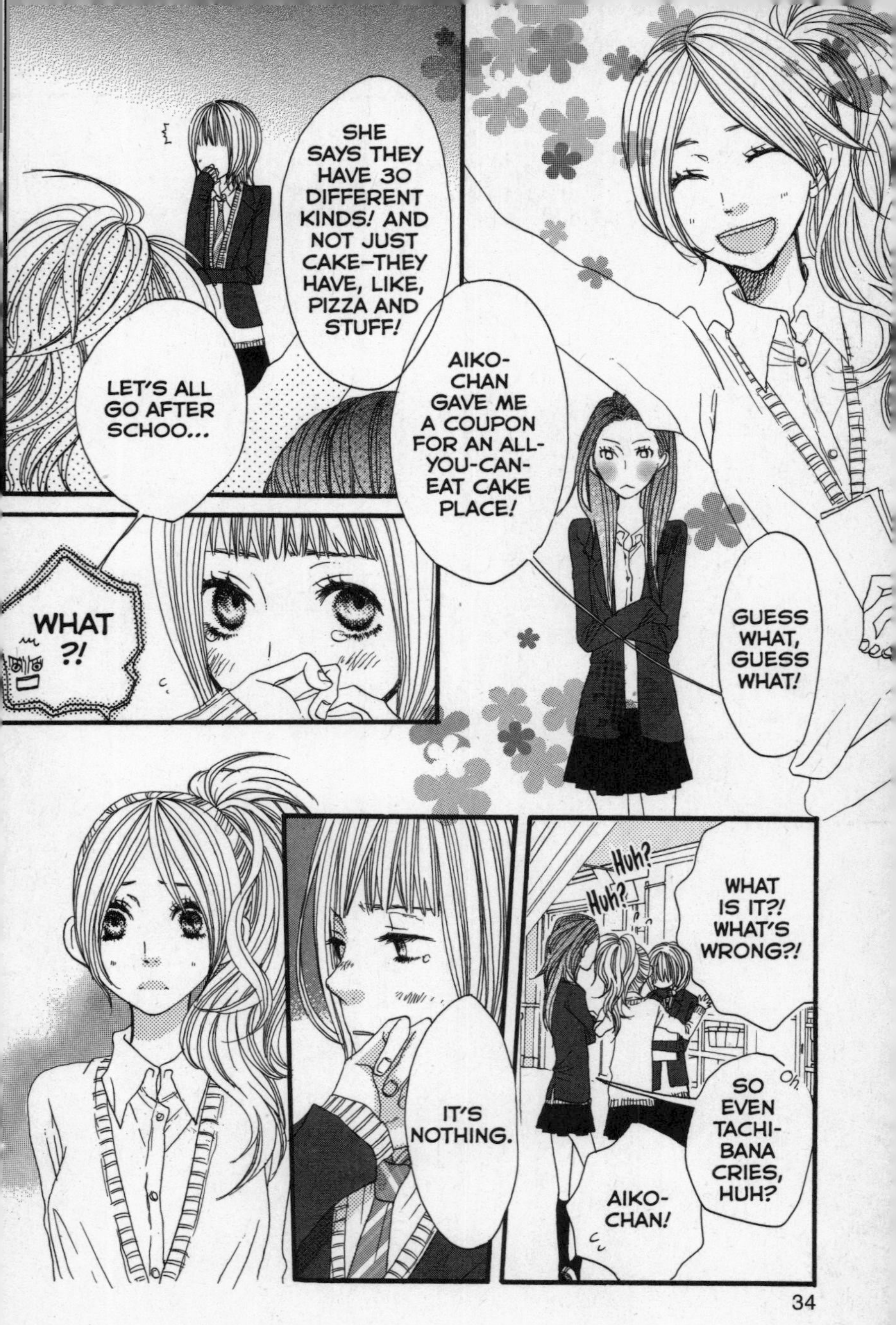
GUESS WHAT, GUESS WHAT!
AIKO-CHAN GAVE ME A COUPON FOR AN ALL-YOU-CAN-EAT CAKE PLACE!
SHE SAYS THEY HAVE 30 DIFFERENT KINDS! AND NOT JUST CAKE—THEY HAVE, LIKE, PIZZA AND STUFF!
LET'S ALL GO AFTER SCHOO...
WHAT ?!
WHAT IS IT?! WHAT'S WRONG?!
Huh?
Huh?
Oh.
SO EVEN TACHIBANA CRIES, HUH?
AIKO-CHAN!
IT'S NOTHING.

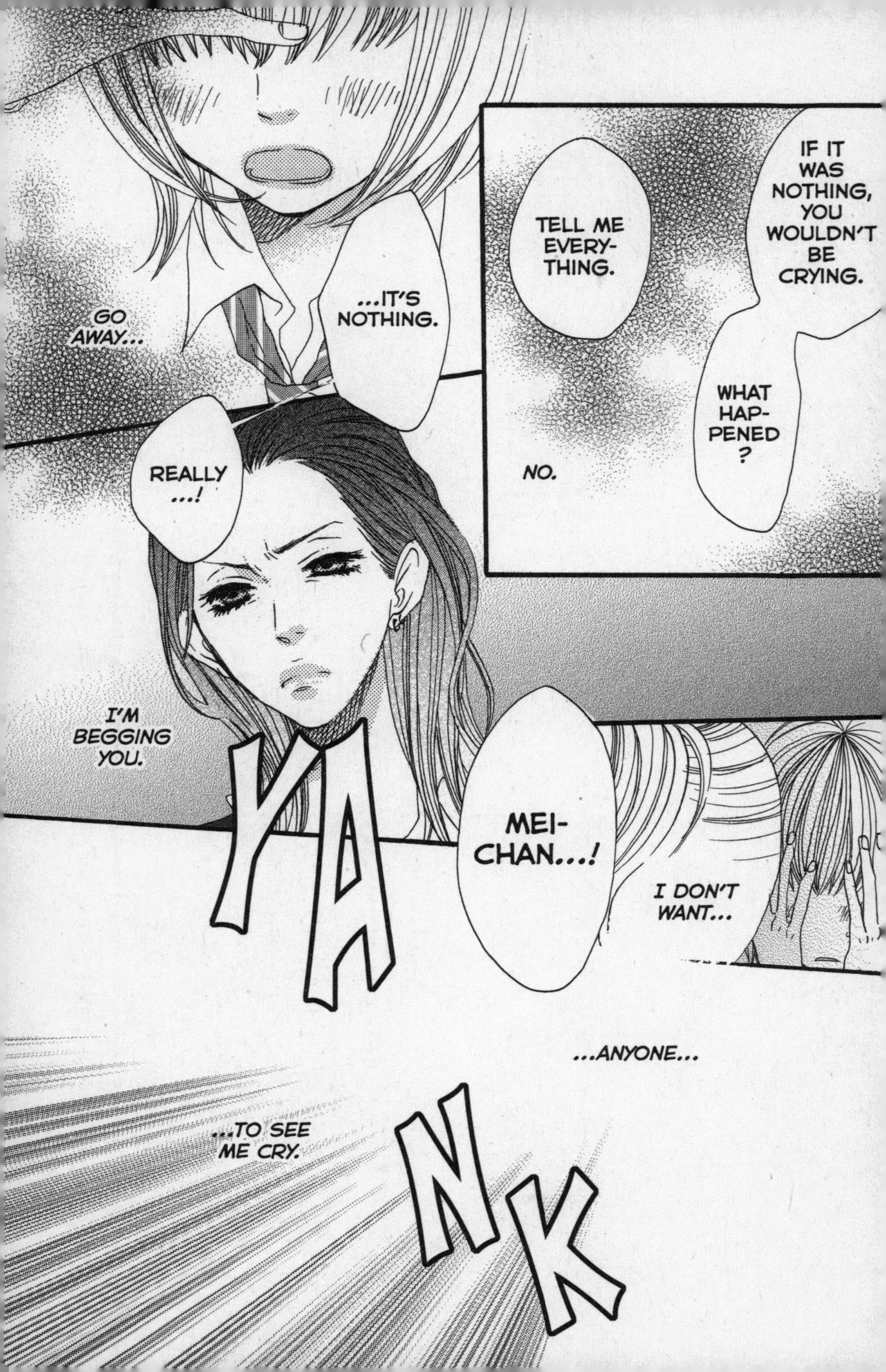
...IT'S NOTHING.
GO AWAY...
IF IT WAS NOTHING, YOU WOULDN'T BE CRYING.
WHAT HAPPENED?
TELL ME EVERYTHING.
NO.
REALLY...!
I'M BEGGING YOU.
MEI-CHAN...!
I DON'T WANT...
YANK
...ANYONE...
...TO SEE ME CRY.

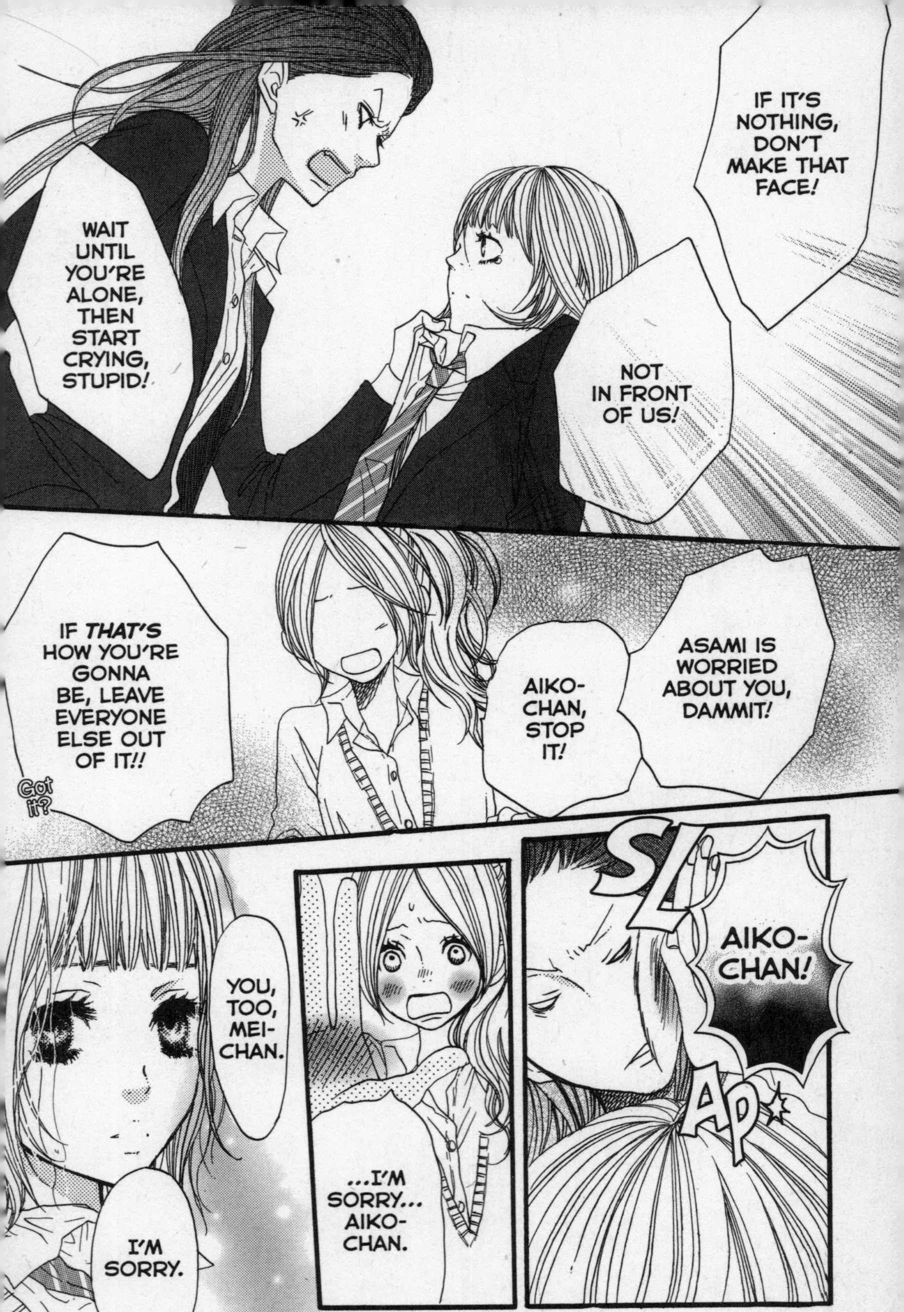
IF IT'S NOTHING, DON'T MAKE THAT FACE!
NOT IN FRONT OF US!
WAIT UNTIL YOU'RE ALONE, THEN START CRYING, STUPID!
ASAMI IS WORRIED ABOUT YOU, DAMMIT!
AIKO-CHAN, STOP IT!
IF *THAT'S* HOW YOU'RE GONNA BE, LEAVE EVERYONE ELSE OUT OF IT!!
Got it?
SLAP
AIKO-CHAN!
...I'M SORRY... AIKO-CHAN.
YOU, TOO, MEI-CHAN.
I'M SORRY.

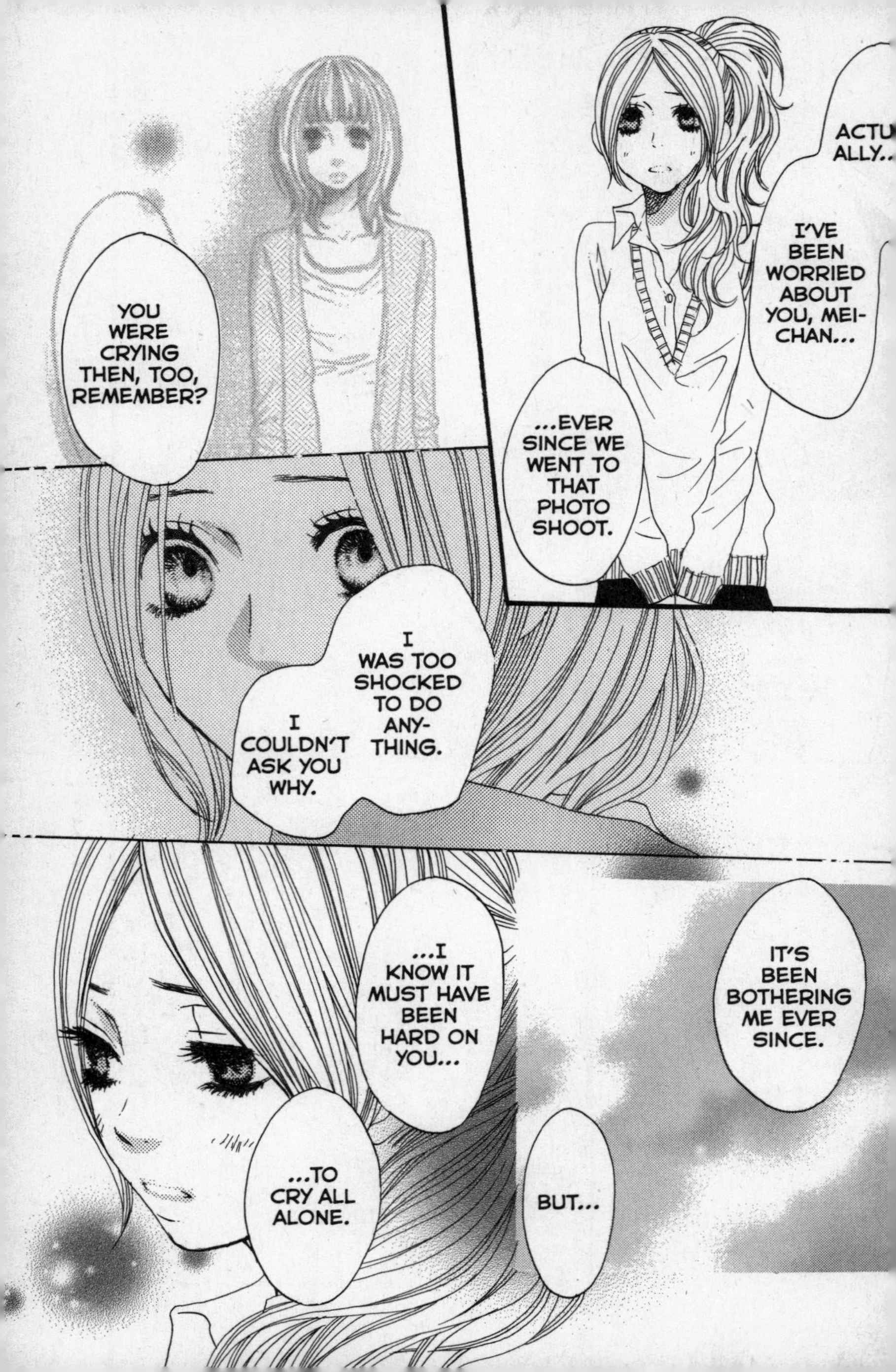
ACTUALLY..
I'VE BEEN WORRIED ABOUT YOU, MEI-CHAN...
...EVER SINCE WE WENT TO THAT PHOTO SHOOT.
YOU WERE CRYING THEN, TOO, REMEMBER?
I WAS TOO SHOCKED TO DO ANYTHING.
I COULDN'T ASK YOU WHY.
IT'S BEEN BOTHERING ME EVER SINCE.
BUT...
...I KNOW IT MUST HAVE BEEN HARD ON YOU...
...TO CRY ALL ALONE.

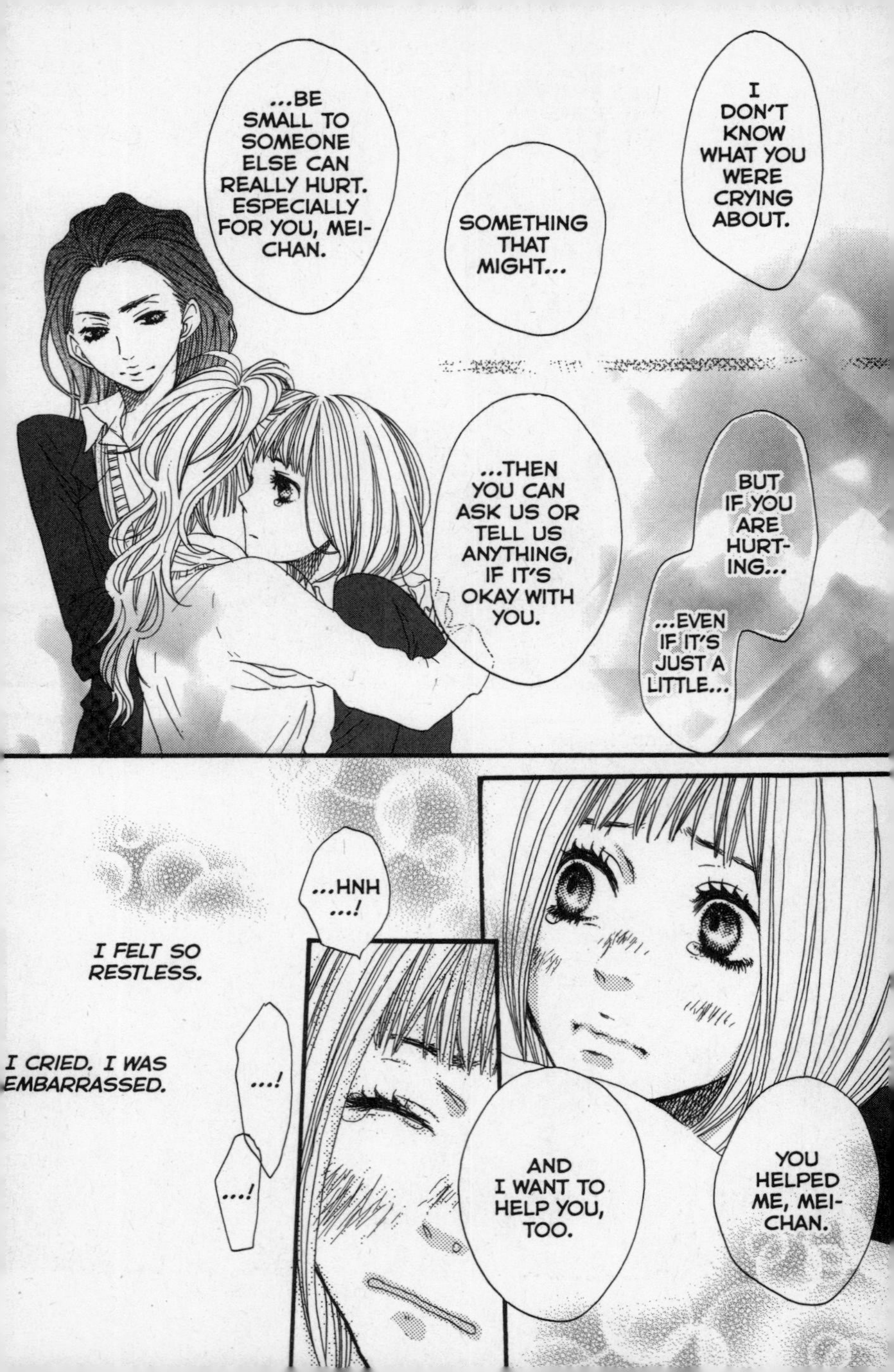
I DON'T KNOW WHAT YOU WERE CRYING ABOUT.
SOMETHING THAT MIGHT...
...BE SMALL TO SOMEONE ELSE CAN REALLY HURT. ESPECIALLY FOR YOU, MEI-CHAN.
BUT IF YOU ARE HURTING...
...EVEN IF IT'S JUST A LITTLE...
...THEN YOU CAN ASK US OR TELL US ANYTHING, IF IT'S OKAY WITH YOU.
...HNH ...!
YOU HELPED ME, MEI-CHAN.
AND I WANT TO HELP YOU, TOO.
...!
...!
I FELT SO RESTLESS.
I CRIED. I WAS EMBARRASSED.

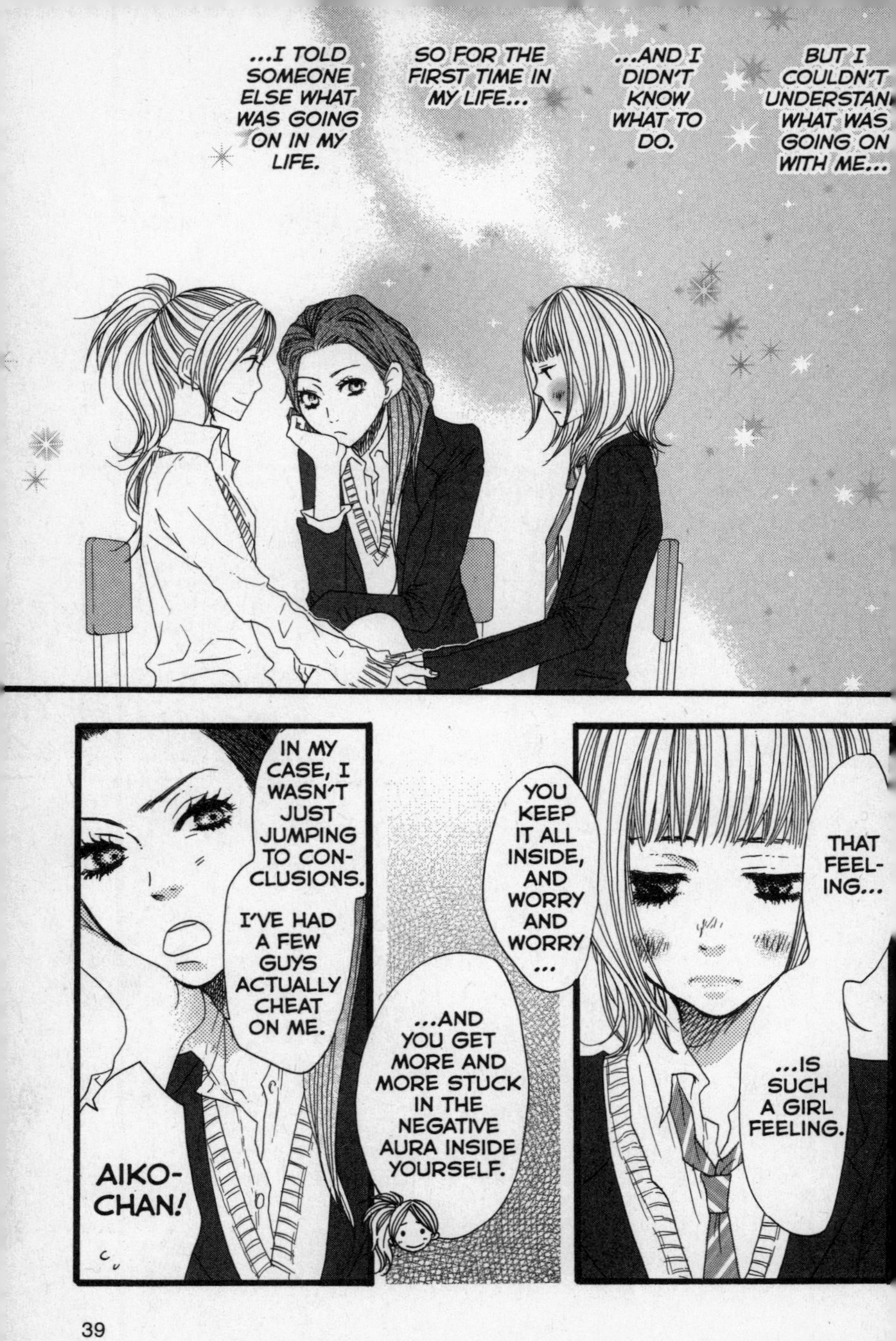
BUT I COULDN'T UNDERSTAN WHAT WAS GOING ON WITH ME...
...AND I DIDN'T KNOW WHAT TO DO.
SO FOR THE FIRST TIME IN MY LIFE...
...I TOLD SOMEONE ELSE WHAT WAS GOING ON IN MY LIFE.
THAT FEEL-ING...
...IS SUCH A GIRL FEELING.
YOU KEEP IT ALL INSIDE, AND WORRY AND WORRY...
...AND YOU GET MORE AND MORE STUCK IN THE NEGATIVE AURA INSIDE YOURSELF.
IN MY CASE, I WASN'T JUST JUMPING TO CON-CLUSIONS.
I'VE HAD A FEW GUYS ACTUALLY CHEAT ON ME.
AIKO-CHAN!

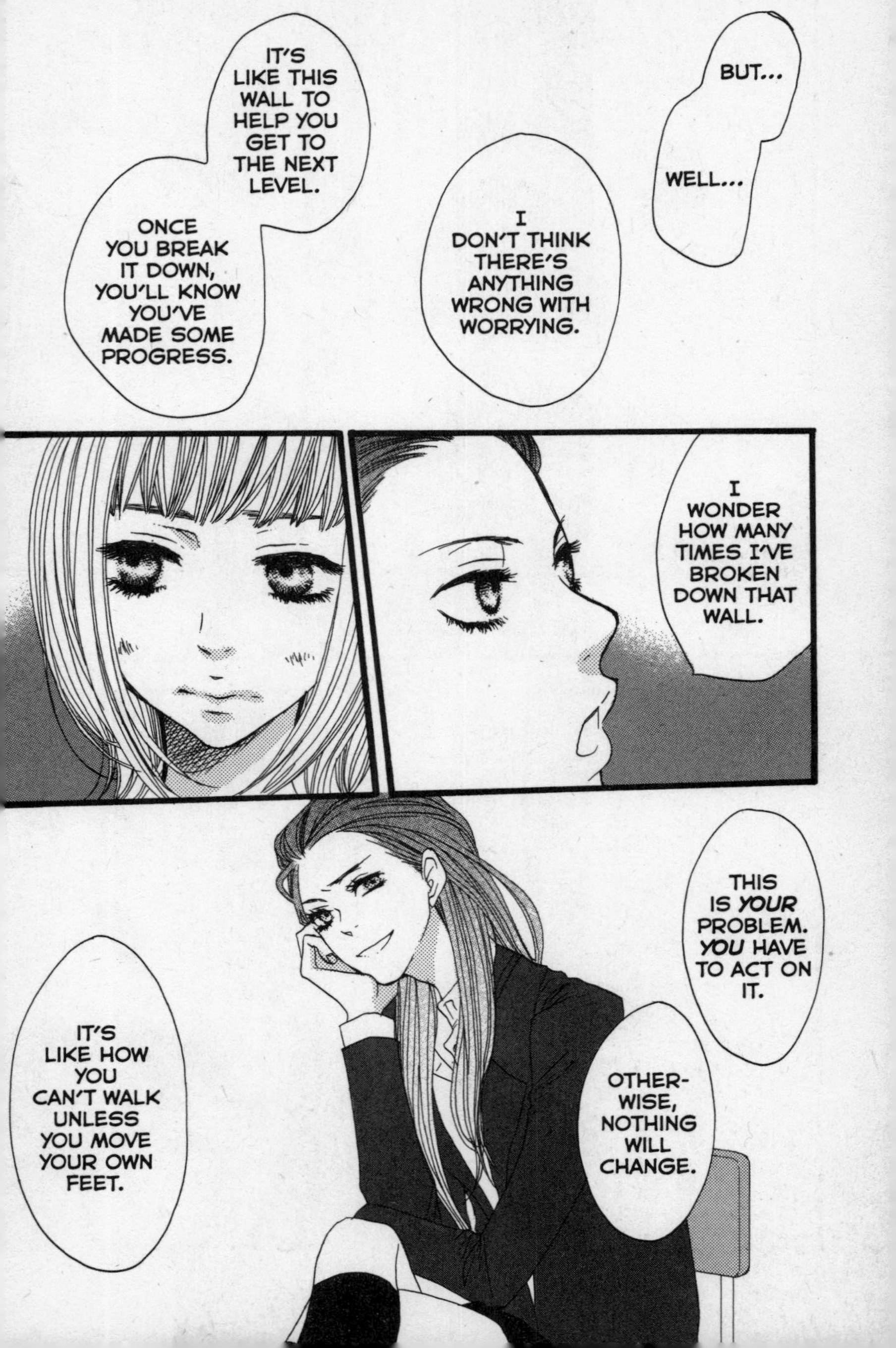
BUT...
WELL...
I DON'T THINK THERE'S ANYTHING WRONG WITH WORRYING.
IT'S LIKE THIS WALL TO HELP YOU GET TO THE NEXT LEVEL.
ONCE YOU BREAK IT DOWN, YOU'LL KNOW YOU'VE MADE SOME PROGRESS.
I WONDER HOW MANY TIMES I'VE BROKEN DOWN THAT WALL.
THIS IS *YOUR* PROBLEM. *YOU* HAVE TO ACT ON IT.
OTHER-WISE, NOTHING WILL CHANGE.
IT'S LIKE HOW YOU CAN'T WALK UNLESS YOU MOVE YOUR OWN FEET.

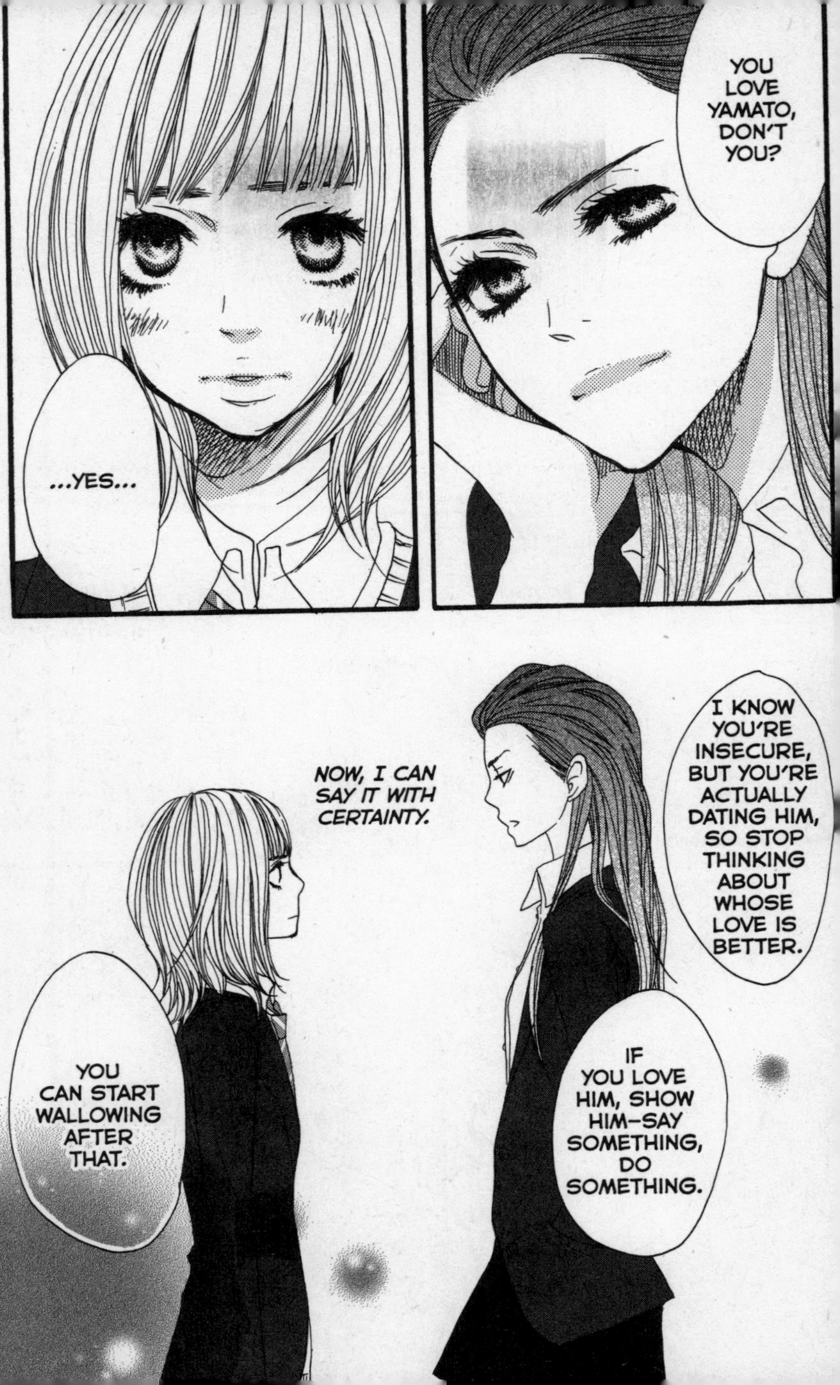
YOU LOVE YAMATO, DON'T YOU?
...YES...
I KNOW YOU'RE INSECURE, BUT YOU'RE ACTUALLY DATING HIM, SO STOP THINKING ABOUT WHOSE LOVE IS BETTER.
NOW, I CAN SAY IT WITH CERTAINTY.
IF YOU LOVE HIM, SHOW HIM–SAY SOMETHING, DO SOMETHING.
YOU CAN START WALLOWING AFTER THAT.

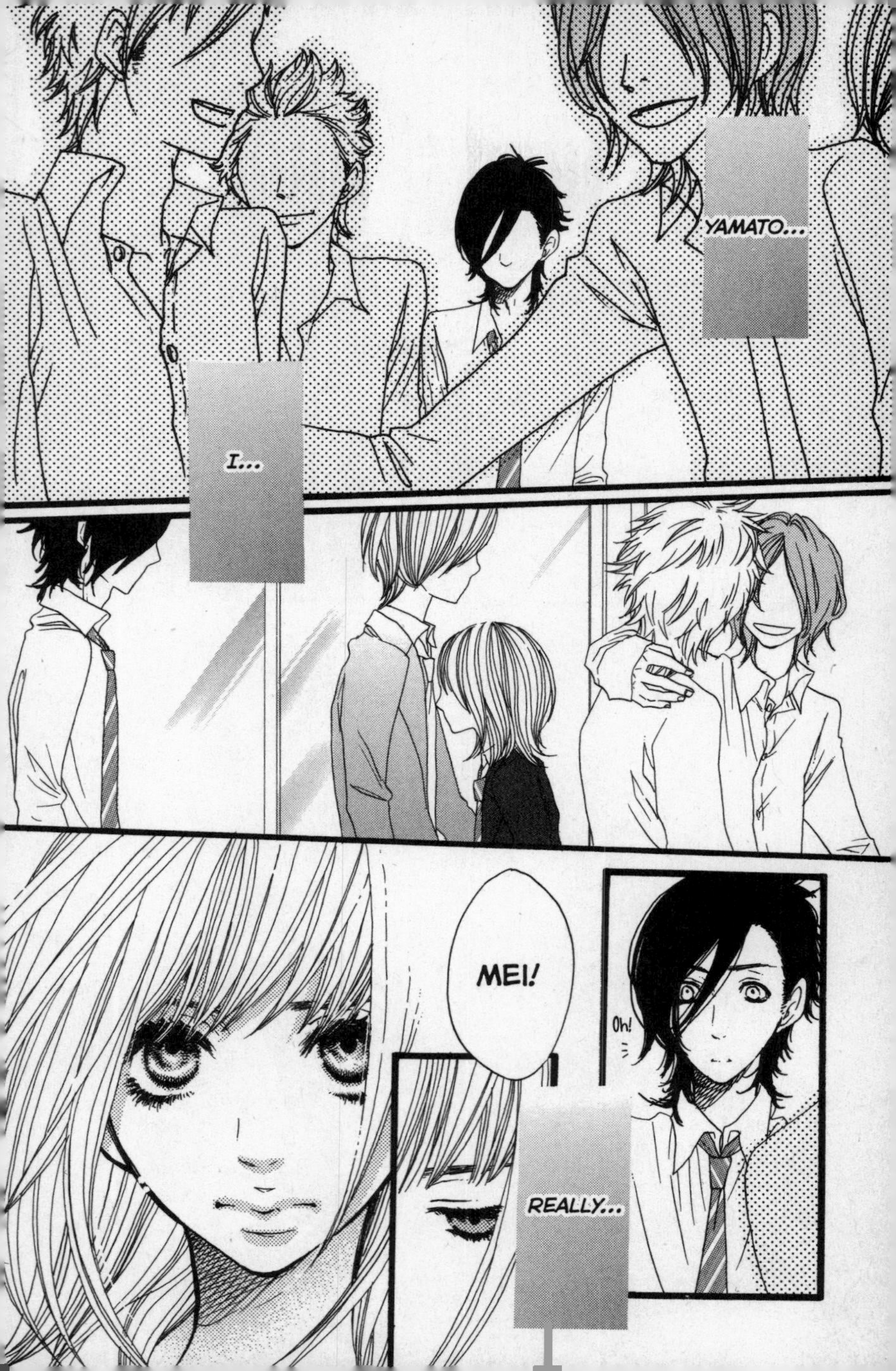
YAMATO...
I...
Oh!
MEI!
REALLY...

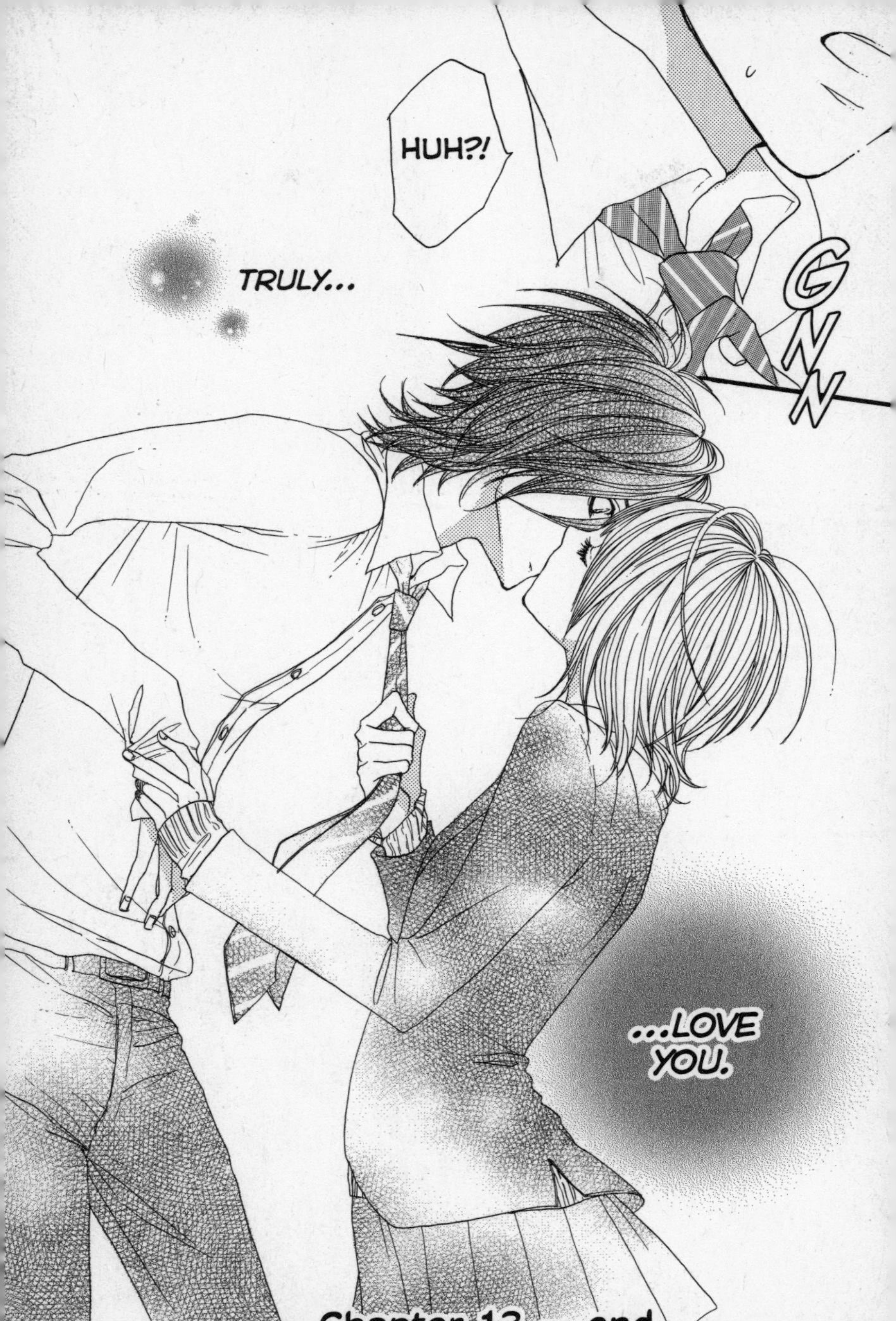
HUH?!
GNN
TRULY...
...LOVE YOU.

Chapter 13 — end

Say
"I love you."
Kanae Hazuki

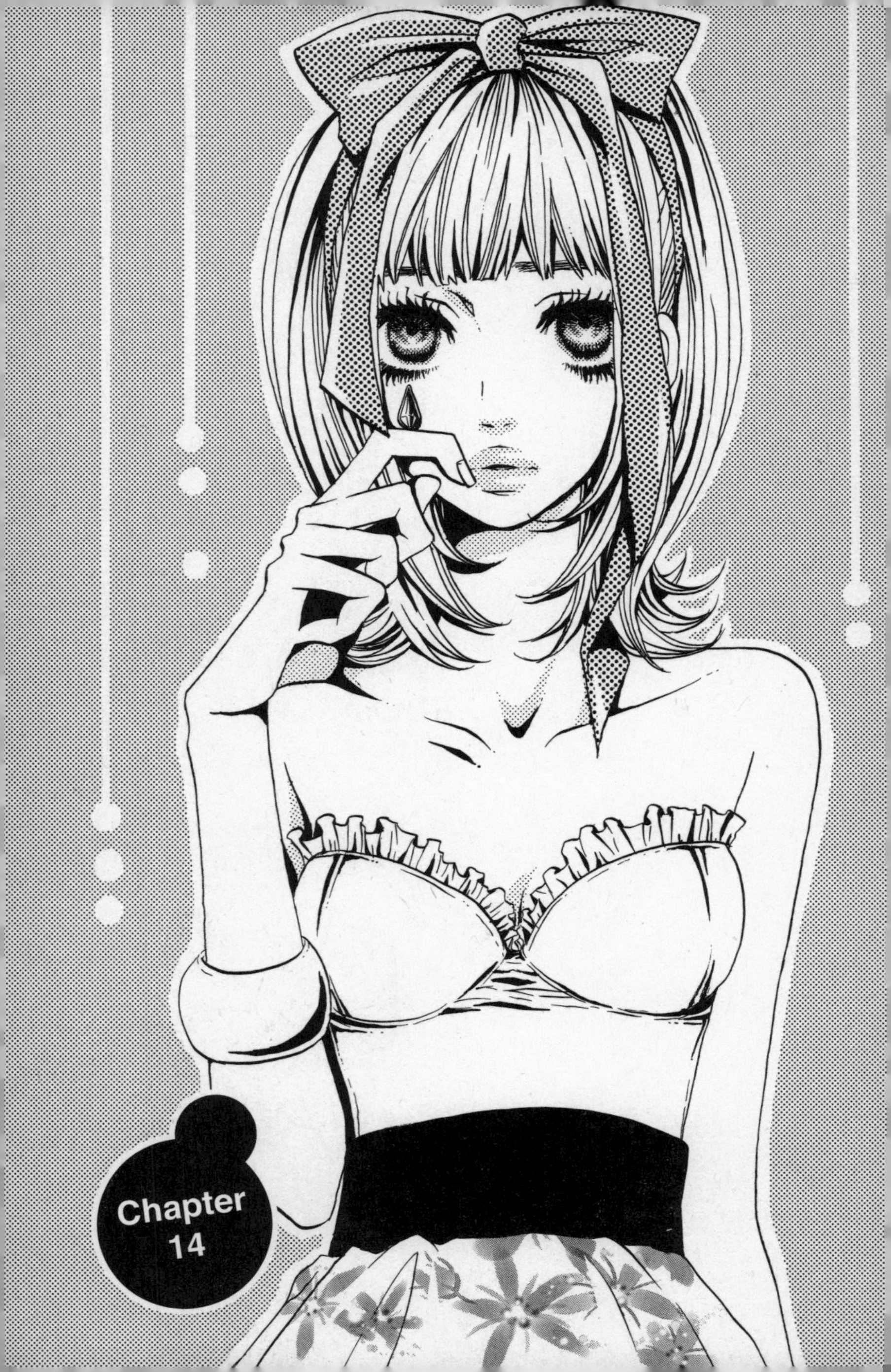
Chapter
14

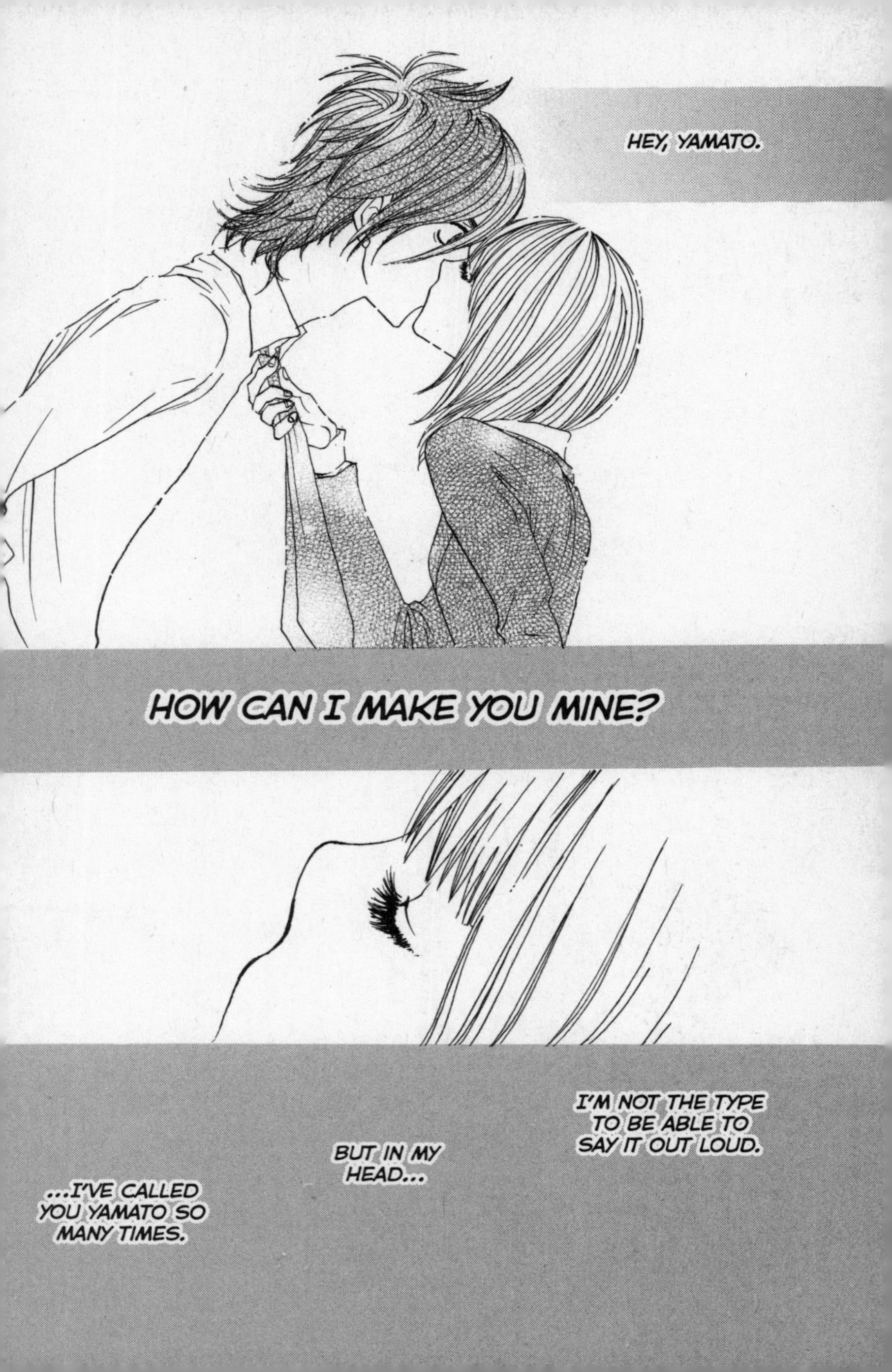
HEY, YAMATO.
HOW CAN I MAKE YOU MINE?
I'M NOT THE TYPE TO BE ABLE TO SAY IT OUT LOUD.
BUT IN MY HEAD...
...I'VE CALLED YOU YAMATO SO MANY TIMES.

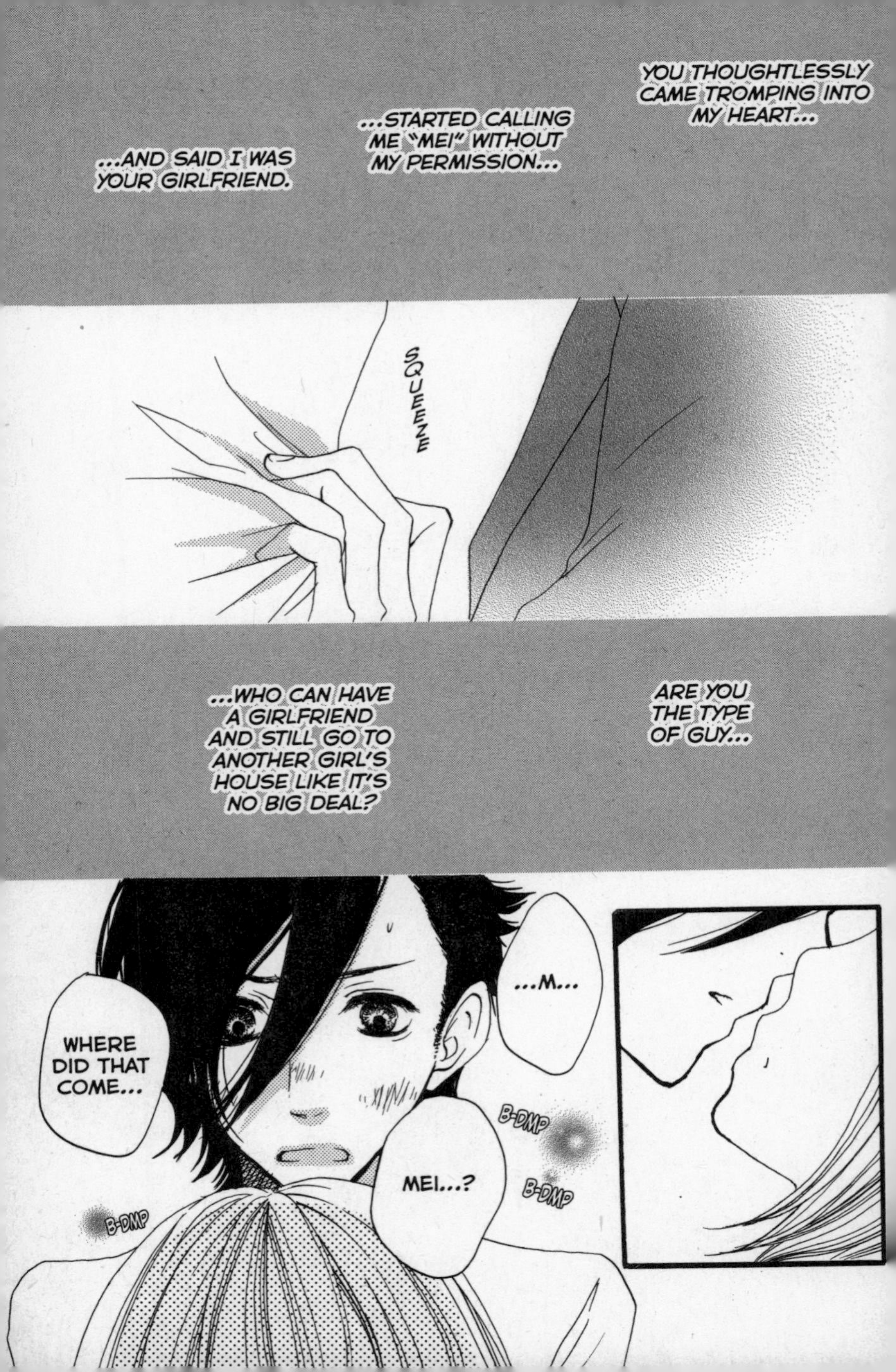
YOU THOUGHTLESSLY CAME TROMPING INTO MY HEART...
...STARTED CALLING ME "MEI" WITHOUT MY PERMISSION...
...AND SAID I WAS YOUR GIRLFRIEND.
SQUEEZE
ARE YOU THE TYPE OF GUY...
...WHO CAN HAVE A GIRLFRIEND AND STILL GO TO ANOTHER GIRL'S HOUSE LIKE IT'S NO BIG DEAL?
...M...
WHERE DID THAT COME...
B-DMP
MEI...?
B-DMP
B-DMP

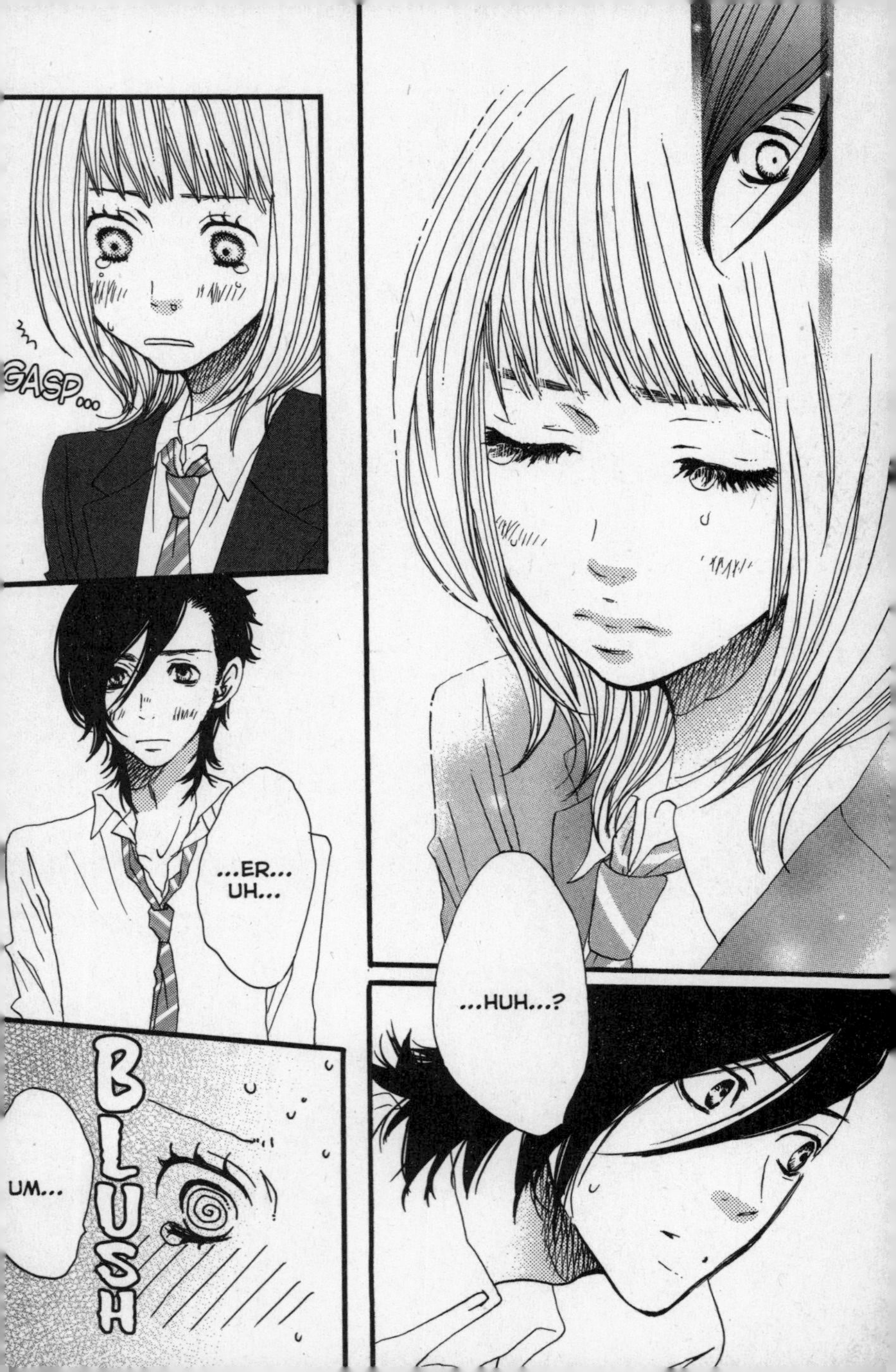
...HUH...?
GASP...
...ER... UH...
BLUSH
UM...

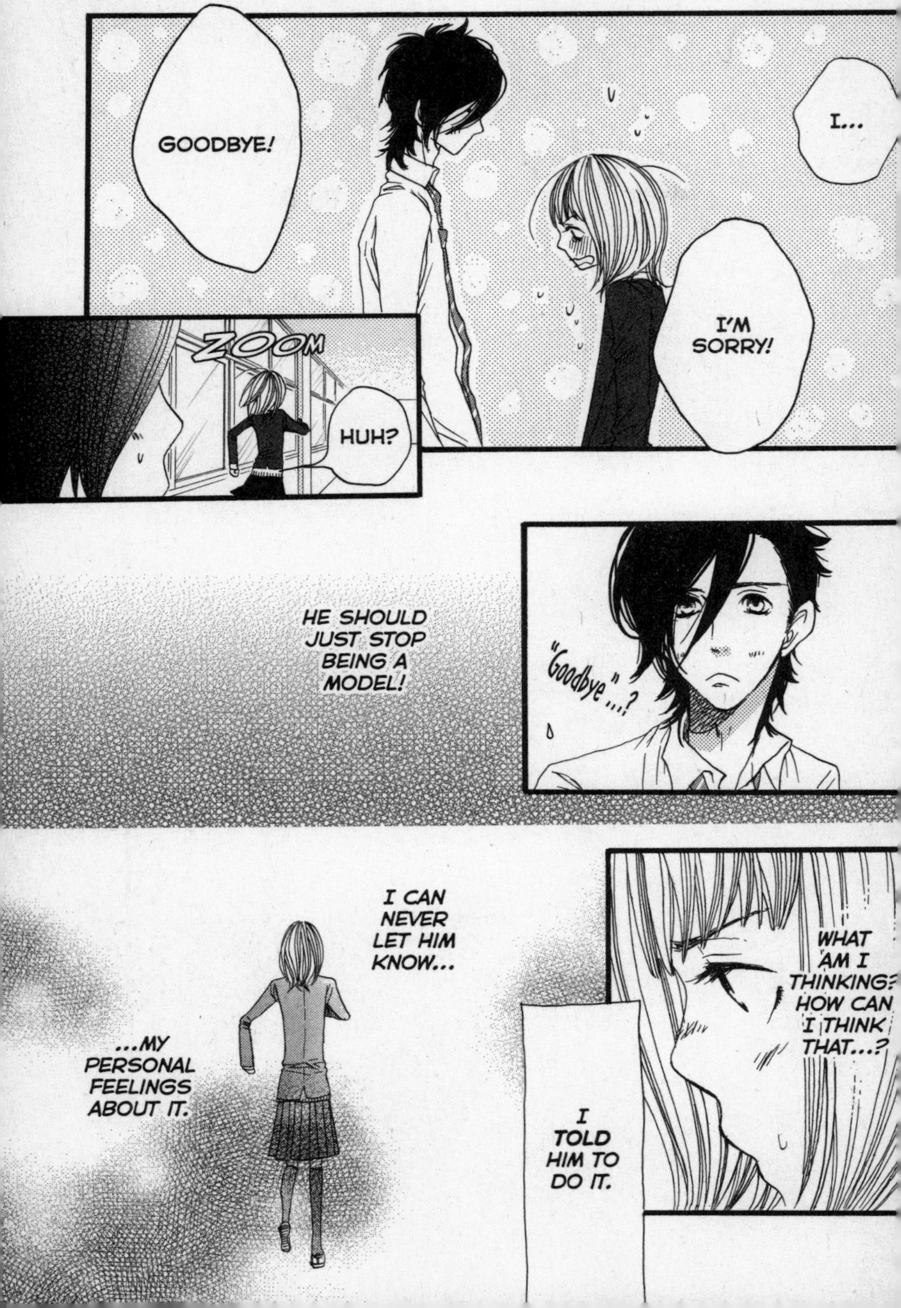
I...
I'M SORRY!
GOODBYE!
ZOOM
HUH?
"Goodbye"...?
HE SHOULD JUST STOP BEING A MODEL!
WHAT AM I THINKING? HOW CAN I THINK THAT...?
I TOLD HIM TO DO IT.
I CAN NEVER LET HIM KNOW...
...MY PERSONAL FEELINGS ABOUT IT.

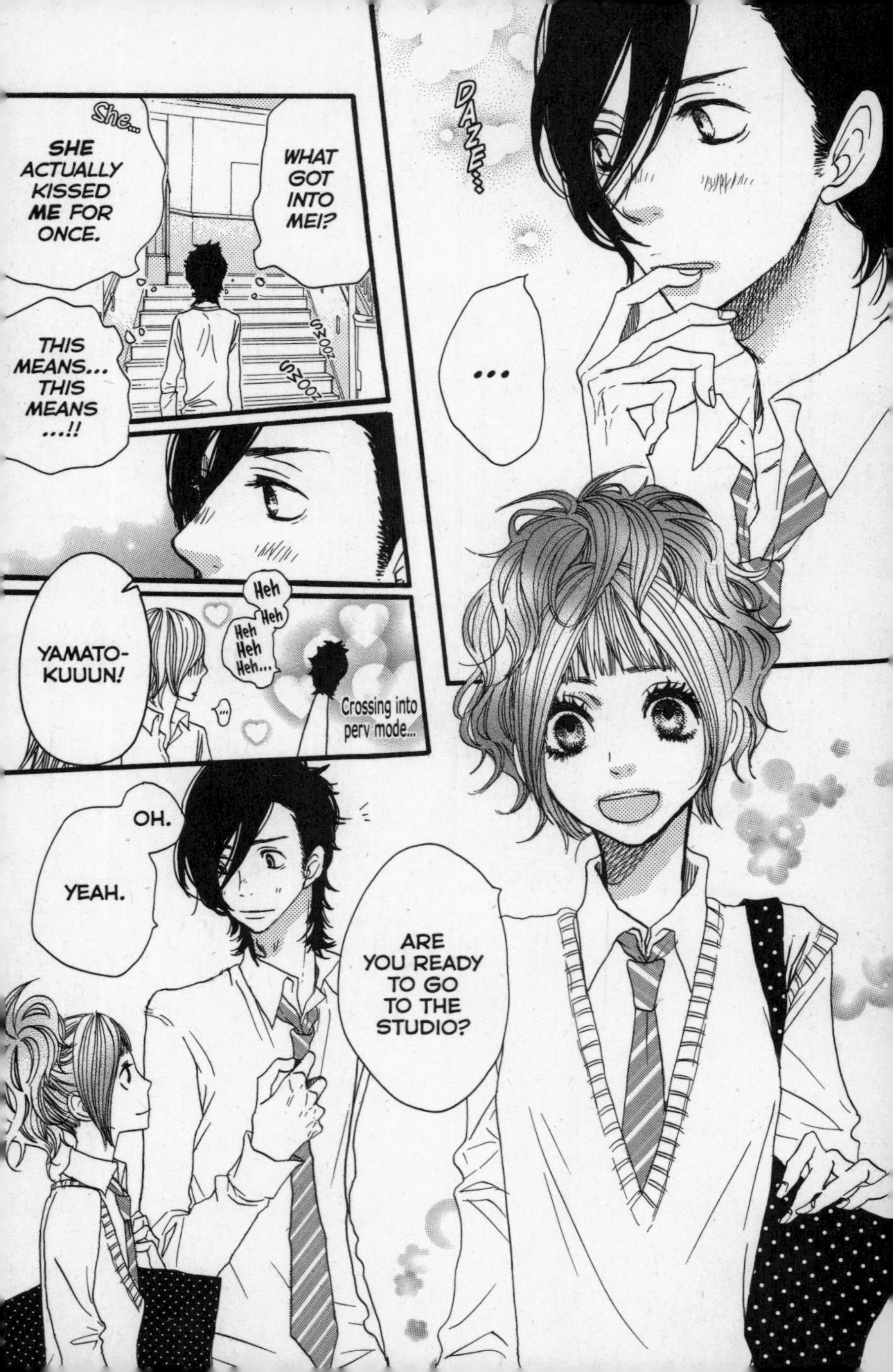
DAZE...
...
WHAT GOT INTO MEI?
She...
SHE ACTUALLY KISSED ME FOR ONCE.
THIS MEANS... THIS MEANS ...!!
Heh Heh Heh Heh Heh...
Crossing into perv mode...
...
YAMATO-KUUUN!
ARE YOU READY TO GO TO THE STUDIO?
OH.
YEAH.

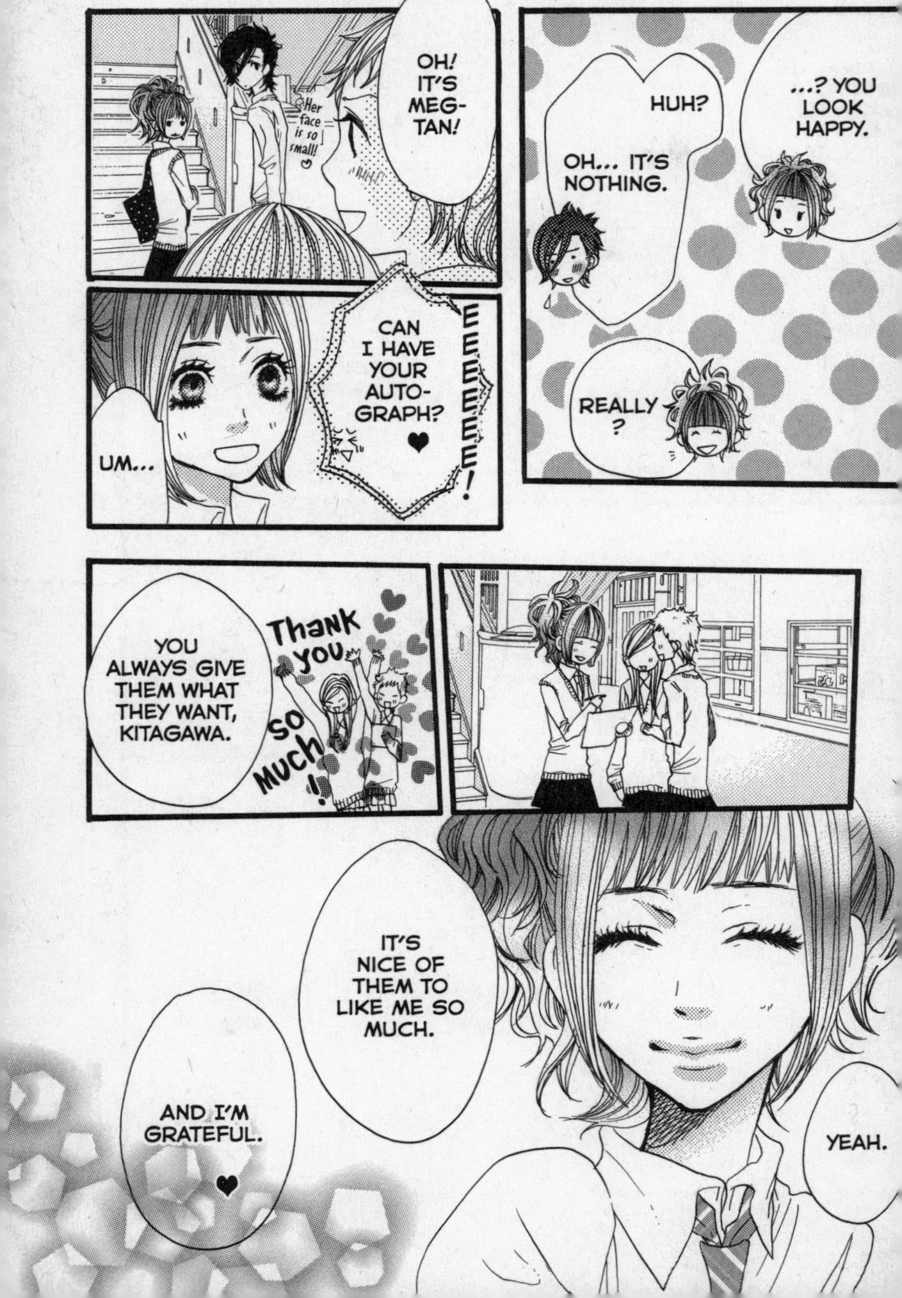
...? YOU LOOK HAPPY.
HUH?
OH... IT'S NOTHING.
REALLY?
OH! IT'S MEG-TAN!
Her face is so small!
EEEEEEE!
CAN I HAVE YOUR AUTO-GRAPH? ♥
UM...
Thank you so much!
YOU ALWAYS GIVE THEM WHAT THEY WANT, KITAGAWA.
YEAH.
IT'S NICE OF THEM TO LIKE ME SO MUCH.
AND I'M GRATEFUL. ♥

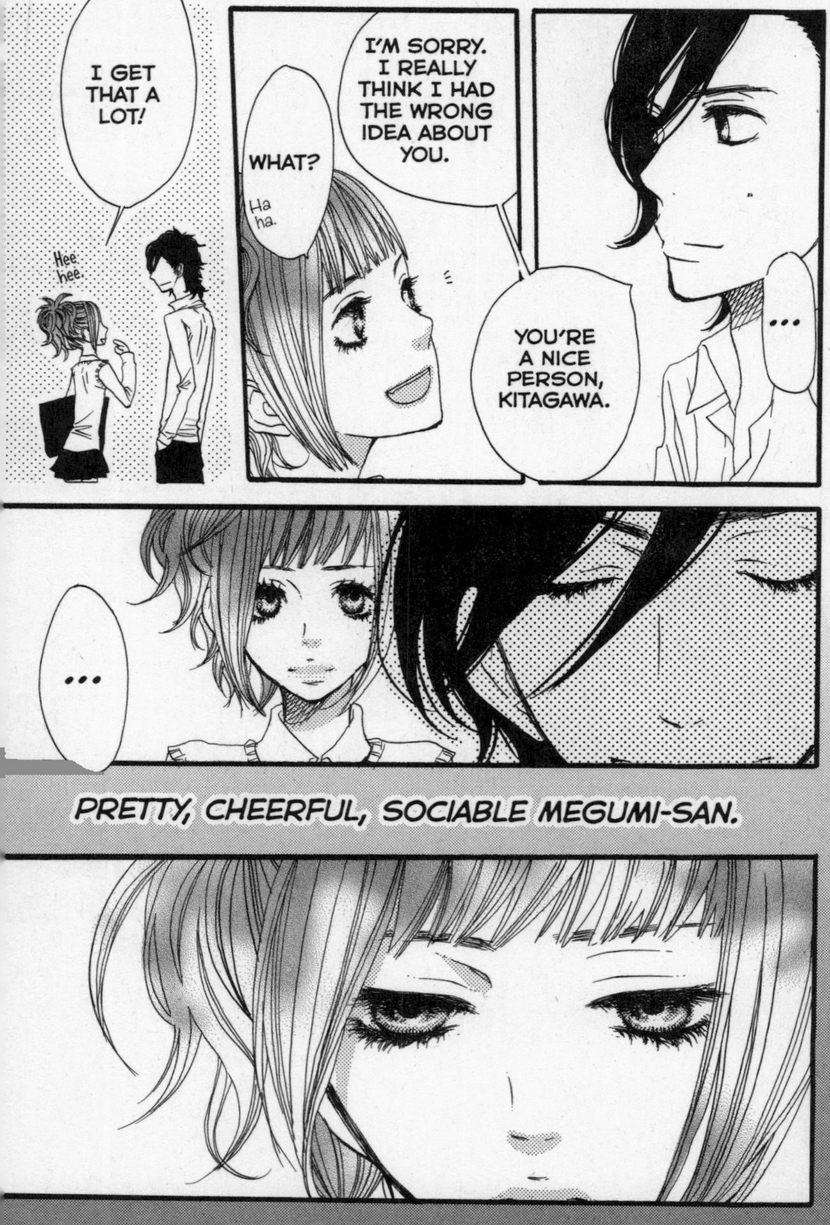
...
YOU'RE A NICE PERSON, KITAGAWA.
I'M SORRY. I REALLY THINK I HAD THE WRONG IDEA ABOUT YOU.
WHAT?
Ha ha.
I GET THAT A LOT!
Hee hee.
...
PRETTY, CHEERFUL, SOCIABLE MEGUMI-SAN.

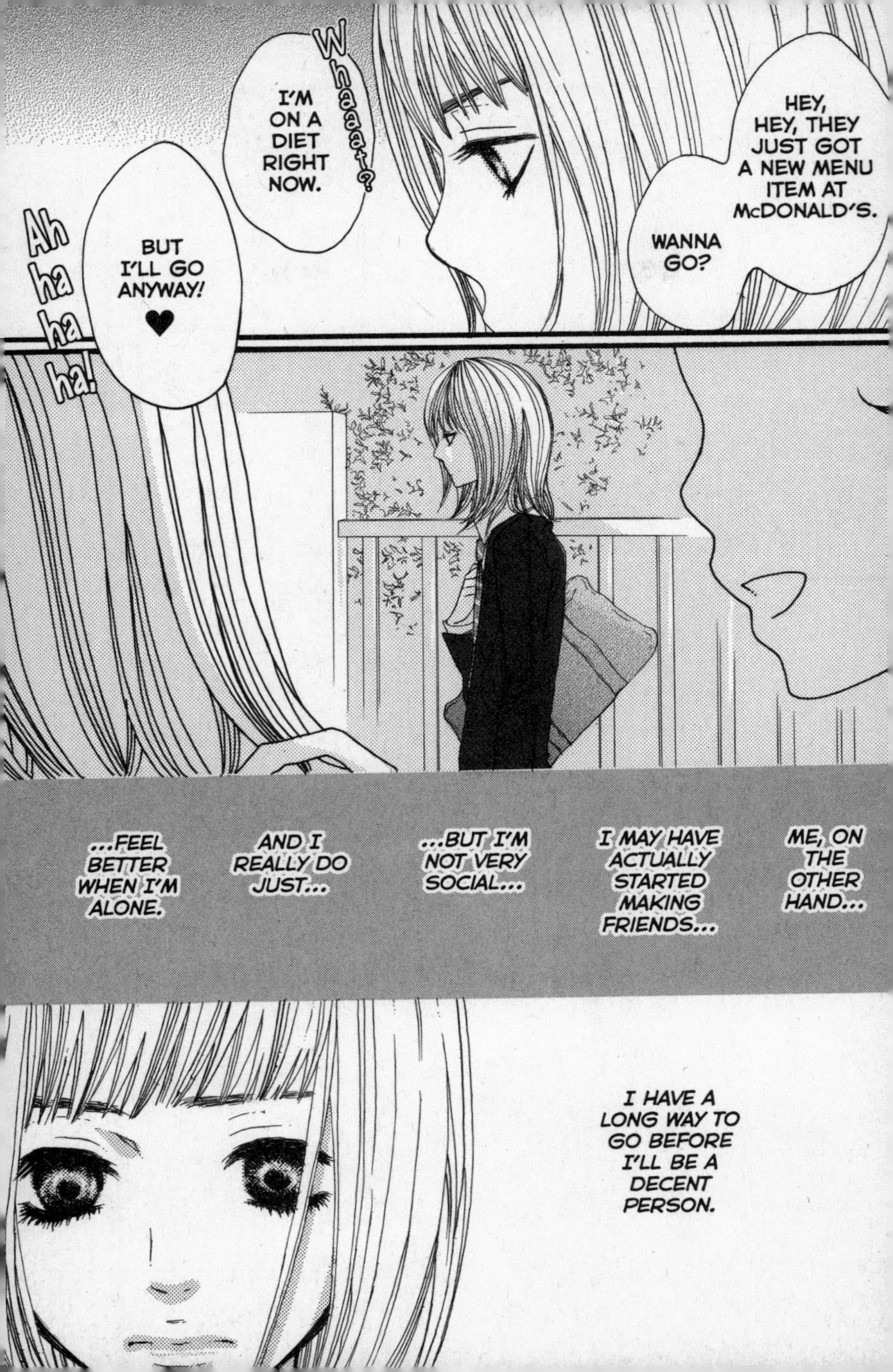
HEY, HEY, THEY JUST GOT A NEW MENU ITEM AT McDONALD'S.
WANNA GO?
I'M ON A DIET RIGHT NOW.
Whaaat?
BUT I'LL GO ANYWAY! ♥
Ah ha ha ha!
ME, ON THE OTHER HAND...
I MAY HAVE ACTUALLY STARTED MAKING FRIENDS...
...BUT I'M NOT VERY SOCIAL...
AND I REALLY DO JUST...
...FEEL BETTER WHEN I'M ALONE.
I HAVE A LONG WAY TO GO BEFORE I'LL BE A DECENT PERSON.

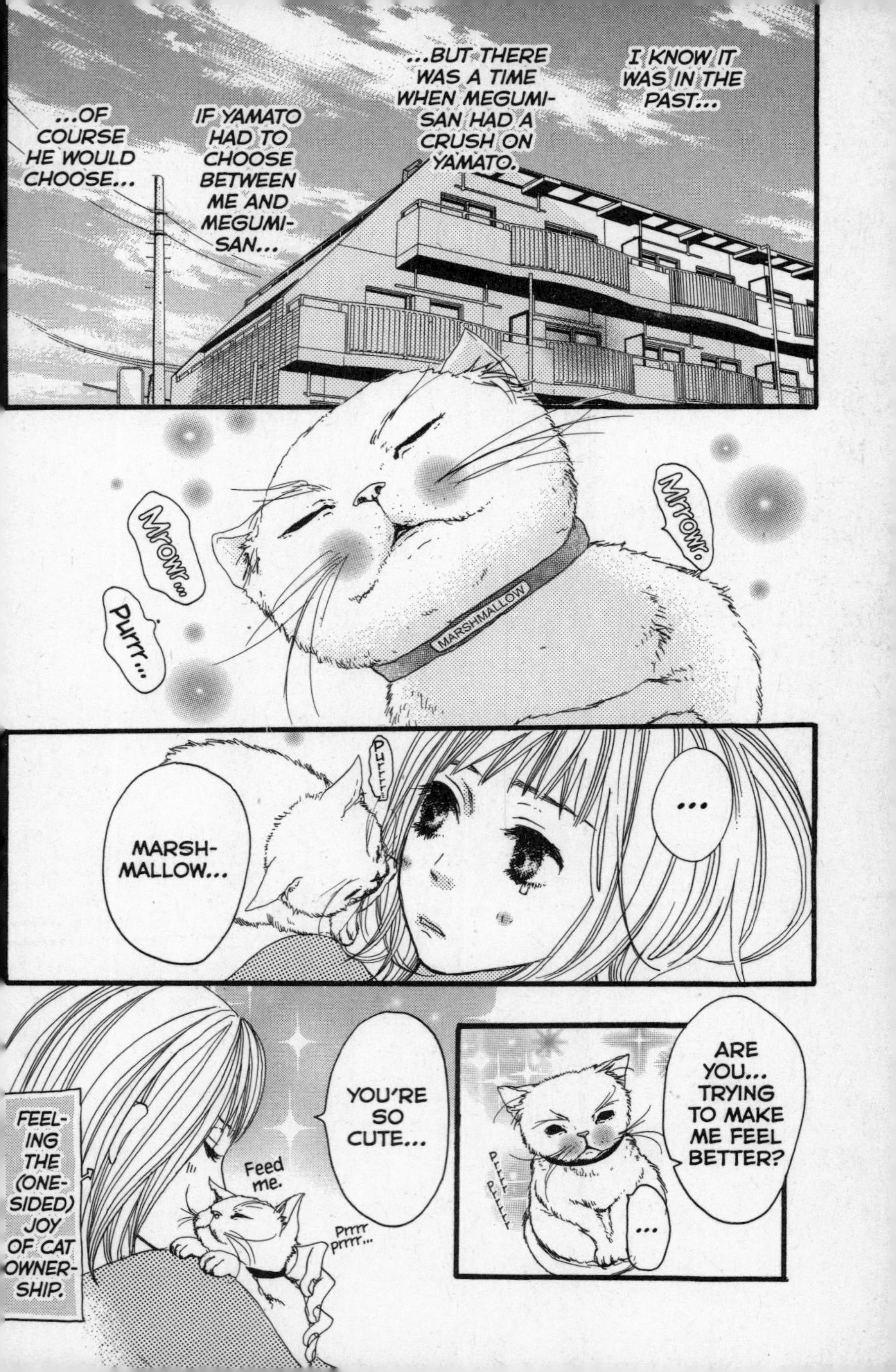
I KNOW IT WAS IN THE PAST...
...BUT THERE WAS A TIME WHEN MEGUMI-SAN HAD A CRUSH ON YAMATO.
IF YAMATO HAD TO CHOOSE BETWEEN ME AND MEGUMI-SAN...
...OF COURSE HE WOULD CHOOSE...
Mrrowr.
MARSHMALLOW
Mrrowr...
Purrr...
...
MARSH-MALLOW...
ARE YOU... TRYING TO MAKE ME FEEL BETTER?
...
YOU'RE SO CUTE...
Feed me.
Prrrr prrrr...
FEELING THE (ONE-SIDED) JOY OF CAT OWNERSHIP.

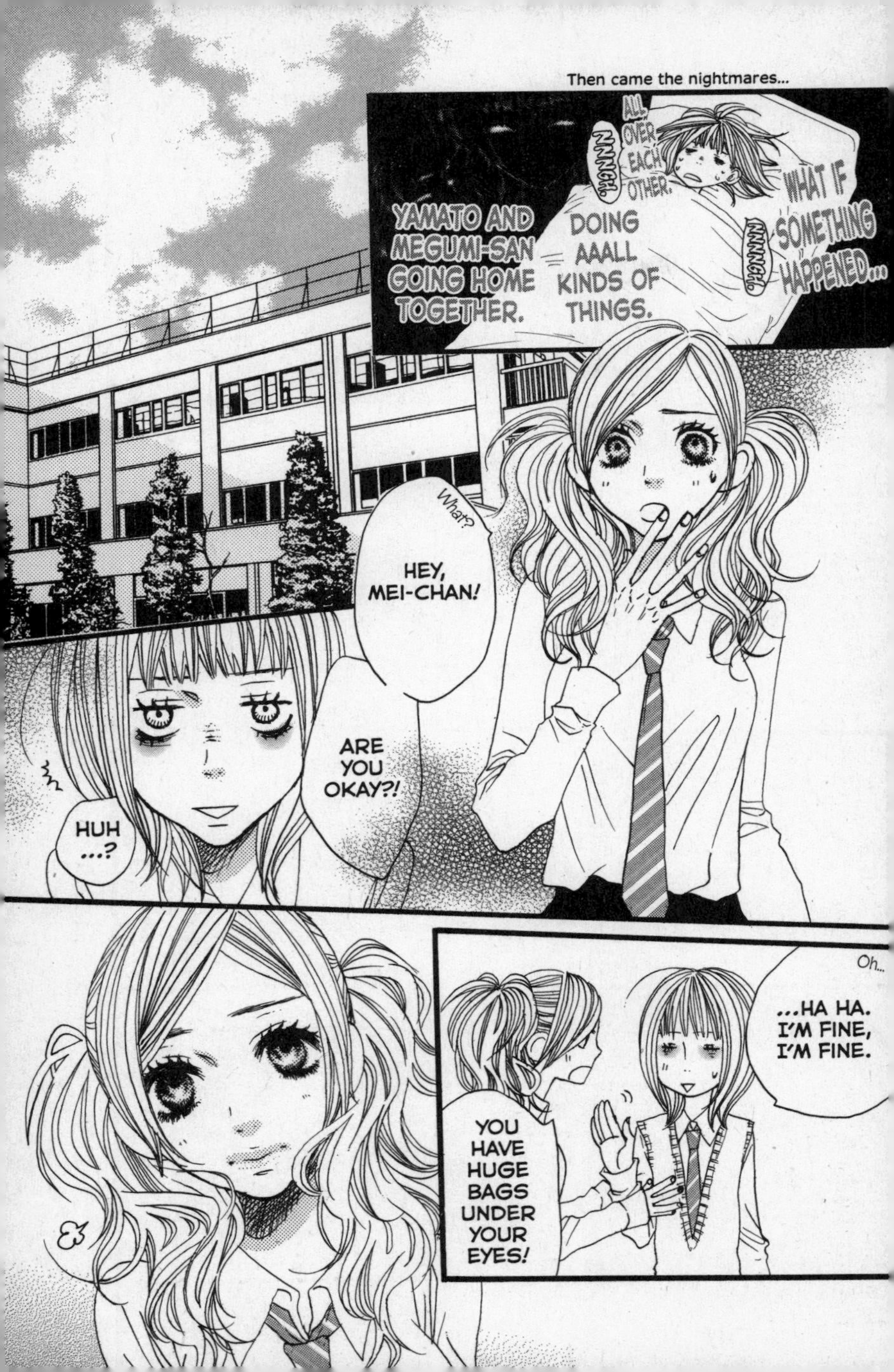
Then came the nightmares...
WHAT IF SOMETHING HAPPENED...
NNNGH!
ALL OVER EACH OTHER.
NNNGH!
DOING AAALL KINDS OF THINGS.
YAMATO AND MEGUMI-SAN GOING HOME TOGETHER.
What?
HEY, MEI-CHAN!
ARE YOU OKAY?!
HUH ...?
Oh...
...HA HA. I'M FINE, I'M FINE.
YOU HAVE HUGE BAGS UNDER YOUR EYES!

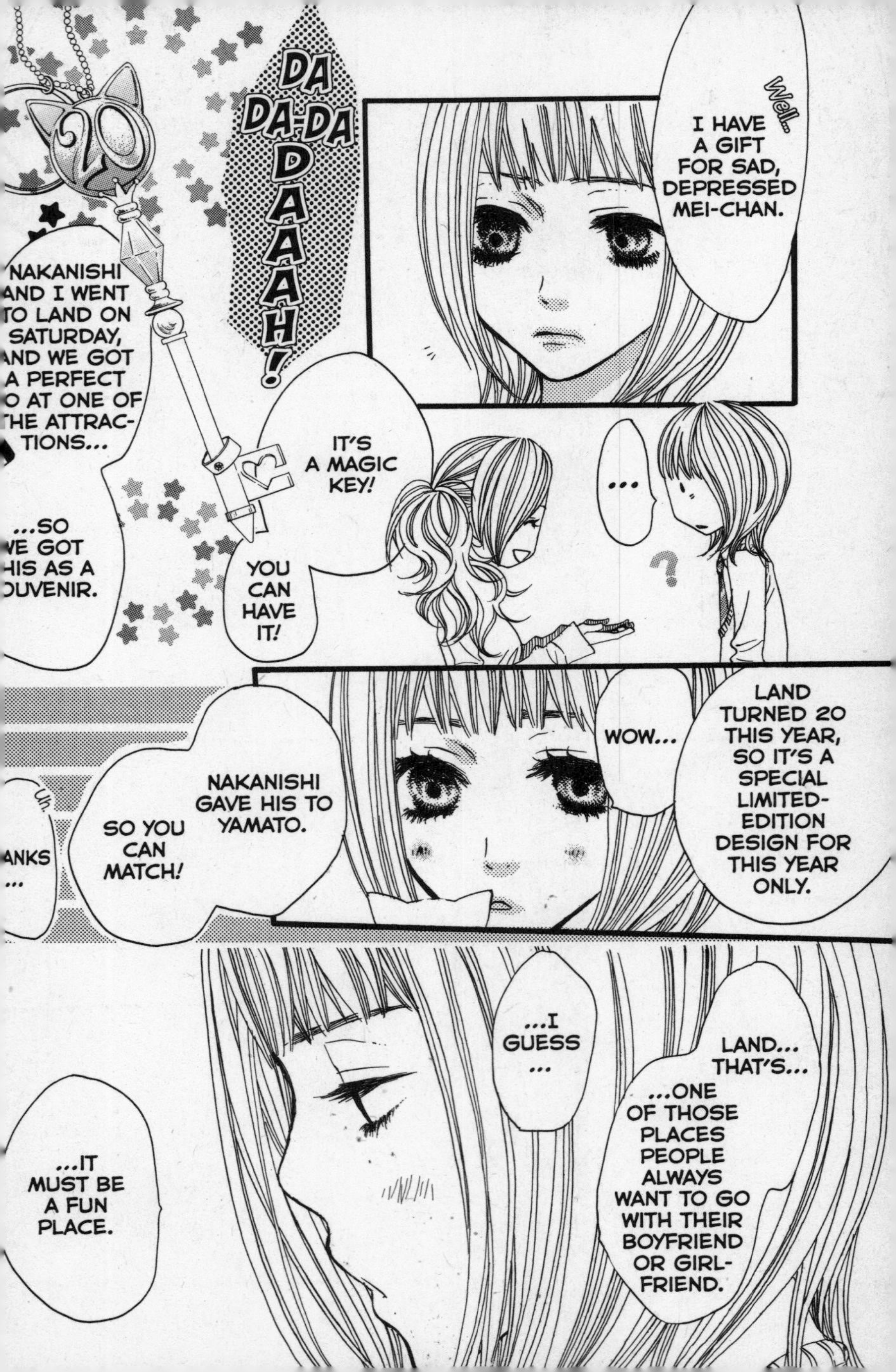
Well...
I HAVE A GIFT FOR SAD, DEPRESSED MEI-CHAN.
...
?
IT'S A MAGIC KEY!
YOU CAN HAVE IT!
DA DA-DA DADAAAAH!
20
NAKANISHI AND I WENT TO LAND ON SATURDAY, AND WE GOT A PERFECT O AT ONE OF THE ATTRAC-TIONS...
...SO WE GOT HIS AS A OUVENIR.
LAND TURNED 20 THIS YEAR, SO IT'S A SPECIAL LIMITED-EDITION DESIGN FOR THIS YEAR ONLY.
WOW...
NAKANISHI GAVE HIS TO YAMATO.
SO YOU CAN MATCH!
Uh.
ANKS...
LAND... THAT'S...
...ONE OF THOSE PLACES PEOPLE ALWAYS WANT TO GO WITH THEIR BOYFRIEND OR GIRL-FRIEND.
...I GUESS...
...IT MUST BE A FUN PLACE.

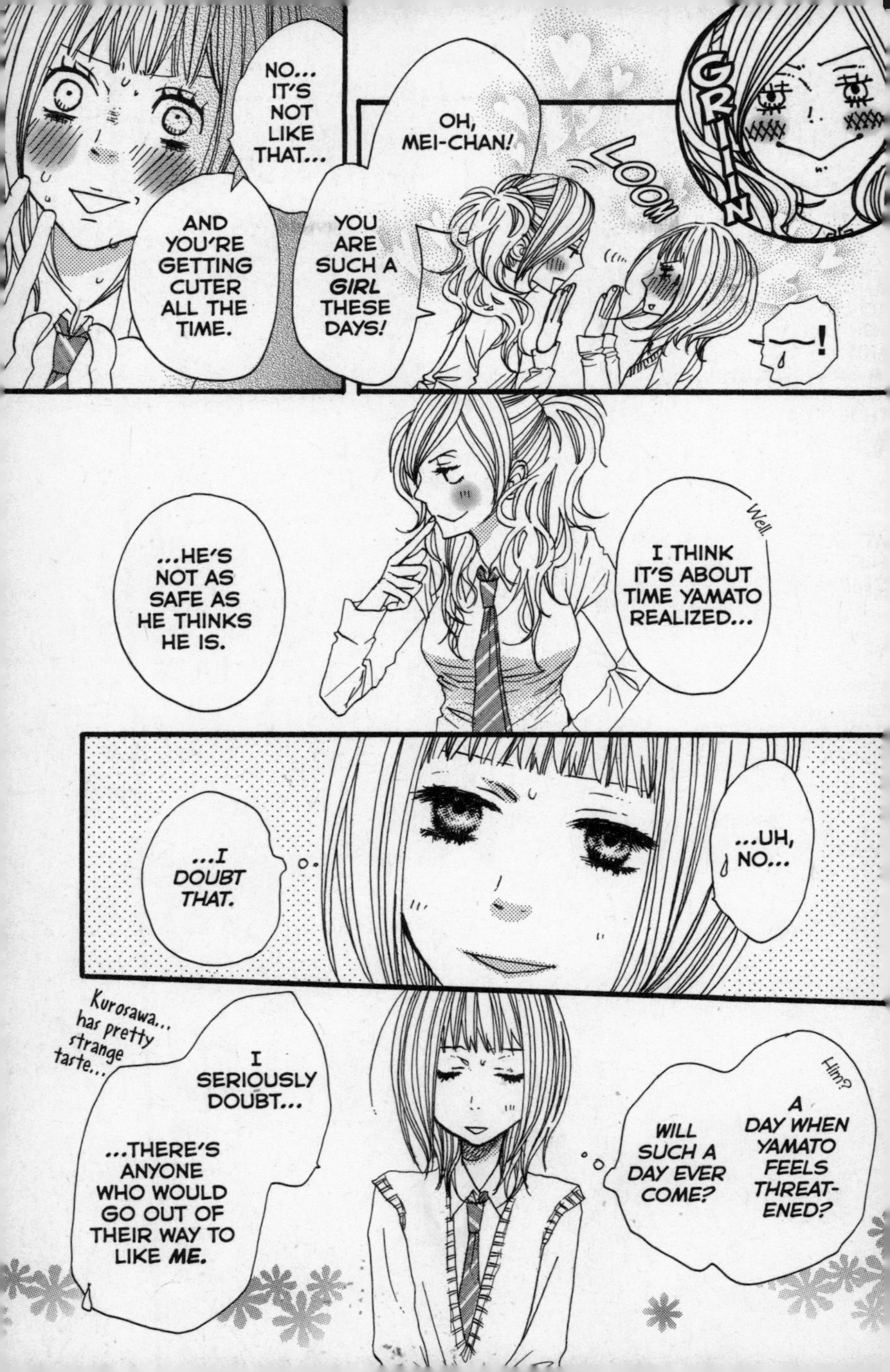
GRIN
LOOM
OH, MEI-CHAN!
YOU ARE SUCH A GIRL THESE DAYS!
—!
NO... IT'S NOT LIKE THAT...
AND YOU'RE GETTING CUTER ALL THE TIME.
Well.
I THINK IT'S ABOUT TIME YAMATO REALIZED...
...HE'S NOT AS SAFE AS HE THINKS HE IS.
...UH, NO...
...I DOUBT THAT.
Him?
A DAY WHEN YAMATO FEELS THREAT-ENED?
WILL SUCH A DAY EVER COME?
I SERIOUSLY DOUBT...
...THERE'S ANYONE WHO WOULD GO OUT OF THEIR WAY TO LIKE ME.
Kurosawa... has pretty strange taste...

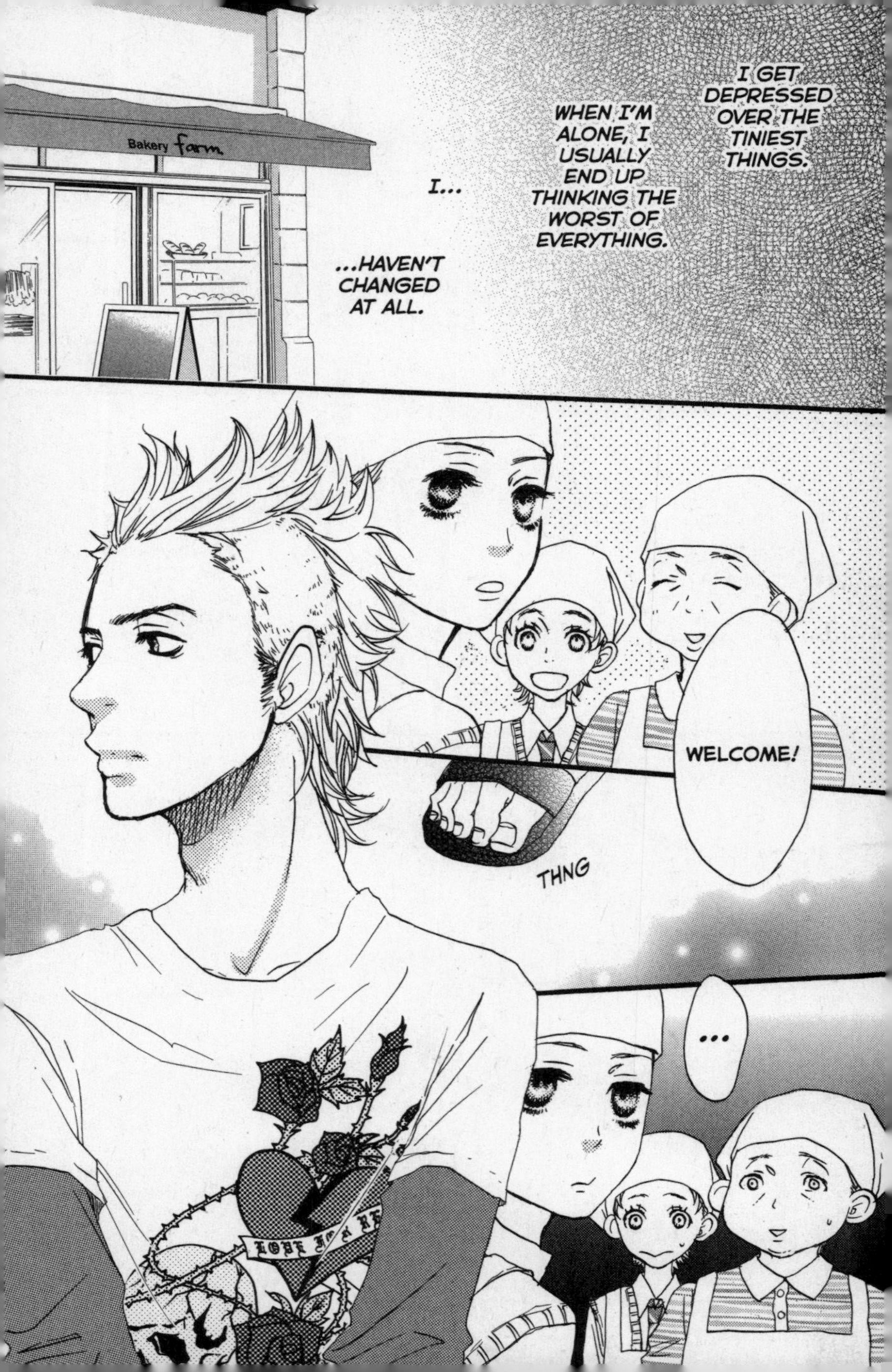
I GET DEPRESSED OVER THE TINIEST THINGS.
WHEN I'M ALONE, I USUALLY END UP THINKING THE WORST OF EVERYTHING.
I...
...HAVEN'T CHANGED AT ALL.
Bakery farm
WELCOME!
THNG
...

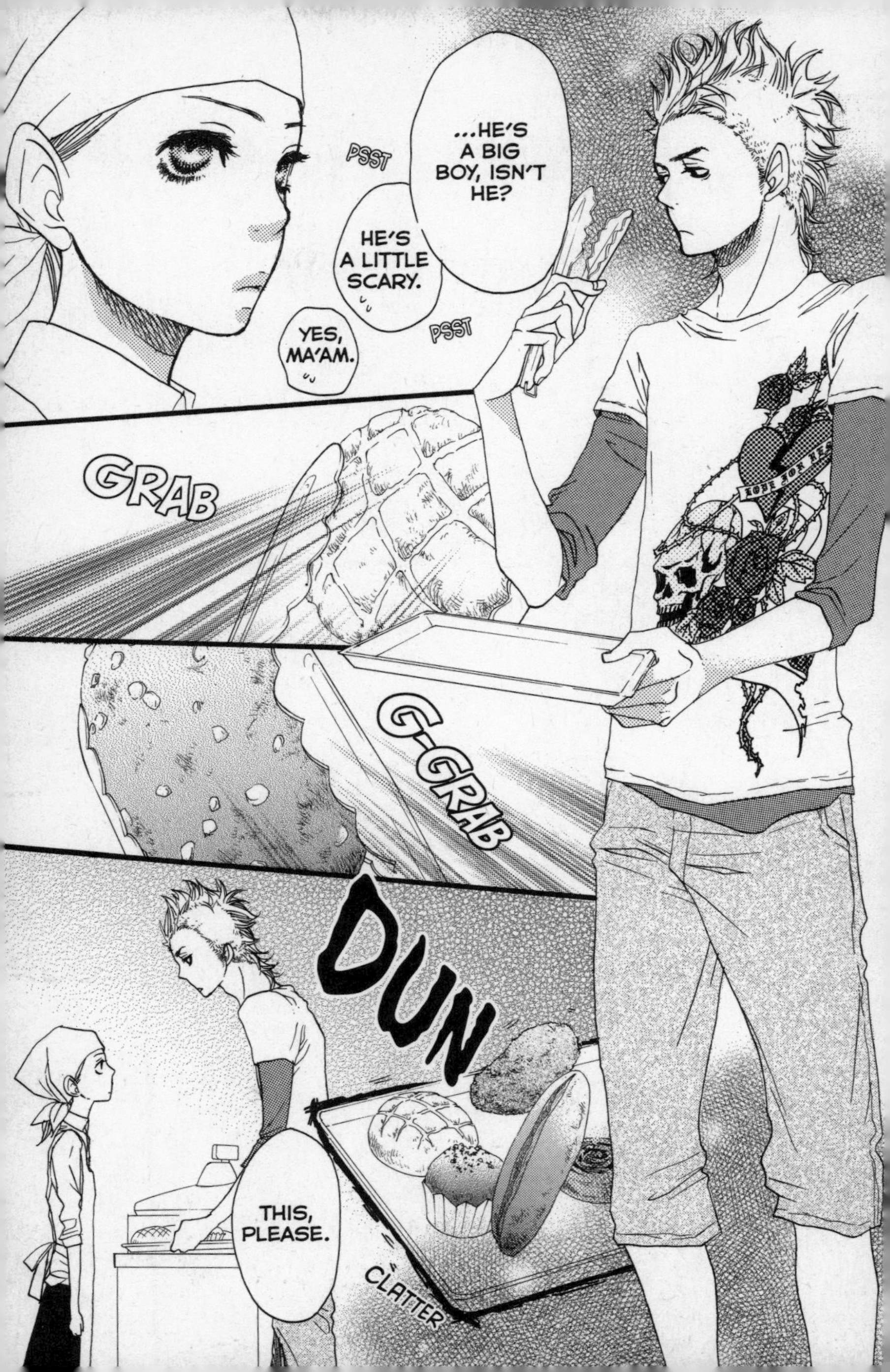
...HE'S A BIG BOY, ISN'T HE?
PSST
HE'S A LITTLE SCARY.
PSST
YES, MA'AM.
GRAB
G-GRAB
DUN
THIS, PLEASE.
CLATTER

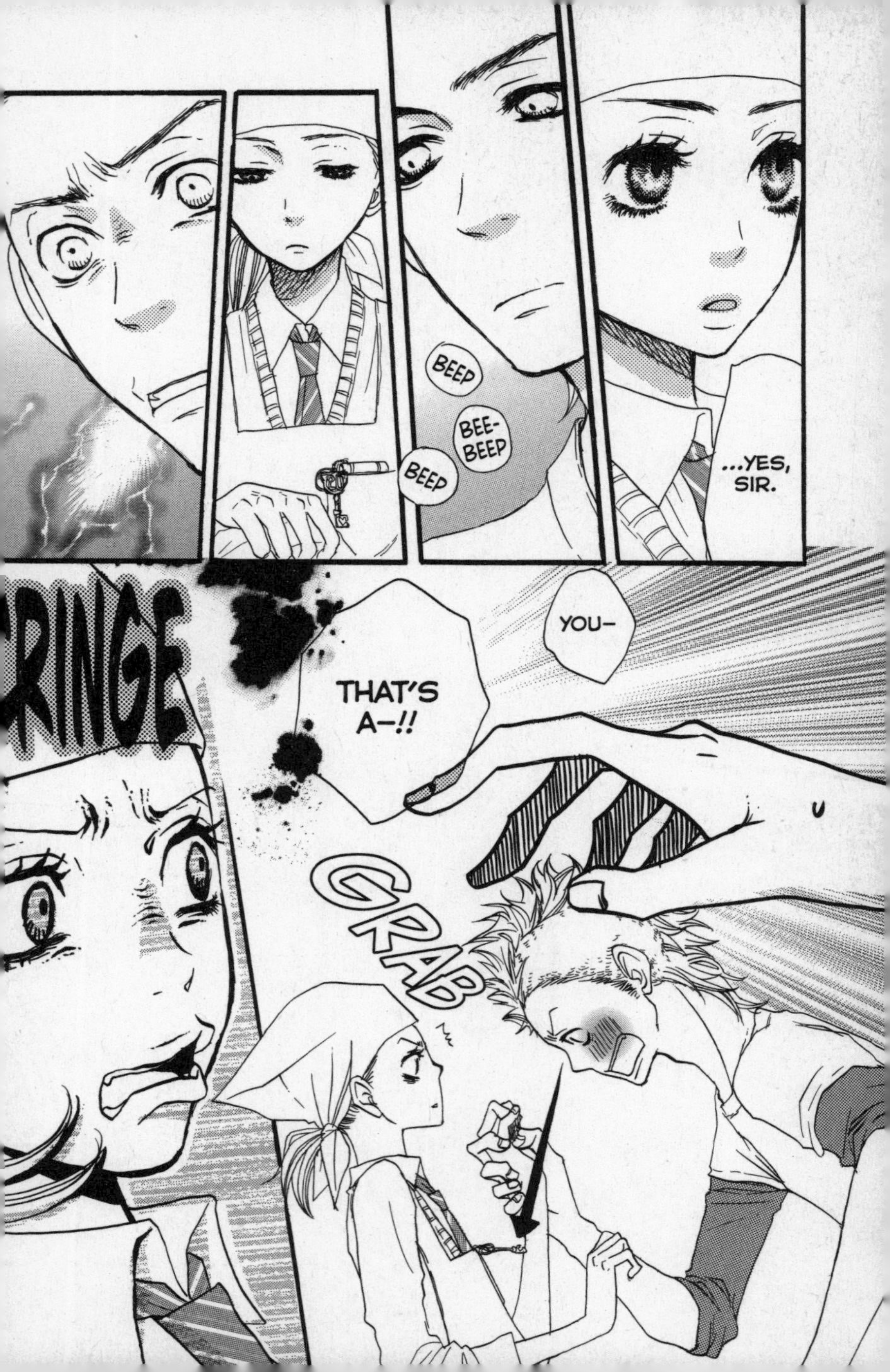

...YES, SIR.
BEEP
BEE-BEEP
BEEP
YOU-
THAT'S A-!!
GRAB
RINGE

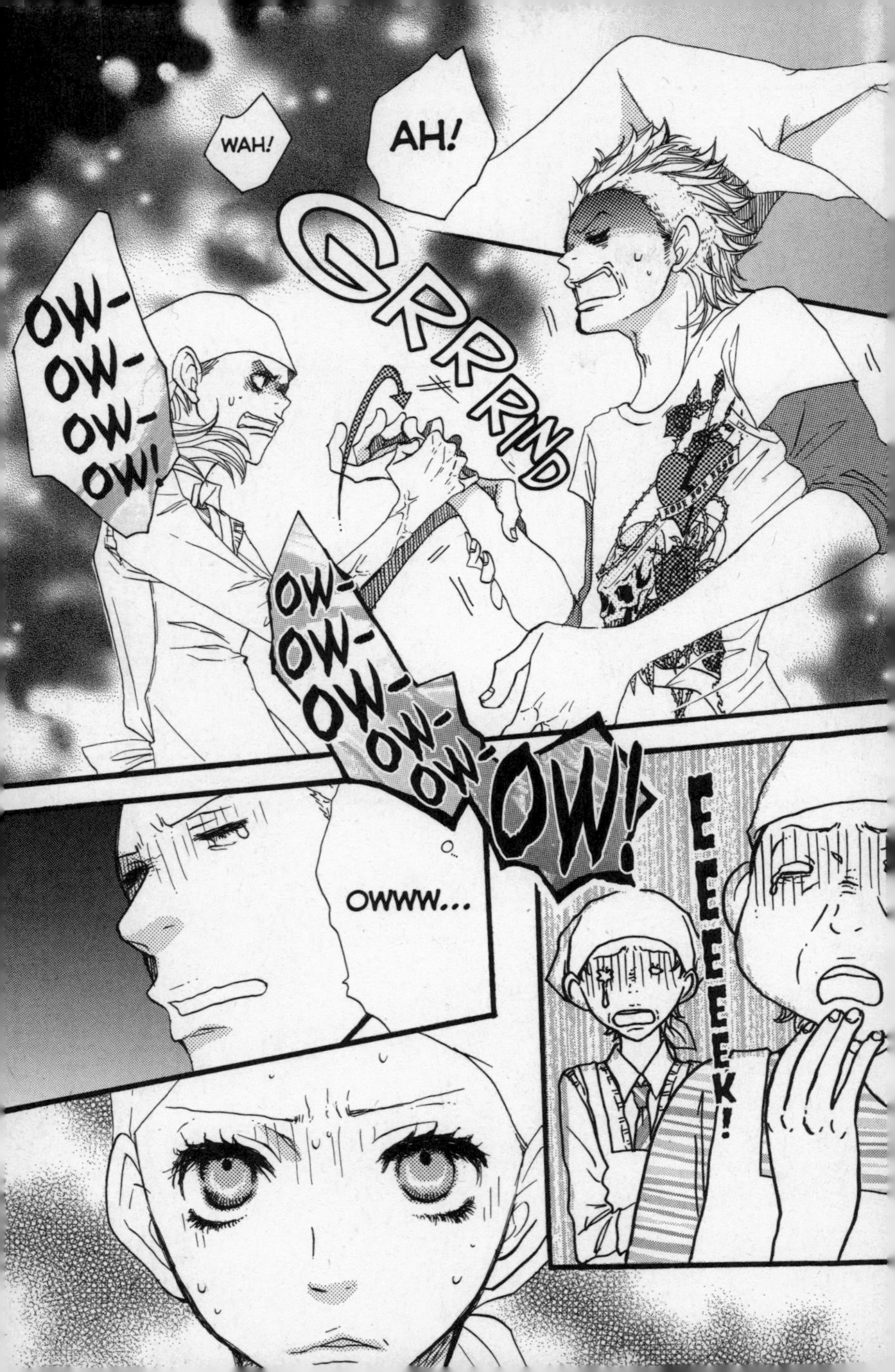
AH!
WAH!
GRRRIND
OW-OW-OW-OW!
OW-OW-OW-OW-OW-OW-OW
OW!
EEEEEEEK!!
OWWW...

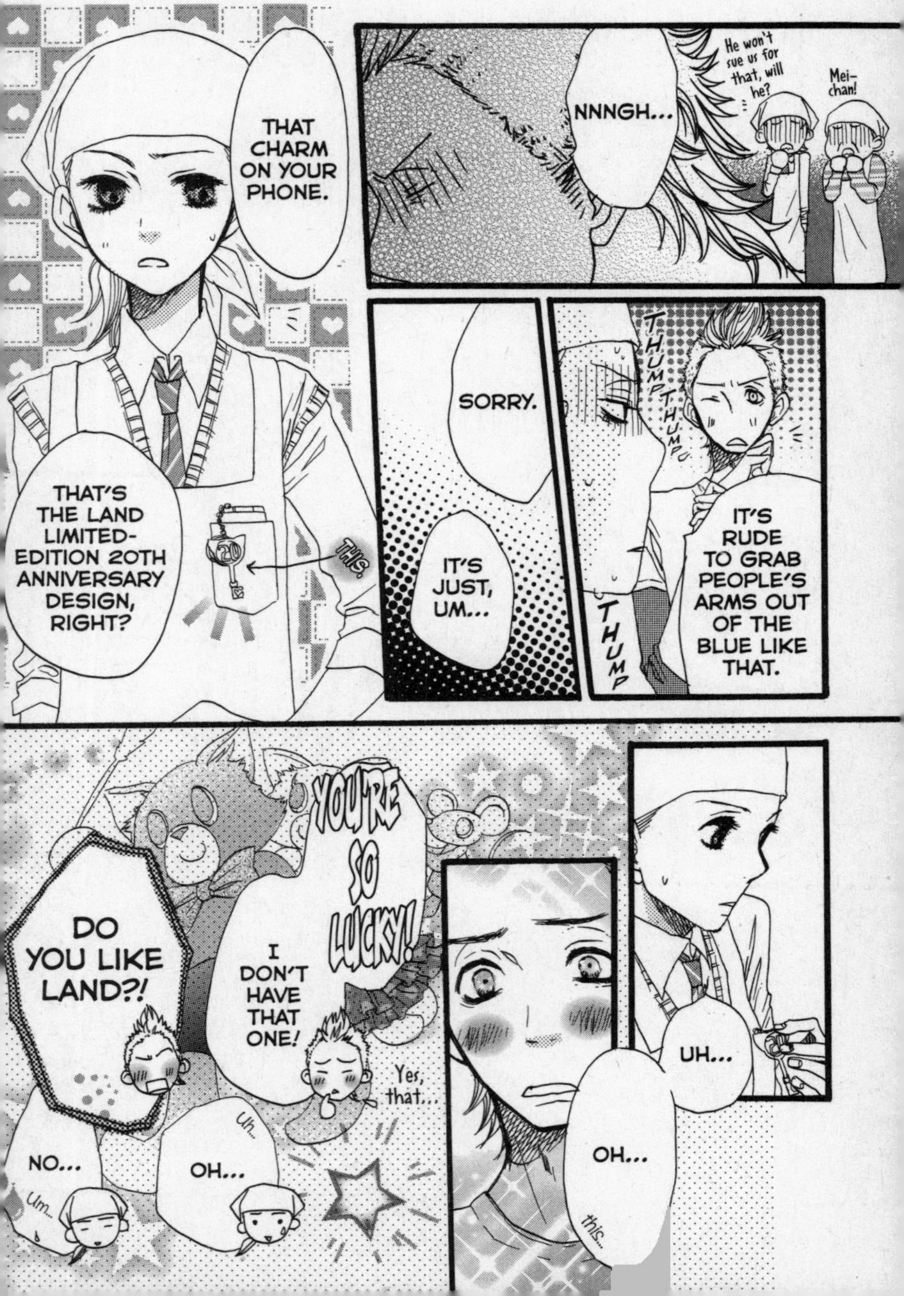
NNNGH...
He won't sue us for that, will he?
Mei-chan!
THUMP THUMP THUMP
IT'S RUDE TO GRAB PEOPLE'S ARMS OUT OF THE BLUE LIKE THAT.
THUMP
SORRY.
IT'S JUST, UM...
THAT CHARM ON YOUR PHONE.
THAT'S THE LAND LIMITED-EDITION 20TH ANNIVERSARY DESIGN, RIGHT?
THIS.
UH...
OH...
this...
YOU'RE SO LUCKY!
I DON'T HAVE THAT ONE!
DO YOU LIKE LAND?!
Yes, that...
Uh.
OH...
NO...
Um...

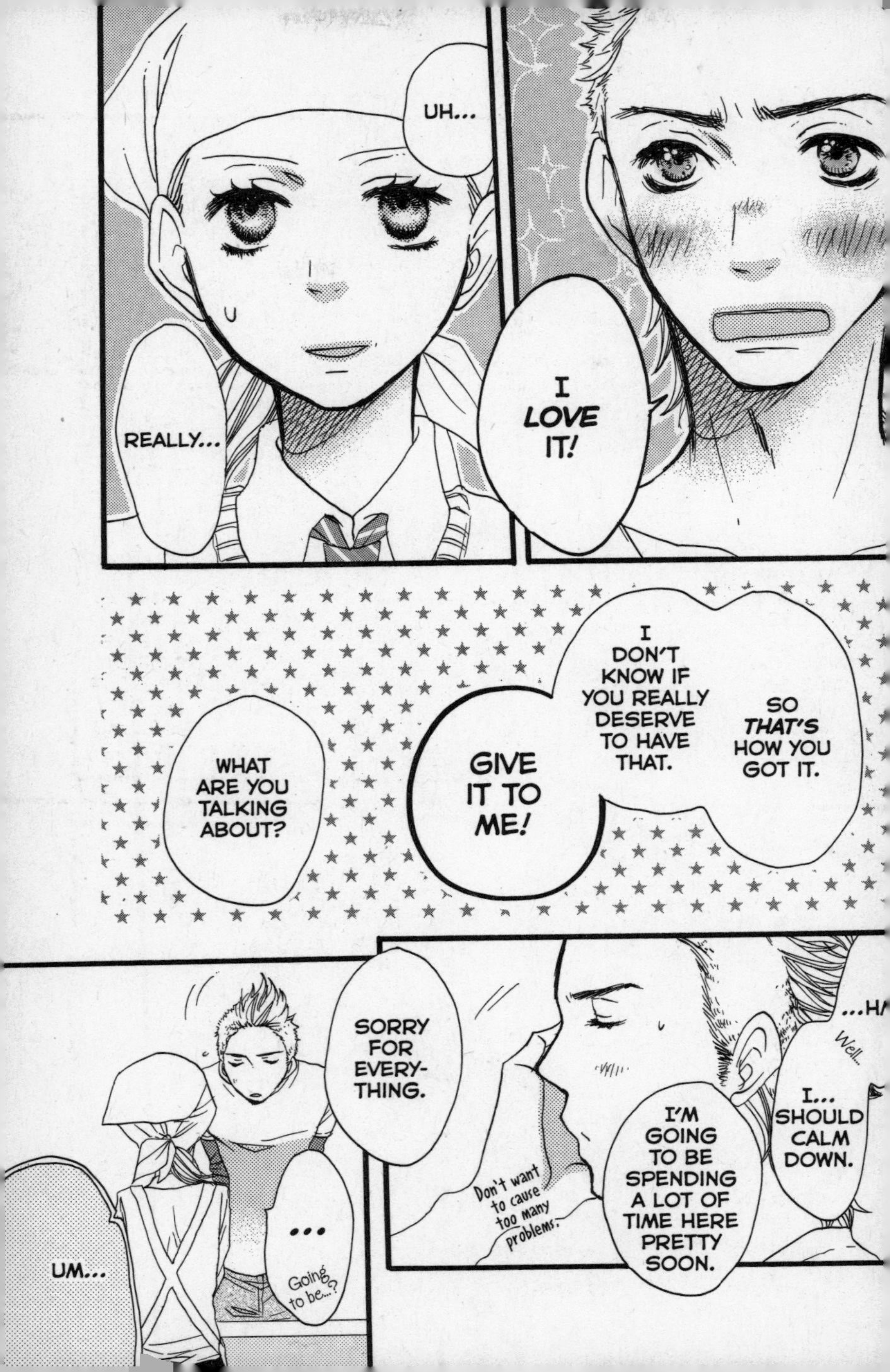
I LOVE IT!
UH...
REALLY...
SO THAT'S HOW YOU GOT IT.
I DON'T KNOW IF YOU REALLY DESERVE TO HAVE THAT.
GIVE IT TO ME!
WHAT ARE YOU TALKING ABOUT?
...H
Well...
I... SHOULD CALM DOWN.
I'M GOING TO BE SPENDING A LOT OF TIME HERE PRETTY SOON.
Don't want to cause too many problems.
SORRY FOR EVERY-THING.
...
Going to be...?
UM...

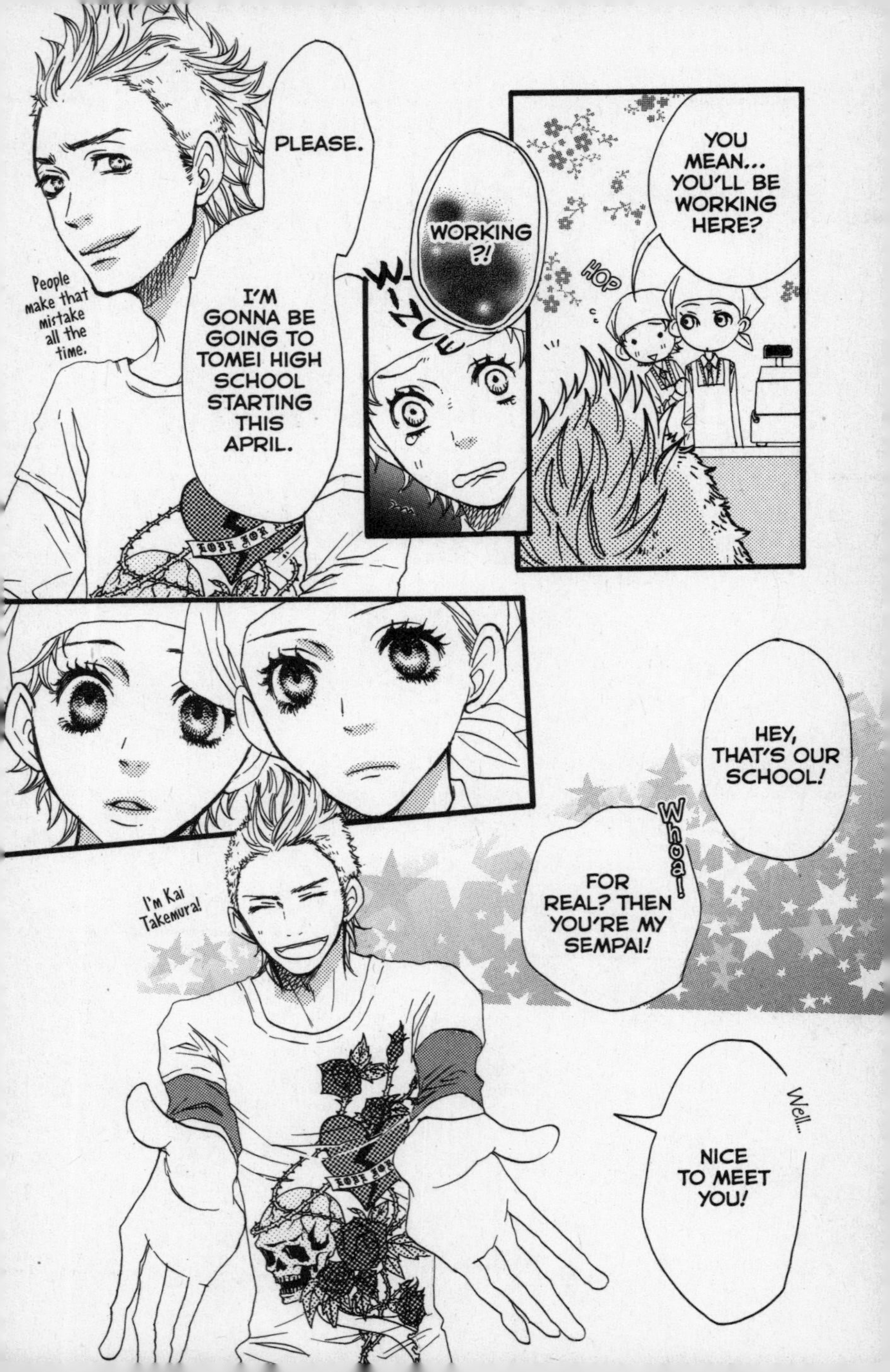
YOU MEAN... YOU'LL BE WORKING HERE?
HOP
WORKING ?!
W-ZUE
PLEASE.
I'M GONNA BE GOING TO TOMEI HIGH SCHOOL STARTING THIS APRIL.
People make that mistake all the time.
HEY, THAT'S OUR SCHOOL!
Whoa!
FOR REAL? THEN YOU'RE MY SEMPAI!
I'm Kai Takemura!
Well...
NICE TO MEET YOU!

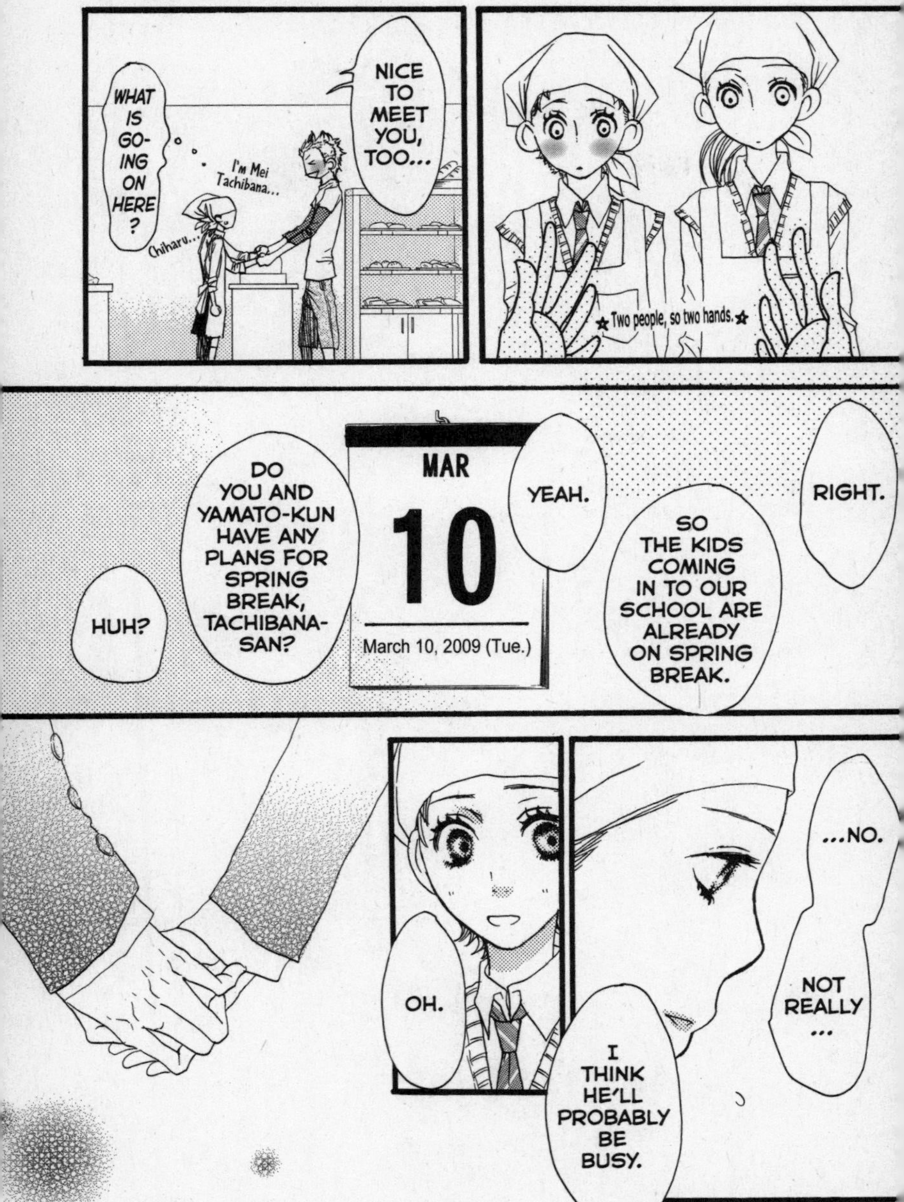

Two people, so two hands.
NICE TO MEET YOU, TOO...
WHAT IS GO-ING ON HERE?
I'm Mei Tachibana...
Chiharu...
RIGHT.
SO THE KIDS COMING IN TO OUR SCHOOL ARE ALREADY ON SPRING BREAK.
YEAH.
MAR
10
March 10, 2009 (Tue.)
DO YOU AND YAMATO-KUN HAVE ANY PLANS FOR SPRING BREAK, TACHIBANA-SAN?
HUH?
...NO.
NOT REALLY...
I THINK HE'LL PROBABLY BE BUSY.
OH.

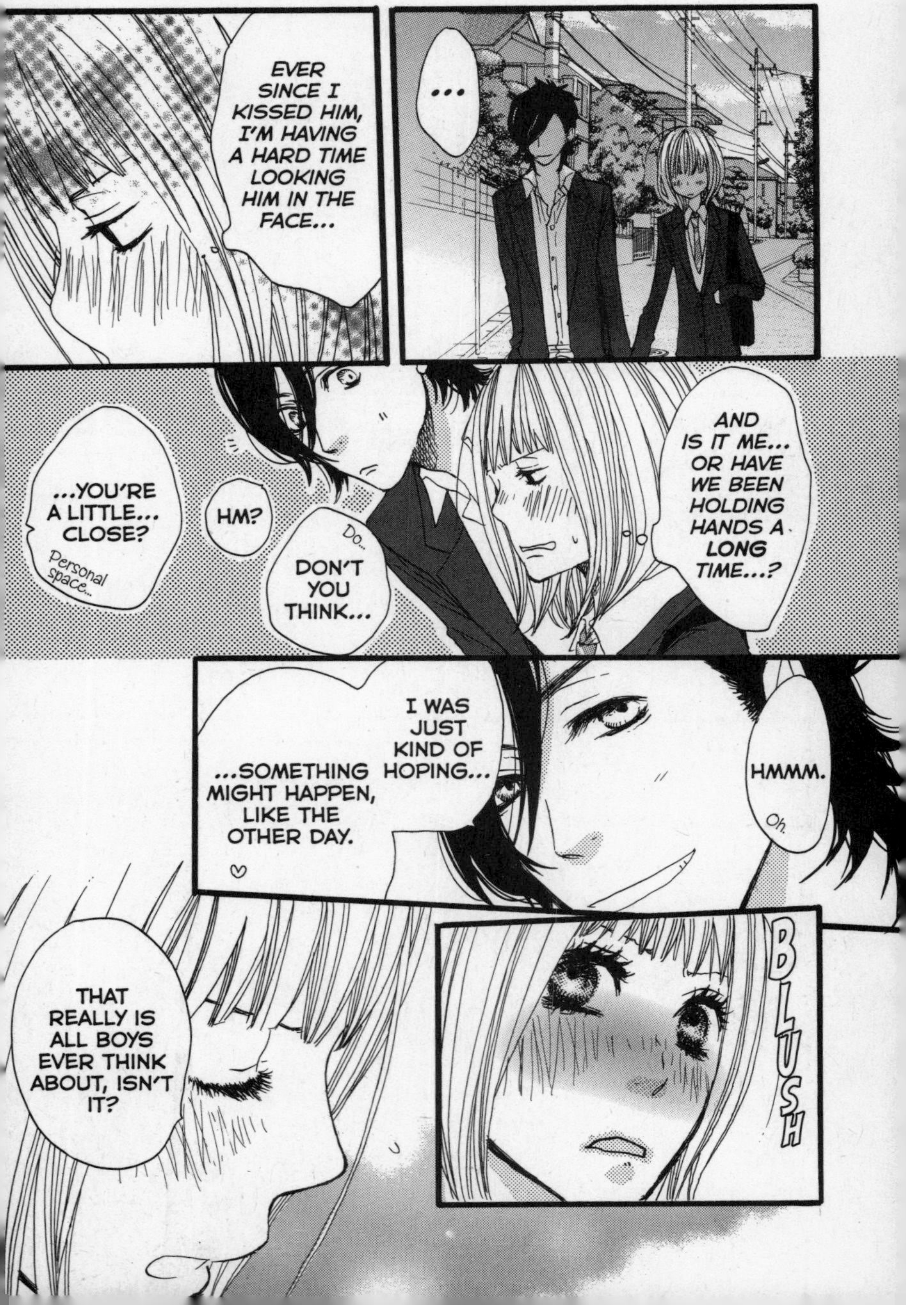
...
EVER SINCE I KISSED HIM, I'M HAVING A HARD TIME LOOKING HIM IN THE FACE...
AND IS IT ME... OR HAVE WE BEEN HOLDING HANDS A LONG TIME...?
Do...
DON'T YOU THINK...
HM?
...YOU'RE A LITTLE... CLOSE?
Personal space...
HMMM.
Oh.
I WAS JUST KIND OF HOPING...
...SOMETHING MIGHT HAPPEN, LIKE THE OTHER DAY.
BLUSH
THAT REALLY IS ALL BOYS EVER THINK ABOUT, ISN'T IT?

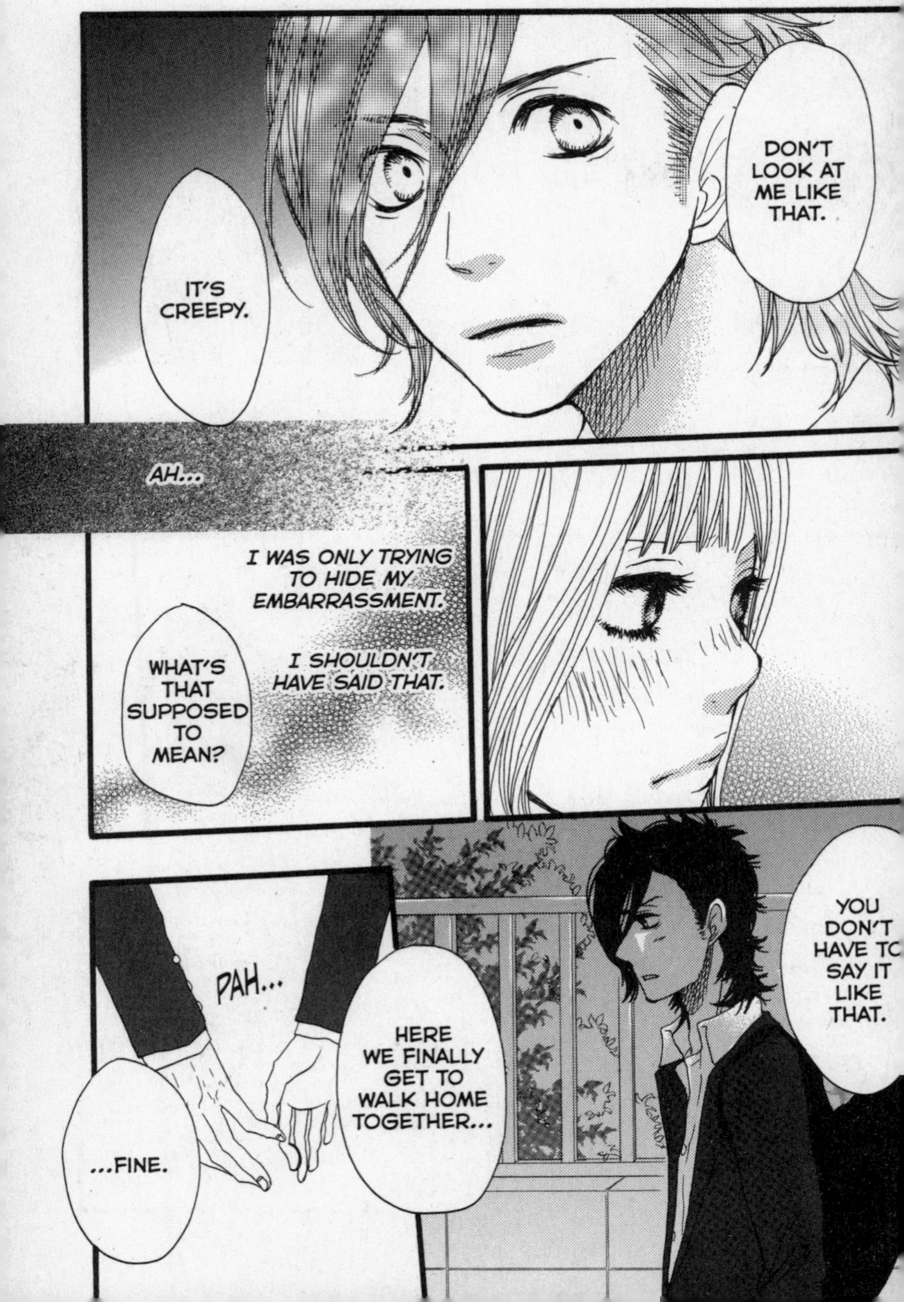
DON'T LOOK AT ME LIKE THAT.
IT'S CREEPY.
AH...
I WAS ONLY TRYING TO HIDE MY EMBARRASSMENT.
I SHOULDN'T HAVE SAID THAT.
WHAT'S THAT SUPPOSED TO MEAN?
YOU DON'T HAVE TO SAY IT LIKE THAT.
HERE WE FINALLY GET TO WALK HOME TOGETHER...
PAH...
...FINE.

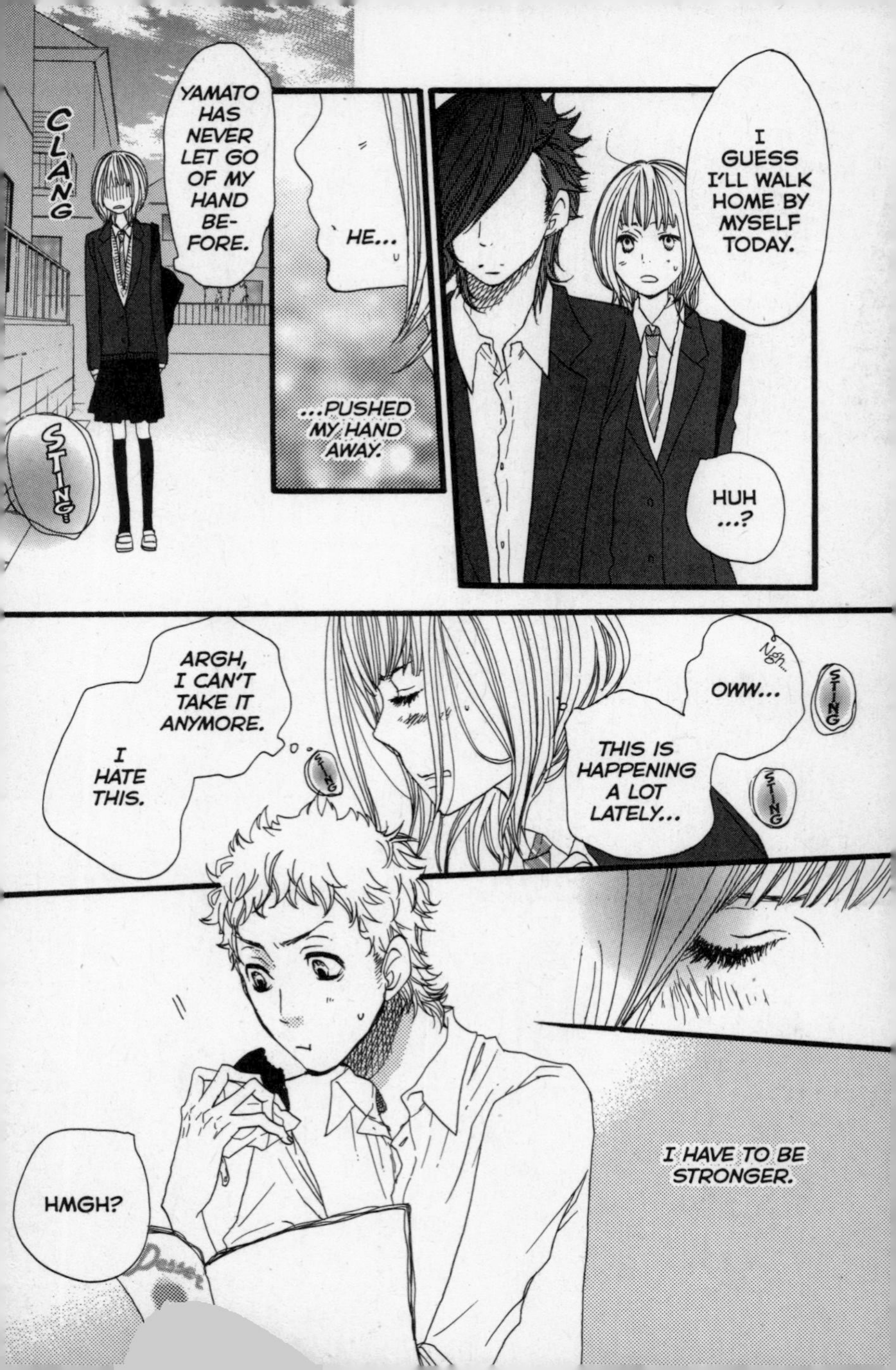
I GUESS I'LL WALK HOME BY MYSELF TODAY.
HUH ...?
HE...
...PUSHED MY HAND AWAY.
CLANG
YAMATO HAS NEVER LET GO OF MY HAND BE-FORE.
STING
Ngh...
OWW...
STING
THIS IS HAPPENING A LOT LATELY...
STING
ARGH, I CAN'T TAKE IT ANYMORE.
I HATE THIS.
STING
I HAVE TO BE STRONGER.
HMGH?

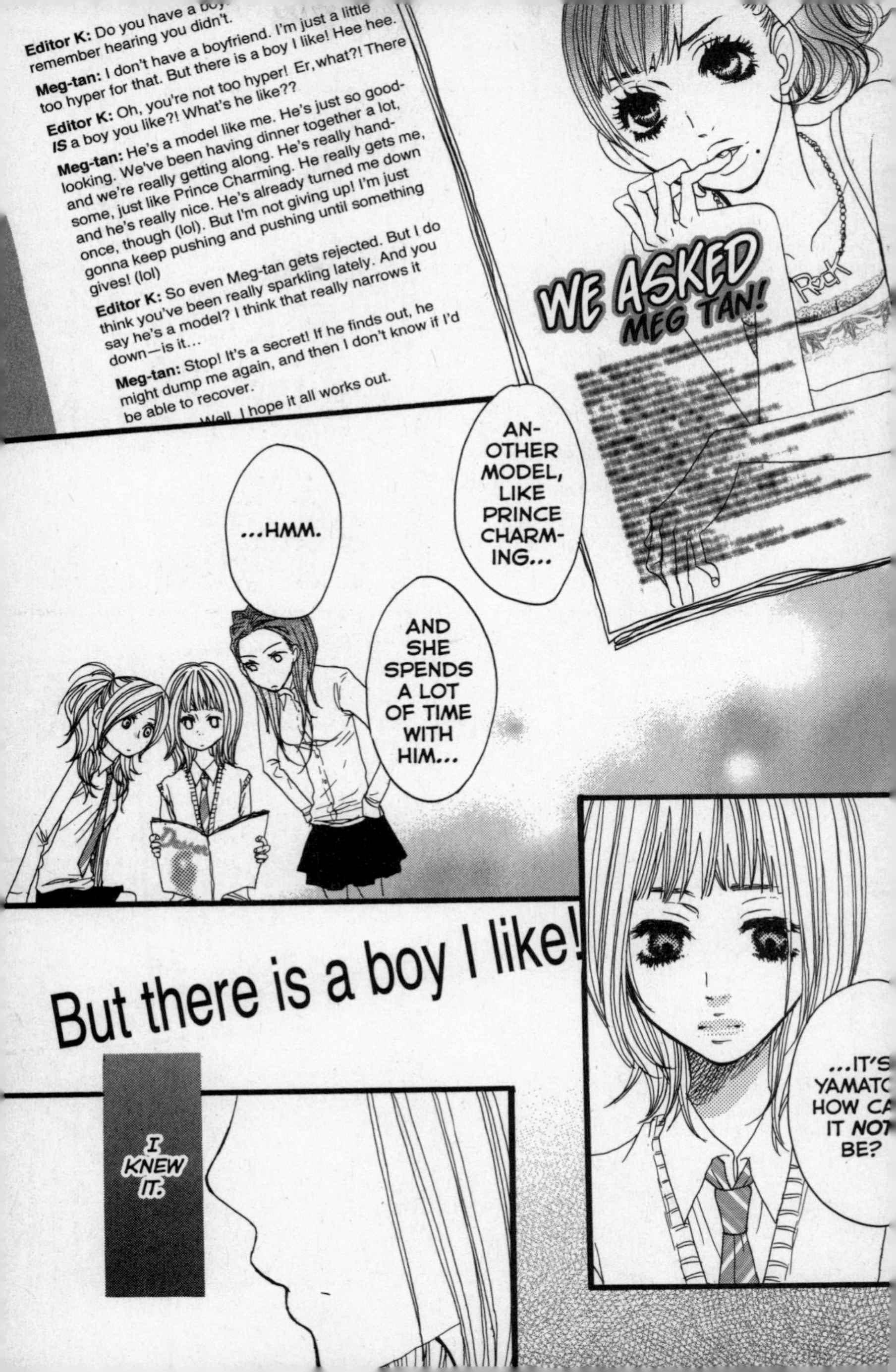
Editor K: Do you have a boy... remember hearing you didn't.
Meg-tan: I don't have a boyfriend. I'm just a little too hyper for that. But there is a boy I like! Hee hee.
Editor K: Oh, you're not too hyper! Er, what?! There IS a boy you like?! What's he like??
Meg-tan: He's a model like me. He's just so good-looking. We've been having dinner together a lot, and we're really getting along. He's really handsome, just like Prince Charming. He really gets me, and he's really nice. He's already turned me down once, though (lol). But I'm not giving up! I'm just gonna keep pushing and pushing until something gives! (lol)
Editor K: So even Meg-tan gets rejected. But I do think you've been really sparkling lately. And you say he's a model? I think that really narrows it down—is it...
Meg-tan: Stop! It's a secret! If he finds out, he might dump me again, and then I don't know if I'd be able to recover.
Well, I hope it all works out.
WE ASKED MEG TAN!
ANOTHER MODEL, LIKE PRINCE CHARMING...
AND SHE SPENDS A LOT OF TIME WITH HIM...
...HMM.
But there is a boy I like!
...IT'S YAMATO
HOW CA
IT NOT BE?
I KNEW IT.

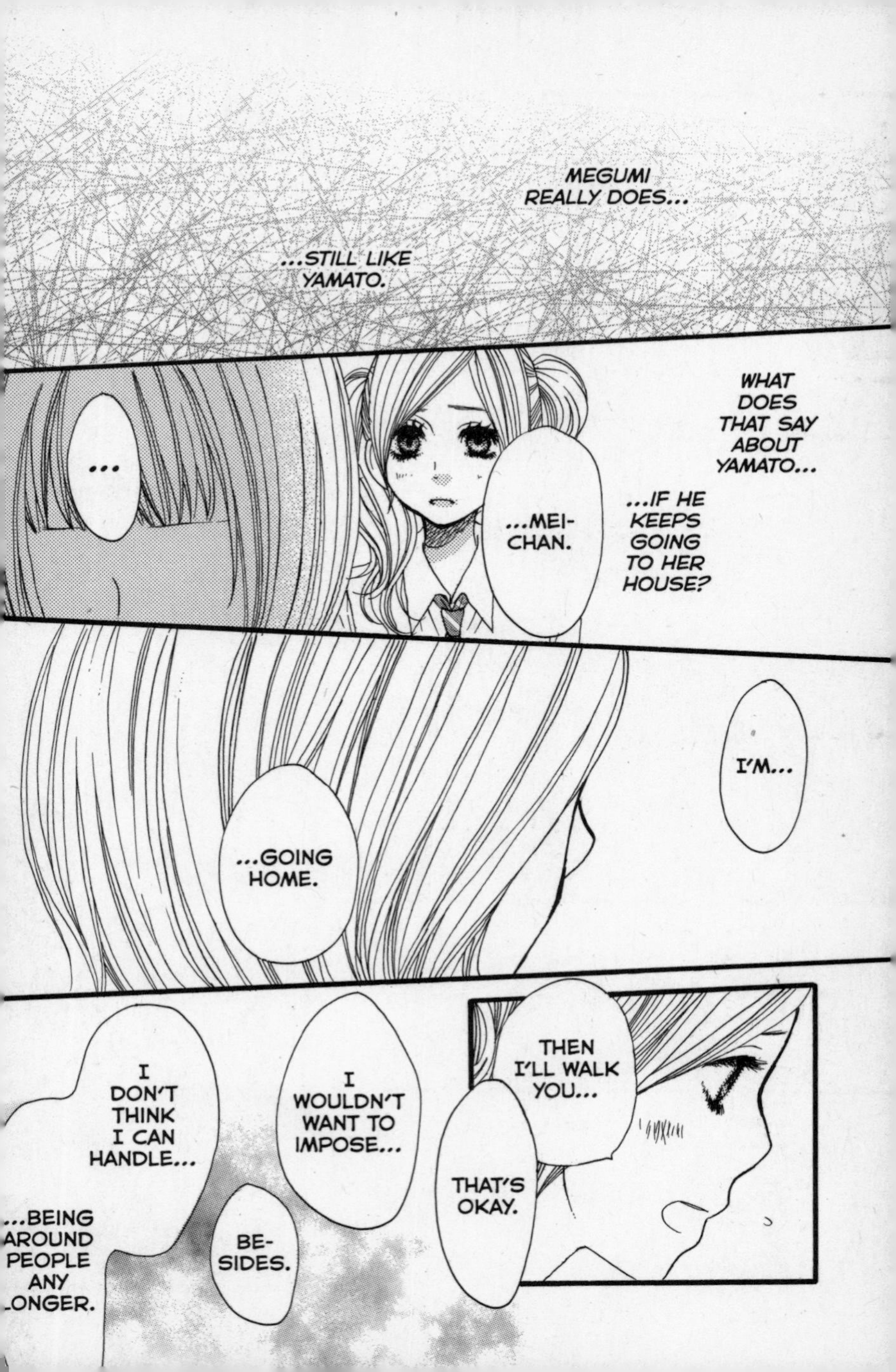
MEGUMI REALLY DOES...
...STILL LIKE YAMATO.
WHAT DOES THAT SAY ABOUT YAMATO...
...IF HE KEEPS GOING TO HER HOUSE?
...MEI-CHAN.
...
I'M...
...GOING HOME.
THEN I'LL WALK YOU...
THAT'S OKAY.
I WOULDN'T WANT TO IMPOSE...
BE-SIDES.
I DON'T THINK I CAN HANDLE...
...BEING AROUND PEOPLE ANY LONGER.

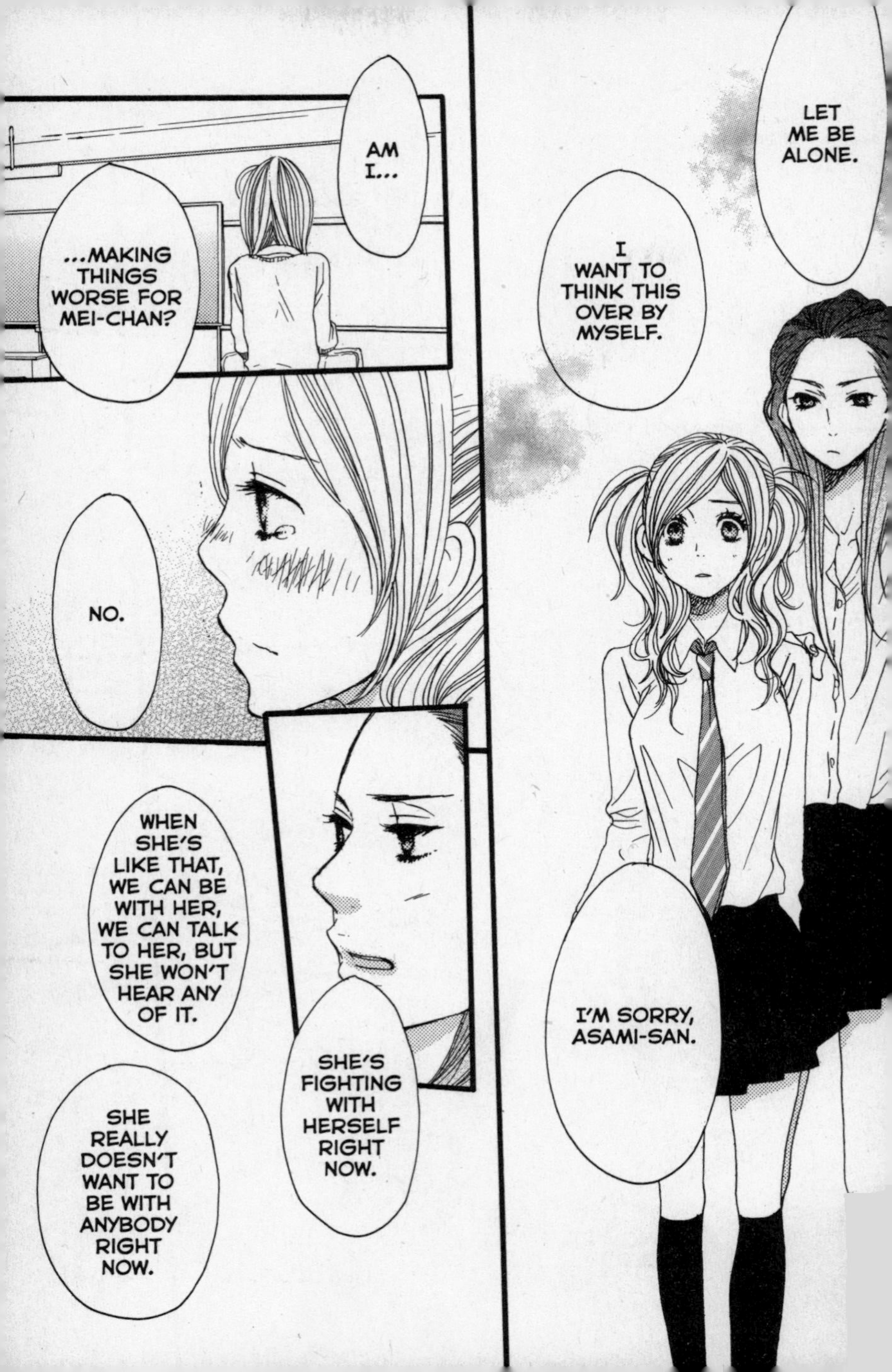
LET ME BE ALONE.
I WANT TO THINK THIS OVER BY MYSELF.
I'M SORRY, ASAMI-SAN.
AM I...
...MAKING THINGS WORSE FOR MEI-CHAN?
NO.
SHE'S FIGHTING WITH HERSELF RIGHT NOW.
WHEN SHE'S LIKE THAT, WE CAN BE WITH HER, WE CAN TALK TO HER, BUT SHE WON'T HEAR ANY OF IT.
SHE REALLY DOESN'T WANT TO BE WITH ANYBODY RIGHT NOW.

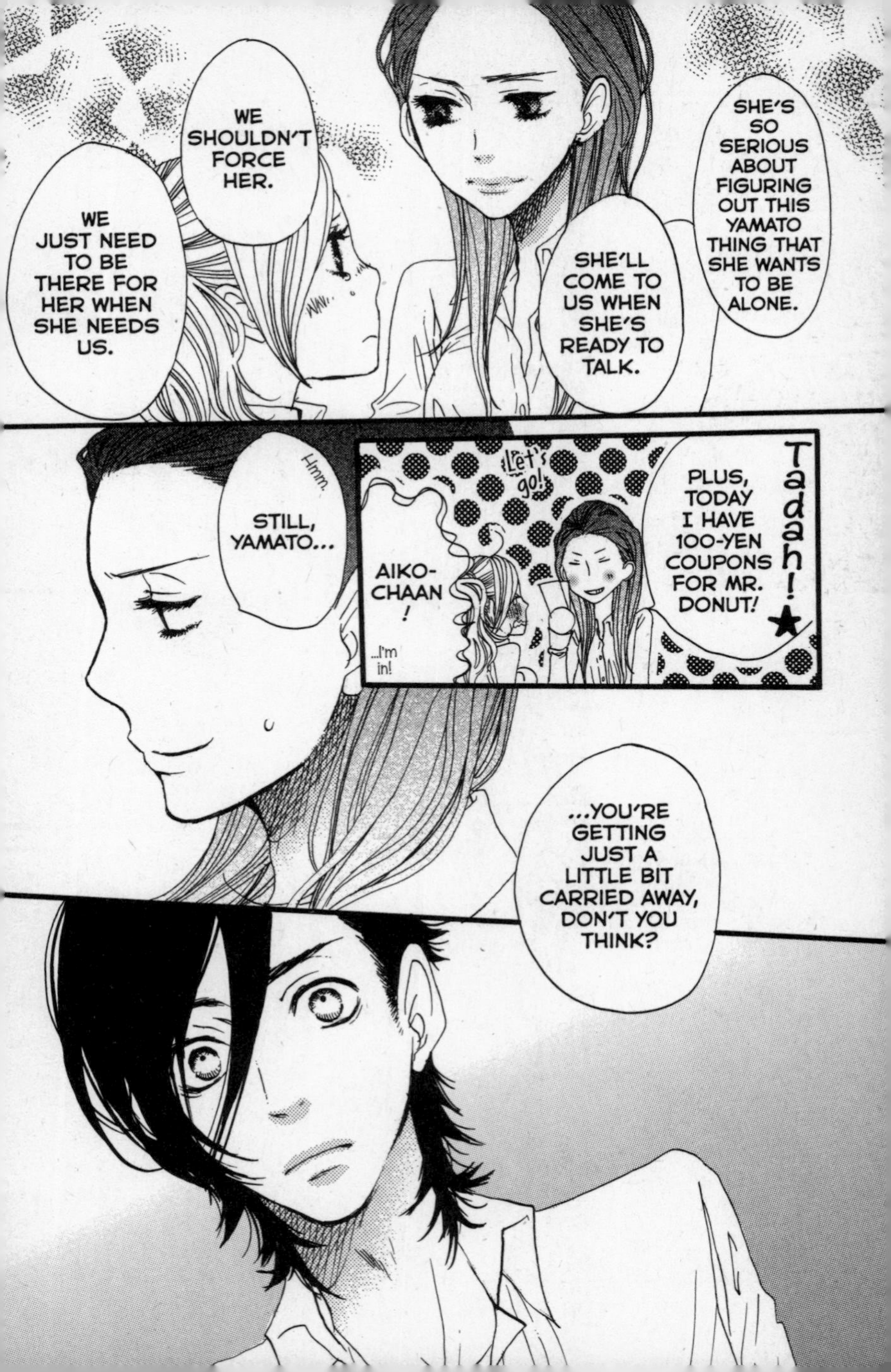
SHE'S SO SERIOUS ABOUT FIGURING OUT THIS YAMATO THING THAT SHE WANTS TO BE ALONE.
SHE'LL COME TO US WHEN SHE'S READY TO TALK.
WE SHOULDN'T FORCE HER.
WE JUST NEED TO BE THERE FOR HER WHEN SHE NEEDS US.
Tadaah!★
PLUS, TODAY I HAVE 100-YEN COUPONS FOR MR. DONUT!
Let's go!
AIKO-CHAAN!
...I'm in!
Hmm.
STILL, YAMATO...
...YOU'RE GETTING JUST A LITTLE BIT CARRIED AWAY, DON'T YOU THINK?

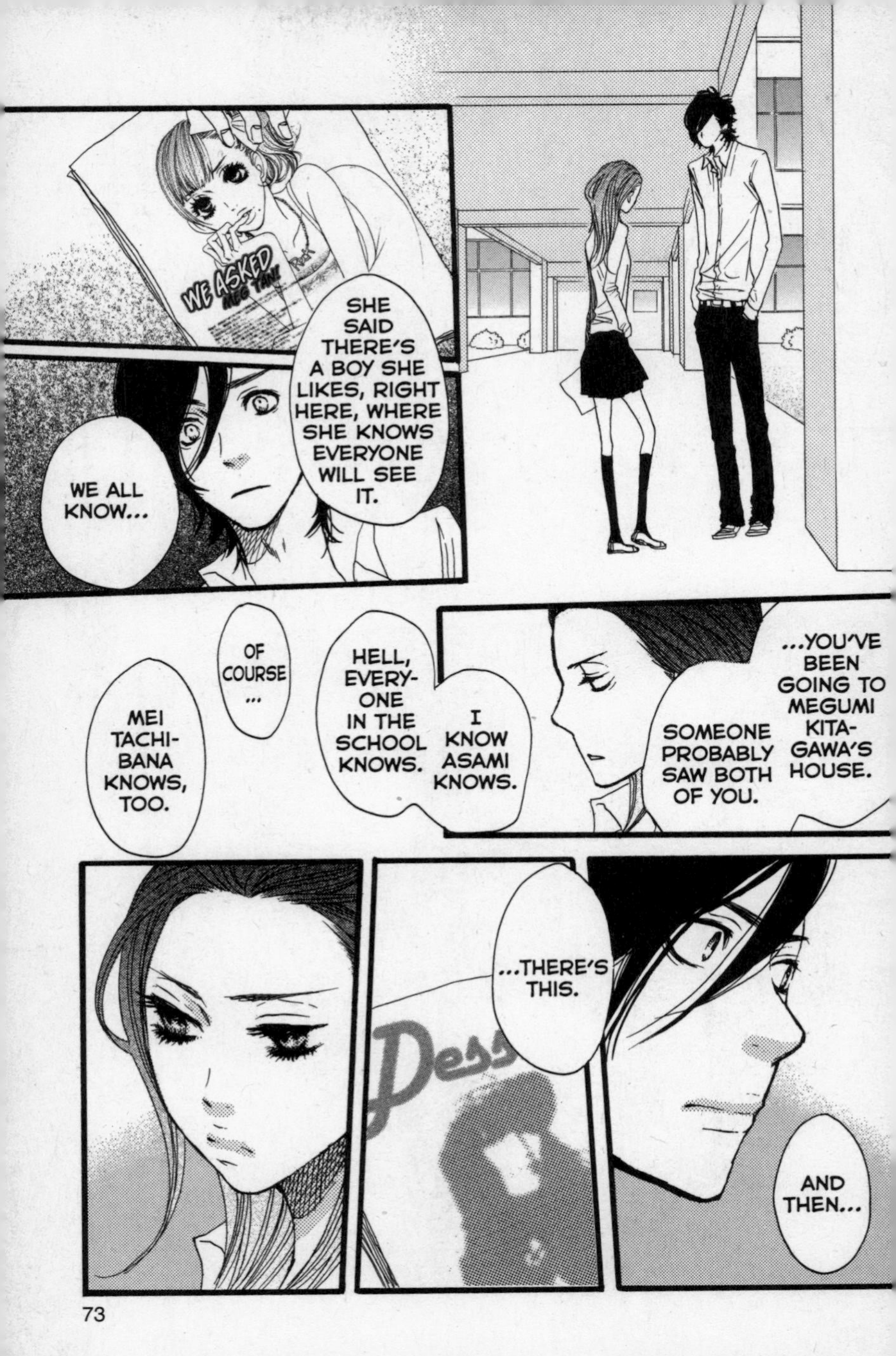
WE ASKED
MEG TANI
ROCK
SHE SAID THERE'S A BOY SHE LIKES, RIGHT HERE, WHERE SHE KNOWS EVERYONE WILL SEE IT.
WE ALL KNOW...
...YOU'VE BEEN GOING TO MEGUMI KITA-GAWA'S HOUSE.
SOMEONE PROBABLY SAW BOTH OF YOU.
I KNOW ASAMI KNOWS.
HELL, EVERY-ONE IN THE SCHOOL KNOWS.
OF COURSE...
MEI TACHI-BANA KNOWS, TOO.
...THERE'S THIS.
AND THEN...
Dess

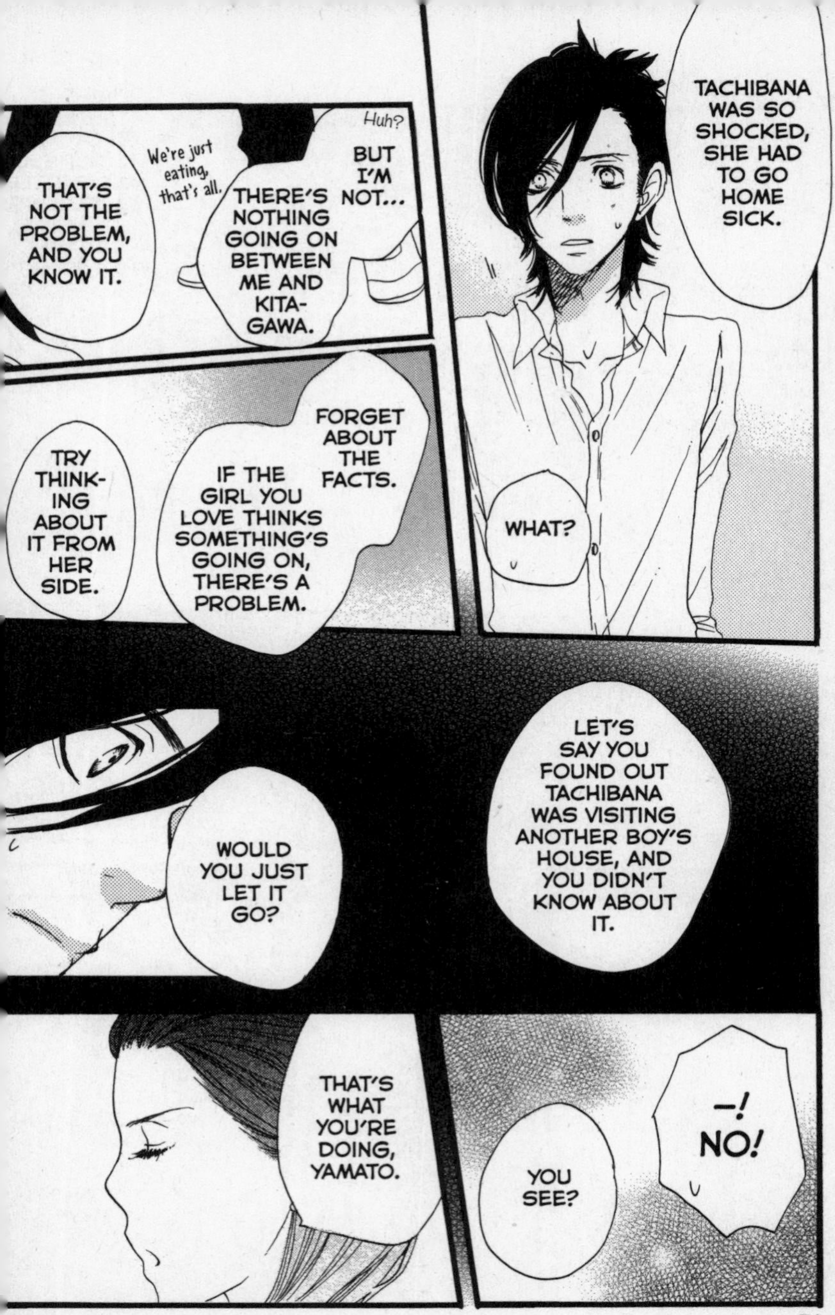
TACHIBANA WAS SO SHOCKED, SHE HAD TO GO HOME SICK.
WHAT?
Huh?
BUT I'M NOT...
THERE'S NOTHING GOING ON BETWEEN ME AND KITA-GAWA.
We're just eating, that's all.
THAT'S NOT THE PROBLEM, AND YOU KNOW IT.
FORGET ABOUT THE FACTS.
IF THE GIRL YOU LOVE THINKS SOMETHING'S GOING ON, THERE'S A PROBLEM.
TRY THINK-ING ABOUT IT FROM HER SIDE.
LET'S SAY YOU FOUND OUT TACHIBANA WAS VISITING ANOTHER BOY'S HOUSE, AND YOU DIDN'T KNOW ABOUT IT.
WOULD YOU JUST LET IT GO?
—! NO!
YOU SEE?
THAT'S WHAT YOU'RE DOING, YAMATO.

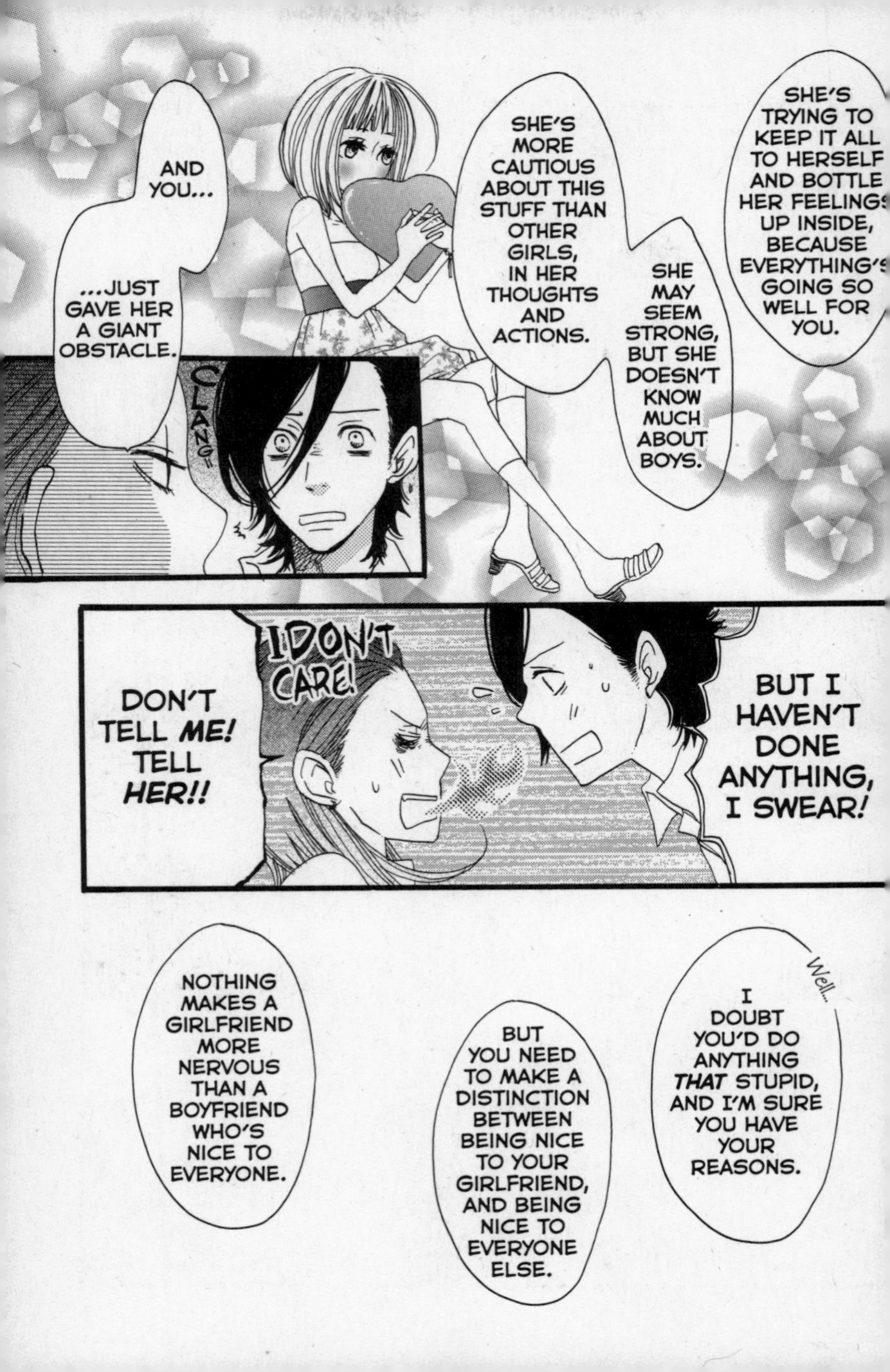
SHE'S TRYING TO KEEP IT ALL TO HERSELF AND BOTTLE HER FEELINGS UP INSIDE, BECAUSE EVERYTHING'S GOING SO WELL FOR YOU.
SHE MAY SEEM STRONG, BUT SHE DOESN'T KNOW MUCH ABOUT BOYS.
SHE'S MORE CAUTIOUS ABOUT THIS STUFF THAN OTHER GIRLS, IN HER THOUGHTS AND ACTIONS.
AND YOU...
...JUST GAVE HER A GIANT OBSTACLE.
CLANG!!
BUT I HAVEN'T DONE ANYTHING, I SWEAR!
I DON'T CARE!
DON'T TELL *ME*! TELL *HER*!!
Well...
I DOUBT YOU'D DO ANYTHING *THAT* STUPID, AND I'M SURE YOU HAVE YOUR REASONS.
BUT YOU NEED TO MAKE A DISTINCTION BETWEEN BEING NICE TO YOUR GIRLFRIEND, AND BEING NICE TO EVERYONE ELSE.
NOTHING MAKES A GIRLFRIEND MORE NERVOUS THAN A BOYFRIEND WHO'S NICE TO EVERYONE.

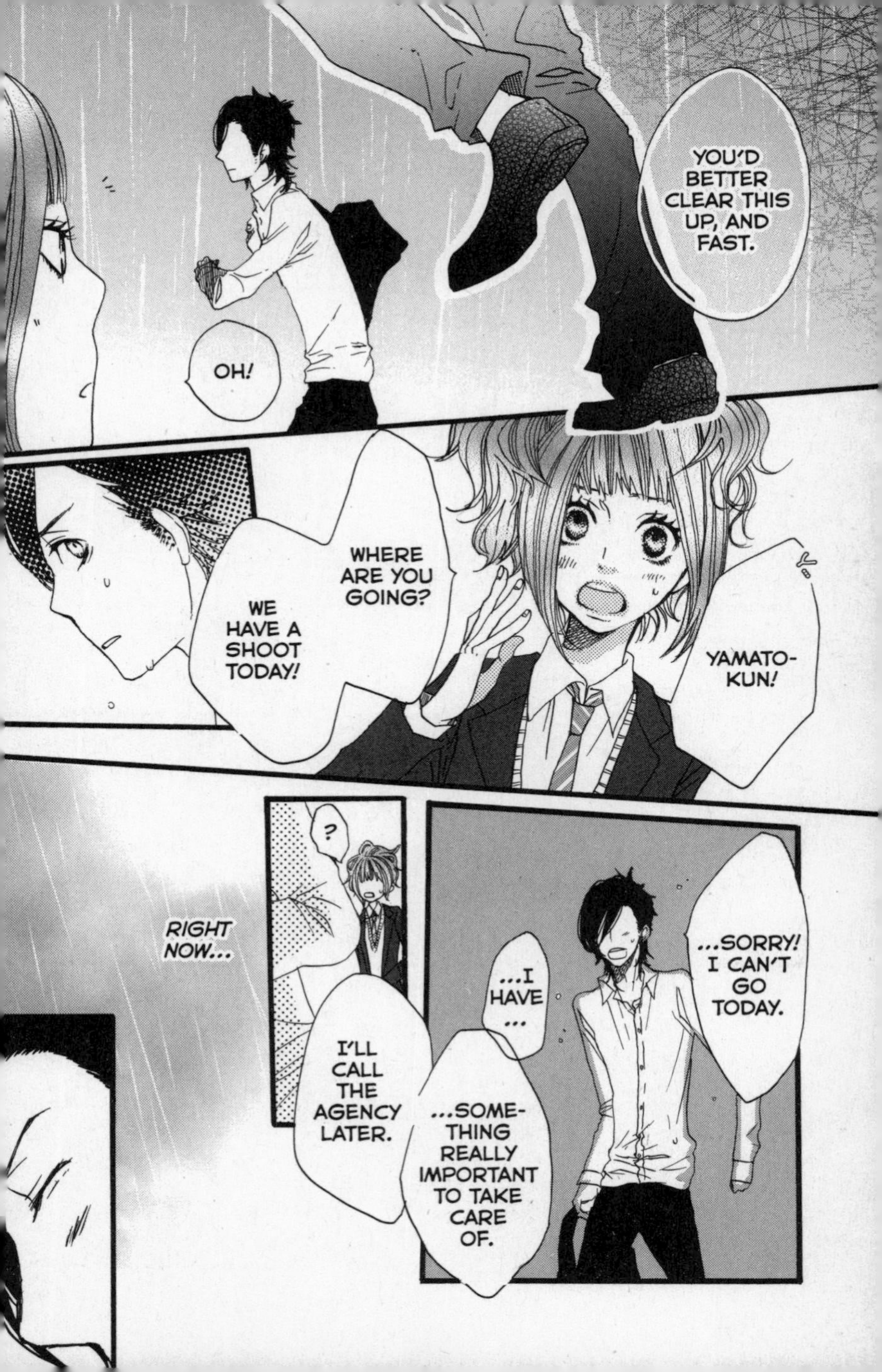
YOU'D BETTER CLEAR THIS UP, AND FAST.
OH!
YAMATO-KUN!
WHERE ARE YOU GOING?
WE HAVE A SHOOT TODAY!
...SORRY! I CAN'T GO TODAY.
...I HAVE...
...SOME-THING REALLY IMPORTANT TO TAKE CARE OF.
I'LL CALL THE AGENCY LATER.
?
RIGHT NOW...

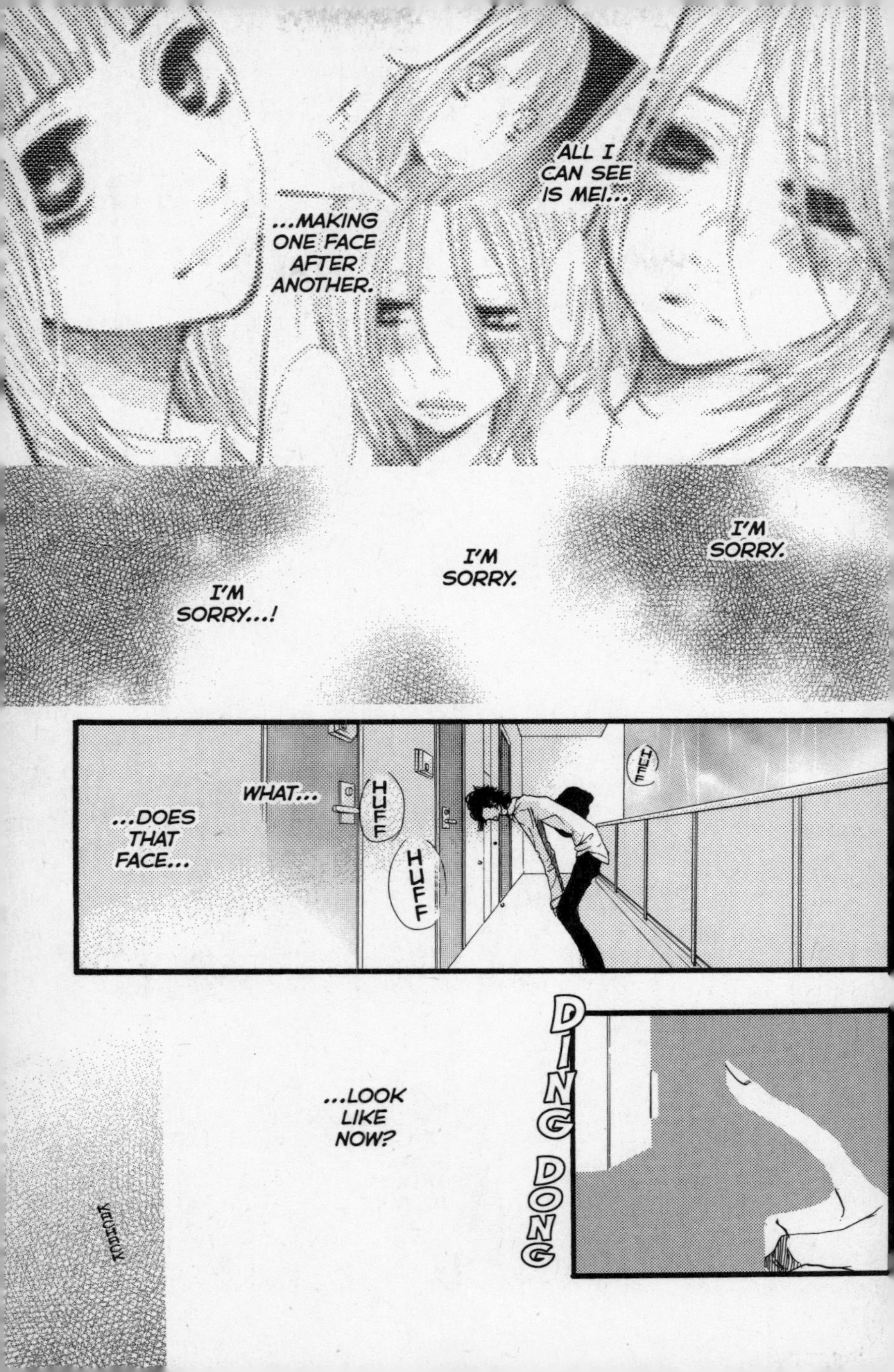
ALL I CAN SEE IS MEI...
...MAKING ONE FACE AFTER ANOTHER.
I'M SORRY.
I'M SORRY.
I'M SORRY...!
HUFF
WHAT...
HUFF
HUFF
...DOES THAT FACE...
DING DONG
...LOOK LIKE NOW?

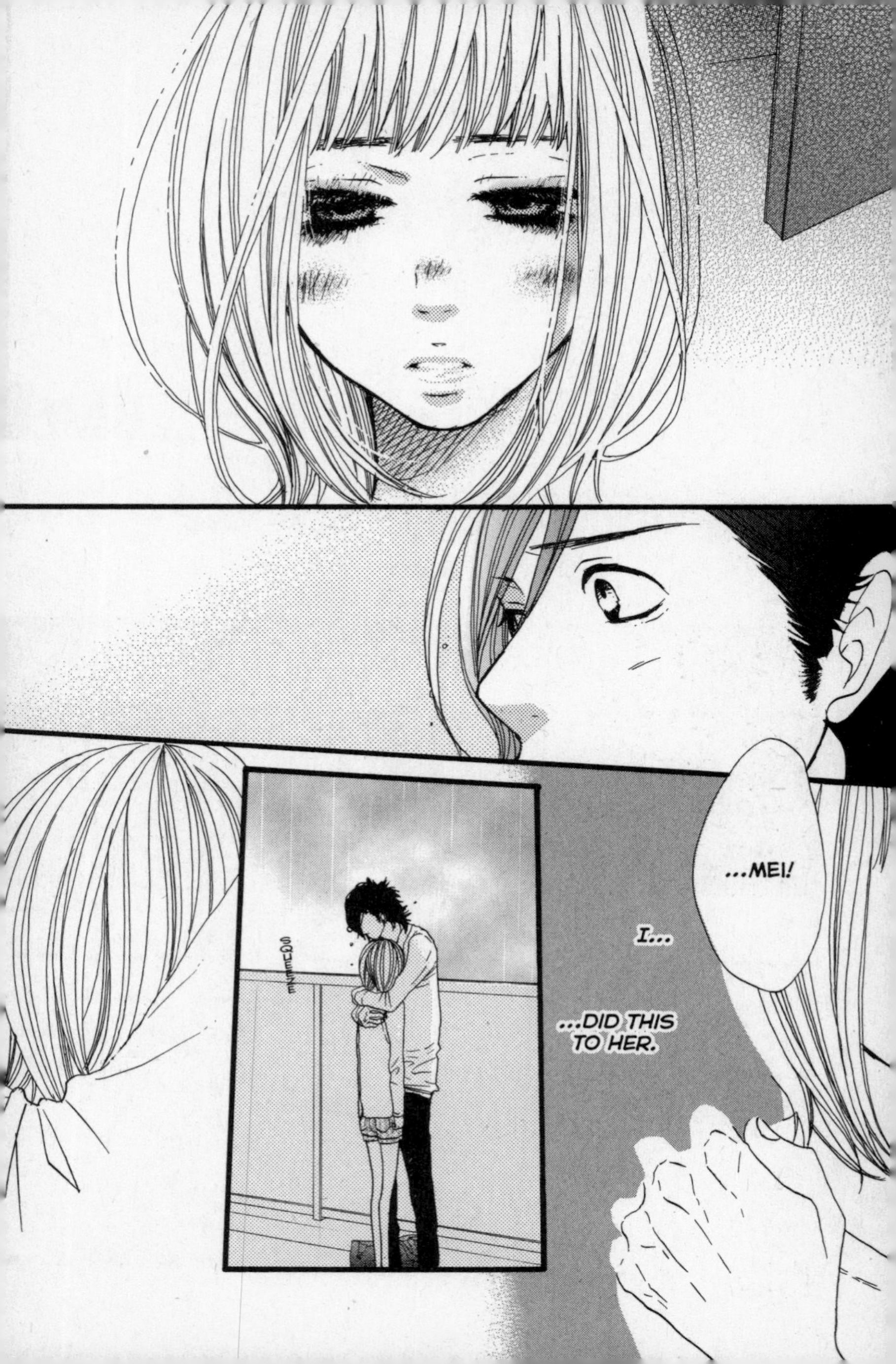
...MEI!
I...
...DID THIS TO HER.
SQUEEZE

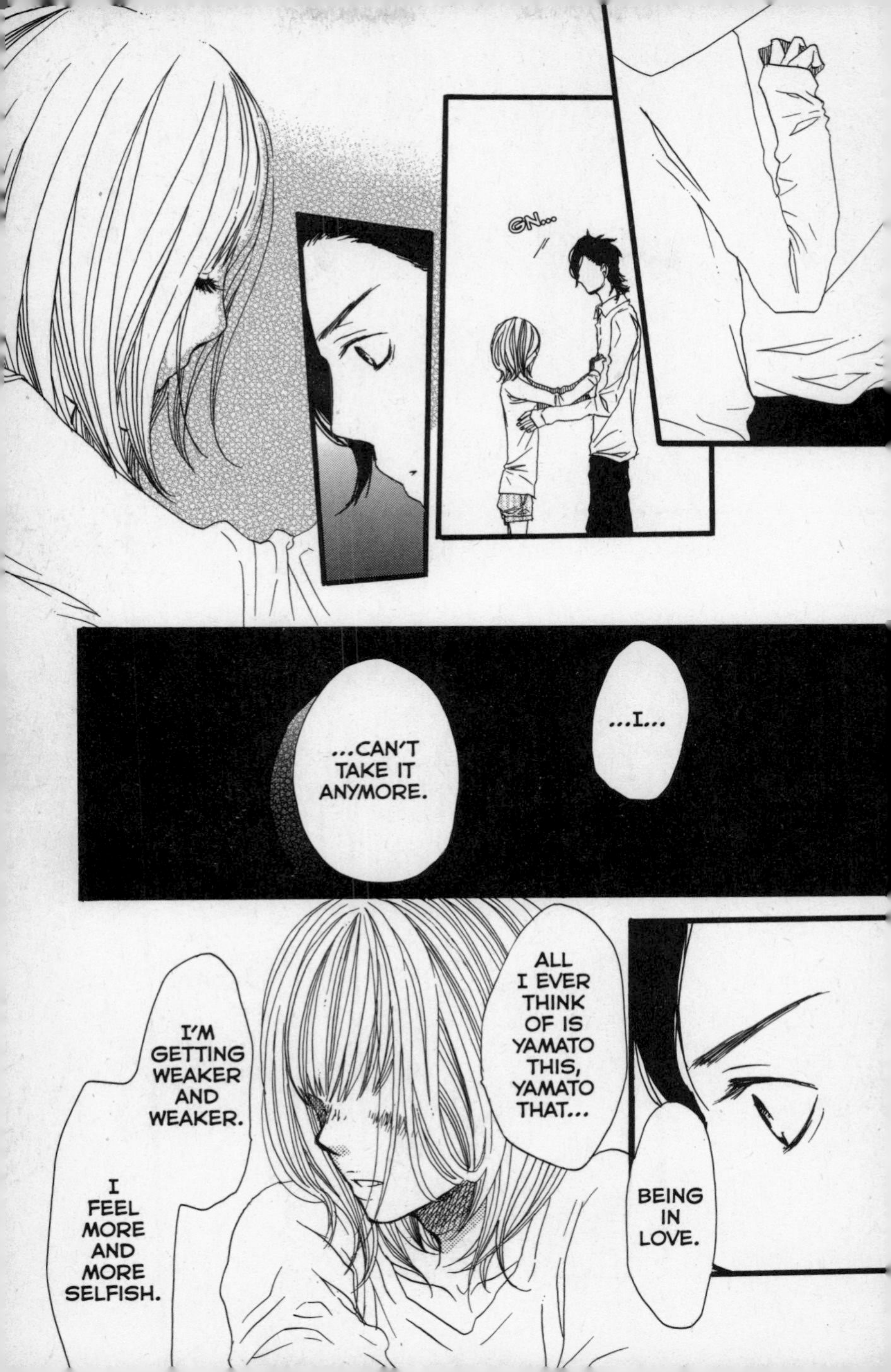
GN...
...I...
...CAN'T TAKE IT ANYMORE.
BEING IN LOVE.
ALL I EVER THINK OF IS YAMATO THIS, YAMATO THAT...
I'M GETTING WEAKER AND WEAKER.
I FEEL MORE AND MORE SELFISH.

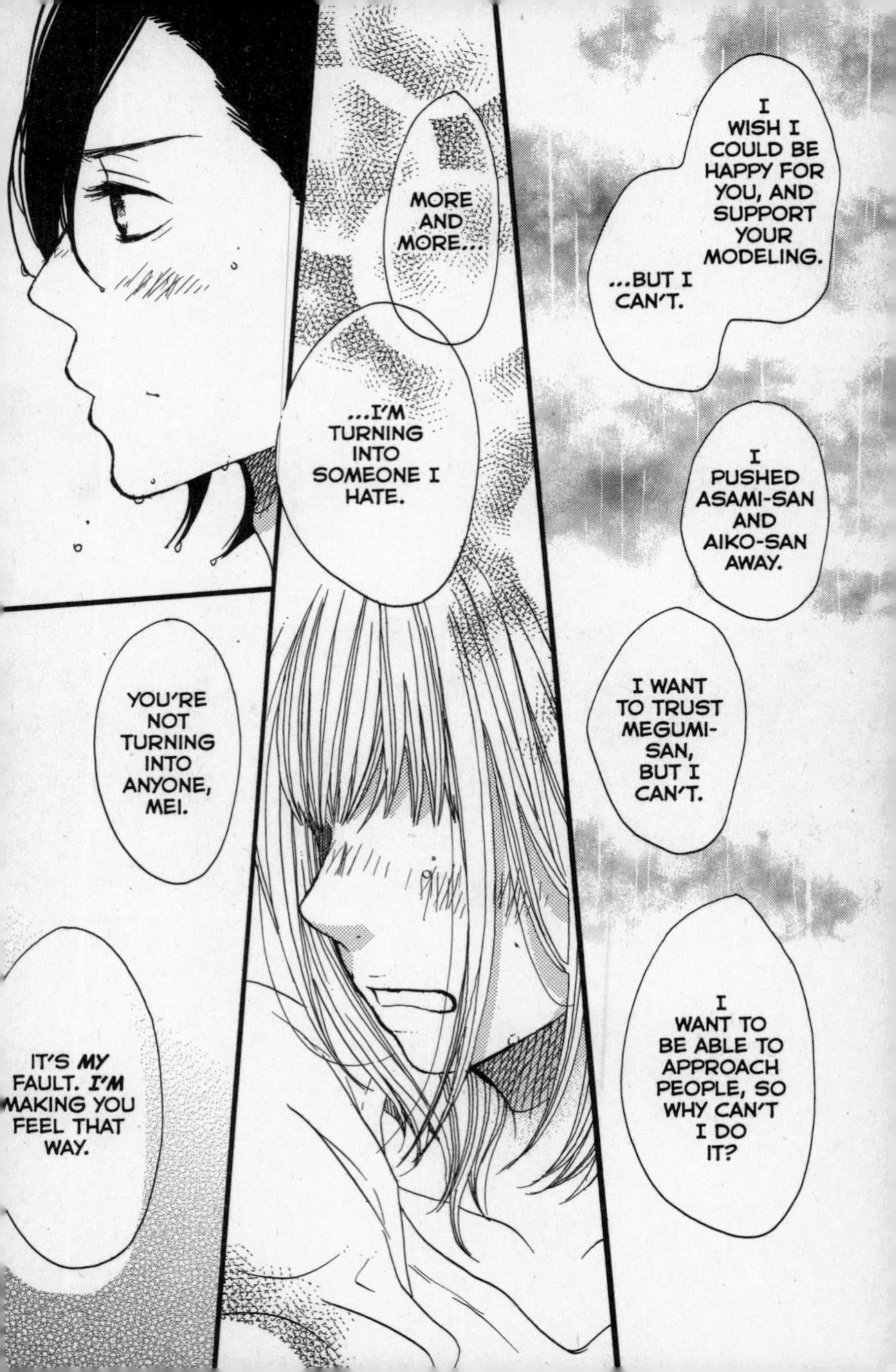
I WISH I COULD BE HAPPY FOR YOU, AND SUPPORT YOUR MODELING.
...BUT I CAN'T.
I PUSHED ASAMI-SAN AND AIKO-SAN AWAY.
I WANT TO TRUST MEGUMI-SAN, BUT I CAN'T.
I WANT TO BE ABLE TO APPROACH PEOPLE, SO WHY CAN'T I DO IT?
MORE AND MORE...
...I'M TURNING INTO SOMEONE I HATE.
YOU'RE NOT TURNING INTO ANYONE, MEI.
IT'S *MY* FAULT. *I'M* MAKING YOU FEEL THAT WAY.

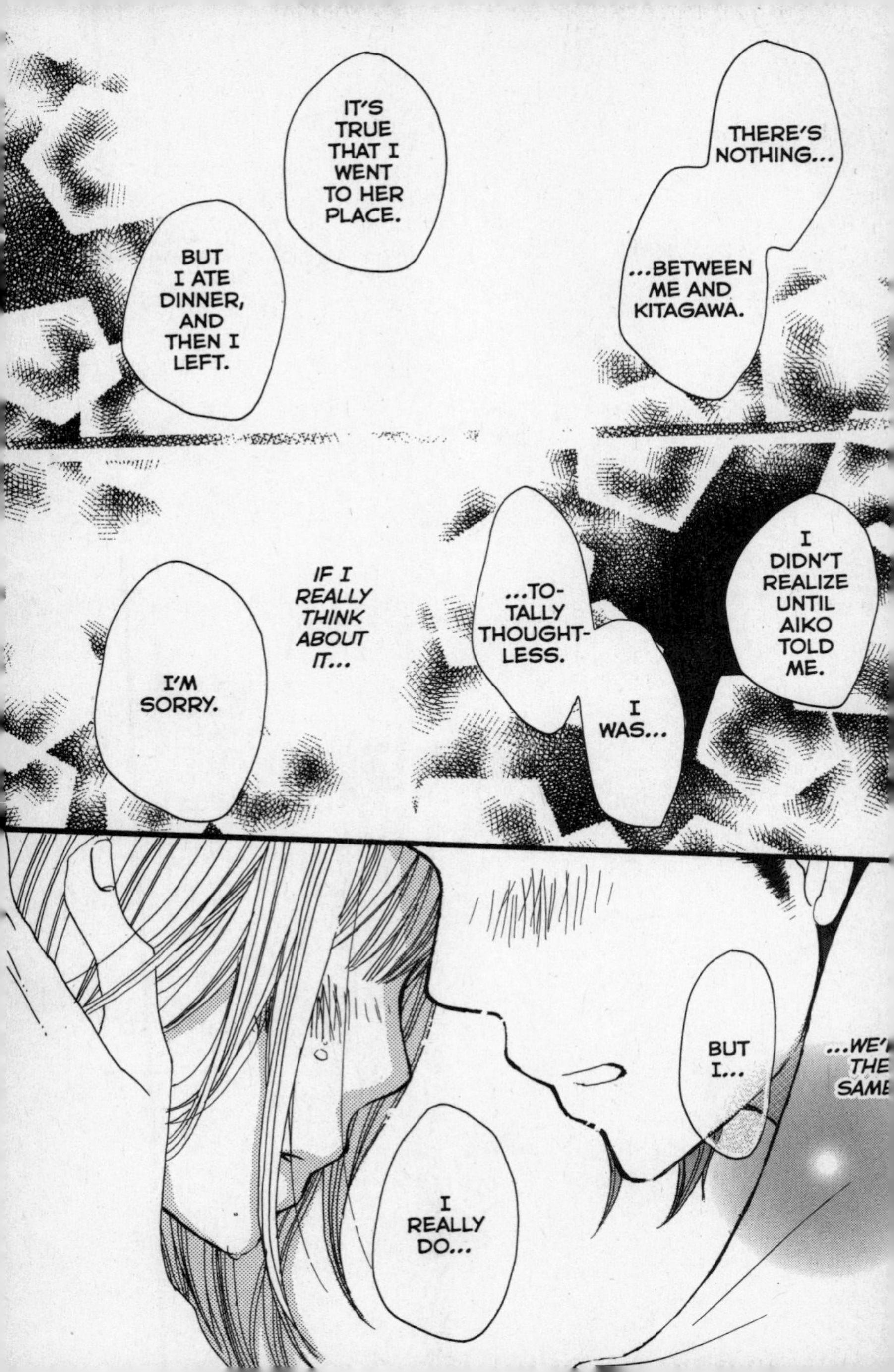
THERE'S NOTHING...
...BETWEEN ME AND KITAGAWA.
IT'S TRUE THAT I WENT TO HER PLACE.
BUT I ATE DINNER, AND THEN I LEFT.
I DIDN'T REALIZE UNTIL AIKO TOLD ME.
I WAS...
...TO-TALLY THOUGHT-LESS.
IF I REALLY THINK ABOUT IT...
I'M SORRY.
...WE' THE SAME
BUT I...
I REALLY DO...

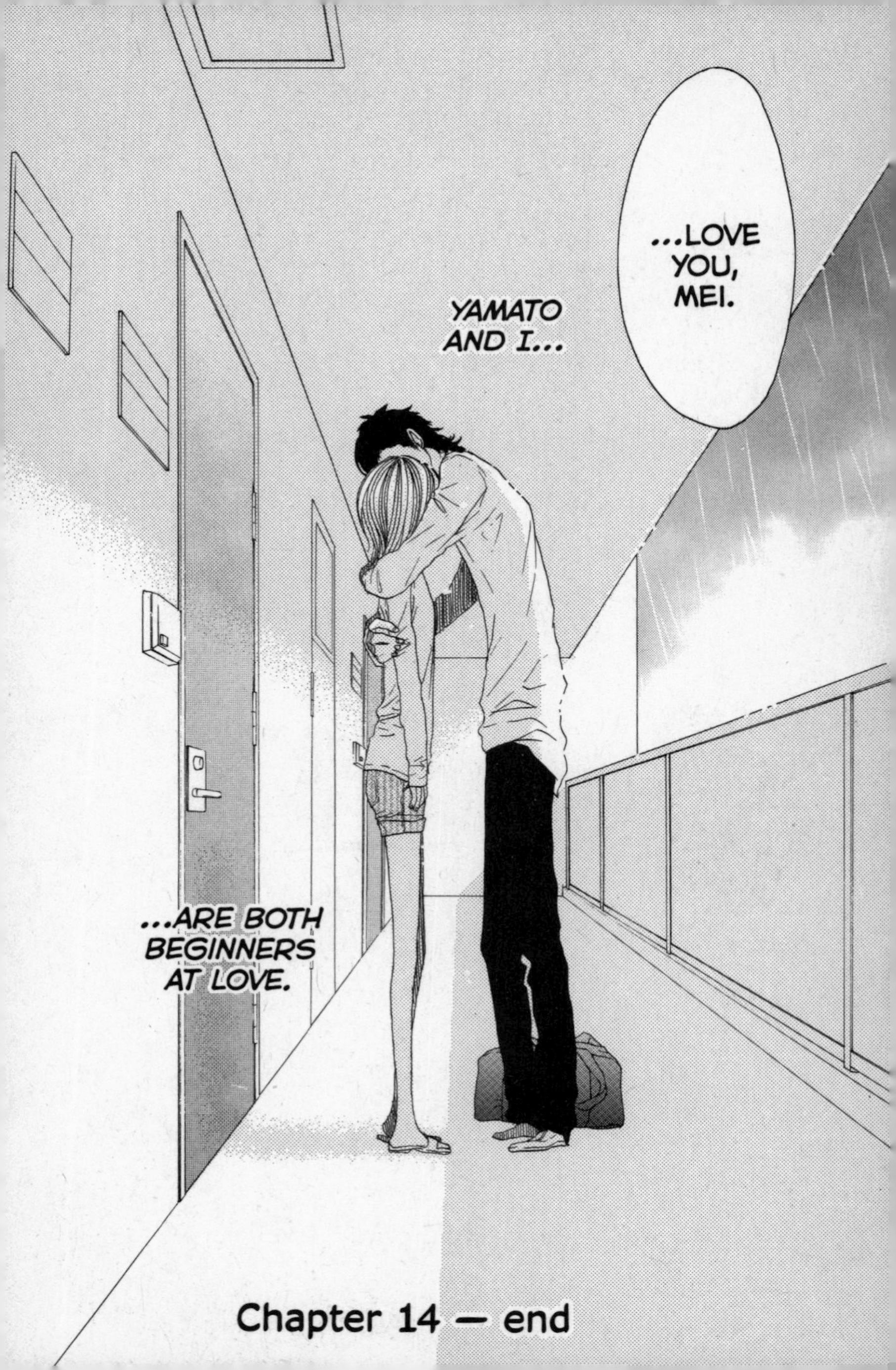
...LOVE YOU, MEI.
YAMATO AND I...
...ARE BOTH BEGINNERS AT LOVE.

Chapter 14 — end

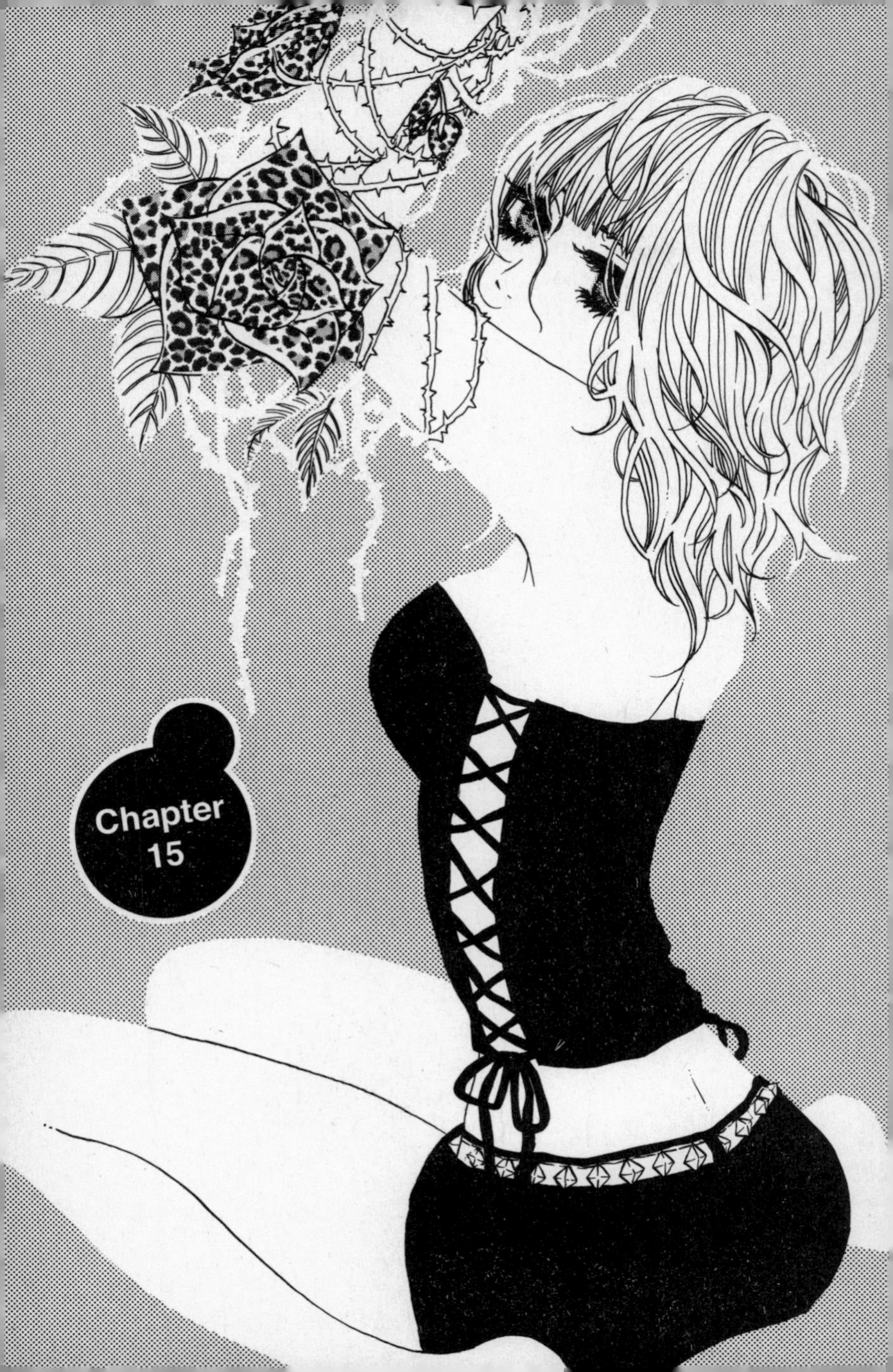
Chapter
15

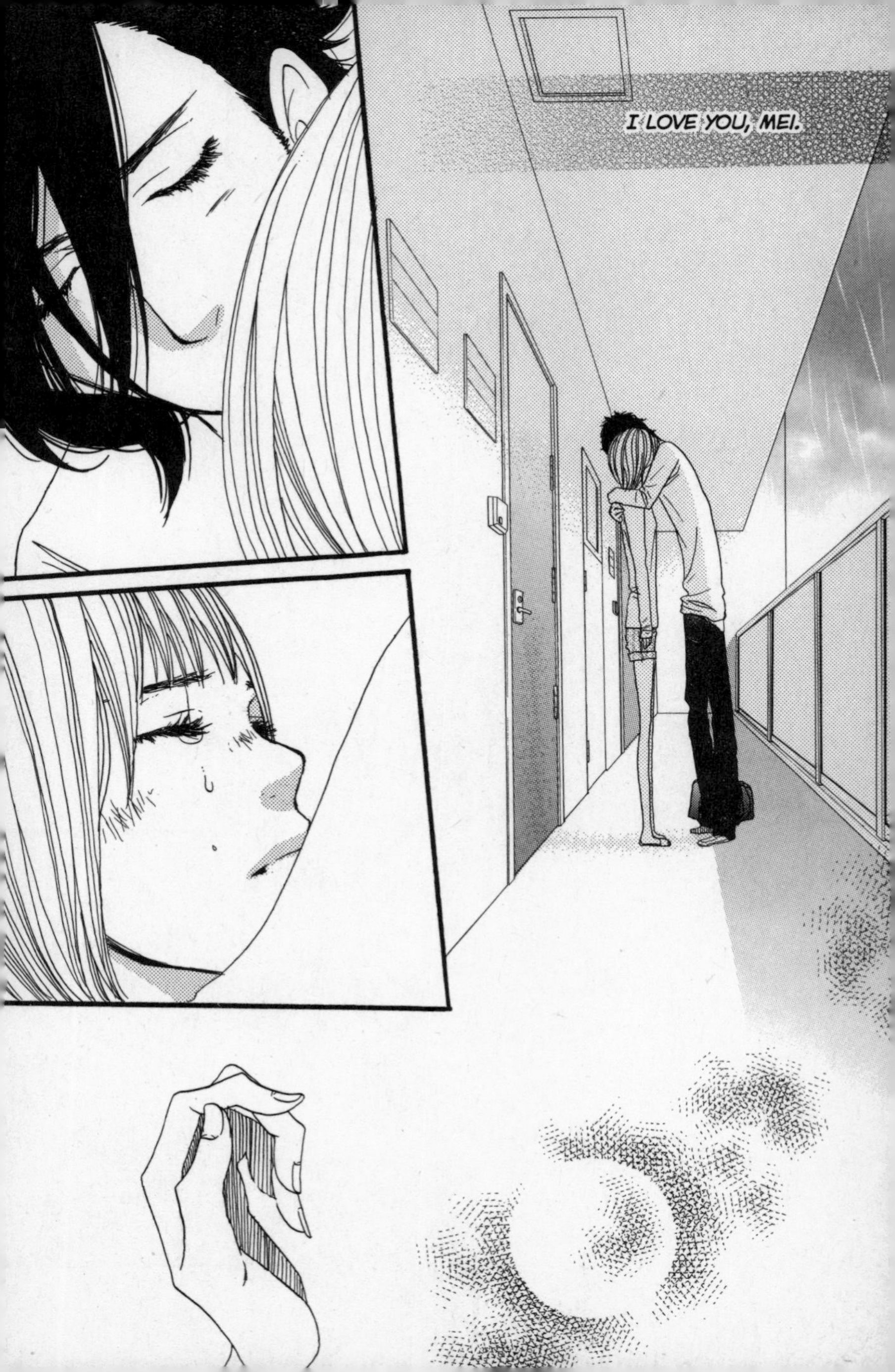
I LOVE YOU, MEI.

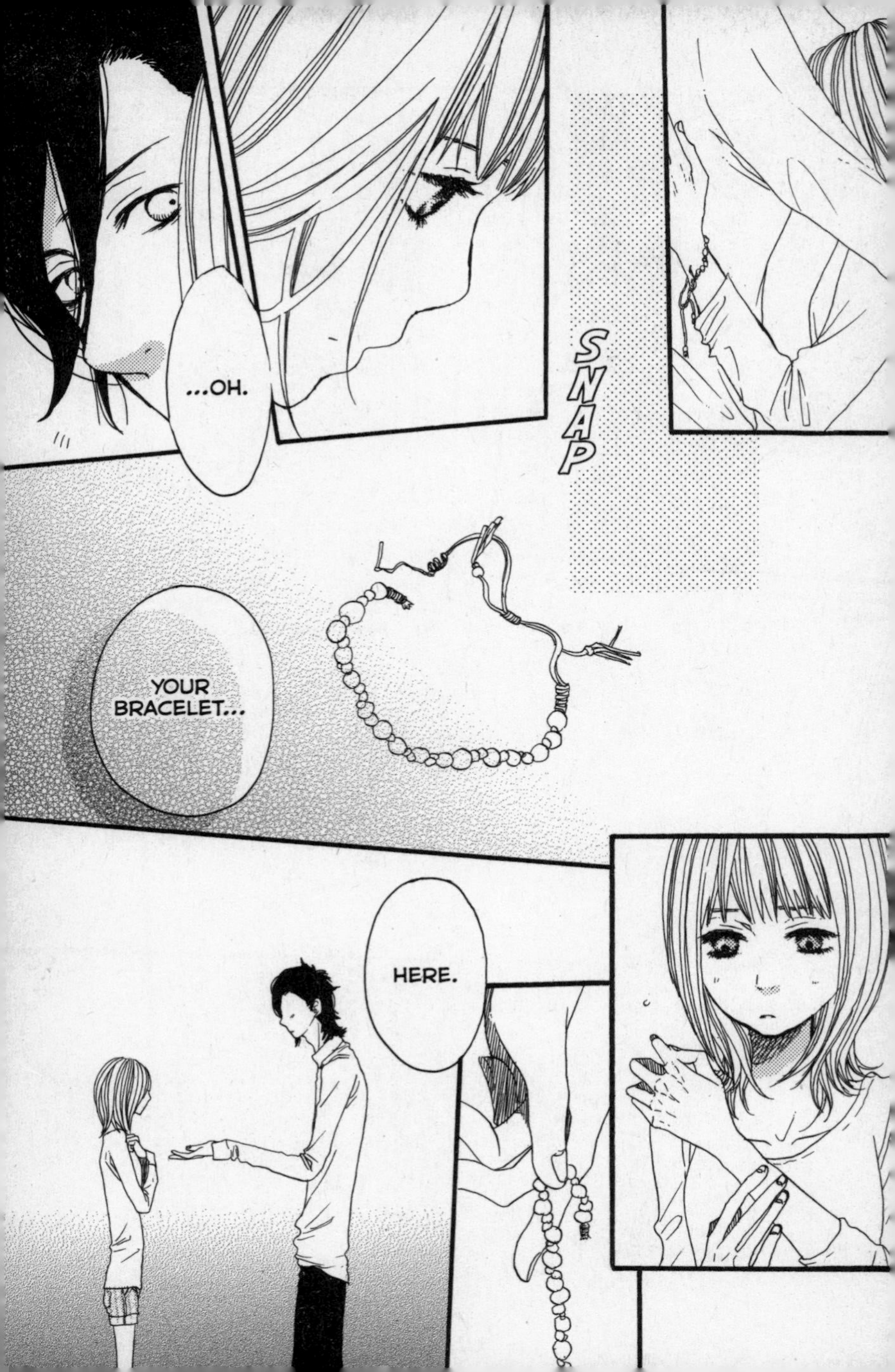
SNAP
...OH.
YOUR BRACELET...
HERE.

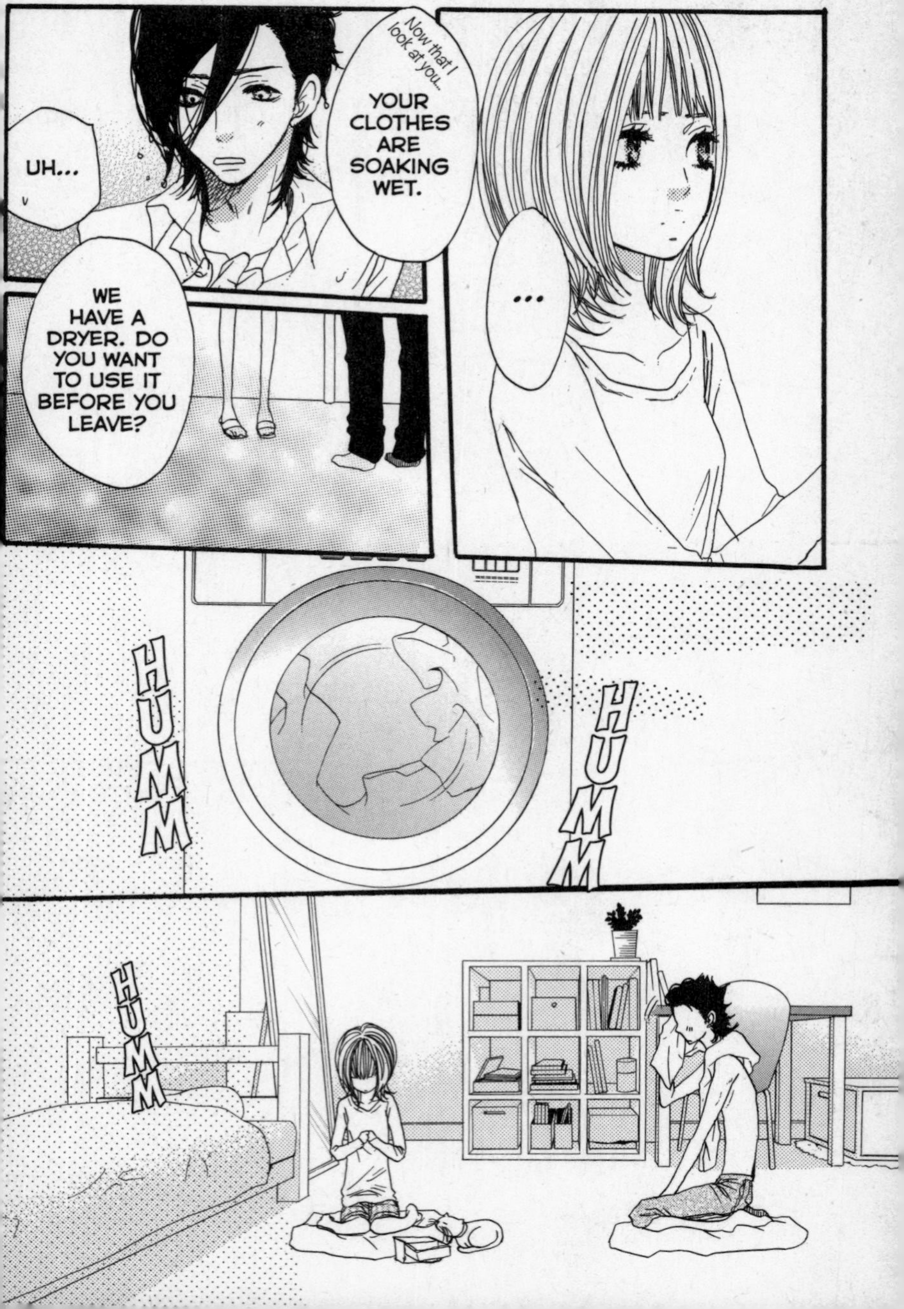
...
Now that I look at you...
YOUR CLOTHES ARE SOAKING WET.
UH...
WE HAVE A DRYER. DO YOU WANT TO USE IT BEFORE YOU LEAVE?
HUMM
HUMM
HUMM

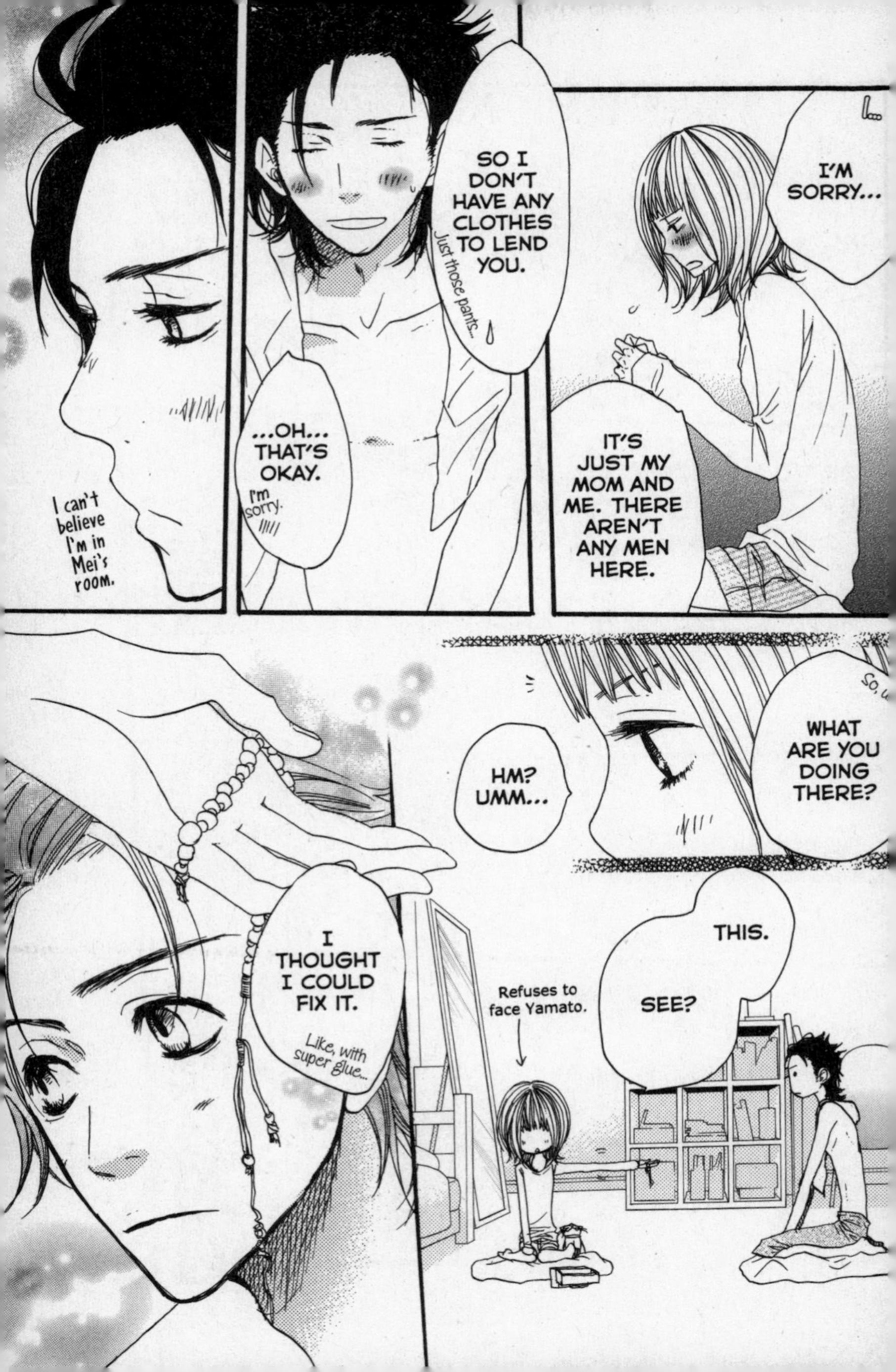
I...
I'M SORRY...
IT'S JUST MY MOM AND ME. THERE AREN'T ANY MEN HERE.
SO I DON'T HAVE ANY CLOTHES TO LEND YOU.
Just those pants...
...OH... THAT'S OKAY.
I'm sorry.
I can't believe I'm in Mei's room.
WHAT ARE YOU DOING THERE?
HM? UMM...
THIS.
SEE?
Refuses to face Yamato.
I THOUGHT I COULD FIX IT.
Like, with super glue...

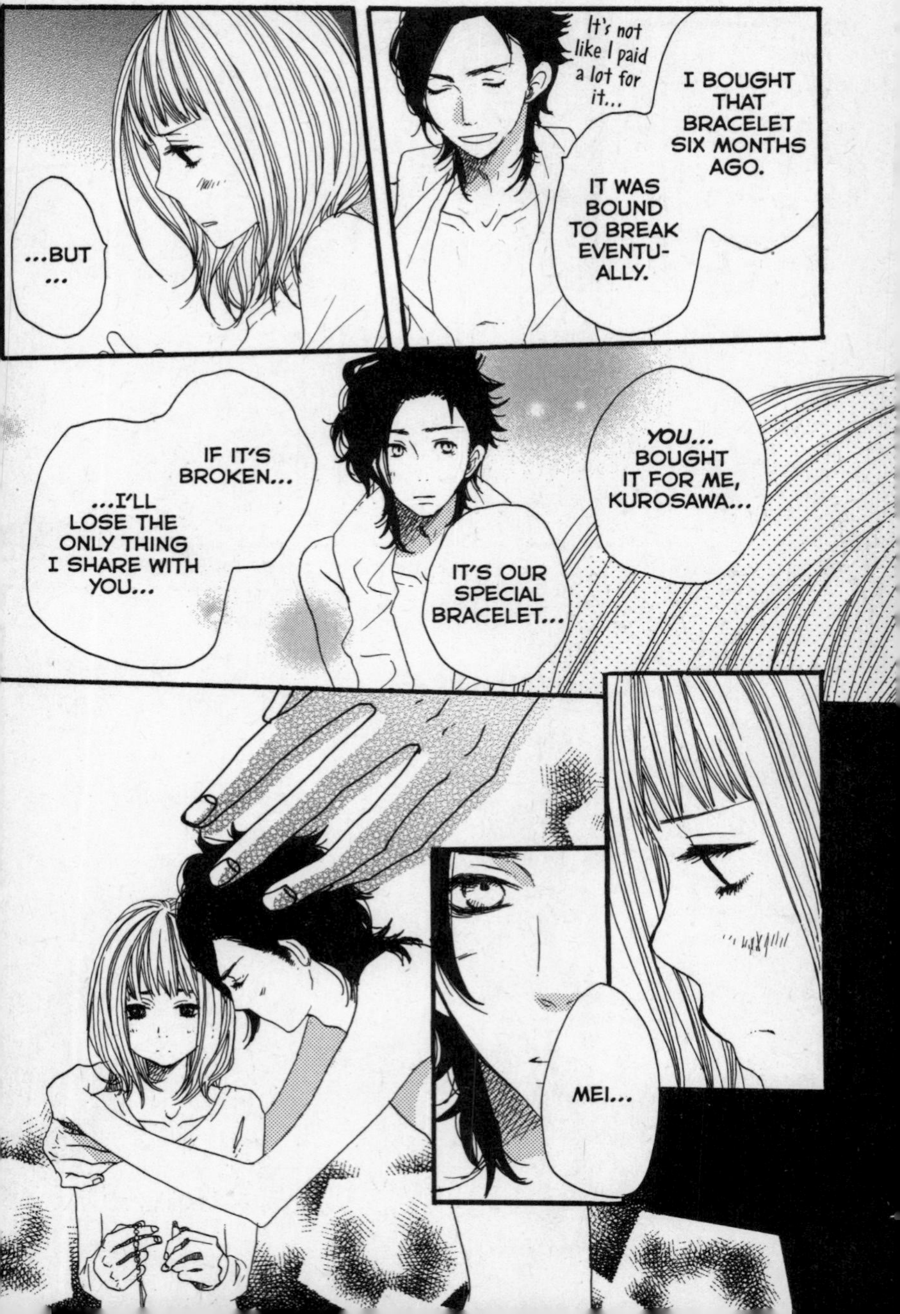
I BOUGHT THAT BRACELET SIX MONTHS AGO.
IT WAS BOUND TO BREAK EVENTU-ALLY.
It's not like I paid a lot for it...
...BUT ...
YOU... BOUGHT IT FOR ME, KUROSAWA...
IT'S OUR SPECIAL BRACELET...
IF IT'S BROKEN...
...I'LL LOSE THE ONLY THING I SHARE WITH YOU...
MEI...

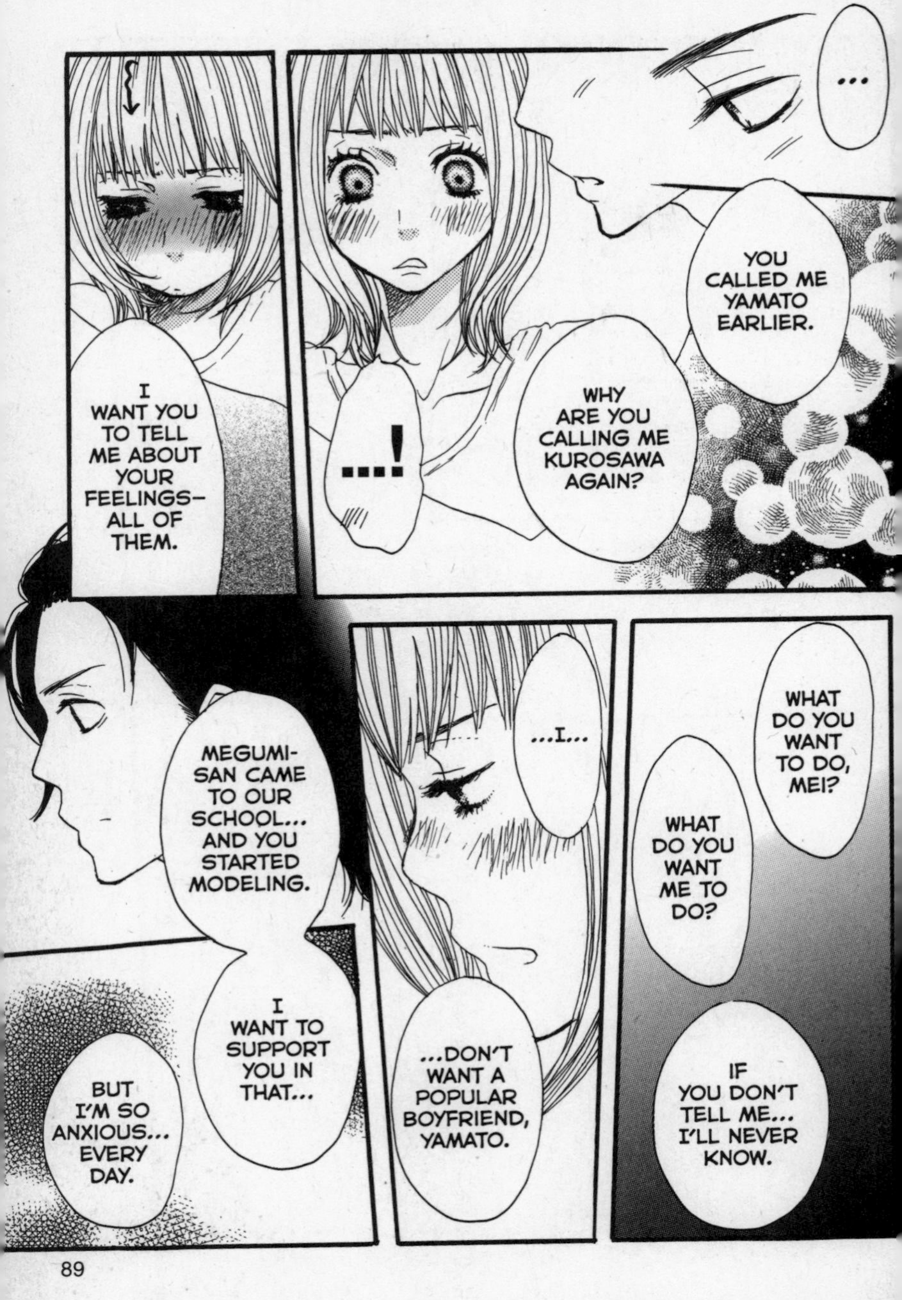
...
YOU CALLED ME YAMATO EARLIER.
WHY ARE YOU CALLING ME KUROSAWA AGAIN?
...!
I WANT YOU TO TELL ME ABOUT YOUR FEELINGS—ALL OF THEM.
WHAT DO YOU WANT TO DO, MEI?
WHAT DO YOU WANT ME TO DO?
IF YOU DON'T TELL ME... I'LL NEVER KNOW.
...I...
...DON'T WANT A POPULAR BOYFRIEND, YAMATO.
MEGUMI-SAN CAME TO OUR SCHOOL... AND YOU STARTED MODELING.
I WANT TO SUPPORT YOU IN THAT...
BUT I'M SO ANXIOUS... EVERY DAY.

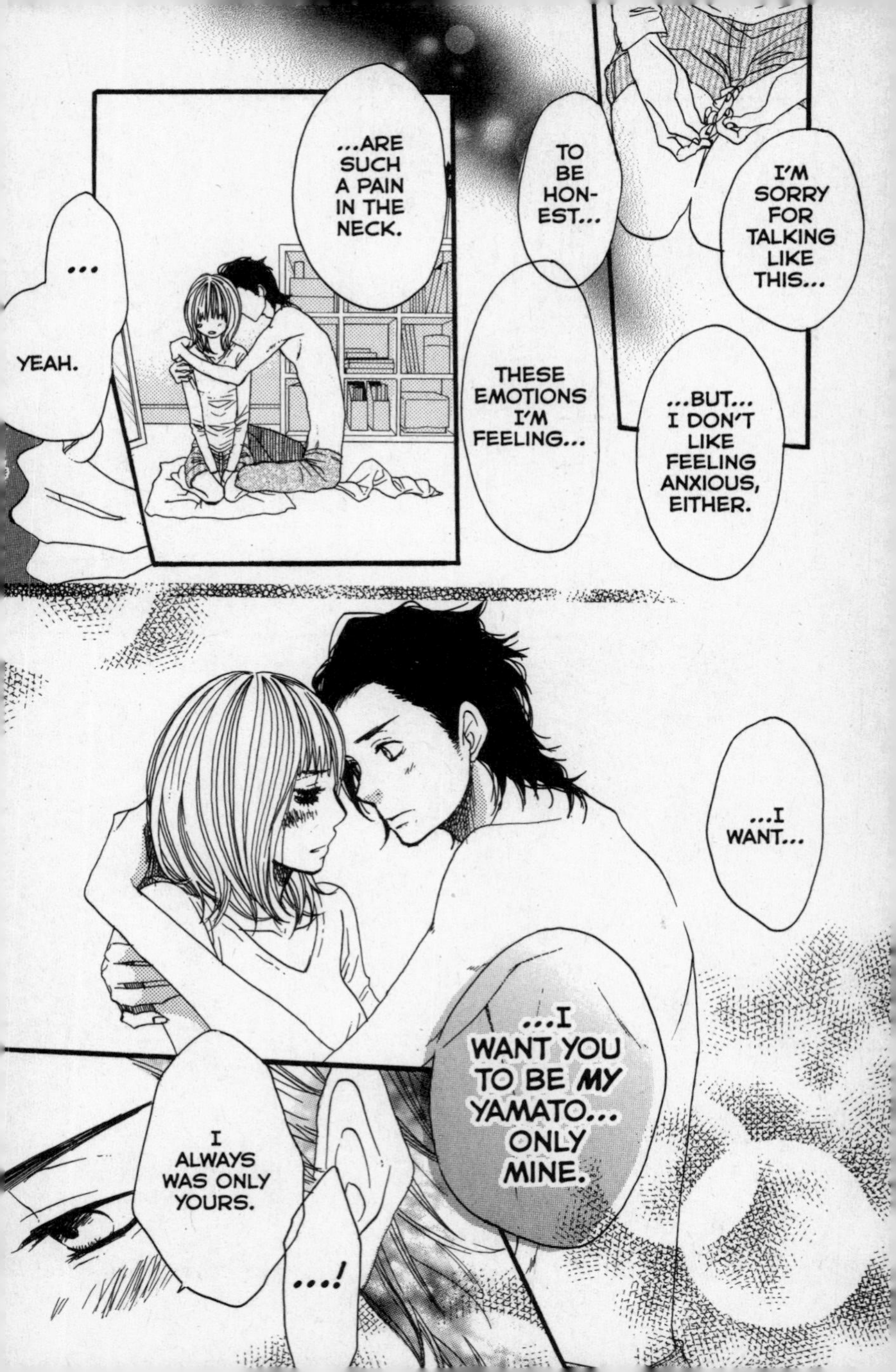
I'M SORRY FOR TALKING LIKE THIS...
TO BE HON-EST...
...BUT... I DON'T LIKE FEELING ANXIOUS, EITHER.
THESE EMOTIONS I'M FEELING...
...ARE SUCH A PAIN IN THE NECK.
...
YEAH.
...I WANT...
...I WANT YOU TO BE *MY* YAMATO... ONLY MINE.
...!
I ALWAYS WAS ONLY YOURS.

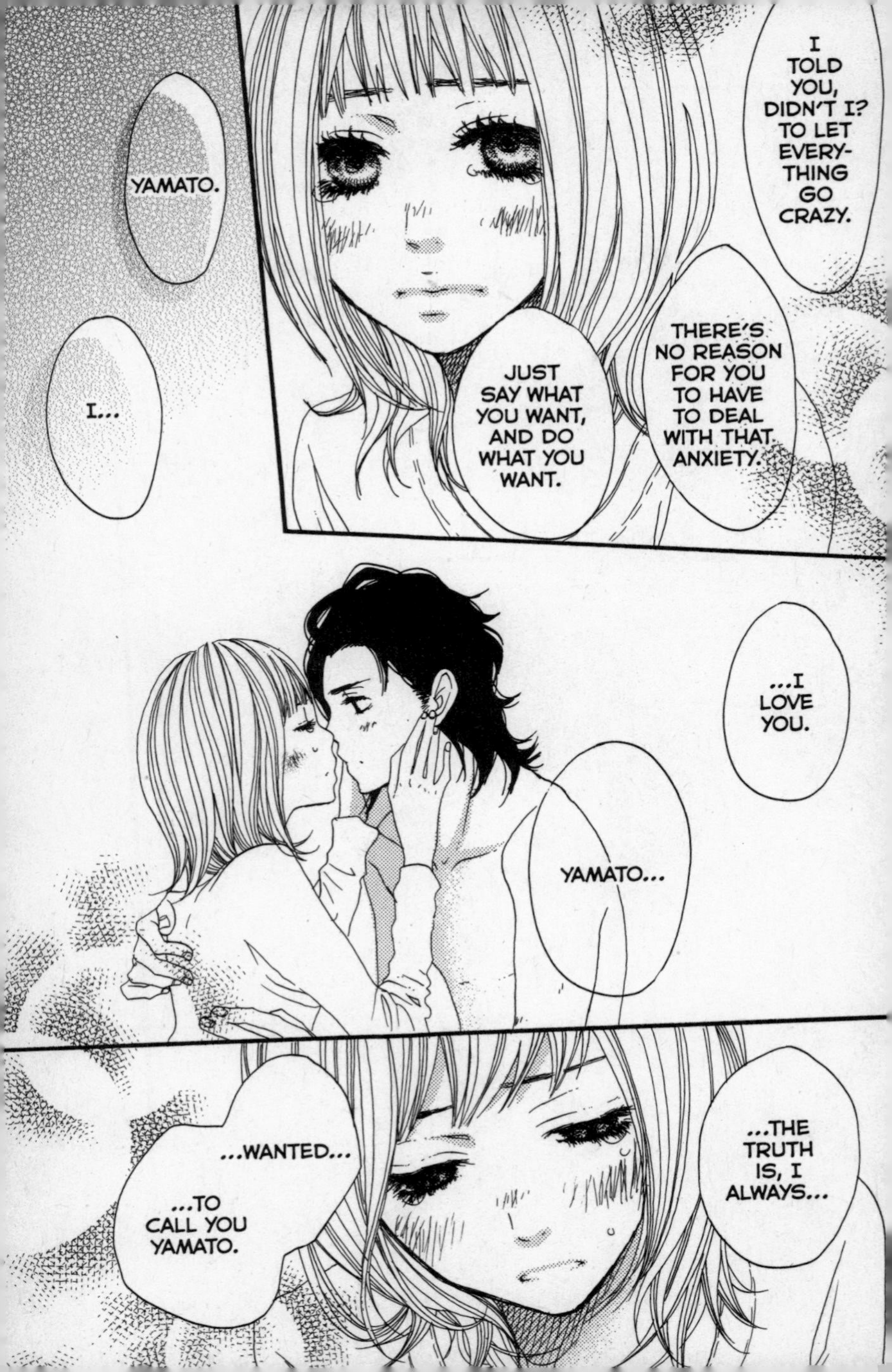
I TOLD YOU, DIDN'T I? TO LET EVERYTHING GO CRAZY.
THERE'S NO REASON FOR YOU TO HAVE TO DEAL WITH THAT ANXIETY.
JUST SAY WHAT YOU WANT, AND DO WHAT YOU WANT.
YAMATO.
I...
...I LOVE YOU.
YAMATO...
...THE TRUTH IS, I ALWAYS...
...WANTED...
...TO CALL YOU YAMATO.

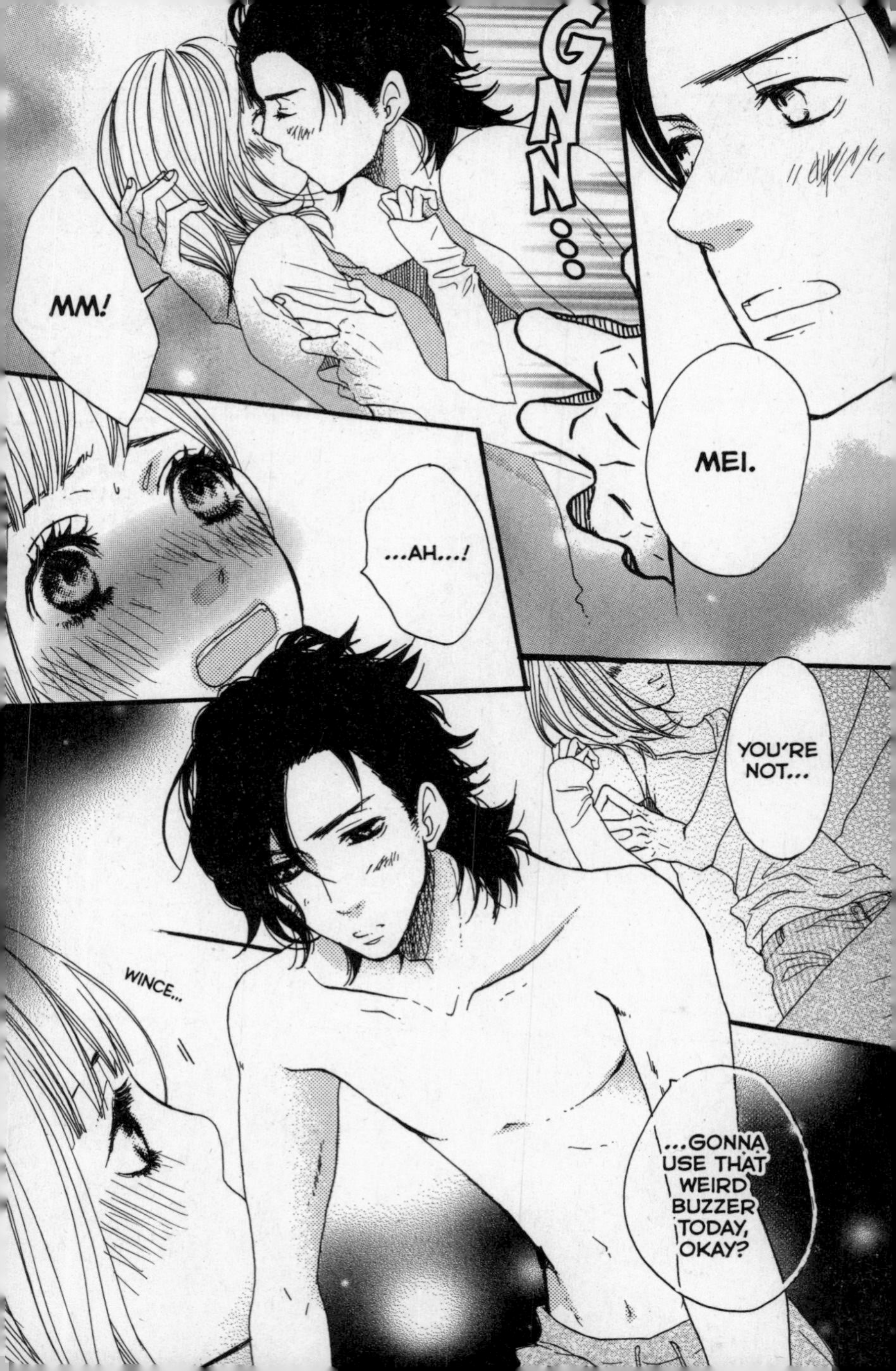
MEI.
GNN...
MM!
...AH...!
YOU'RE NOT...
WINCE...
...GONNA USE THAT WEIRD BUZZER TODAY, OKAY?

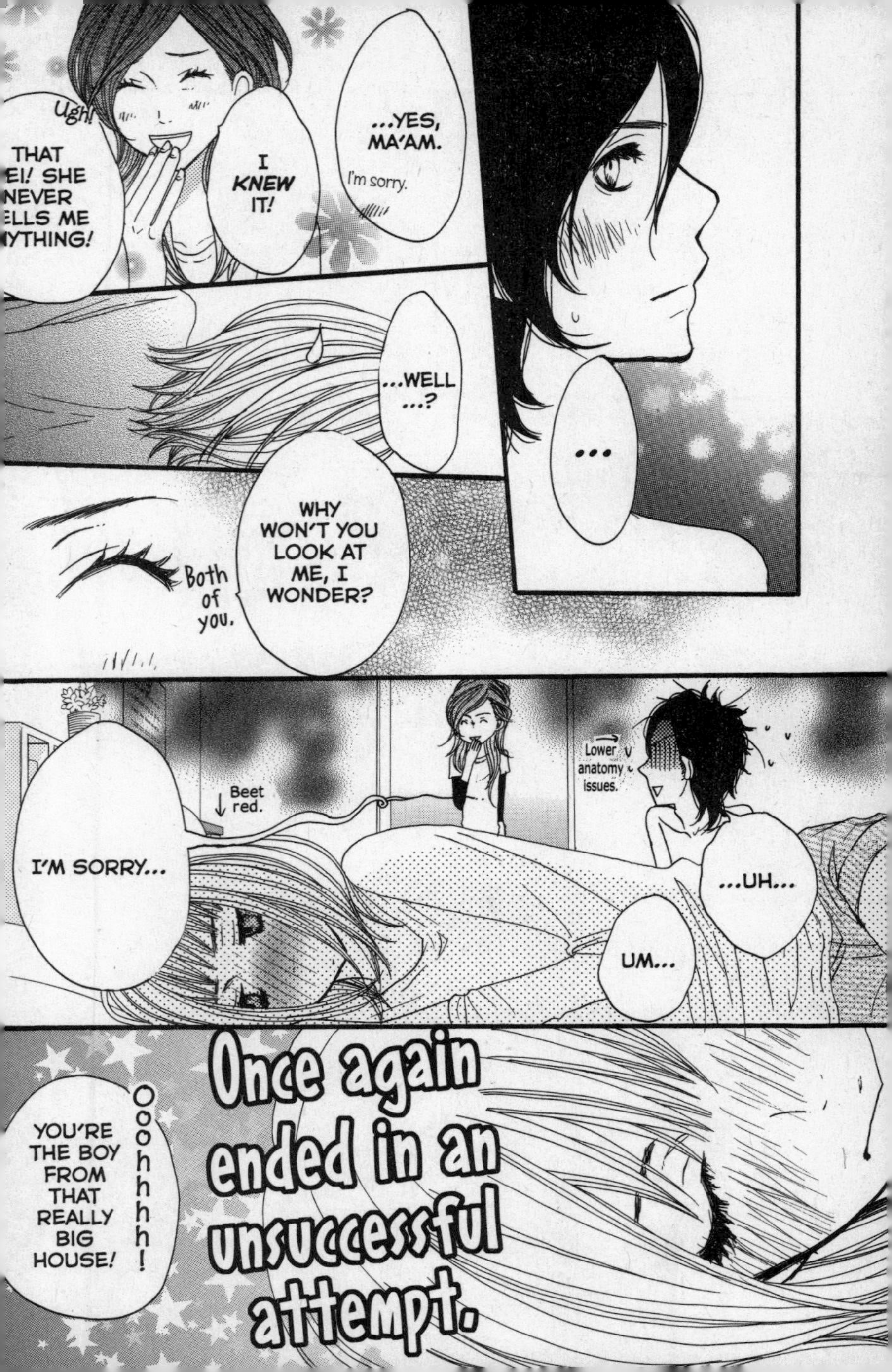
...
...YES, MA'AM.
I'm sorry.
I KNEW IT!
Ugh!
THAT EI! SHE NEVER ELLS ME YTHING!
...WELL ...?
WHY WON'T YOU LOOK AT ME, I WONDER?
Both of you.
...UH...
UM...
Lower anatomy issues.
Beet red.
I'M SORRY...
Once again ended in an unsuccessful attempt.
Ooohhhhh!
YOU'RE THE BOY FROM THAT REALLY BIG HOUSE!

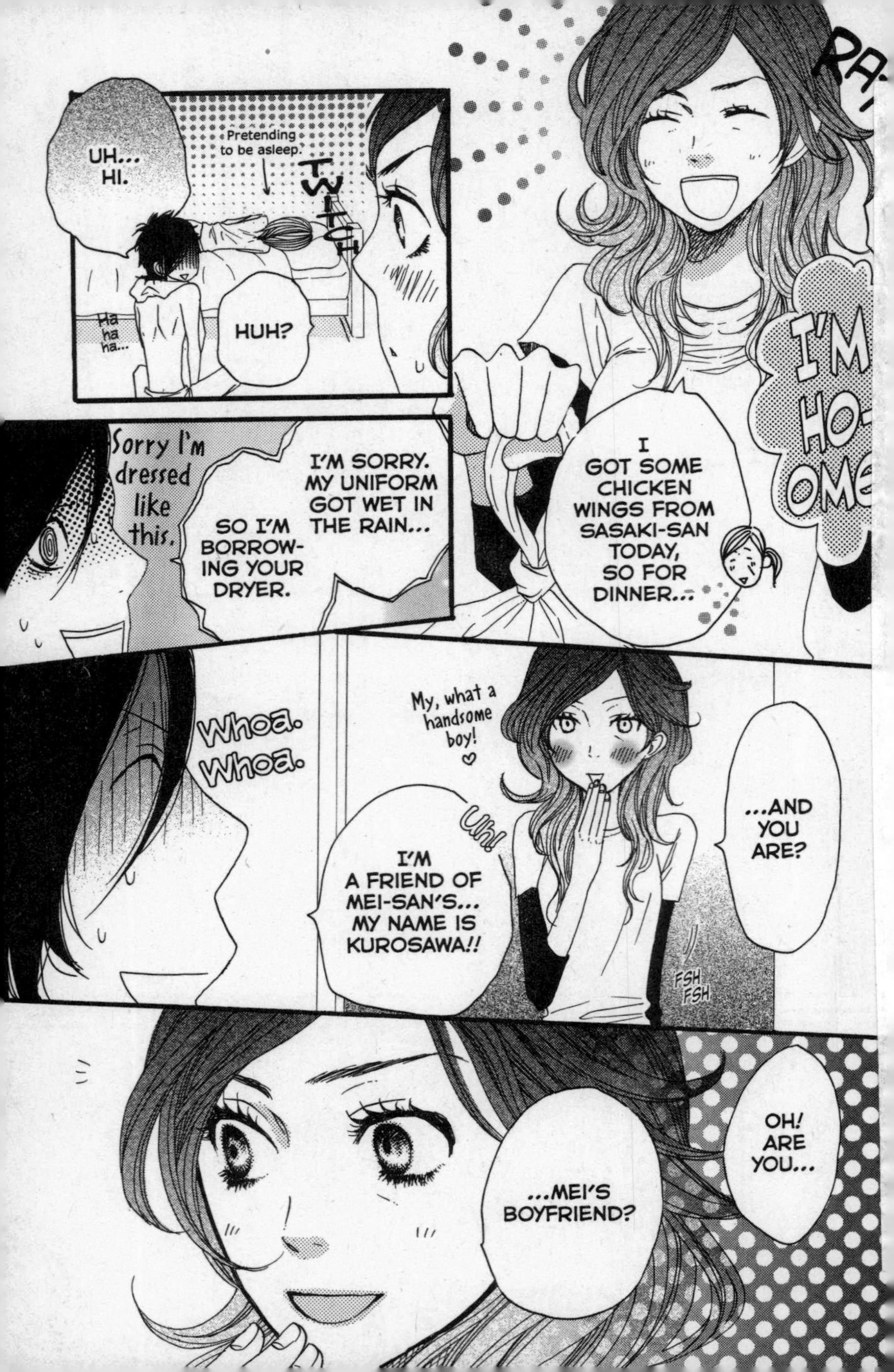
RA
I'M HO-OME
I GOT SOME CHICKEN WINGS FROM SASAKI-SAN TODAY, SO FOR DINNER...
UH... HI.
TWITCH
Pretending to be asleep.
HUH?
Ha ha ha...
I'M SORRY. MY UNIFORM GOT WET IN THE RAIN...
SO I'M BORROWING YOUR DRYER.
Sorry I'm dressed like this.
...AND YOU ARE?
My, what a handsome boy!
Uh!
I'M A FRIEND OF MEI-SAN'S... MY NAME IS KUROSAWA!!
FSH FSH
Whoa. Whoa.
OH! ARE YOU...
...MEI'S BOYFRIEND?

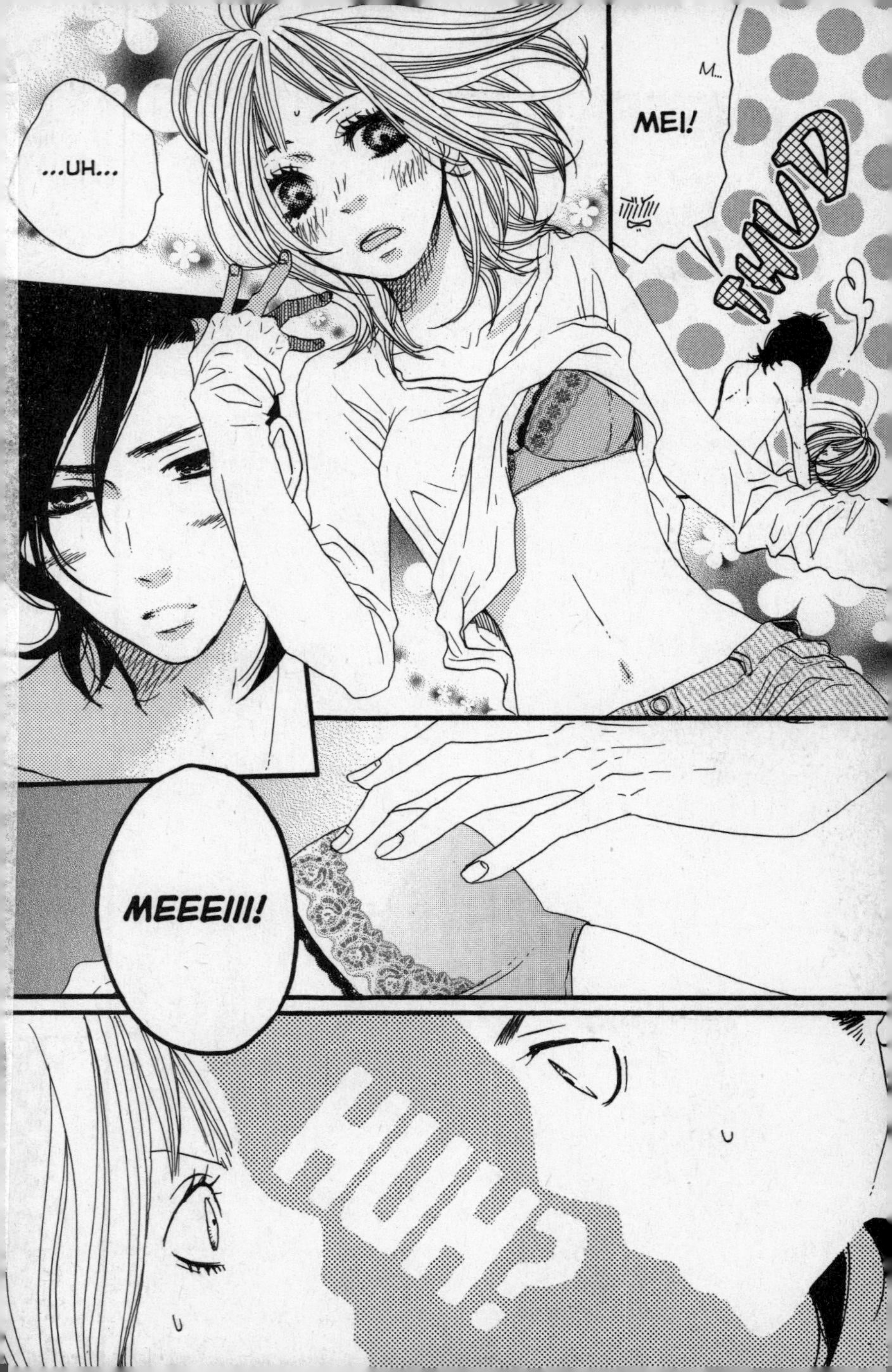
M...
MEI!
THUD
...UH...
MEEEIII!
HUH?

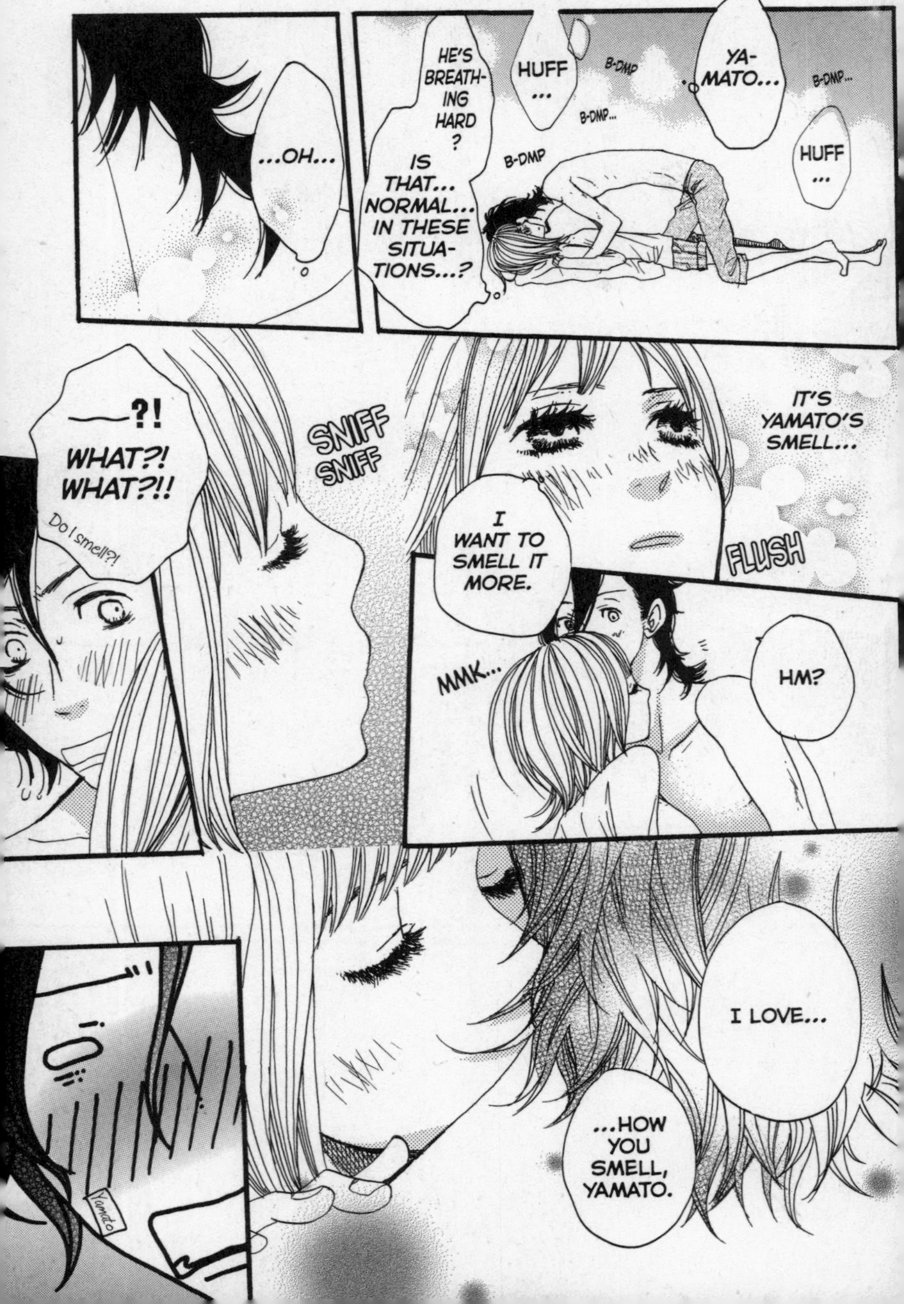
YA-MATO...
B-DMP...
HUFF...
HUFF...
B-DMP
B-DMP...
HE'S BREATHING HARD? IS THAT... NORMAL... IN THESE SITUATIONS...?
B-DMP
...OH...
IT'S YAMATO'S SMELL...
FLUSH
I WANT TO SMELL IT MORE.
SNIFF SNIFF
HM?
MMK...
—?! WHAT?! WHAT?!!
Do I smell?!
I LOVE...
...HOW YOU SMELL, YAMATO.
Yamato

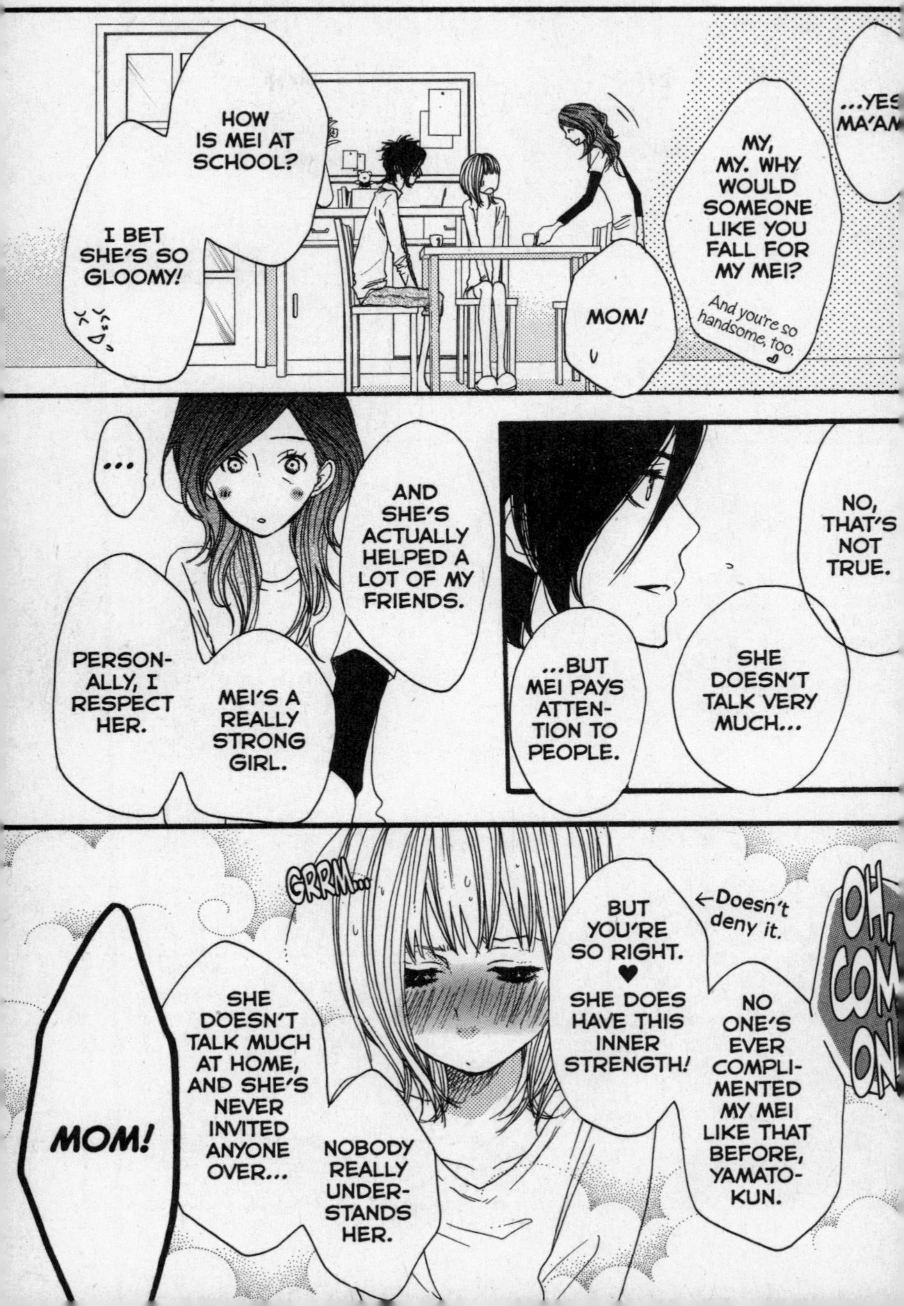

...YES MA'AM
MY, MY. WHY WOULD SOMEONE LIKE YOU FALL FOR MY MEI?
And you're so handsome, too.
MOM!
HOW IS MEI AT SCHOOL?
I BET SHE'S SO GLOOMY!
NO, THAT'S NOT TRUE.
SHE DOESN'T TALK VERY MUCH...
...BUT MEI PAYS ATTENTION TO PEOPLE.
AND SHE'S ACTUALLY HELPED A LOT OF MY FRIENDS.
...
MEI'S A REALLY STRONG GIRL.
PERSONALLY, I RESPECT HER.
OH, COM ON
NO ONE'S EVER COMPLIMENTED MY MEI LIKE THAT BEFORE, YAMATO-KUN.
←Doesn't deny it.
BUT YOU'RE SO RIGHT. ♥ SHE DOES HAVE THIS INNER STRENGTH!
GRRM...
SHE DOESN'T TALK MUCH AT HOME, AND SHE'S NEVER INVITED ANYONE OVER...
NOBODY REALLY UNDERSTANDS HER.
MOM!

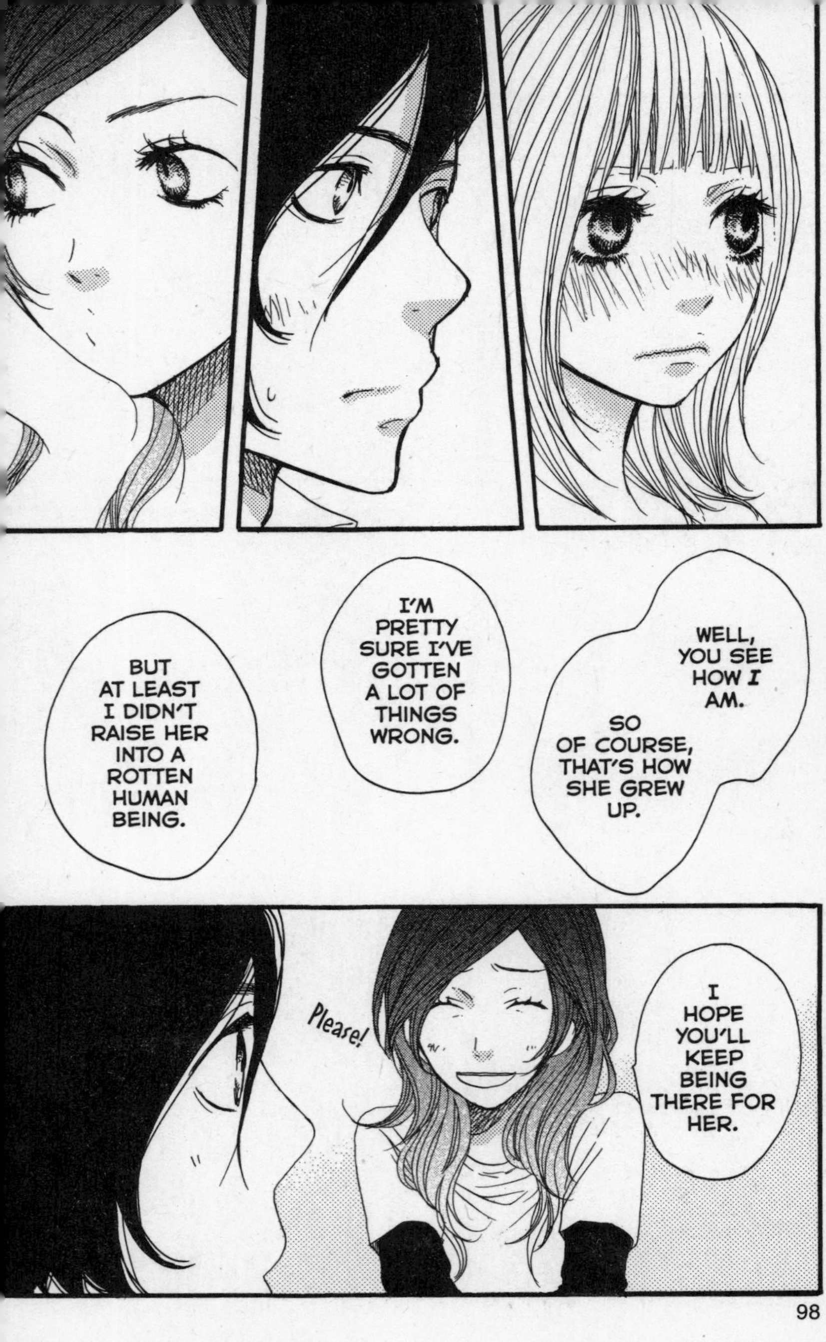
WELL, YOU SEE HOW *I* AM.
SO OF COURSE, THAT'S HOW SHE GREW UP.
I'M PRETTY SURE I'VE GOTTEN A LOT OF THINGS WRONG.
BUT AT LEAST I DIDN'T RAISE HER INTO A ROTTEN HUMAN BEING.
I HOPE YOU'LL KEEP BEING THERE FOR HER.
Please!

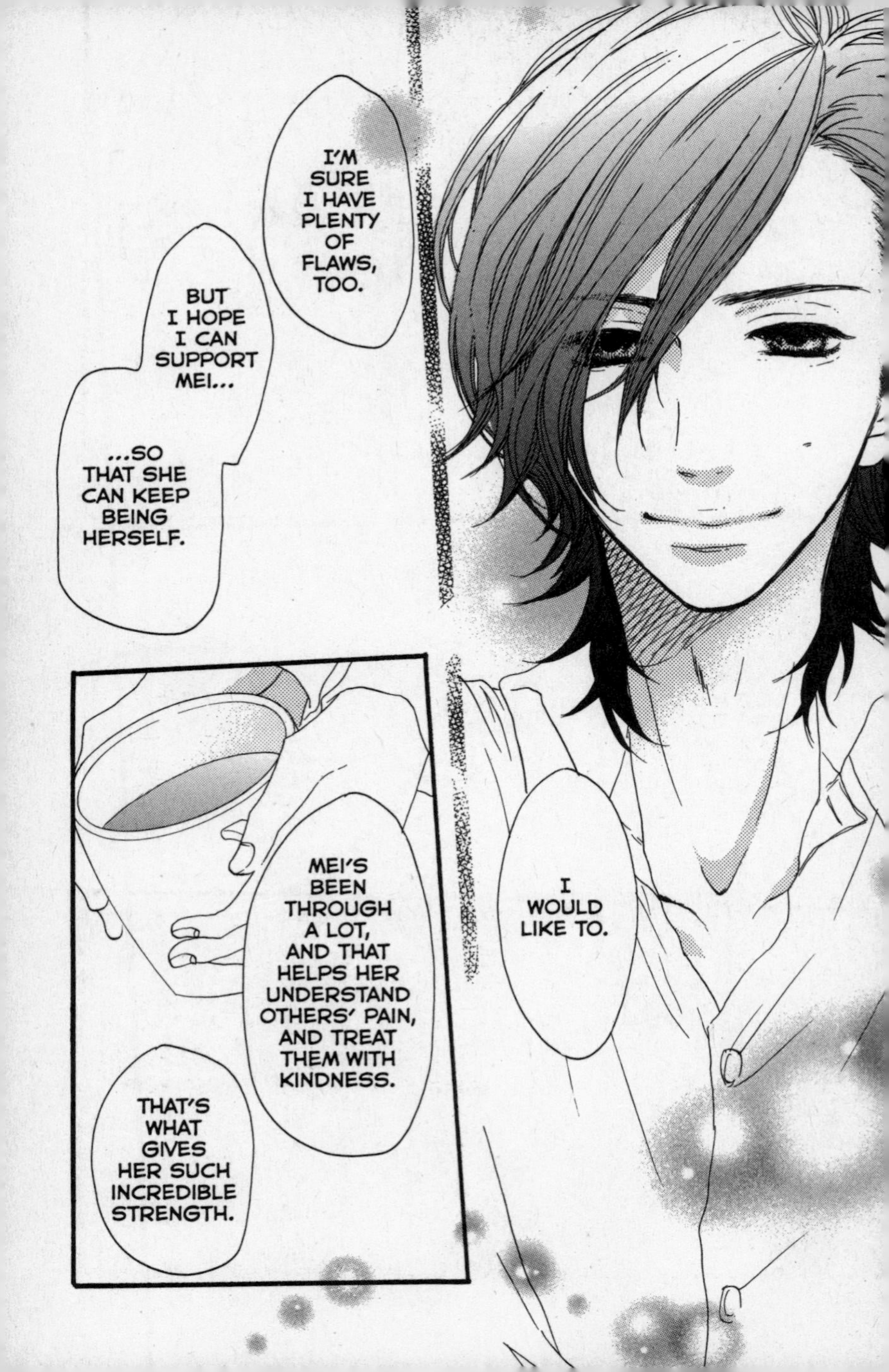
I'M SURE I HAVE PLENTY OF FLAWS, TOO.
BUT I HOPE I CAN SUPPORT MEI...
...SO THAT SHE CAN KEEP BEING HERSELF.
I WOULD LIKE TO.
MEI'S BEEN THROUGH A LOT, AND THAT HELPS HER UNDERSTAND OTHERS' PAIN, AND TREAT THEM WITH KINDNESS.
THAT'S WHAT GIVES HER SUCH INCREDIBLE STRENGTH.

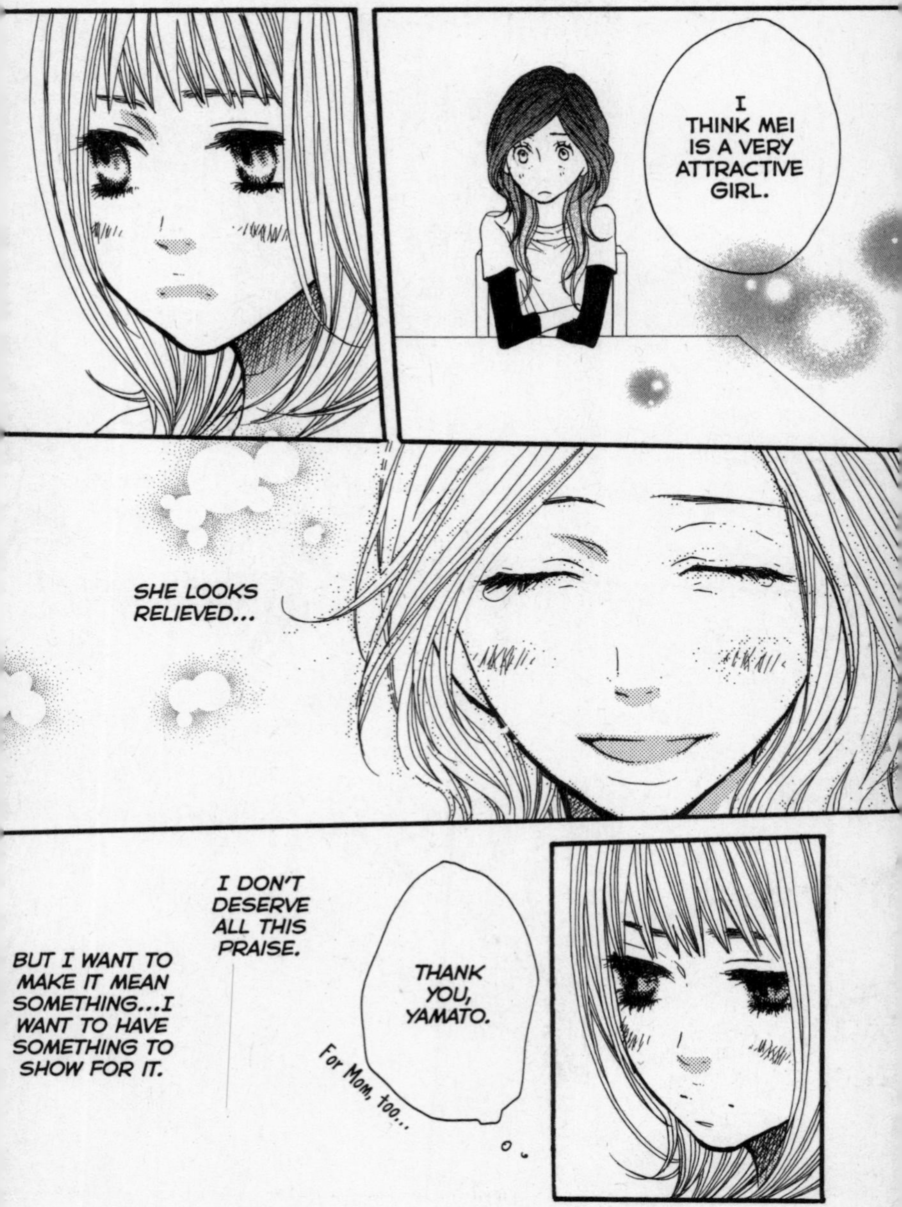
I THINK MEI IS A VERY ATTRACTIVE GIRL.
SHE LOOKS RELIEVED...
THANK YOU, YAMATO.
For Mom, too...
I DON'T DESERVE ALL THIS PRAISE.
BUT I WANT TO MAKE IT MEAN SOMETHING...I WANT TO HAVE SOMETHING TO SHOW FOR IT.

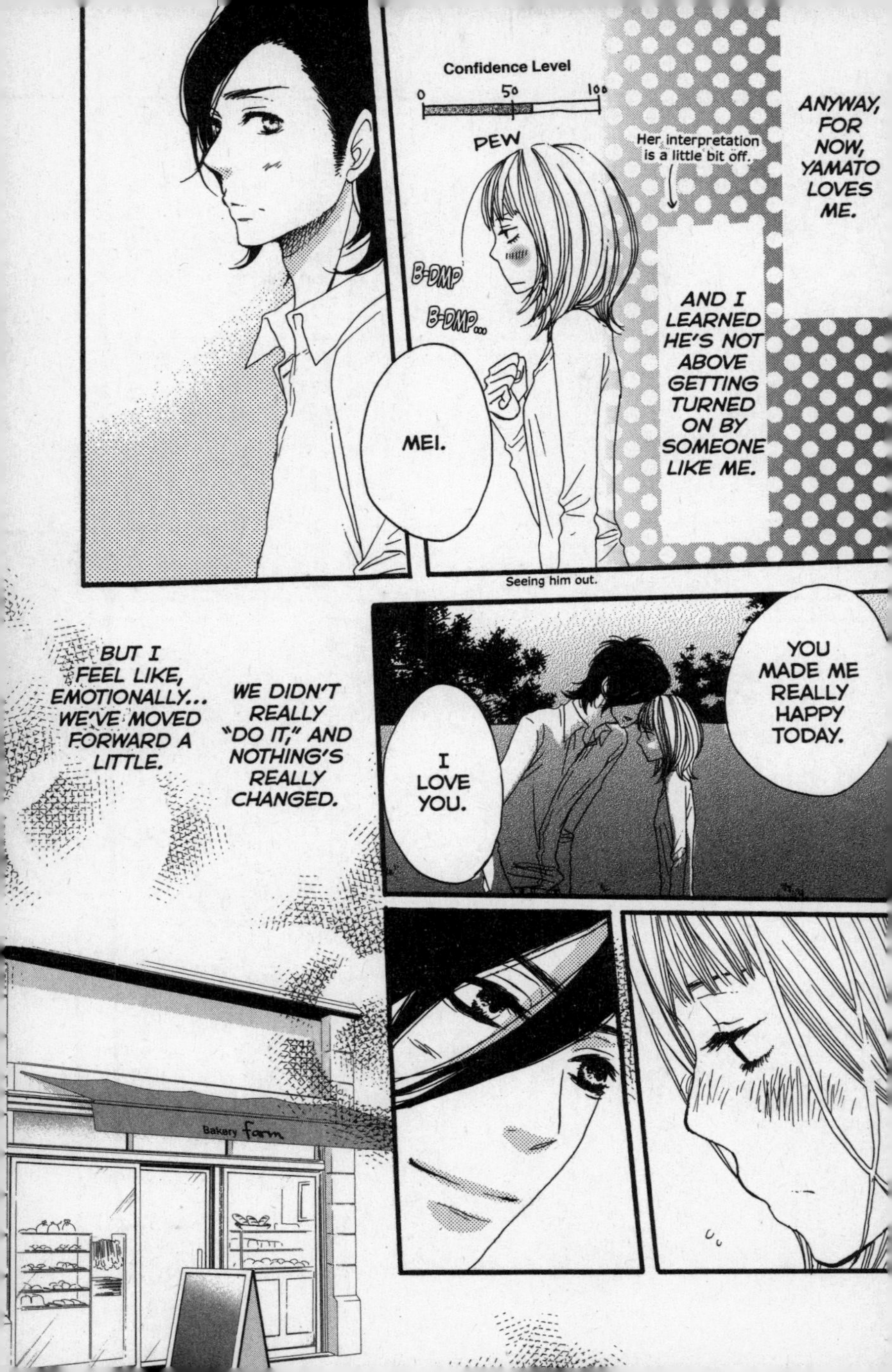
ANYWAY, FOR NOW, YAMATO LOVES ME.
AND I LEARNED HE'S NOT ABOVE GETTING TURNED ON BY SOMEONE LIKE ME.
Her interpretation is a little bit off.
Confidence Level
0
50
100
PEW
B-DMP
B-DMP...
MEI.
Seeing him out.
YOU MADE ME REALLY HAPPY TODAY.
I LOVE YOU.
WE DIDN'T REALLY "DO IT," AND NOTHING'S REALLY CHANGED.
BUT I FEEL LIKE, EMOTIONALLY... WE'VE MOVED FORWARD A LITTLE.
Bakery farm

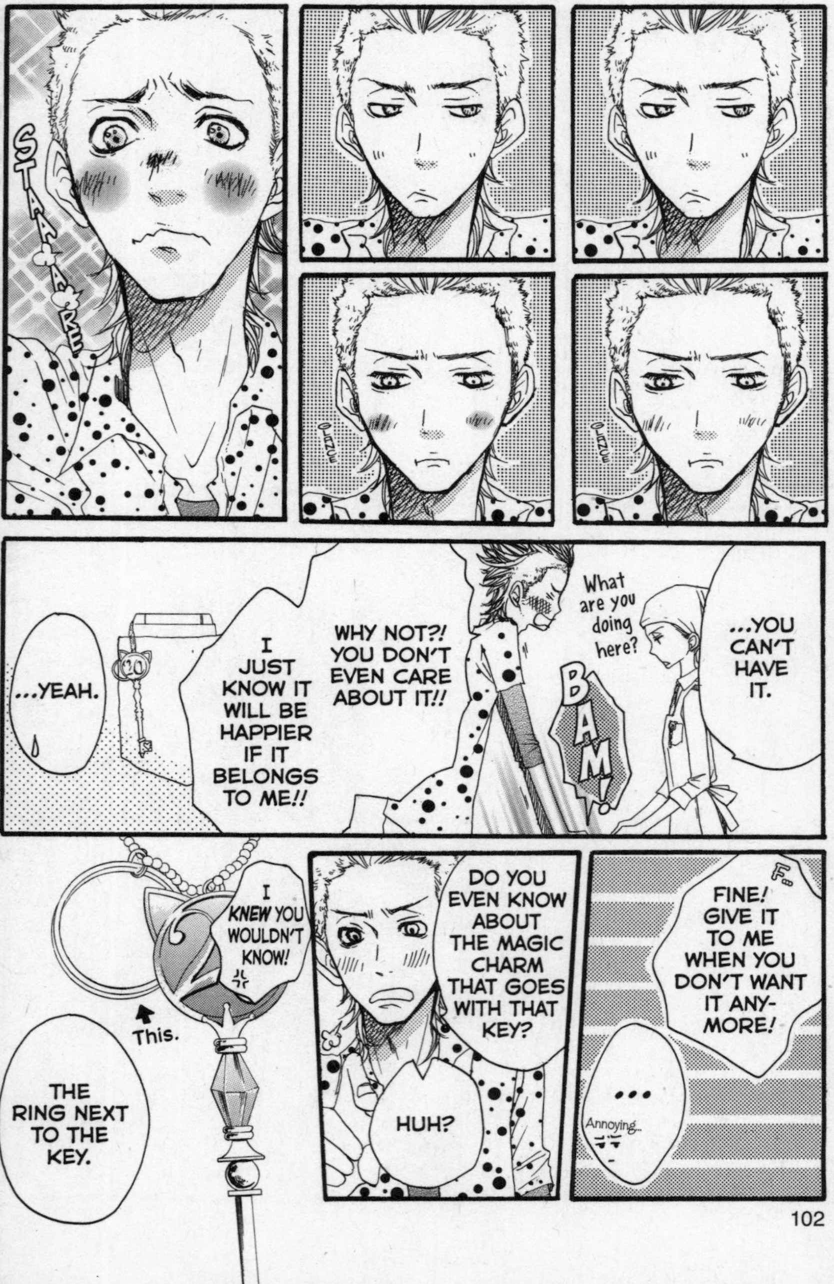
GLANCE
GLANCE
STAAAARE
...YOU CAN'T HAVE IT.
What are you doing here?
BAM!
WHY NOT?! YOU DON'T EVEN CARE ABOUT IT!!
I JUST KNOW IT WILL BE HAPPIER IF IT BELONGS TO ME!!
...YEAH.
F..
FINE! GIVE IT TO ME WHEN YOU DON'T WANT IT ANYMORE!
...
Annoying..
DO YOU EVEN KNOW ABOUT THE MAGIC CHARM THAT GOES WITH THAT KEY?
HUH?
I KNEW YOU WOULDN'T KNOW!
This.
THE RING NEXT TO THE KEY.

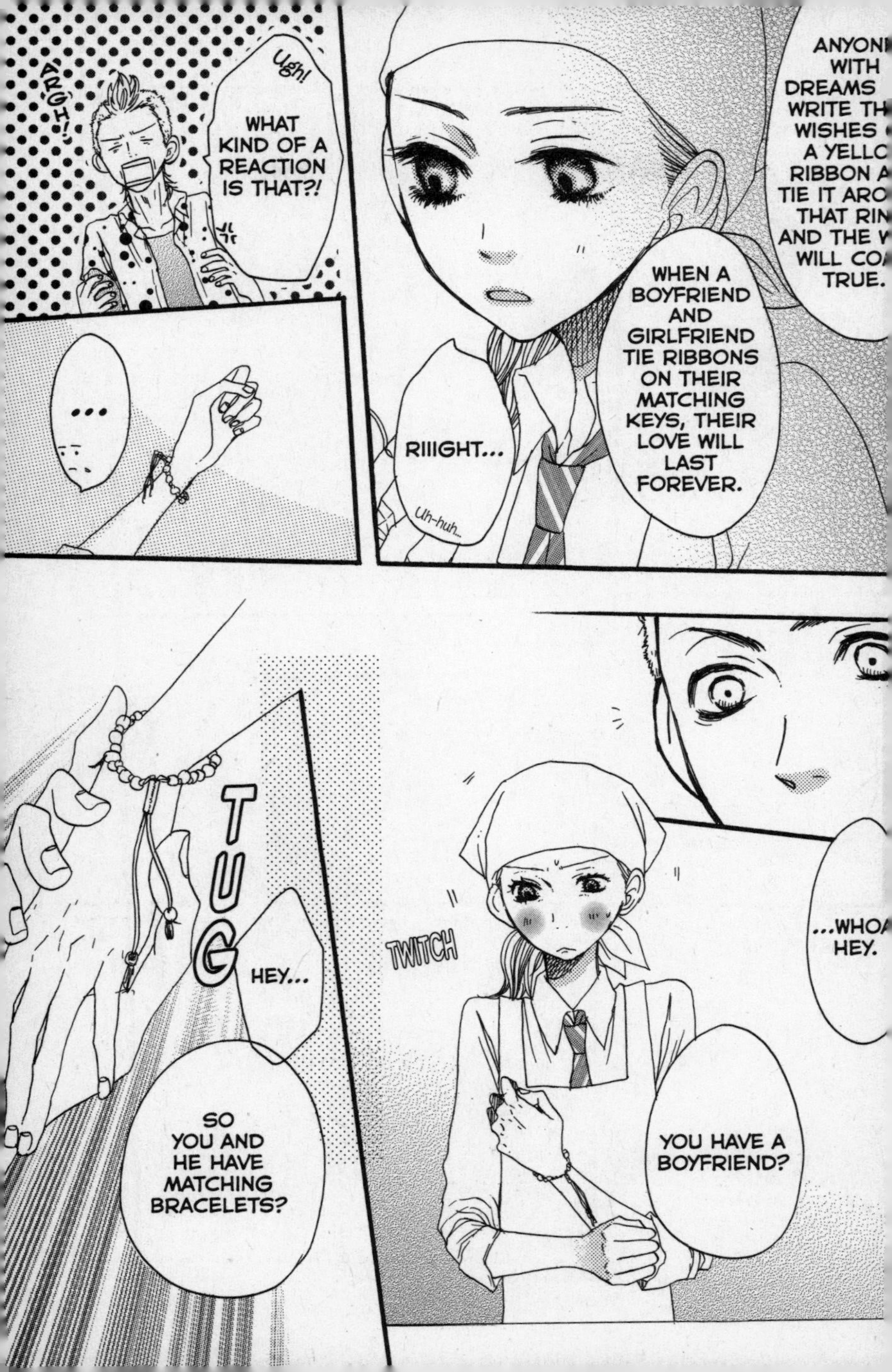
ANYONE WITH DREAMS WRITE TH WISHES A YELLO RIBBON A TIE IT ARO THAT RIN AND THE W WILL CO TRUE.
WHEN A BOYFRIEND AND GIRLFRIEND TIE RIBBONS ON THEIR MATCHING KEYS, THEIR LOVE WILL LAST FOREVER.
RIIIGHT...
Uh-huh...
ARGH!!
Ugh!
WHAT KIND OF A REACTION IS THAT?!
...
...WHOA HEY.
TWITCH
YOU HAVE A BOYFRIEND?
TUG
HEY...
SO YOU AND HE HAVE MATCHING BRACELETS?

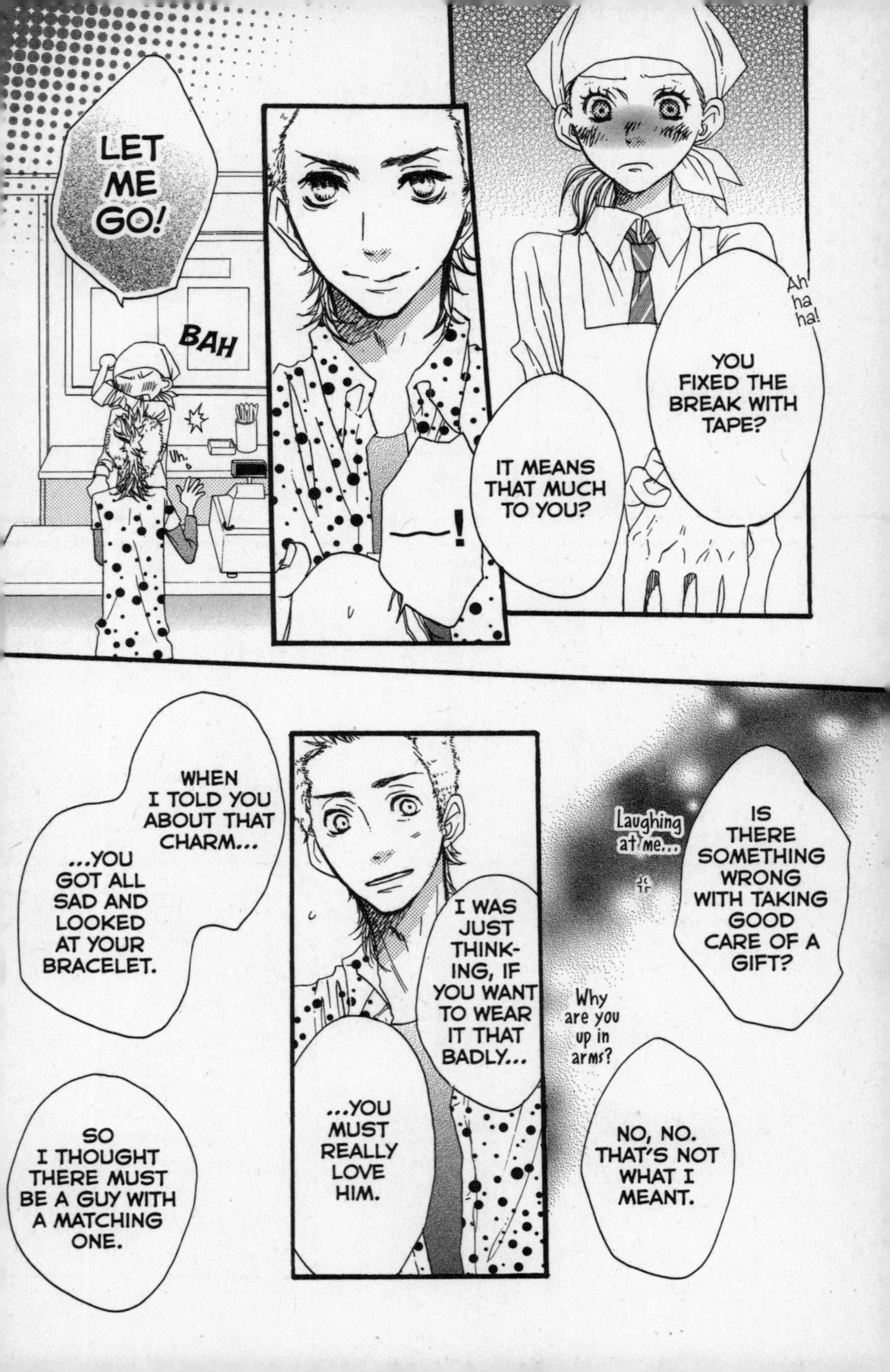
Ah ha ha!
YOU FIXED THE BREAK WITH TAPE?
IT MEANS THAT MUCH TO YOU?
—!
LET ME GO!
BAH
Uh.
IS THERE SOMETHING WRONG WITH TAKING GOOD CARE OF A GIFT?
Laughing at me...
Why are you up in arms?
NO, NO. THAT'S NOT WHAT I MEANT.
I WAS JUST THINKING, IF YOU WANT TO WEAR IT THAT BADLY...
...YOU MUST REALLY LOVE HIM.
WHEN I TOLD YOU ABOUT THAT CHARM...
...YOU GOT ALL SAD AND LOOKED AT YOUR BRACELET.
SO I THOUGHT THERE MUST BE A GUY WITH A MATCHING ONE.

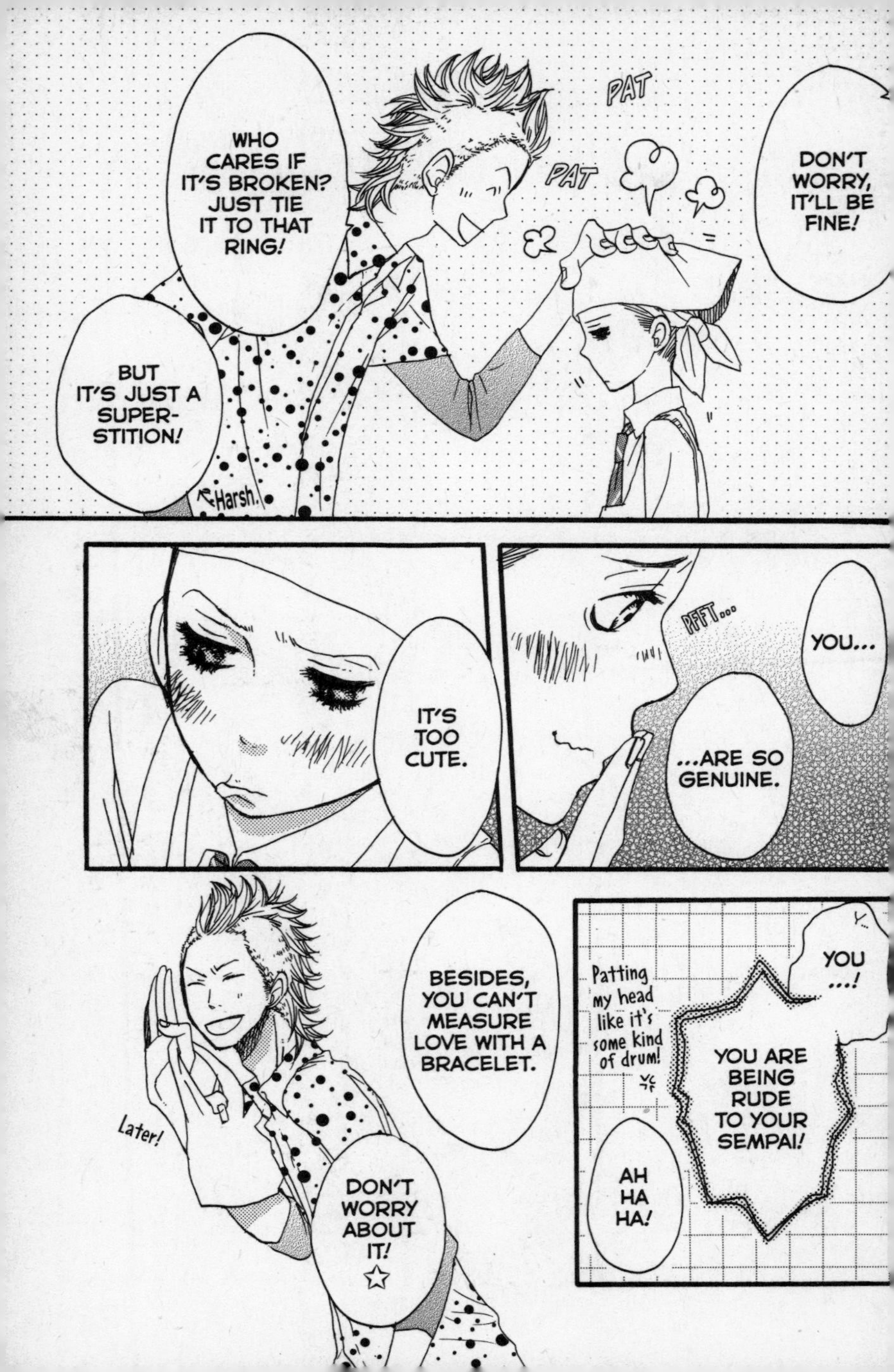
DON'T WORRY, IT'LL BE FINE!
PAT
PAT
WHO CARES IF IT'S BROKEN? JUST TIE IT TO THAT RING!
BUT IT'S JUST A SUPER-STITION!
Harsh.
PFFT...
YOU...
...ARE SO GENUINE.
IT'S TOO CUTE.
Y...
YOU ...!
YOU ARE BEING RUDE TO YOUR SEMPAI!
Patting my head like it's some kind of drum!
AH HA HA!
BESIDES, YOU CAN'T MEASURE LOVE WITH A BRACELET.
Later!
DON'T WORRY ABOUT IT! ☆

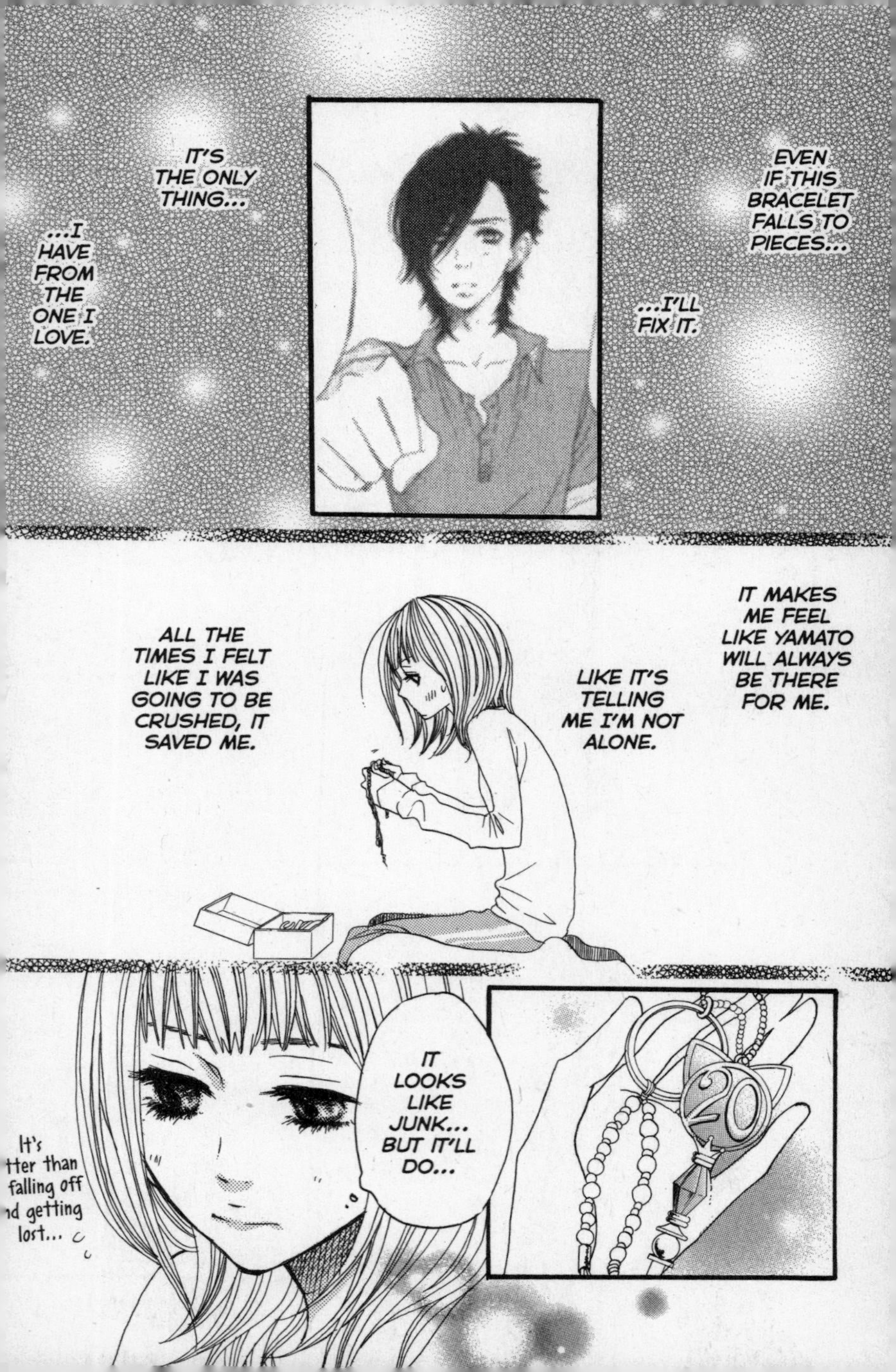
EVEN IF THIS BRACELET FALLS TO PIECES...
...I'LL FIX IT.
IT'S THE ONLY THING...
...I HAVE FROM THE ONE I LOVE.
IT MAKES ME FEEL LIKE YAMATO WILL ALWAYS BE THERE FOR ME.
LIKE IT'S TELLING ME I'M NOT ALONE.
ALL THE TIMES I FELT LIKE I WAS GOING TO BE CRUSHED, IT SAVED ME.
IT LOOKS LIKE JUNK... BUT IT'LL DO...
It's tter than falling off nd getting lost...

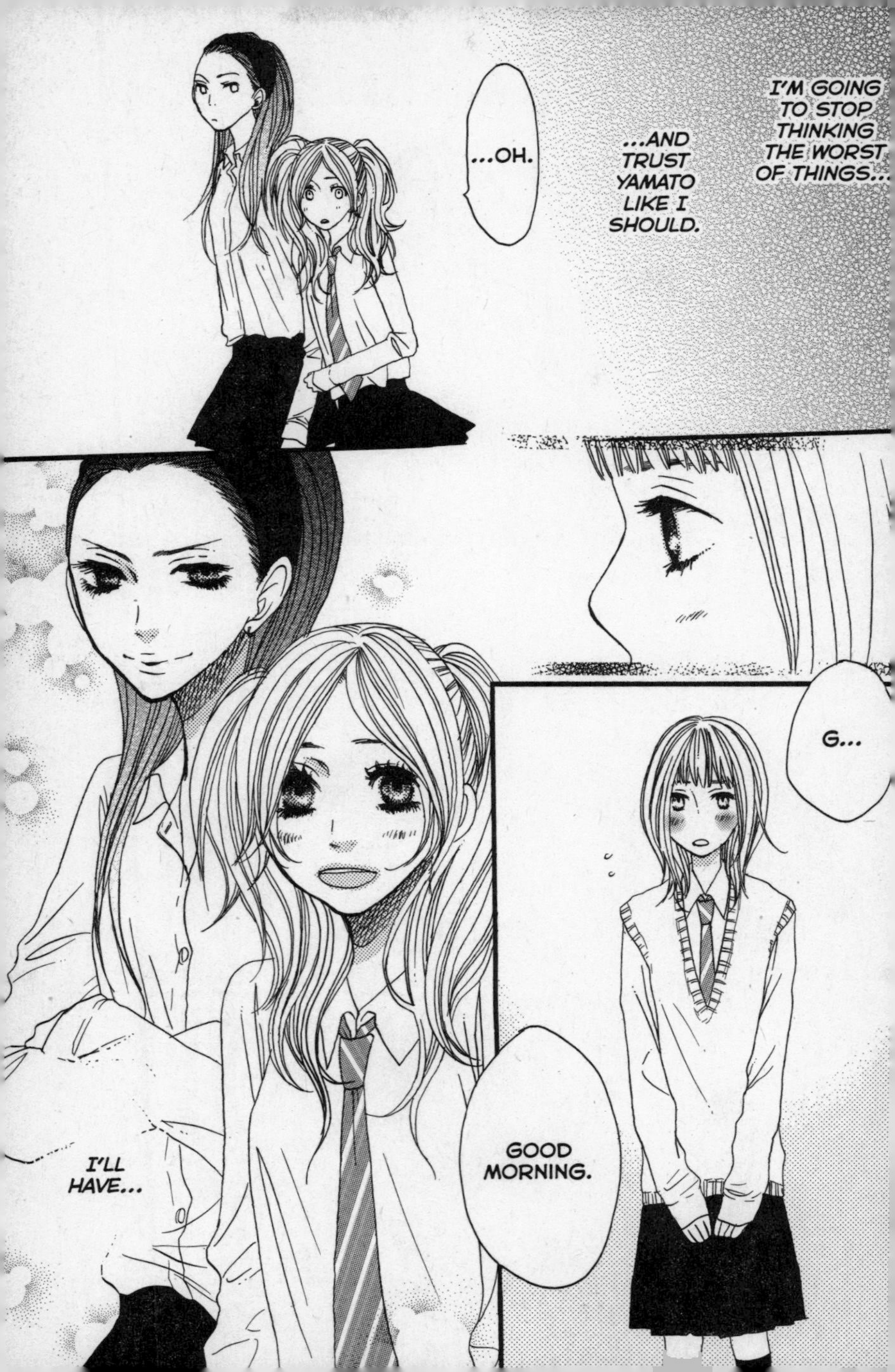
I'M GOING TO STOP THINKING THE WORST OF THINGS...
...AND TRUST YAMATO LIKE I SHOULD.
...OH.
G...
GOOD MORNING.
I'LL HAVE...

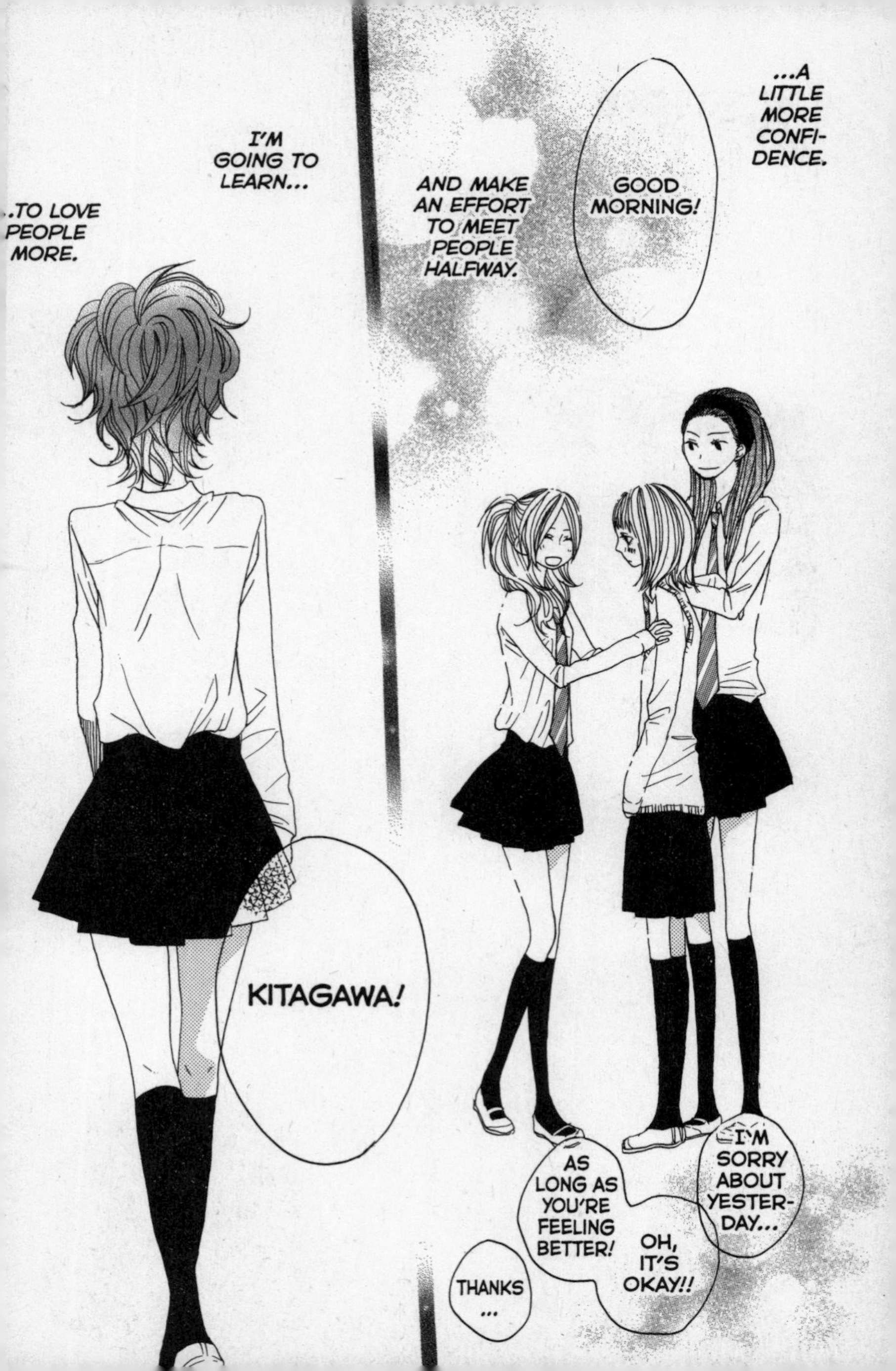
...A LITTLE MORE CONFIDENCE.
GOOD MORNING!
AND MAKE AN EFFORT TO MEET PEOPLE HALFWAY.
I'M SORRY ABOUT YESTERDAY...
OH, IT'S OKAY!!
AS LONG AS YOU'RE FEELING BETTER!
THANKS...
I'M GOING TO LEARN...
..TO LOVE PEOPLE MORE.
KITAGAWA!

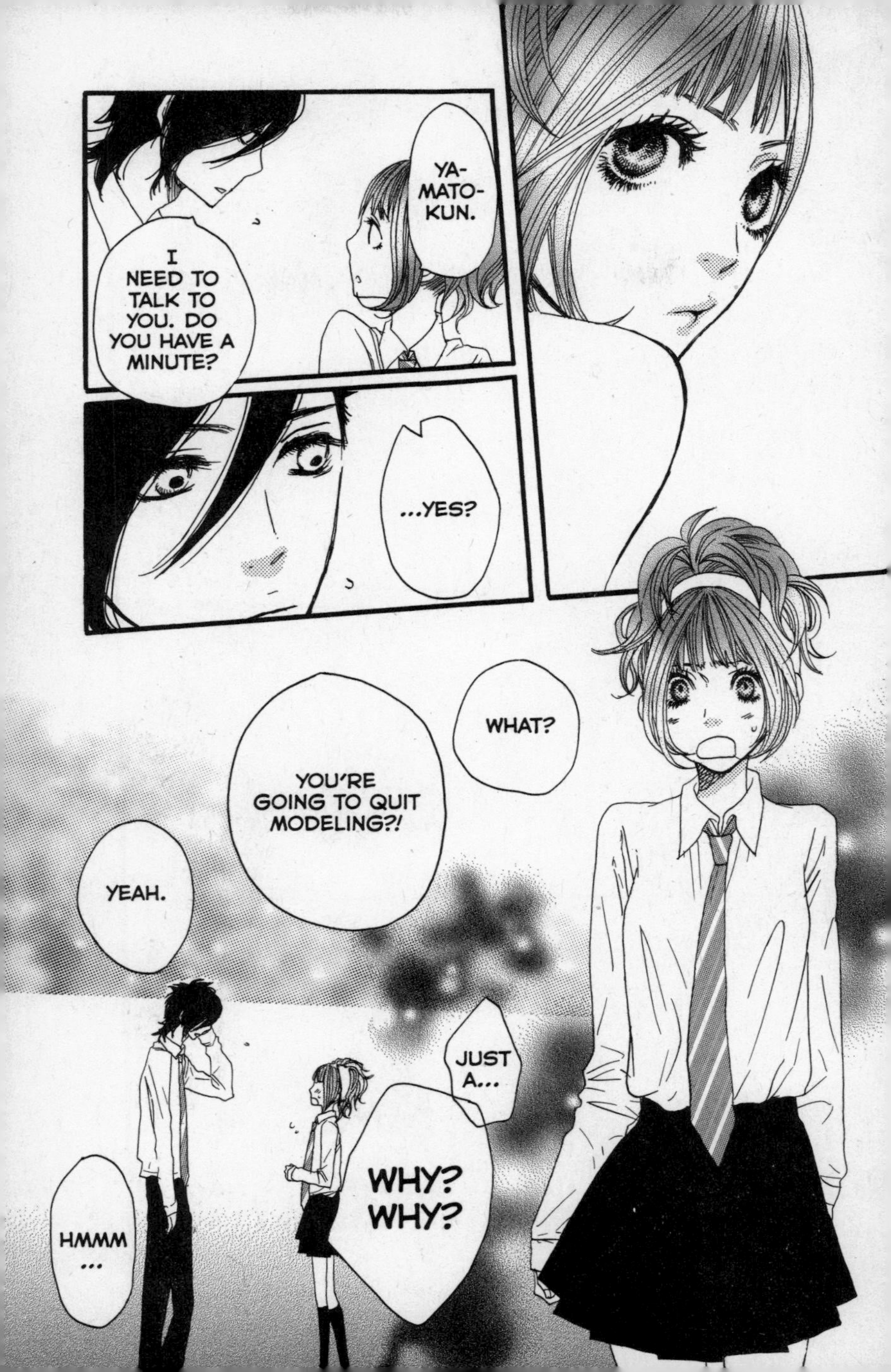
YA-MATO-KUN.
I NEED TO TALK TO YOU. DO YOU HAVE A MINUTE?
...YES?
WHAT?
YOU'RE GOING TO QUIT MODELING?!
YEAH.
JUST A...
WHY? WHY?
HMMM ...

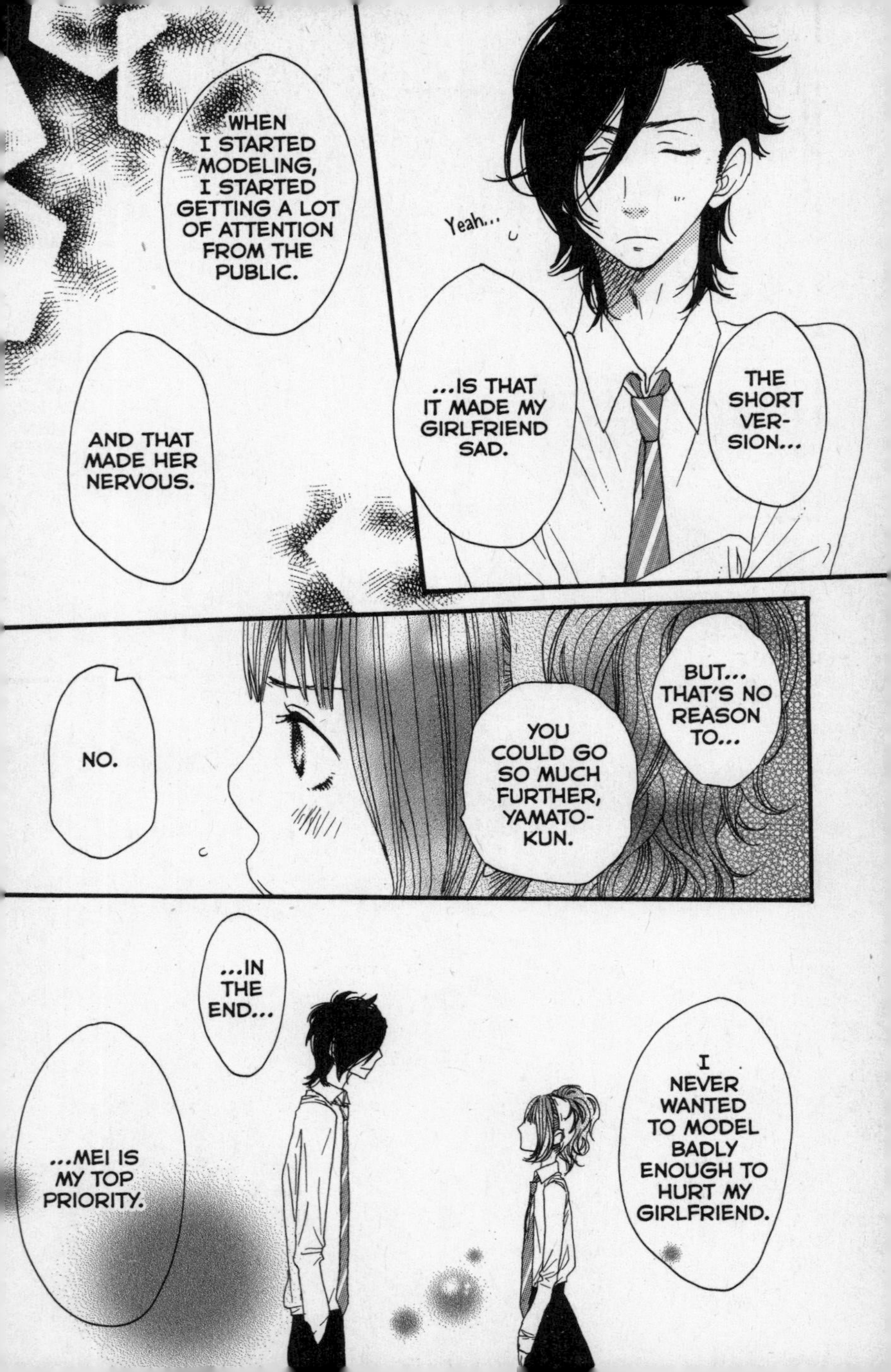
Yeah...
THE SHORT VERSION...
...IS THAT IT MADE MY GIRLFRIEND SAD.
WHEN I STARTED MODELING, I STARTED GETTING A LOT OF ATTENTION FROM THE PUBLIC.
AND THAT MADE HER NERVOUS.
BUT... THAT'S NO REASON TO...
YOU COULD GO SO MUCH FURTHER, YAMATO-KUN.
NO.
I NEVER WANTED TO MODEL BADLY ENOUGH TO HURT MY GIRLFRIEND.
...IN THE END...
...MEI IS MY TOP PRIORITY.

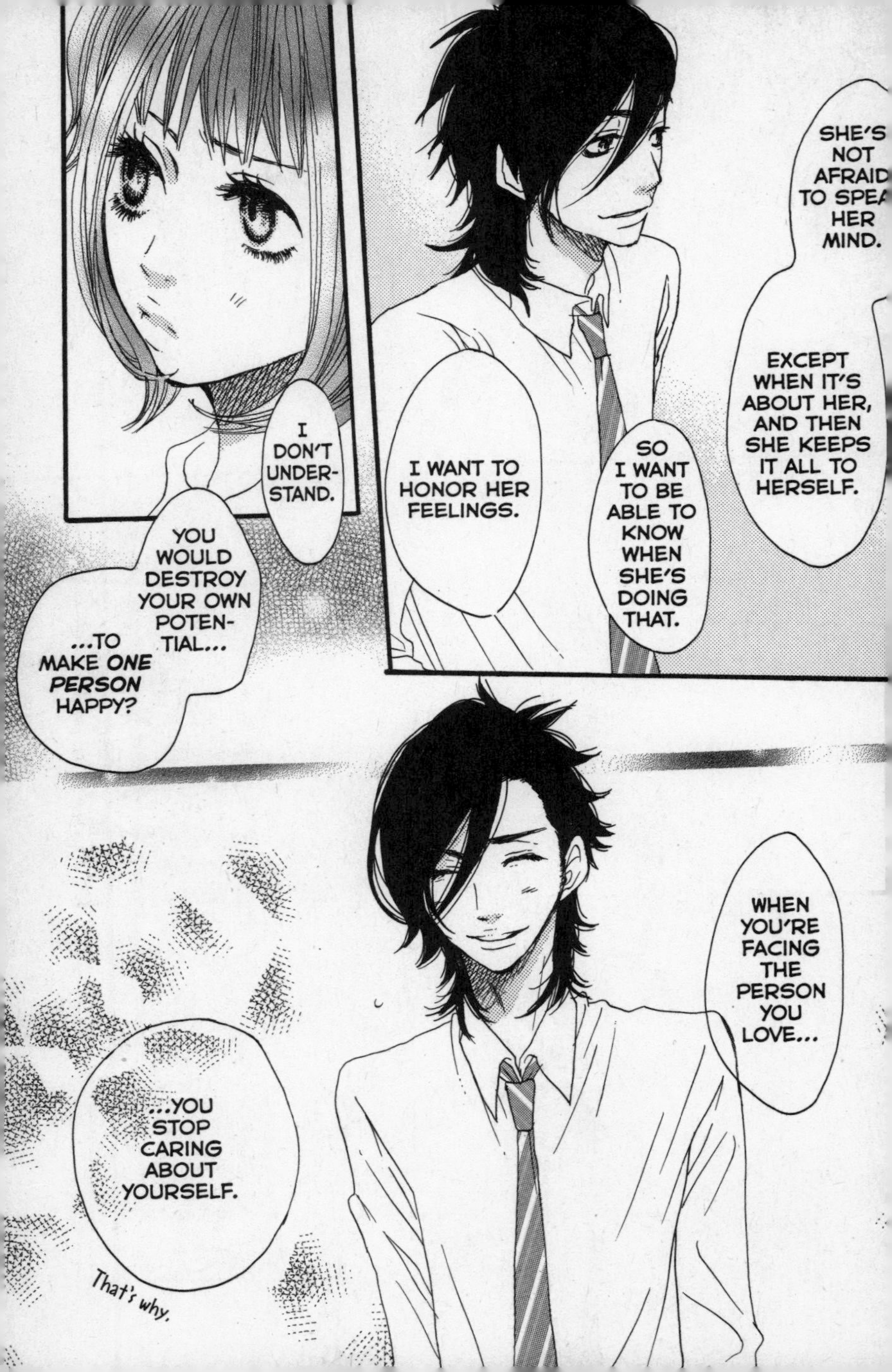
SHE'S NOT AFRAID TO SPEA HER MIND.
EXCEPT WHEN IT'S ABOUT HER, AND THEN SHE KEEPS IT ALL TO HERSELF.
SO I WANT TO BE ABLE TO KNOW WHEN SHE'S DOING THAT.
I WANT TO HONOR HER FEELINGS.
I DON'T UNDER-STAND.
YOU WOULD DESTROY YOUR OWN POTEN-TIAL...
...TO MAKE *ONE PERSON* HAPPY?
WHEN YOU'RE FACING THE PERSON YOU LOVE...
...YOU STOP CARING ABOUT YOURSELF.
That's why.

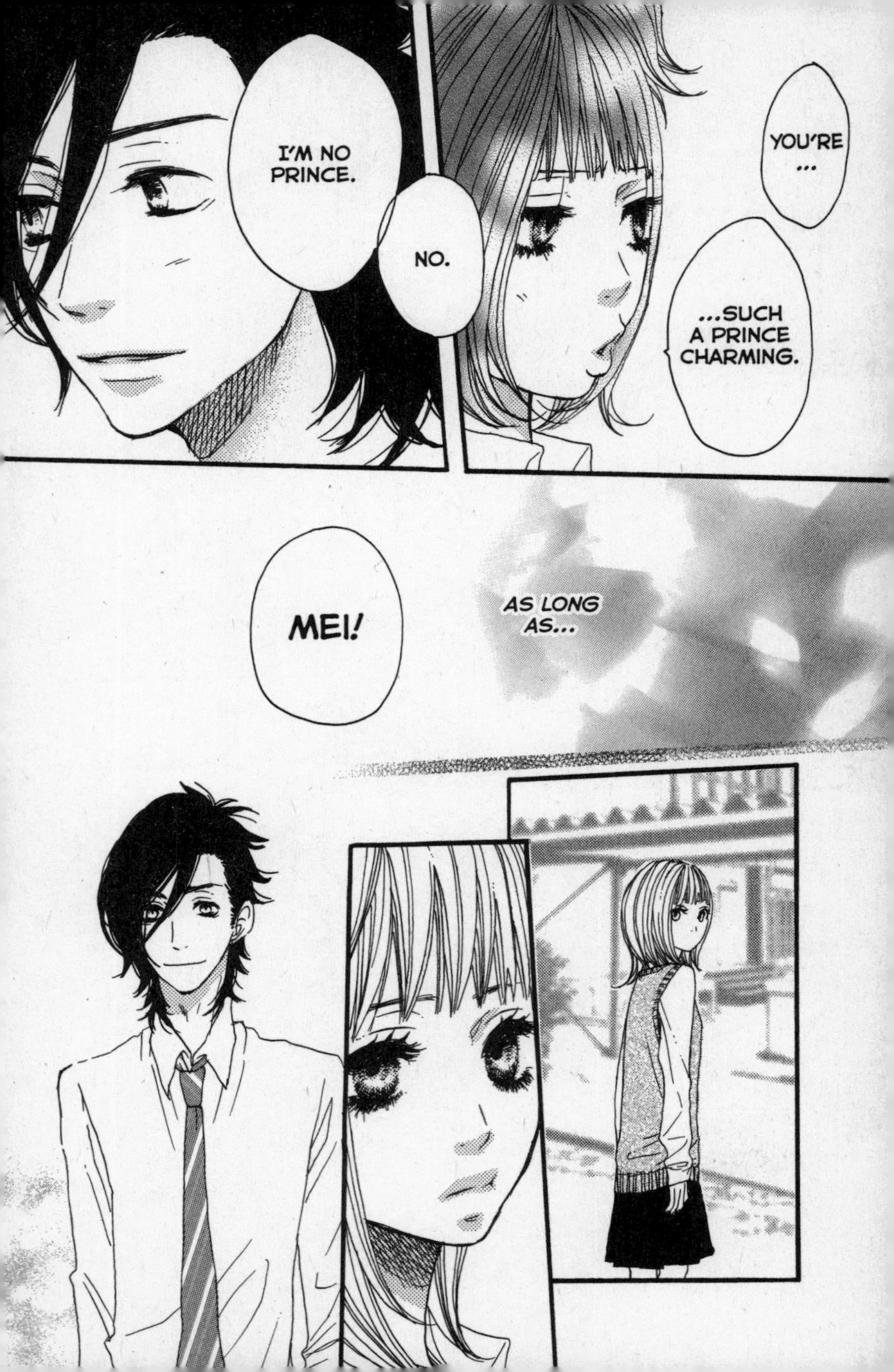
YOU'RE ...
...SUCH A PRINCE CHARMING.
NO.
I'M NO PRINCE.
AS LONG AS...
MEI!

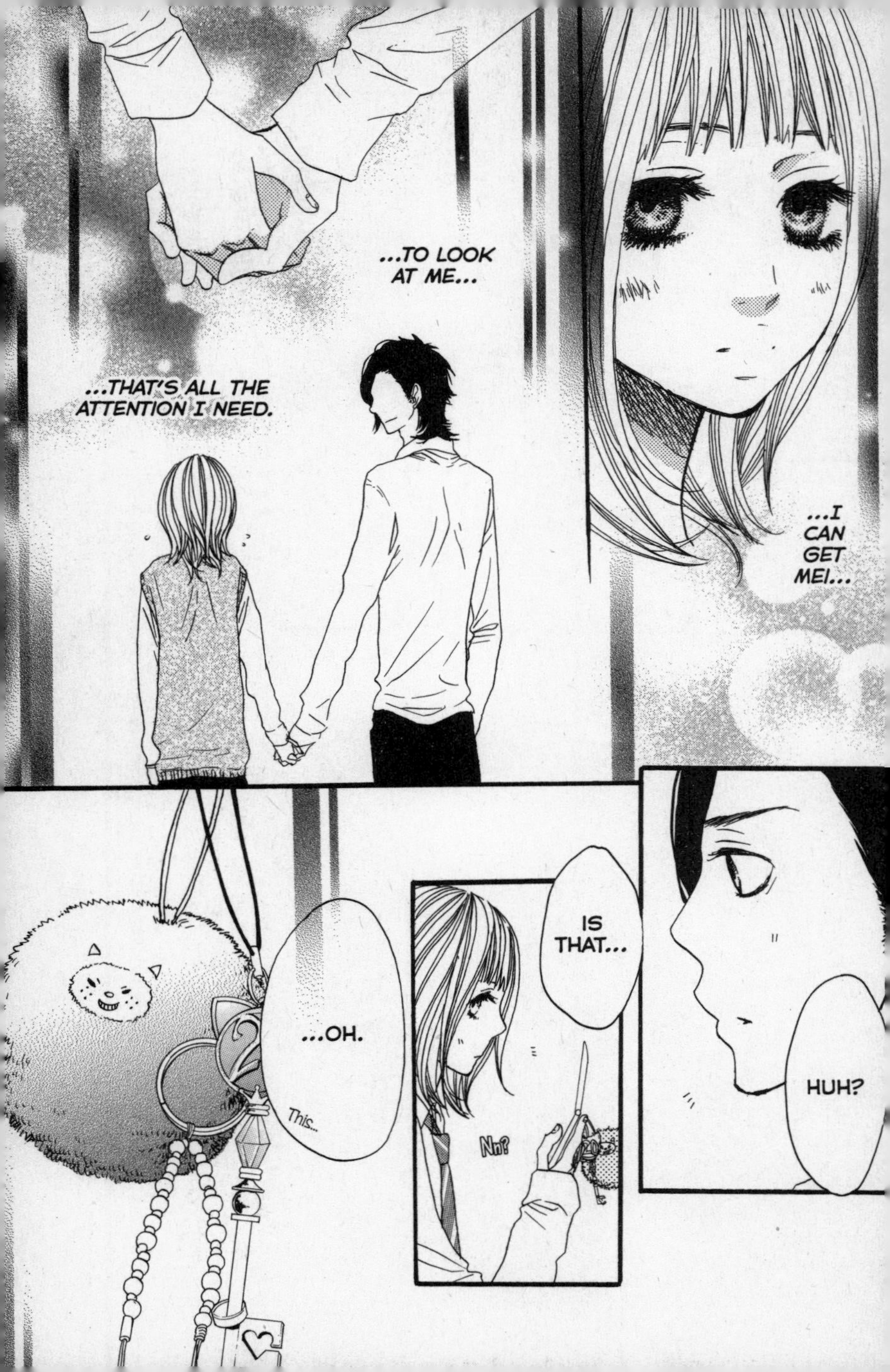
...I CAN GET MEI...
...TO LOOK AT ME...
...THAT'S ALL THE ATTENTION I NEED.
HUH?
IS THAT...
Nn?
...OH.
This...

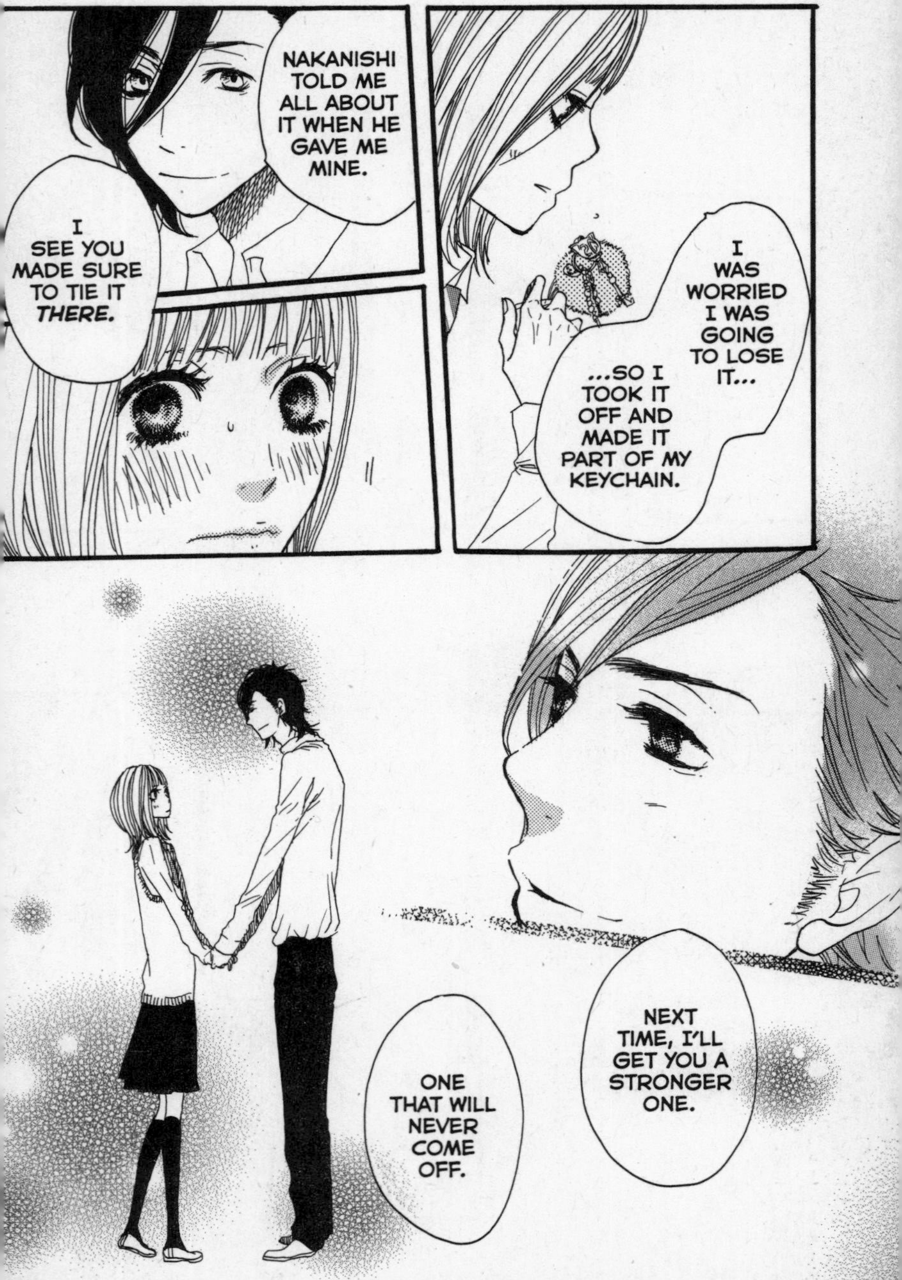
I WAS WORRIED I WAS GOING TO LOSE IT...
...SO I TOOK IT OFF AND MADE IT PART OF MY KEYCHAIN.
NAKANISHI TOLD ME ALL ABOUT IT WHEN HE GAVE ME MINE.
I SEE YOU MADE SURE TO TIE IT *THERE.*
NEXT TIME, I'LL GET YOU A STRONGER ONE.
ONE THAT WILL NEVER COME OFF.

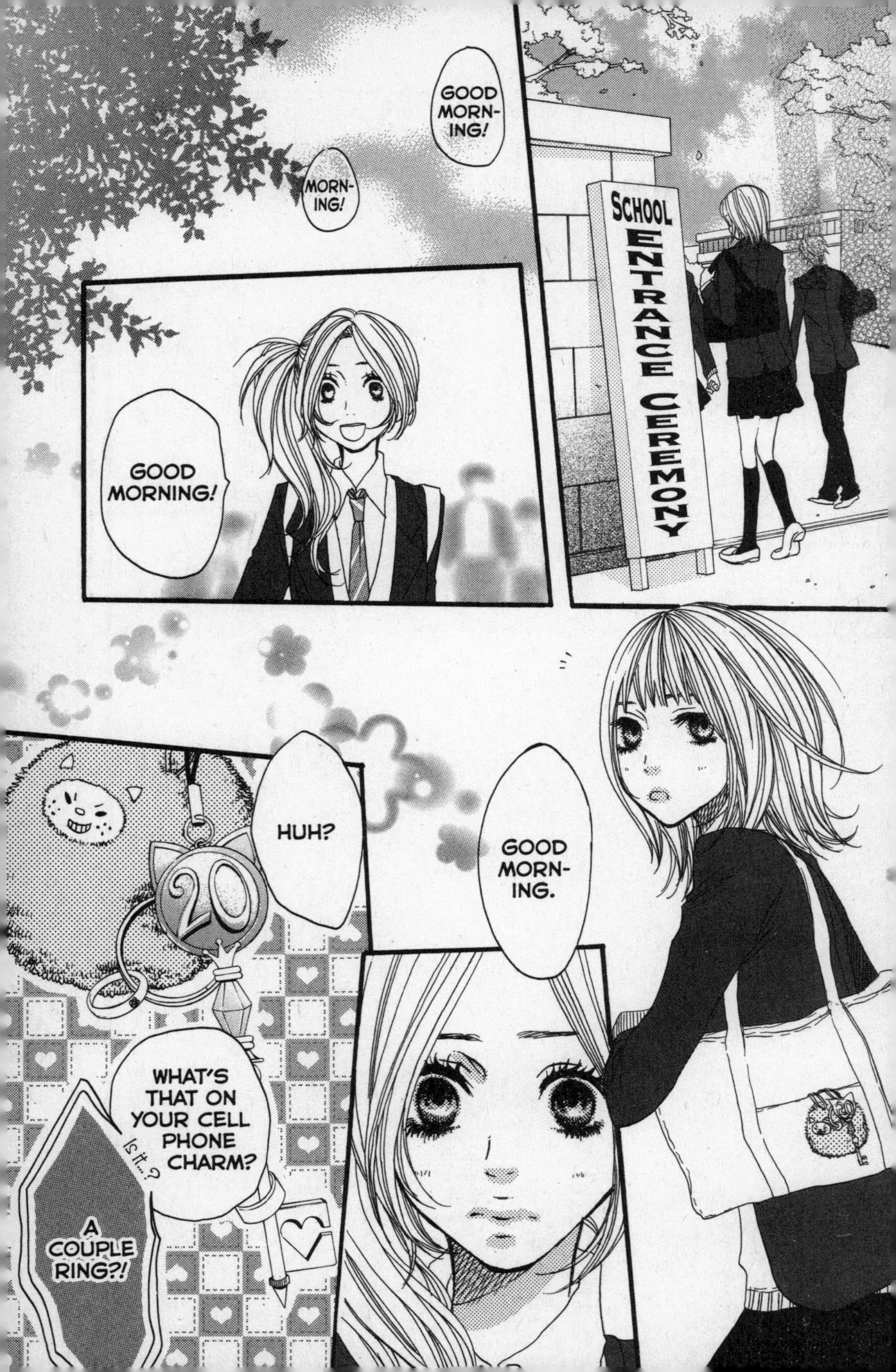
SCHOOL ENTRANCE CEREMONY
GOOD MORNING!
MORNING!
GOOD MORNING!
GOOD MORNING.
HUH?
WHAT'S THAT ON YOUR CELL PHONE CHARM?
Is it...?
A COUPLE RING?!

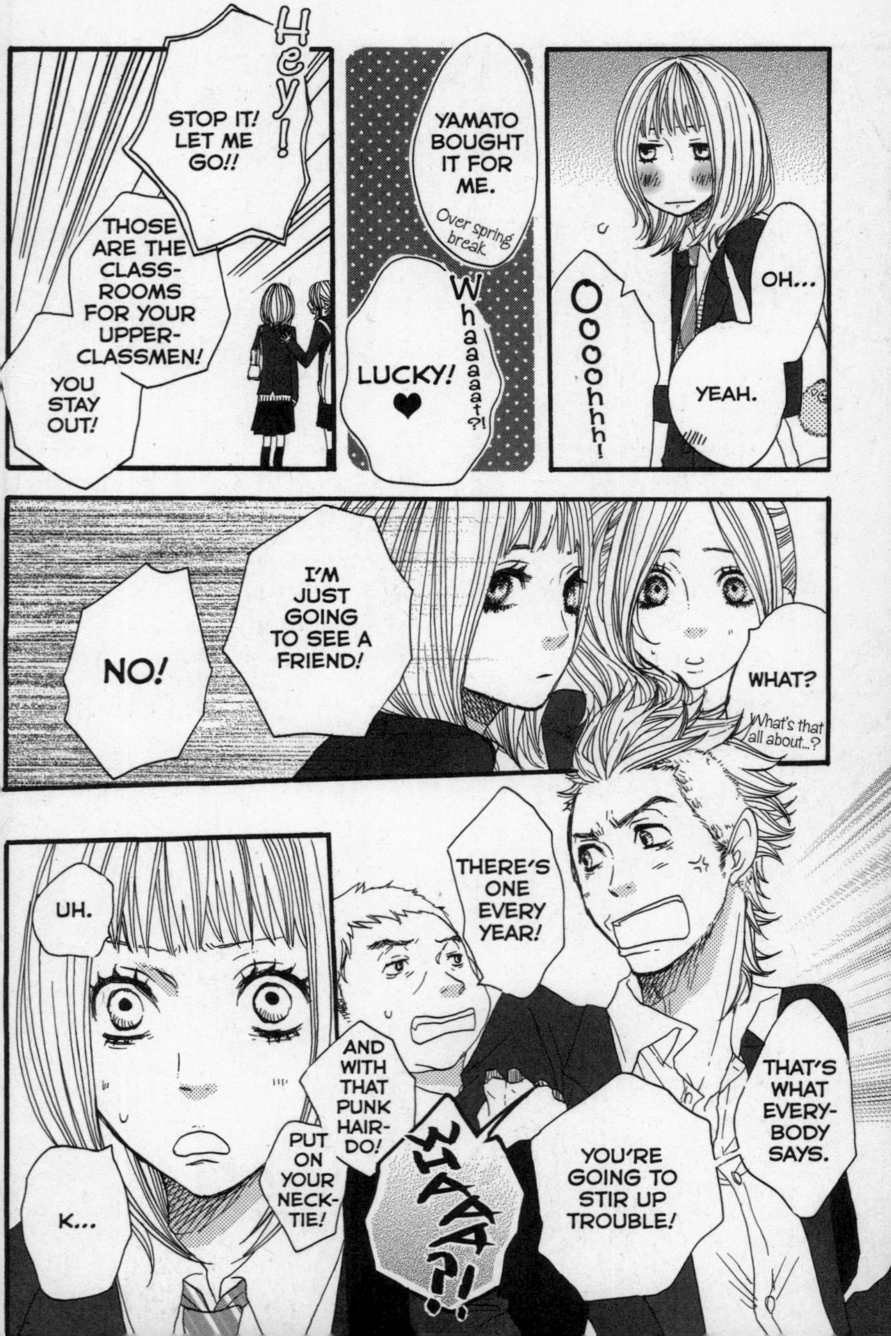
OH...
Oooohh!
YEAH.
YAMATO BOUGHT IT FOR ME.
Over spring break.
Whaaaaat?!
LUCKY! ♥
Hey!
STOP IT! LET ME GO!!
THOSE ARE THE CLASSROOMS FOR YOUR UPPERCLASSMEN!
YOU STAY OUT!
WHAT?
What's that all about...?
I'M JUST GOING TO SEE A FRIEND!
NO!
THERE'S ONE EVERY YEAR!
THAT'S WHAT EVERYBODY SAYS.
YOU'RE GOING TO STIR UP TROUBLE!
AND WITH THAT PUNK HAIRDO!
WAAA?!
PUT ON YOUR NECKTIE!
UH.
K...

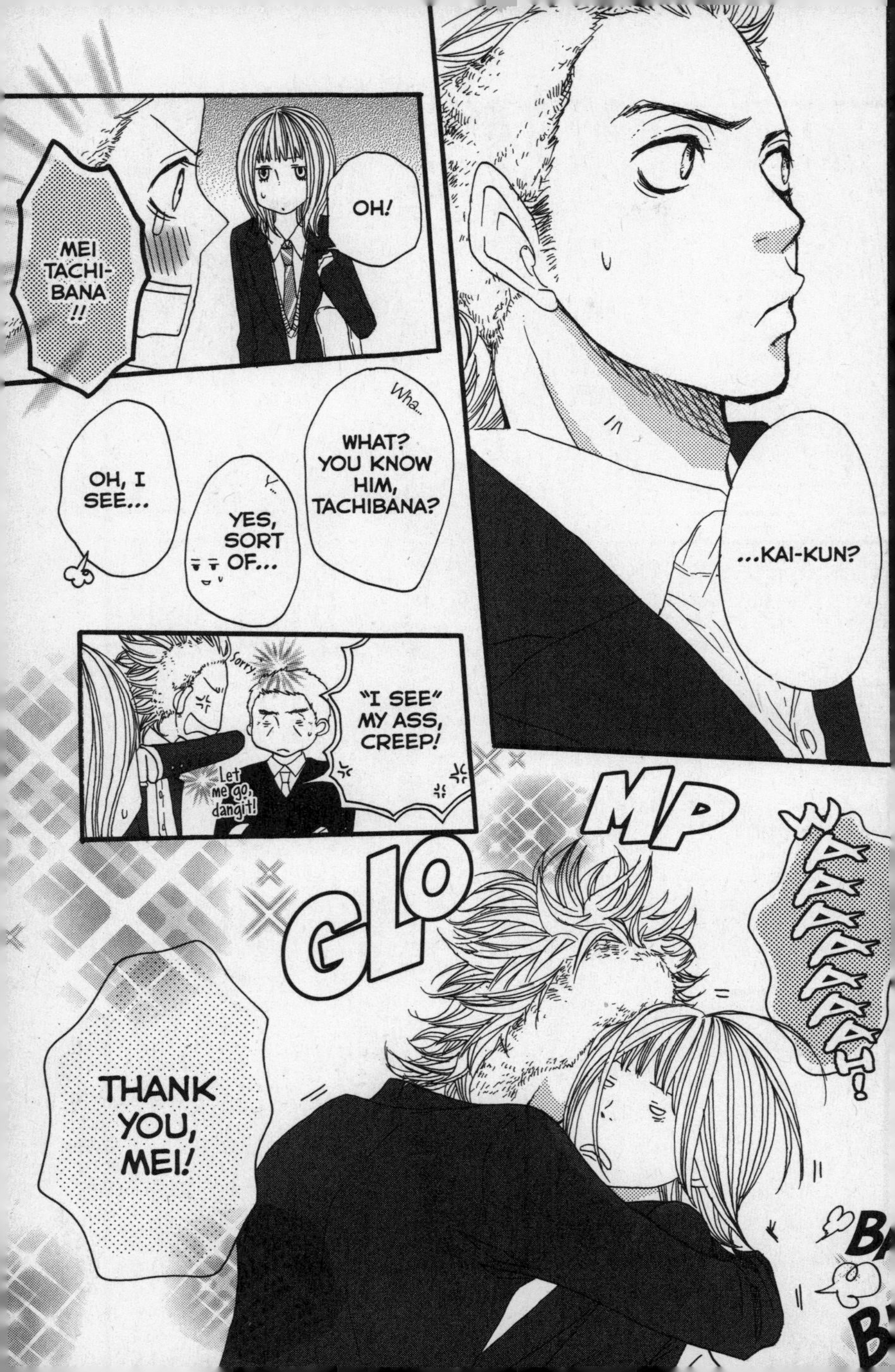

...KAI-KUN?
OH!
MEI TACHIBANA!!
Wha...
WHAT? YOU KNOW HIM, TACHIBANA?
Y...
YES, SORT OF...
OH, I SEE...
"I SEE" MY ASS, CREEP!
Sorry.
Let me go, dangit!
YAAAAAAAH!
GLOMP
THANK YOU, MEI!

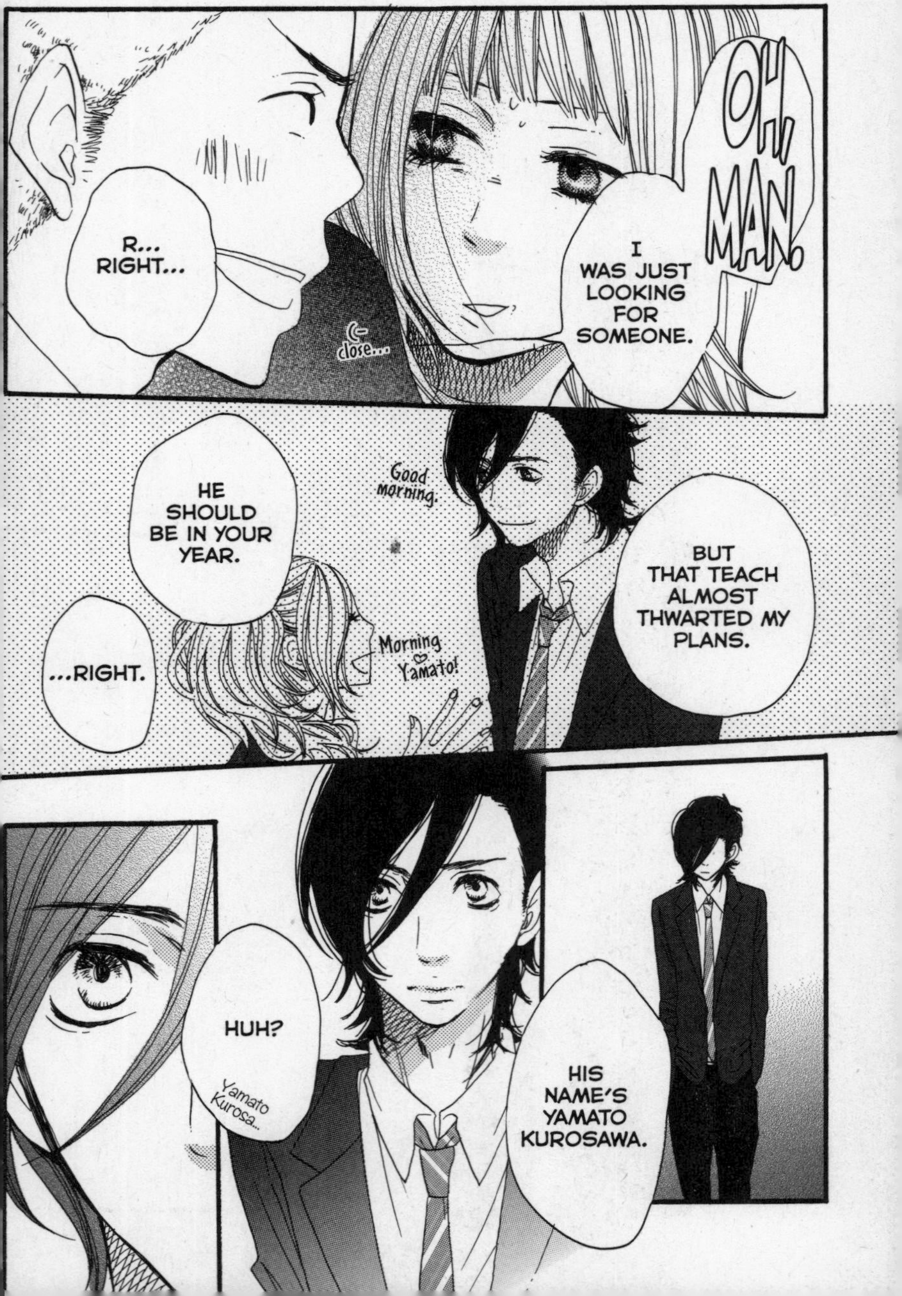
OH, MAN.
I WAS JUST LOOKING FOR SOMEONE.
C-close...
R... RIGHT...
BUT THAT TEACH ALMOST THWARTED MY PLANS.
Good morning.
Morning ♡ Yamato!
HE SHOULD BE IN YOUR YEAR.
...RIGHT.
HIS NAME'S YAMATO KUROSAWA.
HUH?
Yamato Kurosa...

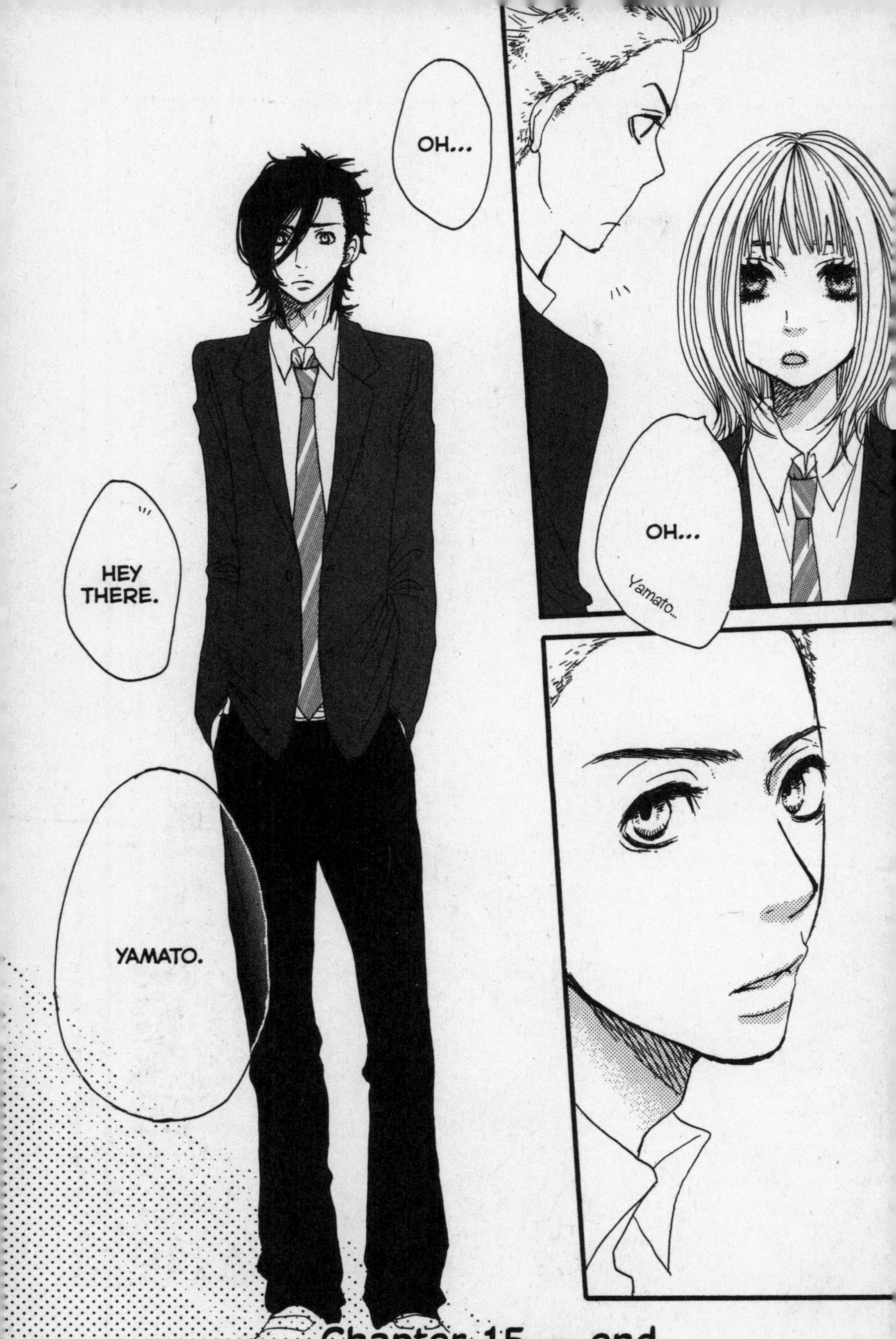
OH...
OH...
Yamato...
HEY THERE.
YAMATO.

Chapter 15 — end

Say
"I love you."
Kanae Hazuki

Chapter 16

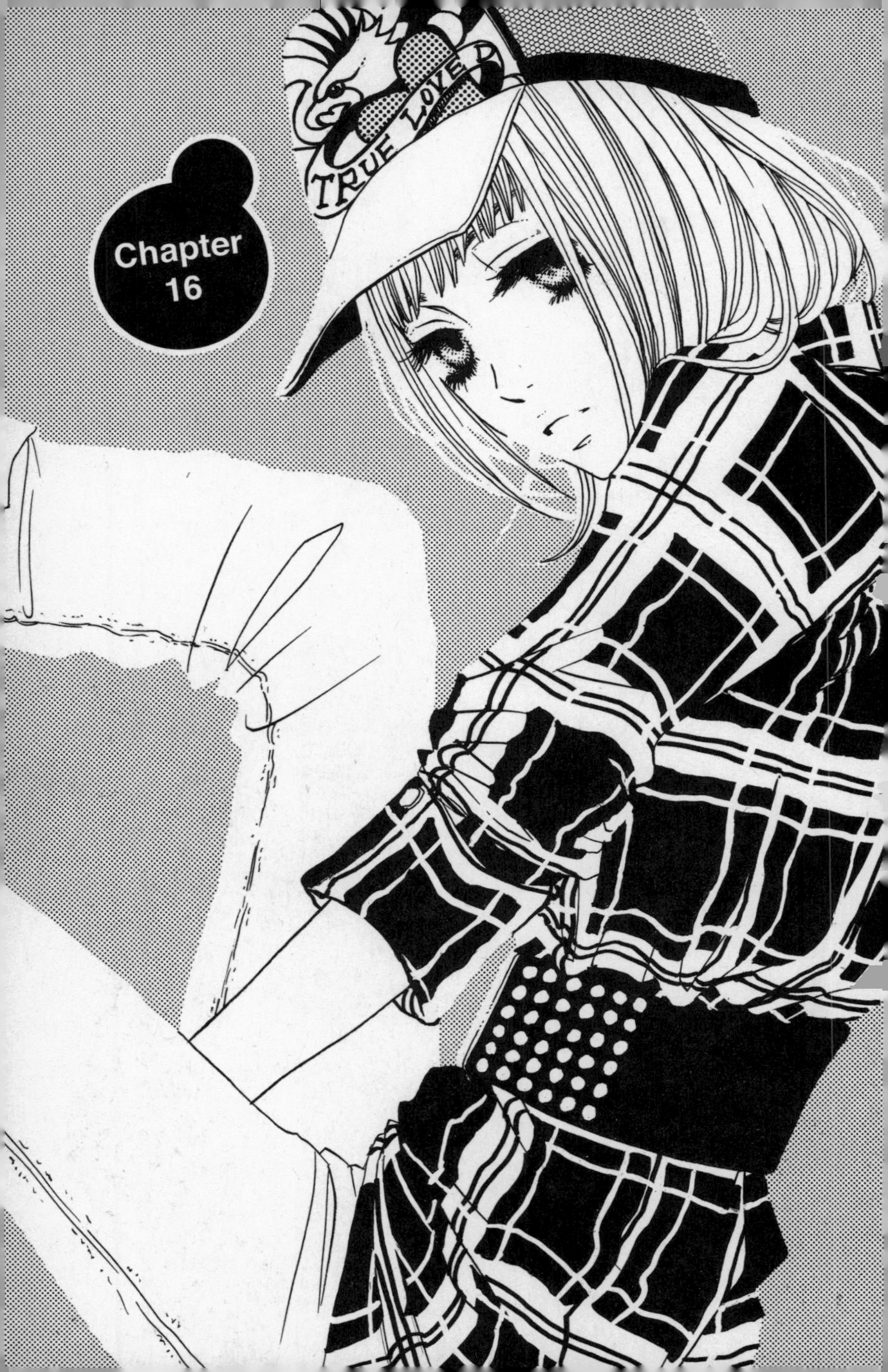
TRUE LOVE

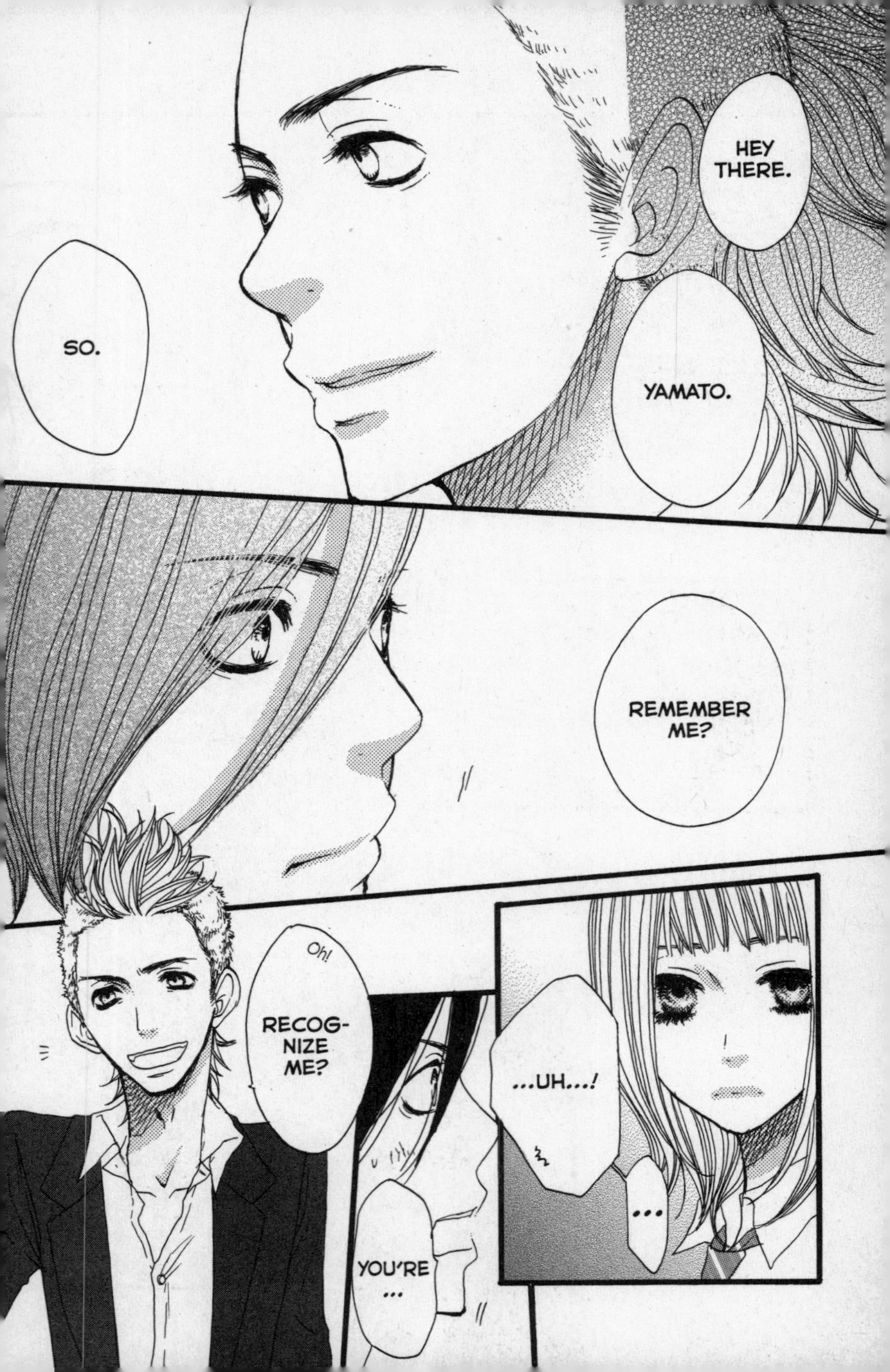
HEY THERE.
YAMATO.
SO.
REMEMBER ME?
...UH...!
...
Oh! RECOG-NIZE ME?
YOU'RE ...

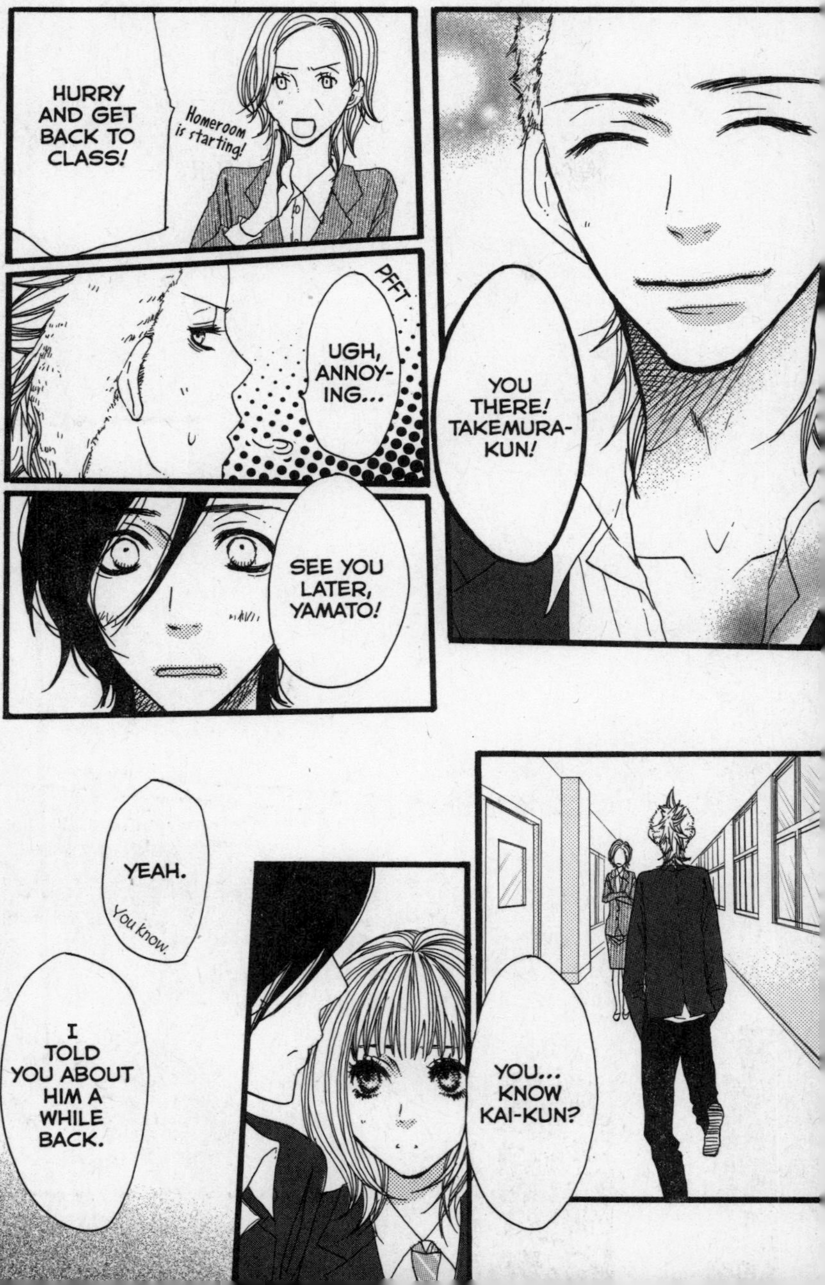
YOU THERE! TAKEMURA-KUN!
HURRY AND GET BACK TO CLASS!
Homeroom is starting!
PFFT
UGH, ANNOYING...
SEE YOU LATER, YAMATO!
YOU... KNOW KAI-KUN?
YEAH.
You know.
I TOLD YOU ABOUT HIM A WHILE BACK.

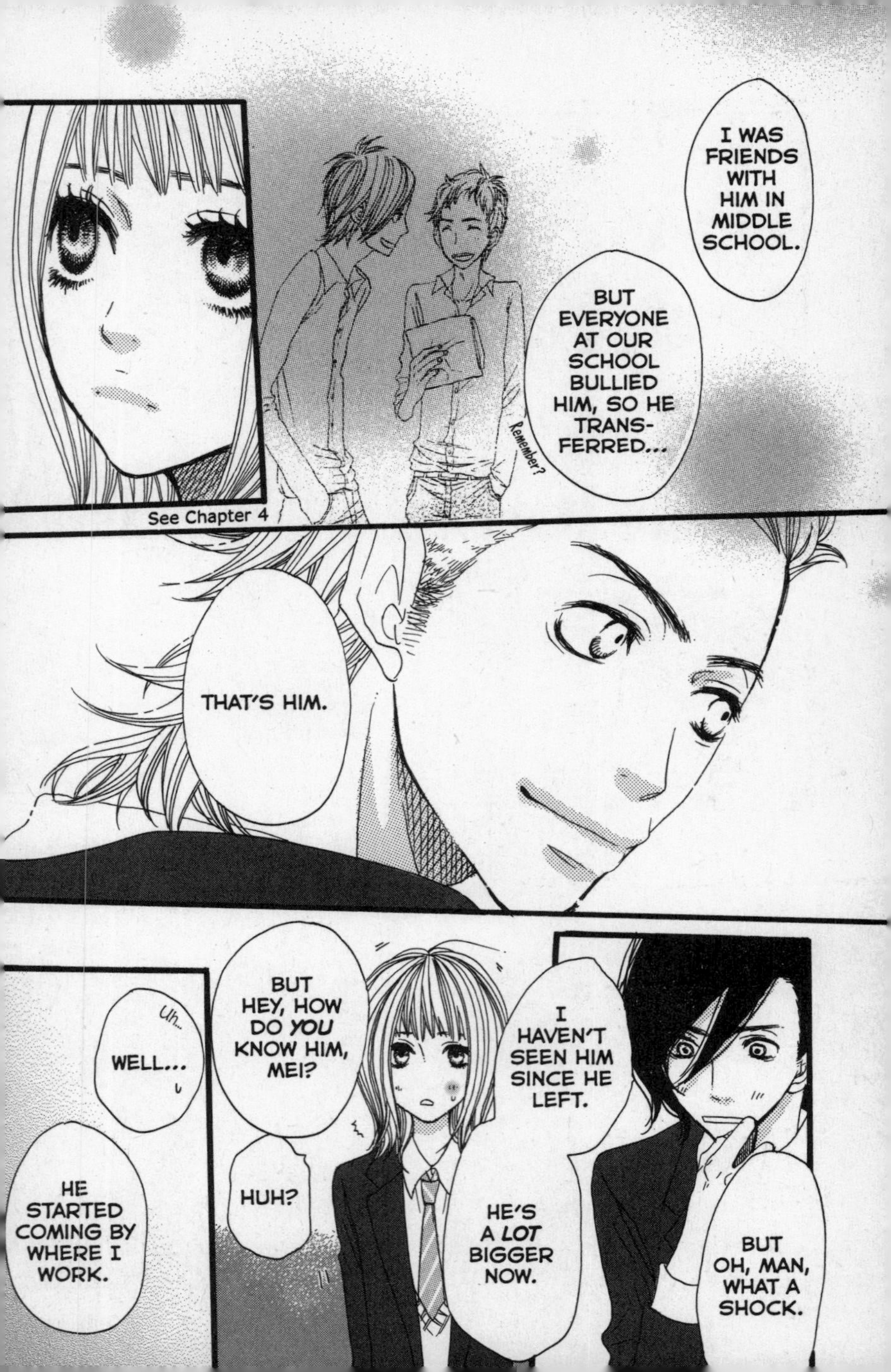
I WAS FRIENDS WITH HIM IN MIDDLE SCHOOL.
BUT EVERYONE AT OUR SCHOOL BULLIED HIM, SO HE TRANSFERRED...
Remember?
See Chapter 4
THAT'S HIM.
I HAVEN'T SEEN HIM SINCE HE LEFT.
BUT OH, MAN, WHAT A SHOCK.
HE'S A *LOT* BIGGER NOW.
BUT HEY, HOW DO *YOU* KNOW HIM, MEI?
HUH?
Uh..
WELL...
HE STARTED COMING BY WHERE I WORK.

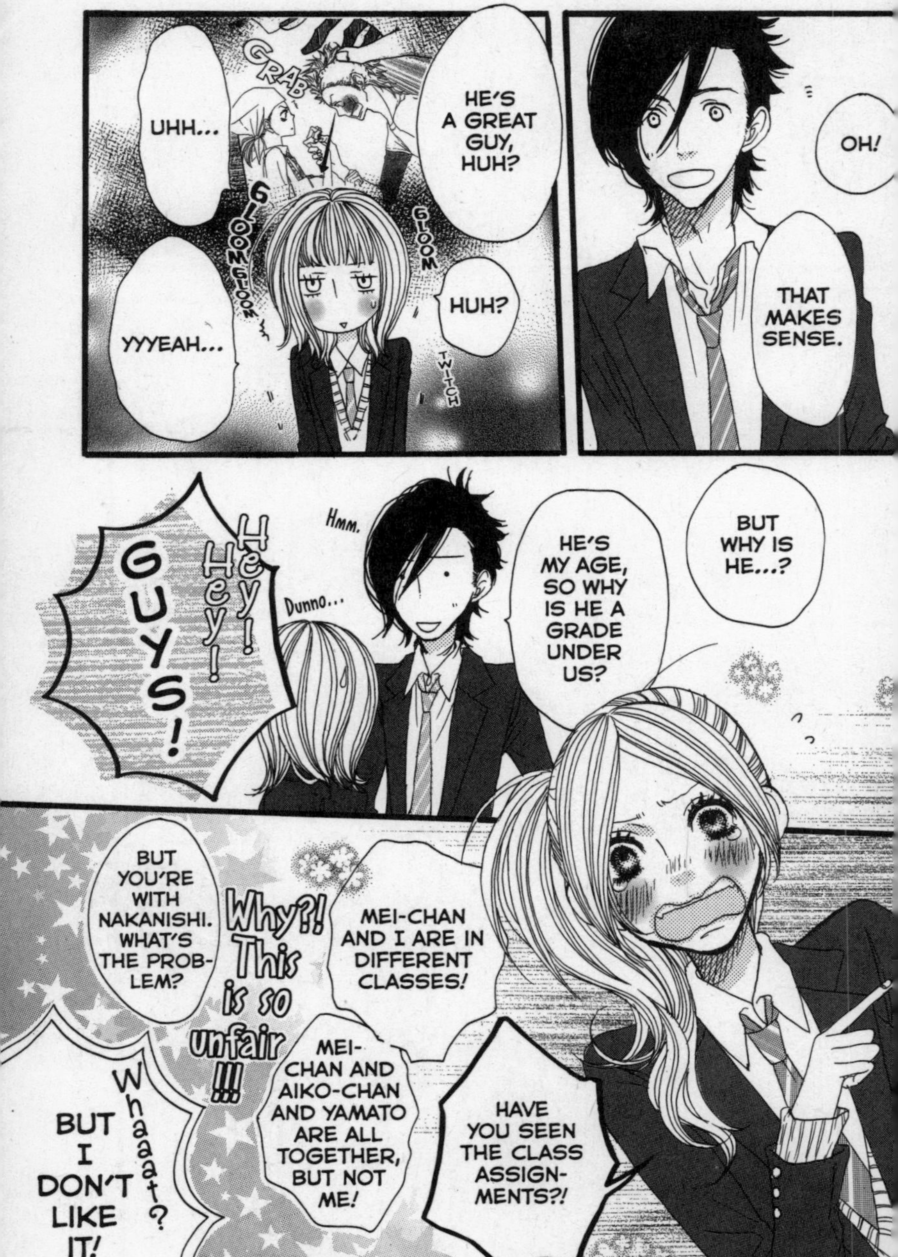
OH!
THAT MAKES SENSE.
HE'S A GREAT GUY, HUH?
GRAB
UHH...
GLOOM GLOOM
GLOOM
HUH?
TWITCH
YYYEAH...
BUT WHY IS HE...?
HE'S MY AGE, SO WHY IS HE A GRADE UNDER US?
Hmm.
Dunno...
Hey! Hey! GUYS!
HAVE YOU SEEN THE CLASS ASSIGNMENTS?!
MEI-CHAN AND I ARE IN DIFFERENT CLASSES!
MEI-CHAN AND AIKO-CHAN AND YAMATO ARE ALL TOGETHER, BUT NOT ME!
Why?! This is so unfair!!!
BUT YOU'RE WITH NAKANISHI. WHAT'S THE PROB-LEM?
Whaaaat?
BUT I DON'T LIKE IT!

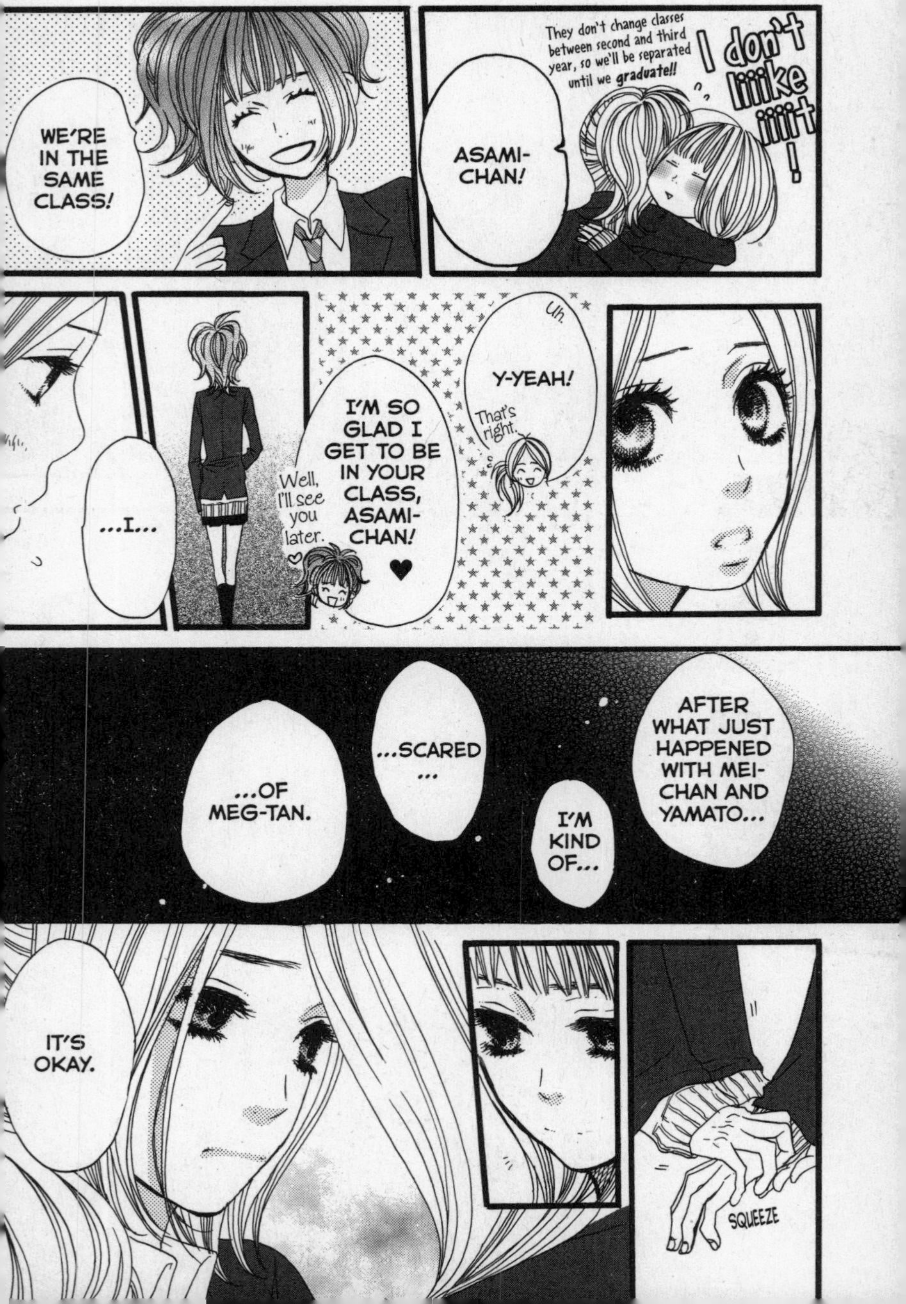
They don't change classes between second and third year, so we'll be separated until we graduate!!
I don't liiiike iiiiit!
ASAMI-CHAN!
WE'RE IN THE SAME CLASS!
Uh.
Y-YEAH!
That's right.
I'M SO GLAD I GET TO BE IN YOUR CLASS, ASAMI-CHAN! ♥
Well, I'll see you later.
...I...
AFTER WHAT JUST HAPPENED WITH MEI-CHAN AND YAMATO...
I'M KIND OF...
...SCARED...
...OF MEG-TAN.
SQUEEZE
IT'S OKAY.

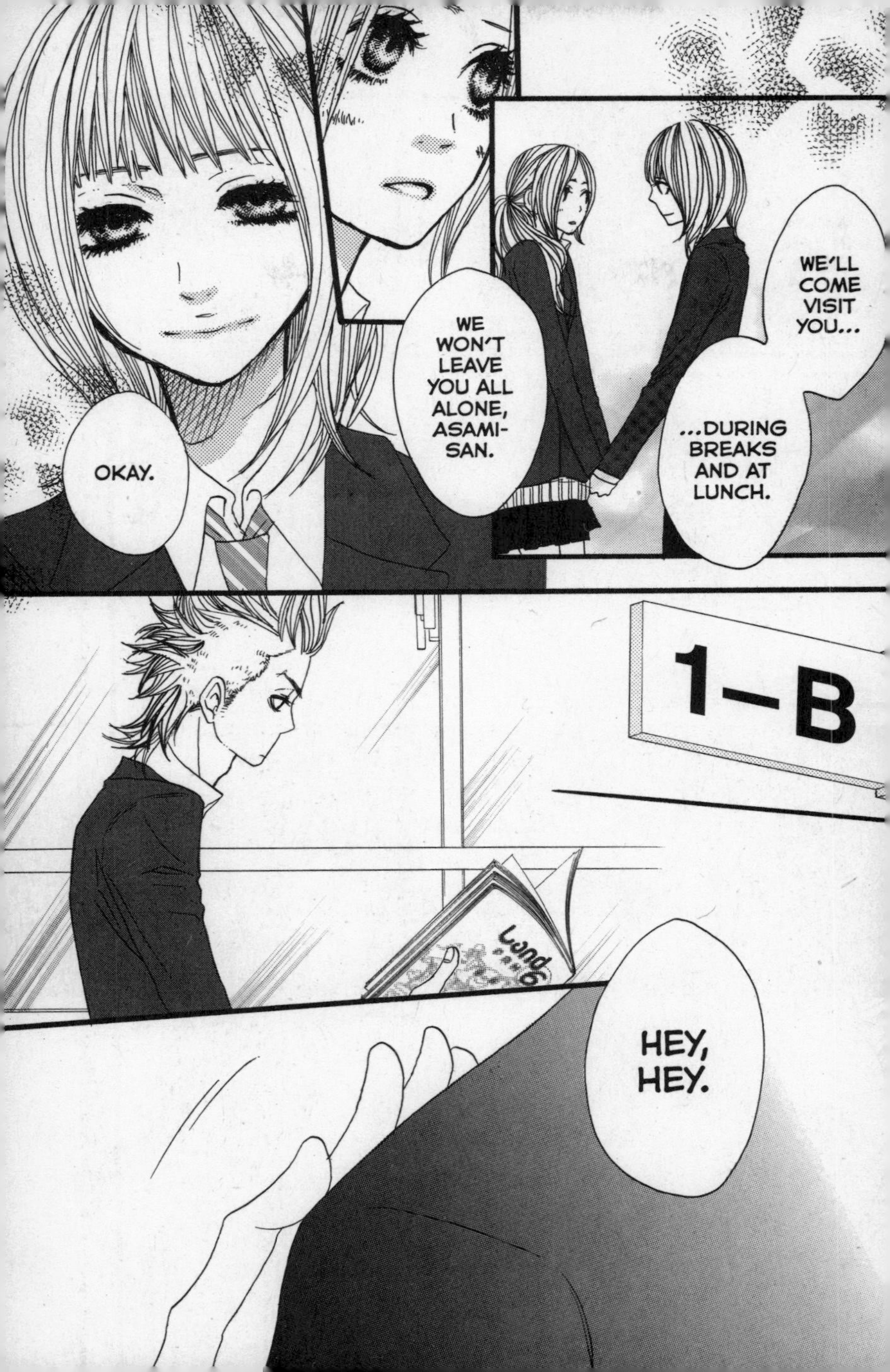
WE'LL COME VISIT YOU...
...DURING BREAKS AND AT LUNCH.
WE WON'T LEAVE YOU ALL ALONE, ASAMI-SAN.
OKAY.
1-B
HEY, HEY.

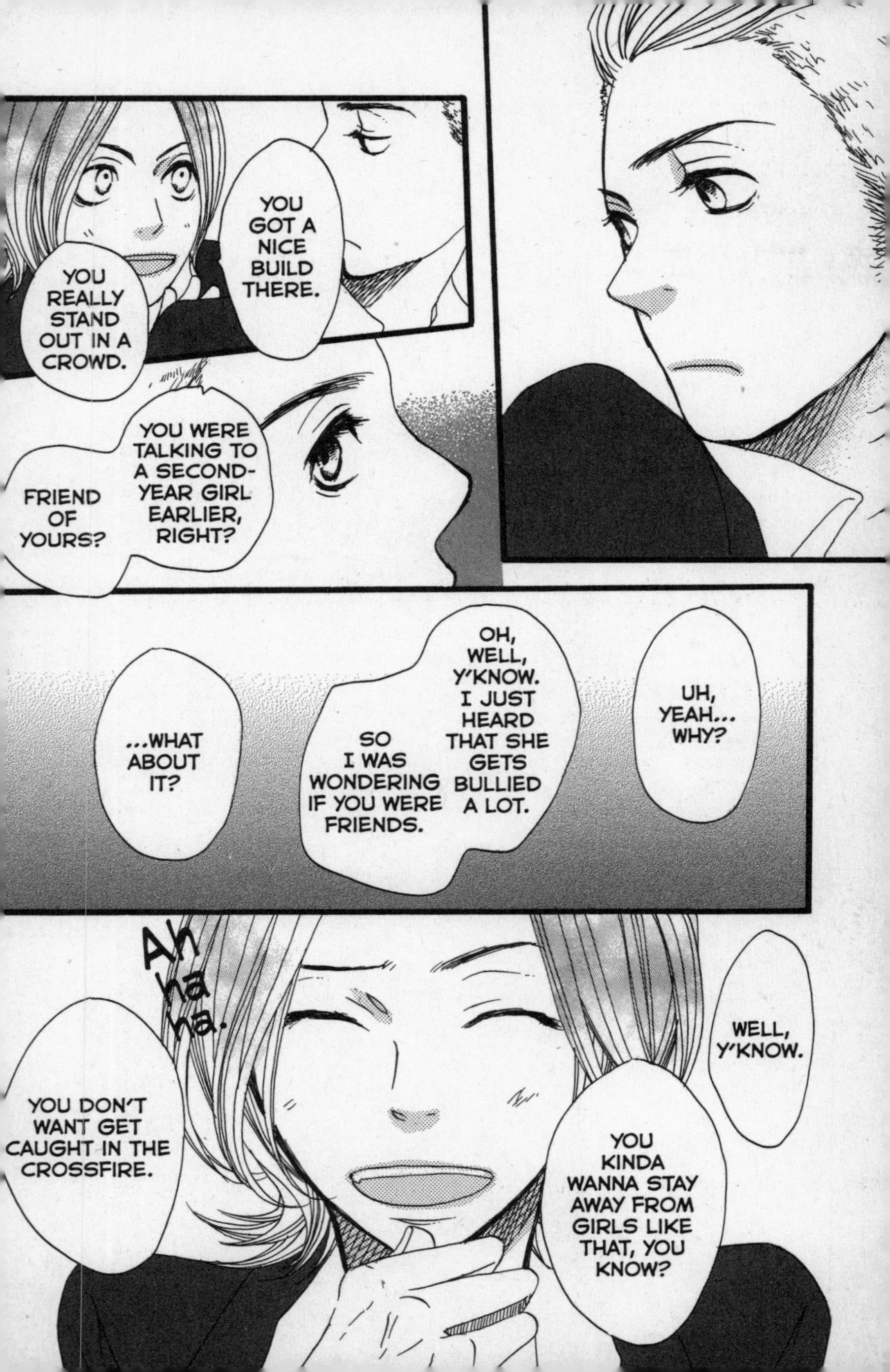
YOU GOT A NICE BUILD THERE.
YOU REALLY STAND OUT IN A CROWD.
YOU WERE TALKING TO A SECOND-YEAR GIRL EARLIER, RIGHT?
FRIEND OF YOURS?
UH, YEAH... WHY?
OH, WELL, Y'KNOW. I JUST HEARD THAT SHE GETS BULLIED A LOT.
SO I WAS WONDERING IF YOU WERE FRIENDS.
...WHAT ABOUT IT?
WELL, Y'KNOW.
YOU KINDA WANNA STAY AWAY FROM GIRLS LIKE THAT, YOU KNOW?
Ah ha ha.
YOU DON'T WANT GET CAUGHT IN THE CROSSFIRE.

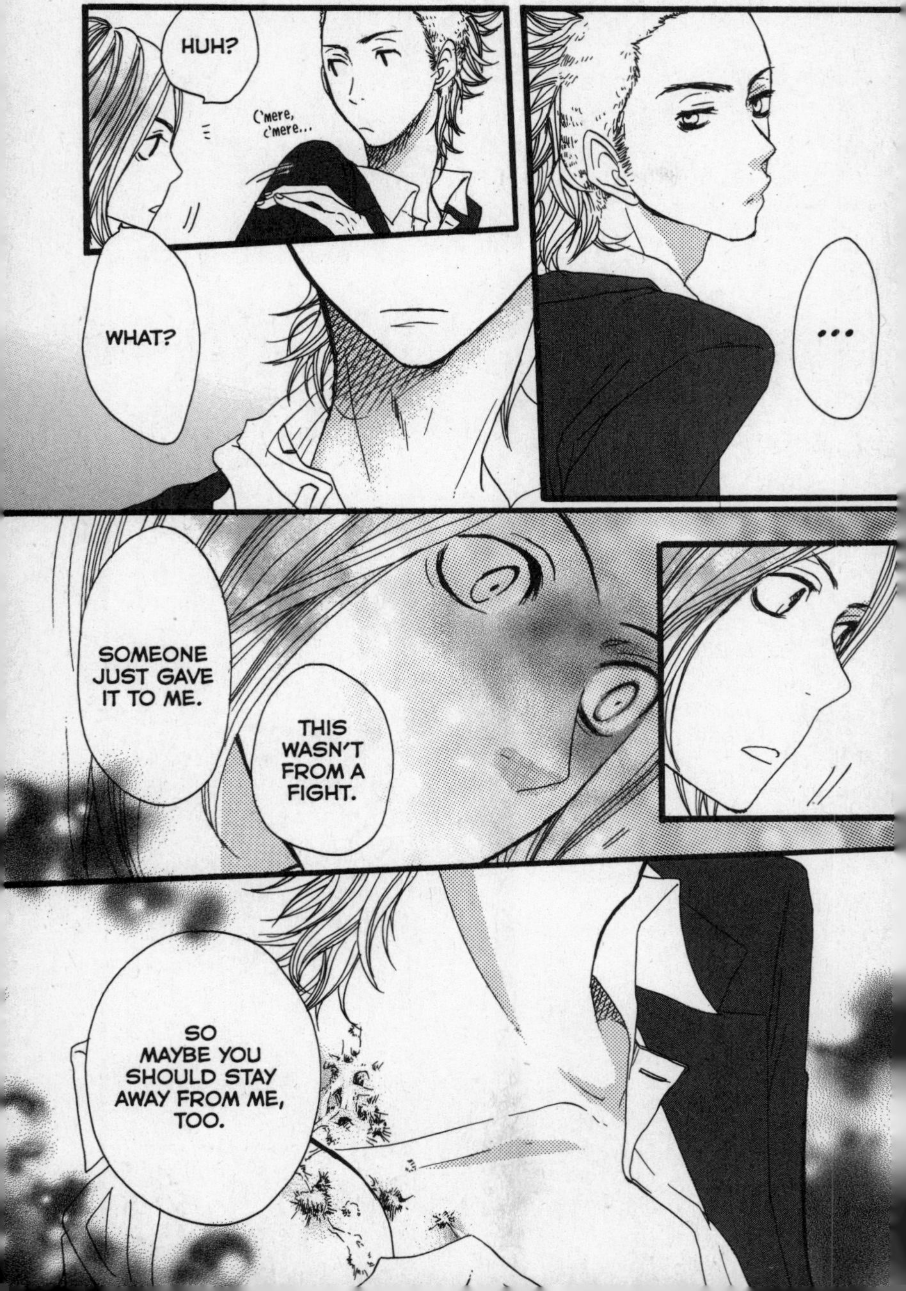
...
HUH?
C'mere, c'mere...
WHAT?
THIS WASN'T FROM A FIGHT.
SOMEONE JUST GAVE IT TO ME.
SO MAYBE YOU SHOULD STAY AWAY FROM ME, TOO.

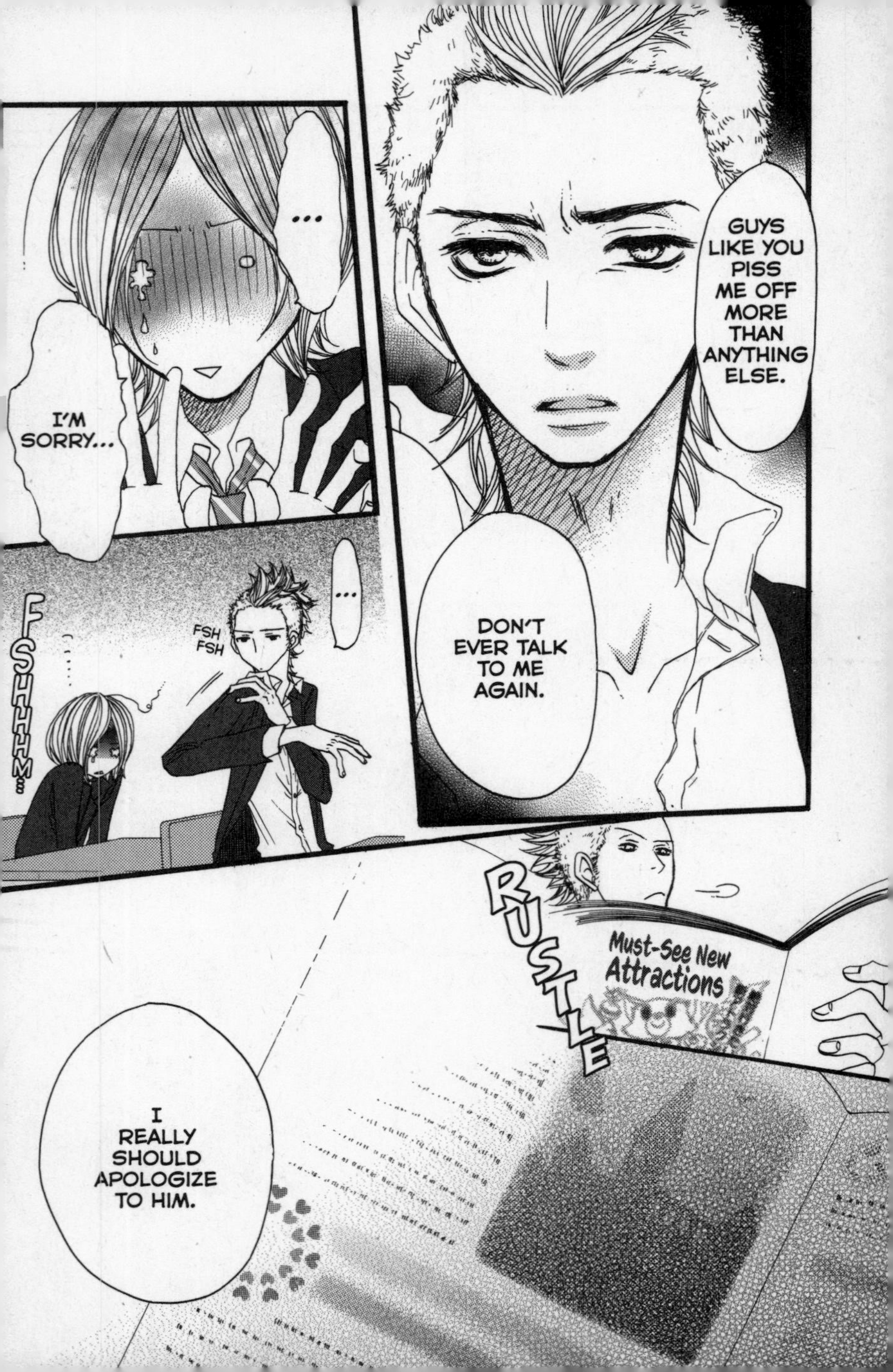
GUYS LIKE YOU PISS ME OFF MORE THAN ANYTHING ELSE.
DON'T EVER TALK TO ME AGAIN.
...
I'M SORRY...
...
FSH FSH
FSHHHM...
RUSTLE
Must-See New Attractions
I REALLY SHOULD APOLOGIZE TO HIM.

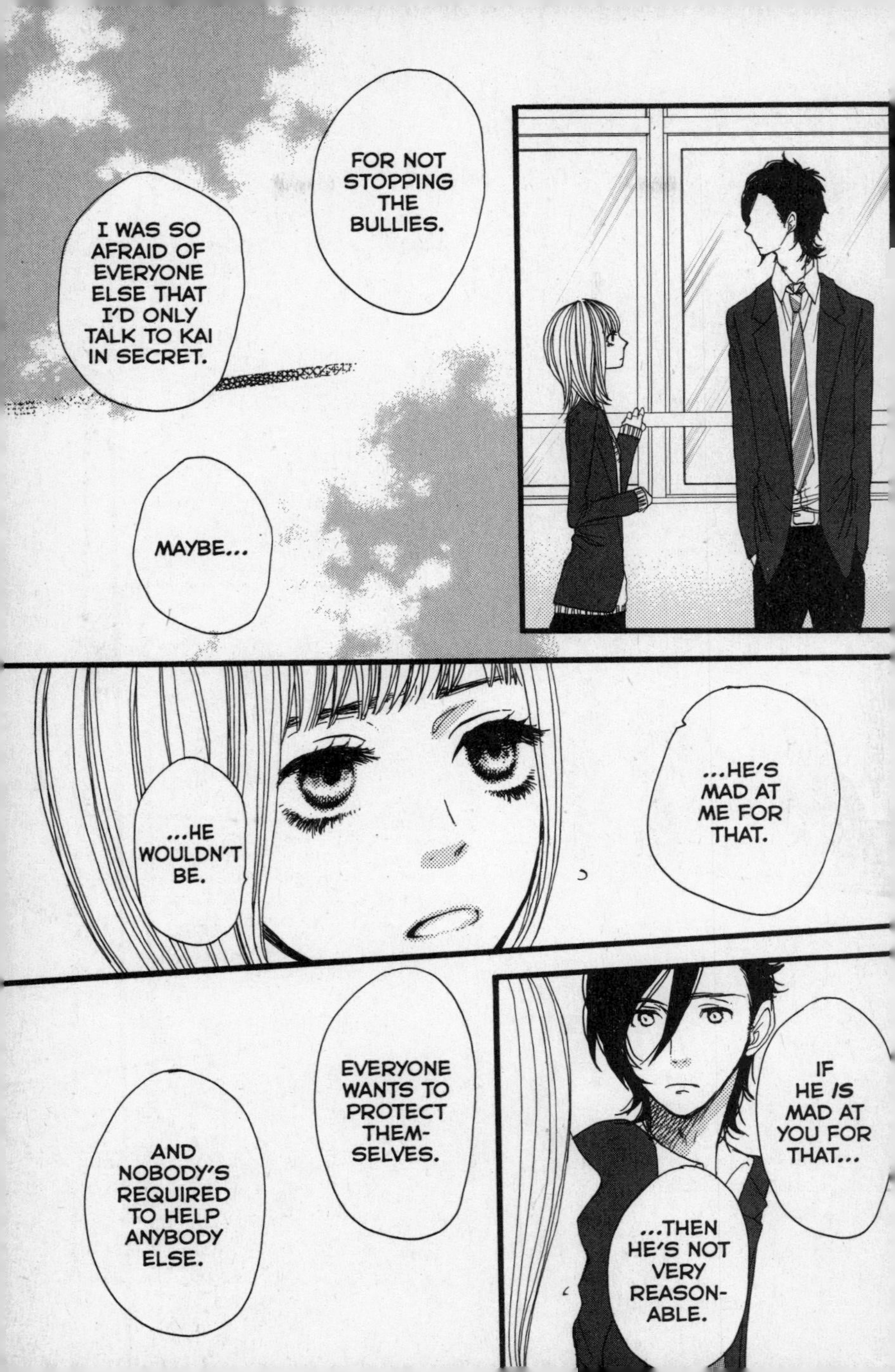
FOR NOT STOPPING THE BULLIES.
I WAS SO AFRAID OF EVERYONE ELSE THAT I'D ONLY TALK TO KAI IN SECRET.
MAYBE...
...HE'S MAD AT ME FOR THAT.
...HE WOULDN'T BE.
IF HE *IS* MAD AT YOU FOR THAT...
...THEN HE'S NOT VERY REASONABLE.
EVERYONE WANTS TO PROTECT THEM-SELVES.
AND NOBODY'S REQUIRED TO HELP ANYBODY ELSE.

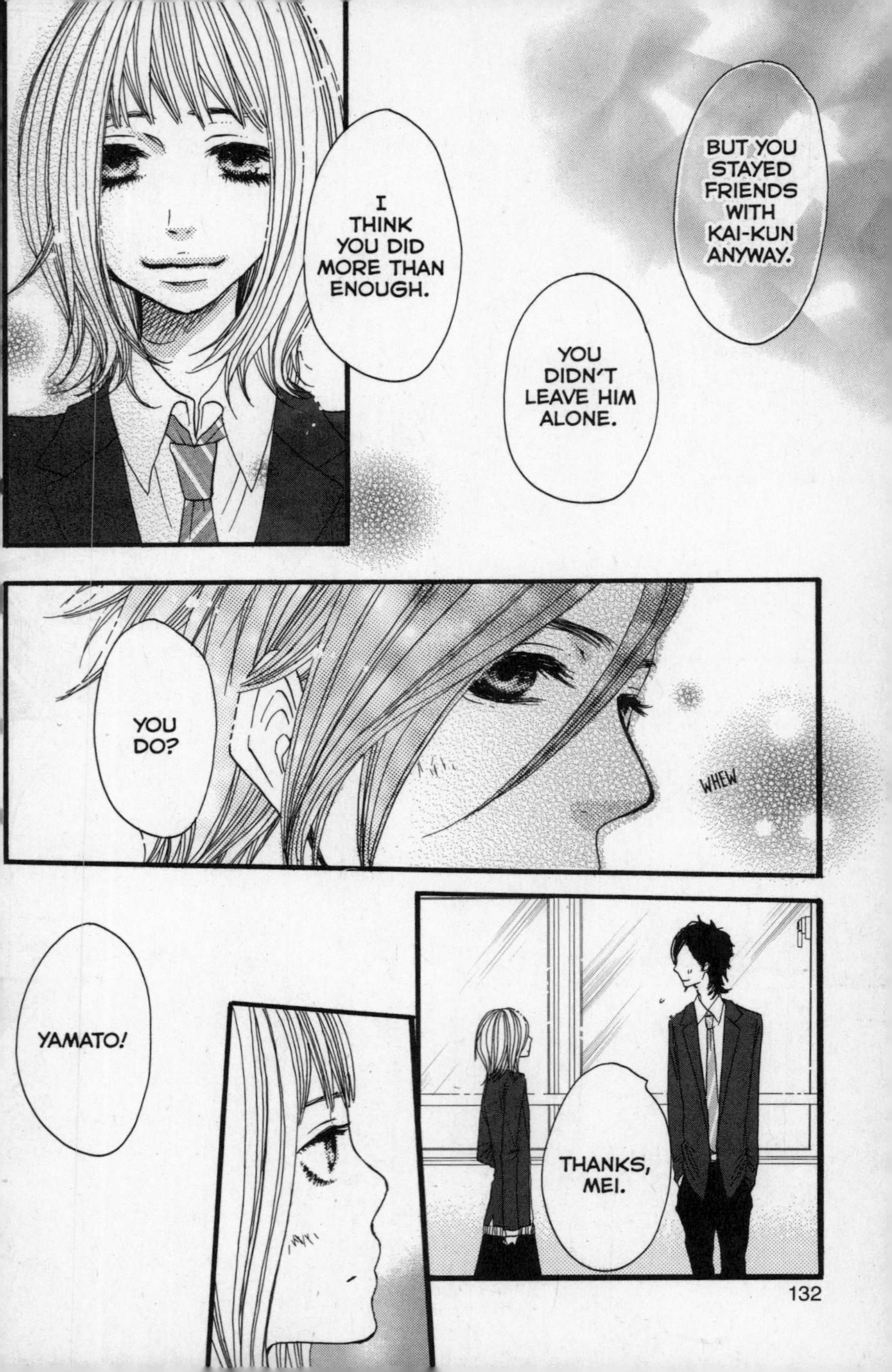
BUT YOU STAYED FRIENDS WITH KAI-KUN ANYWAY.
YOU DIDN'T LEAVE HIM ALONE.
I THINK YOU DID MORE THAN ENOUGH.
WHEW
YOU DO?
THANKS, MEI.
YAMATO!

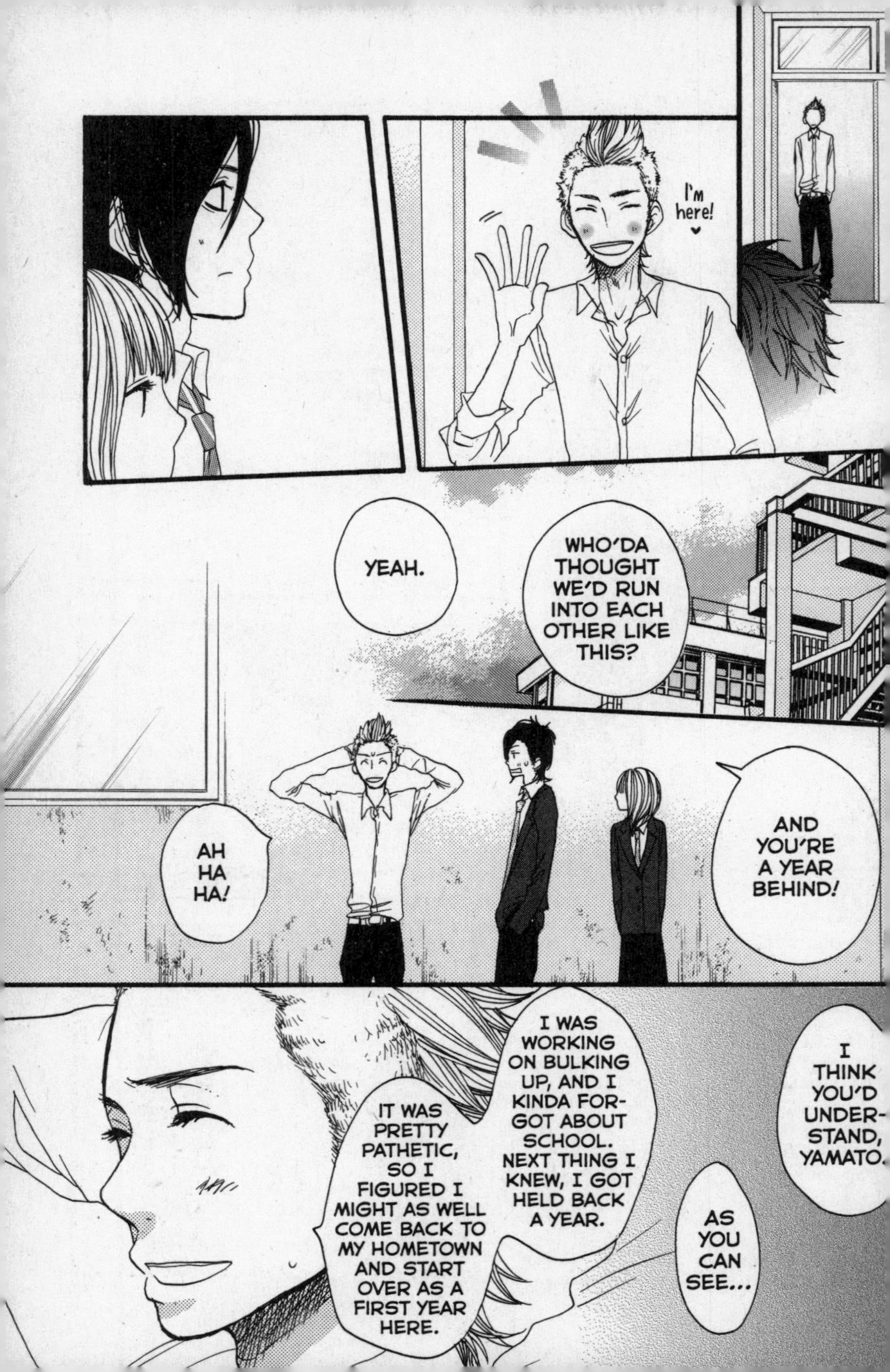
I'm here!
WHO'DA THOUGHT WE'D RUN INTO EACH OTHER LIKE THIS?
YEAH.
AND YOU'RE A YEAR BEHIND!
AH HA HA!
I THINK YOU'D UNDER-STAND, YAMATO.
AS YOU CAN SEE...
I WAS WORKING ON BULKING UP, AND I KINDA FOR-GOT ABOUT SCHOOL. NEXT THING I KNEW, I GOT HELD BACK A YEAR.
IT WAS PRETTY PATHETIC, SO I FIGURED I MIGHT AS WELL COME BACK TO MY HOMETOWN AND START OVER AS A FIRST YEAR HERE.

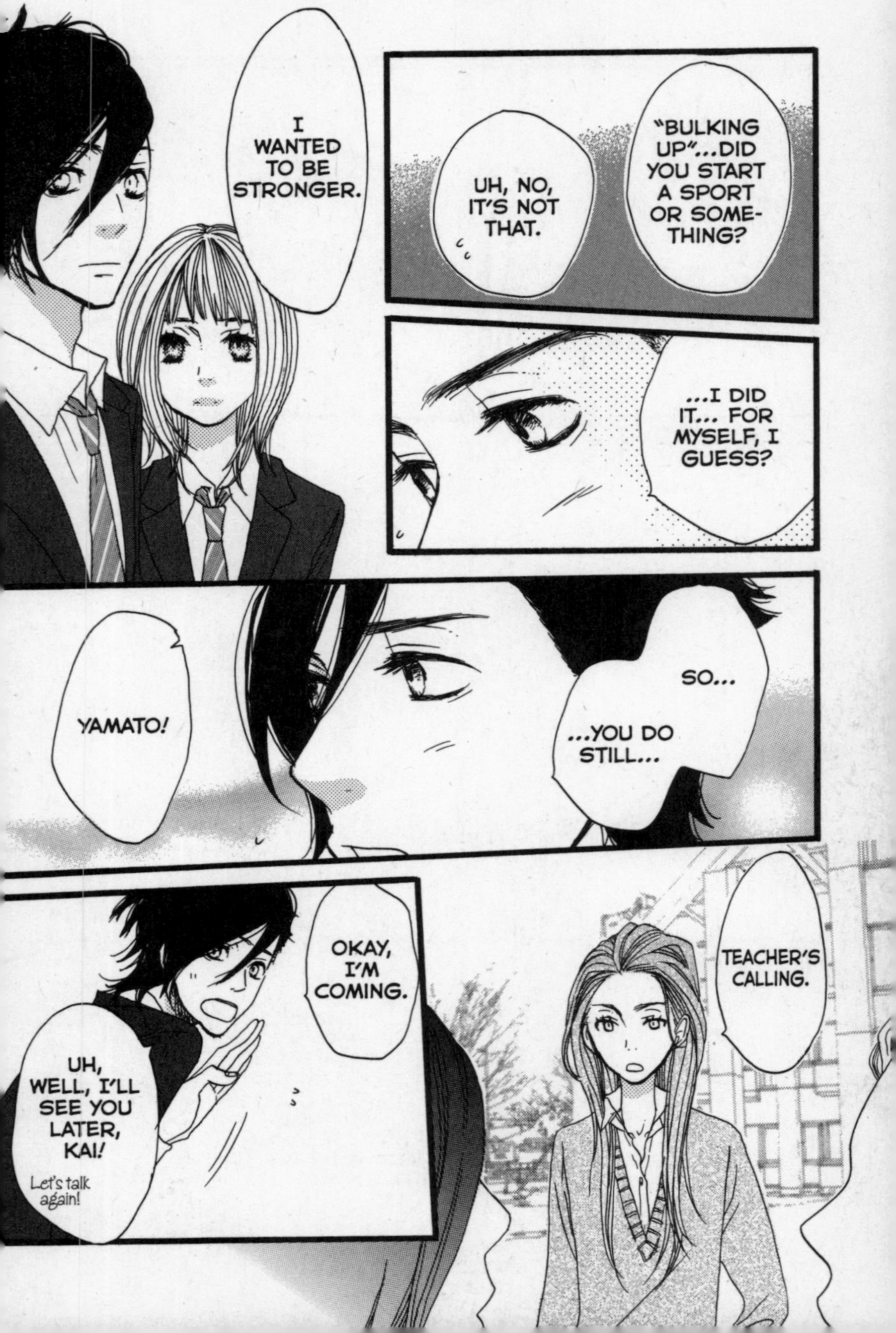
"BULKING UP"...DID YOU START A SPORT OR SOMETHING?
UH, NO, IT'S NOT THAT.
...I DID IT... FOR MYSELF, I GUESS?
I WANTED TO BE STRONGER.
SO...
...YOU DO STILL...
YAMATO!
TEACHER'S CALLING.
OKAY, I'M COMING.
UH, WELL, I'LL SEE YOU LATER, KAI!
Let's talk again!

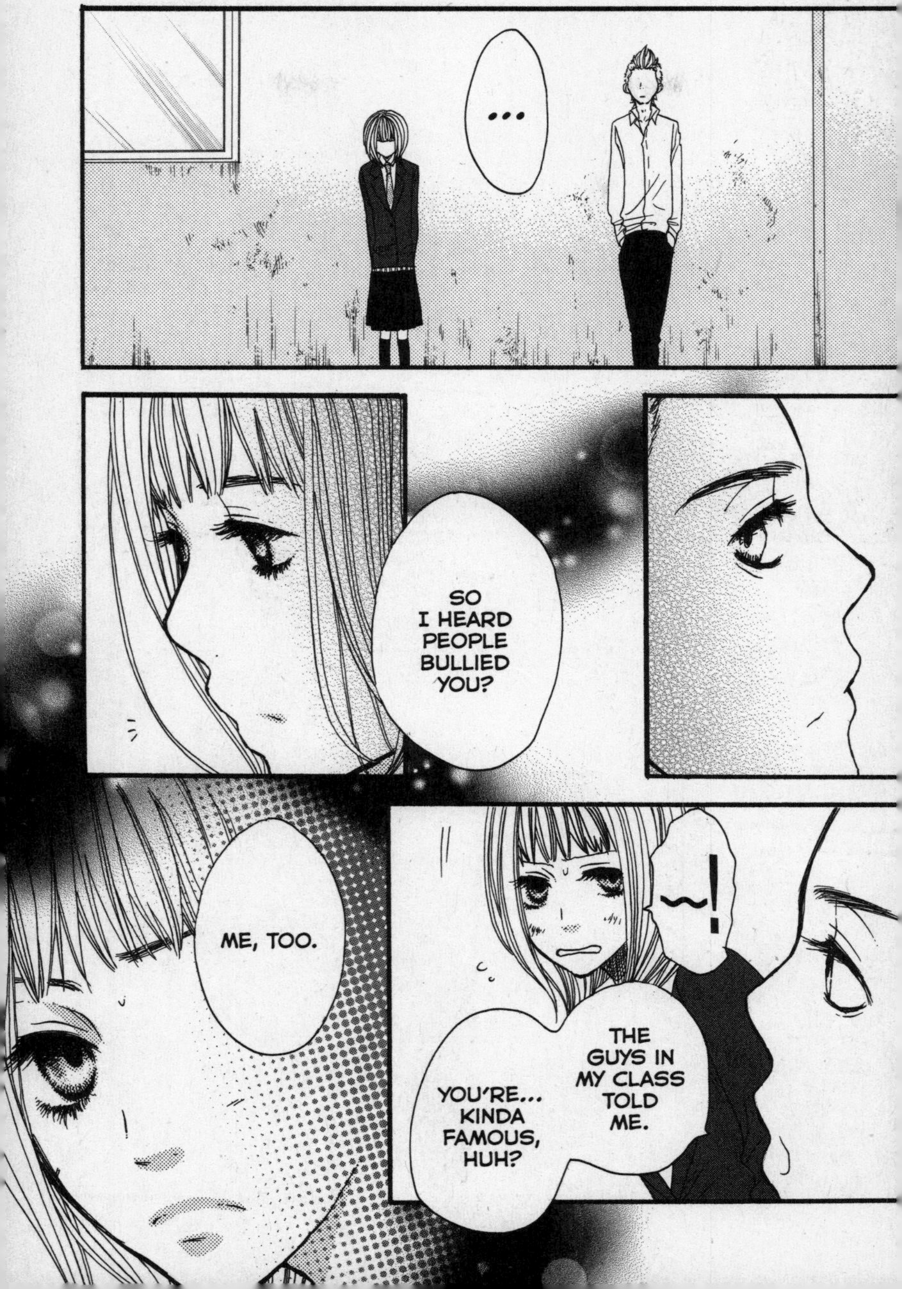
...
SO I HEARD PEOPLE BULLIED YOU?
~!
THE GUYS IN MY CLASS TOLD ME.
YOU'RE... KINDA FAMOUS, HUH?
ME, TOO.

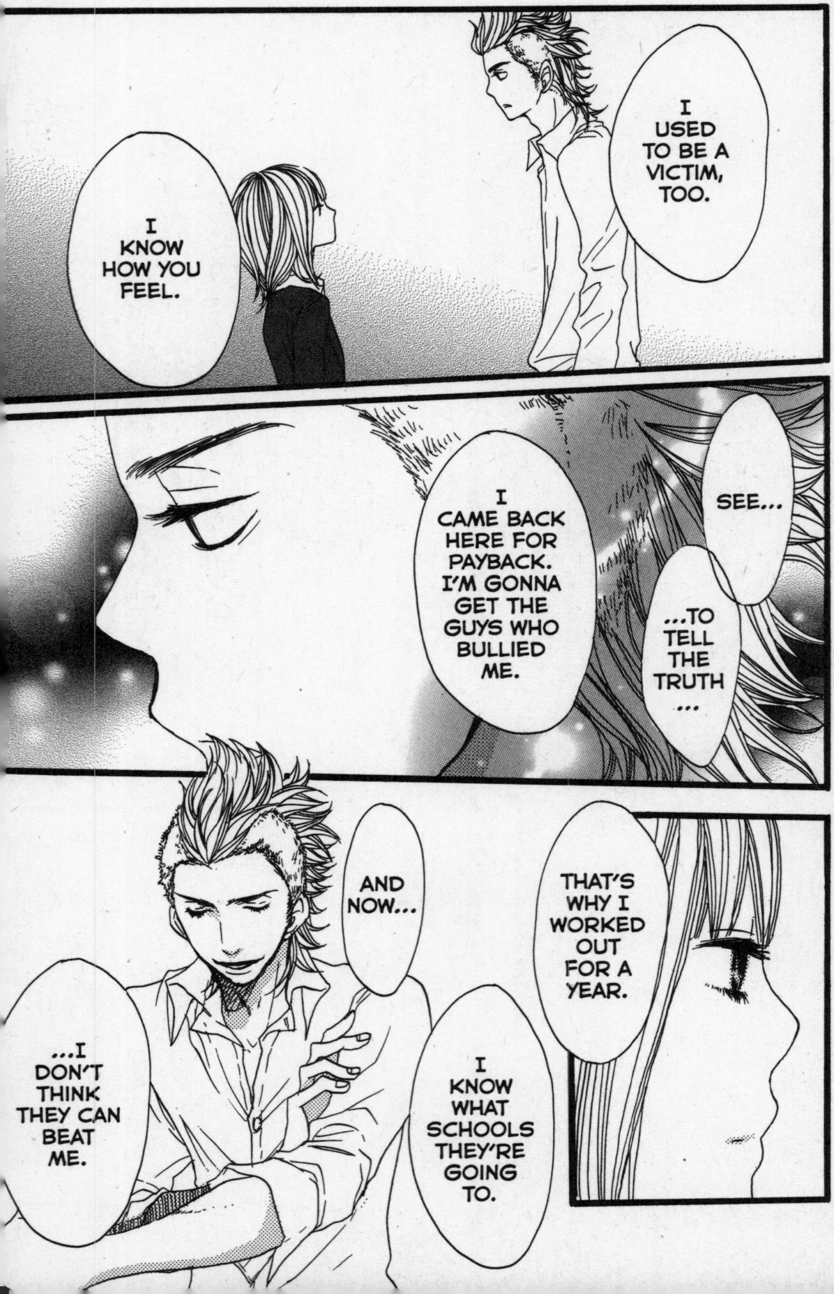
I USED TO BE A VICTIM, TOO.
I KNOW HOW YOU FEEL.
SEE...
...TO TELL THE TRUTH...
I CAME BACK HERE FOR PAYBACK. I'M GONNA GET THE GUYS WHO BULLIED ME.
THAT'S WHY I WORKED OUT FOR A YEAR.
I KNOW WHAT SCHOOLS THEY'RE GOING TO.
AND NOW...
...I DON'T THINK THEY CAN BEAT ME.

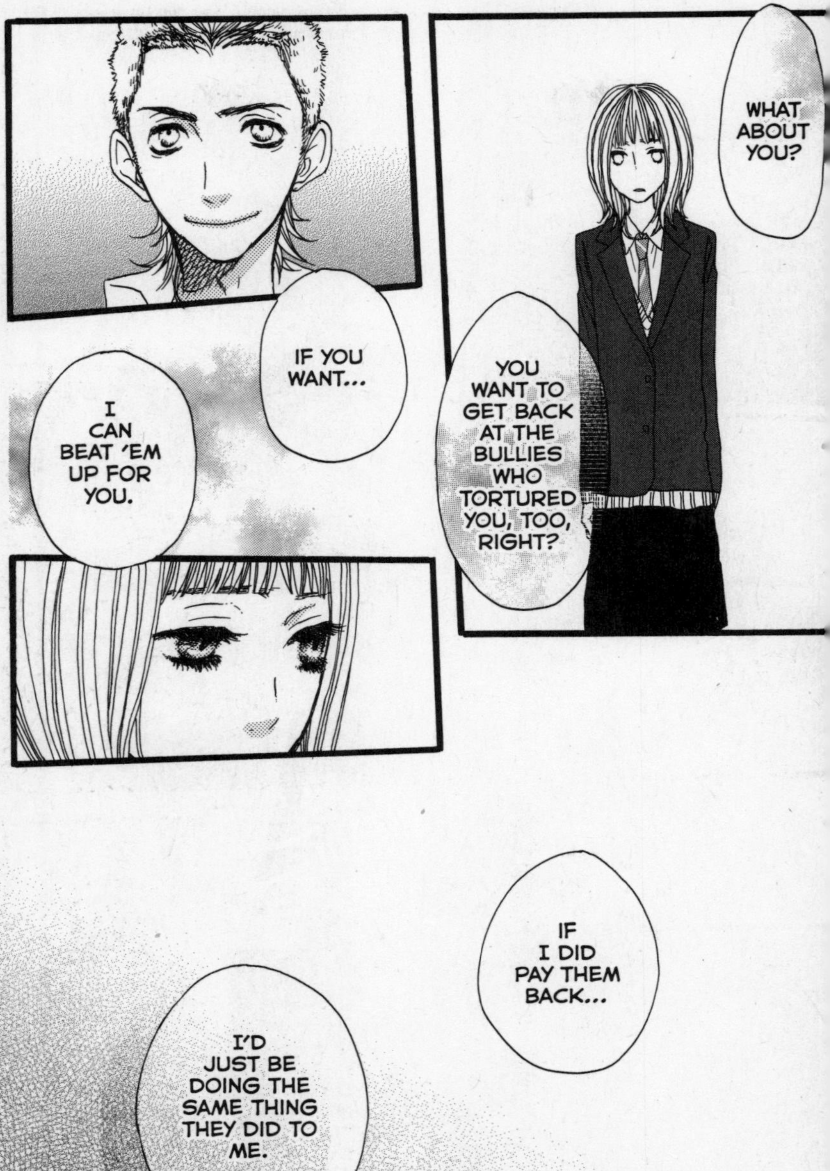
WHAT ABOUT YOU?
YOU WANT TO GET BACK AT THE BULLIES WHO TORTURED YOU, TOO, RIGHT?
IF YOU WANT...
I CAN BEAT 'EM UP FOR YOU.
IF I DID PAY THEM BACK...
I'D JUST BE DOING THE SAME THING THEY DID TO ME.

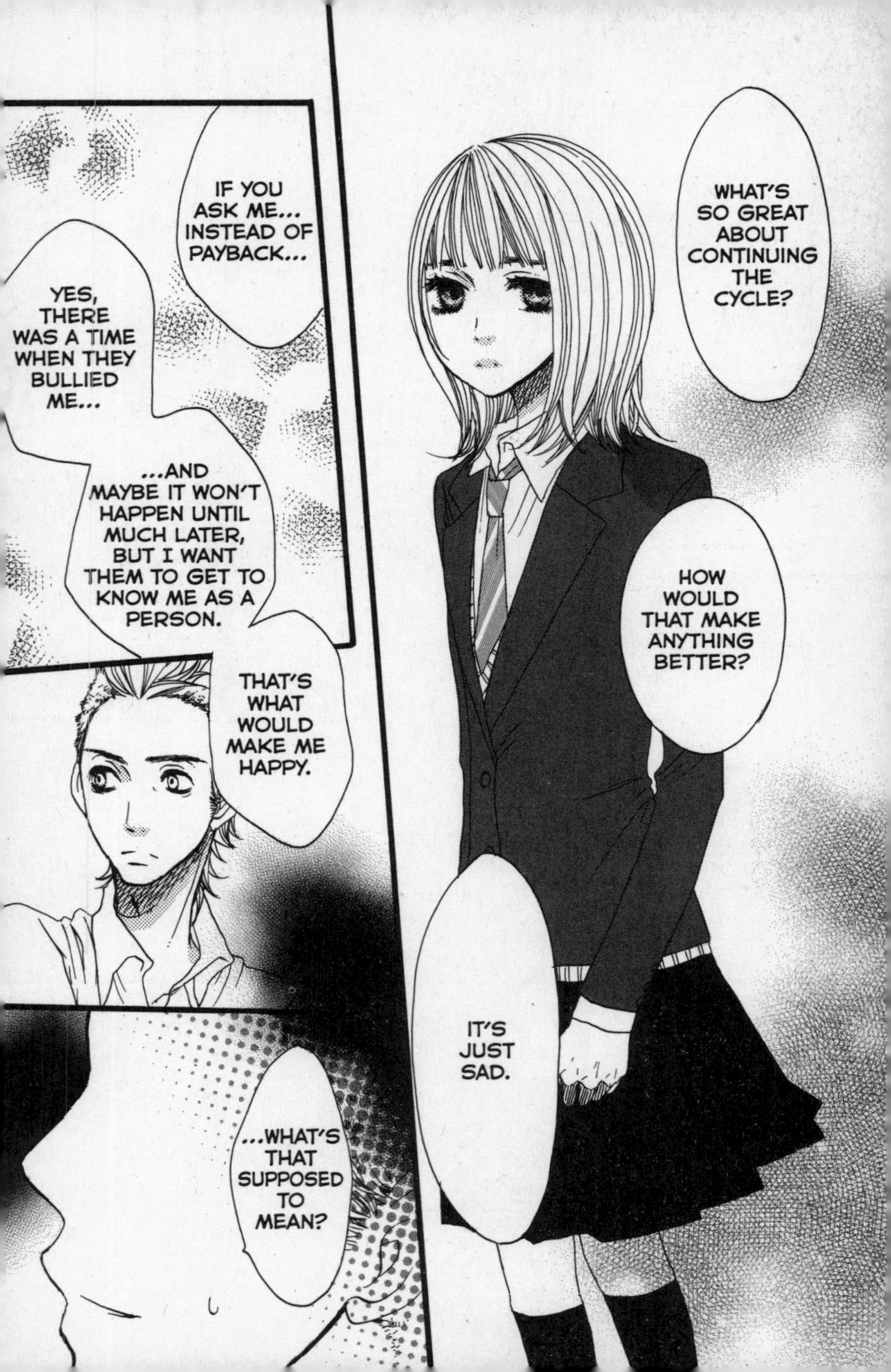
WHAT'S SO GREAT ABOUT CONTINUING THE CYCLE?
HOW WOULD THAT MAKE ANYTHING BETTER?
IT'S JUST SAD.
IF YOU ASK ME... INSTEAD OF PAYBACK...
YES, THERE WAS A TIME WHEN THEY BULLIED ME...
...AND MAYBE IT WON'T HAPPEN UNTIL MUCH LATER, BUT I WANT THEM TO GET TO KNOW ME AS A PERSON.
THAT'S WHAT WOULD MAKE ME HAPPY.
...WHAT'S THAT SUPPOSED TO MEAN?

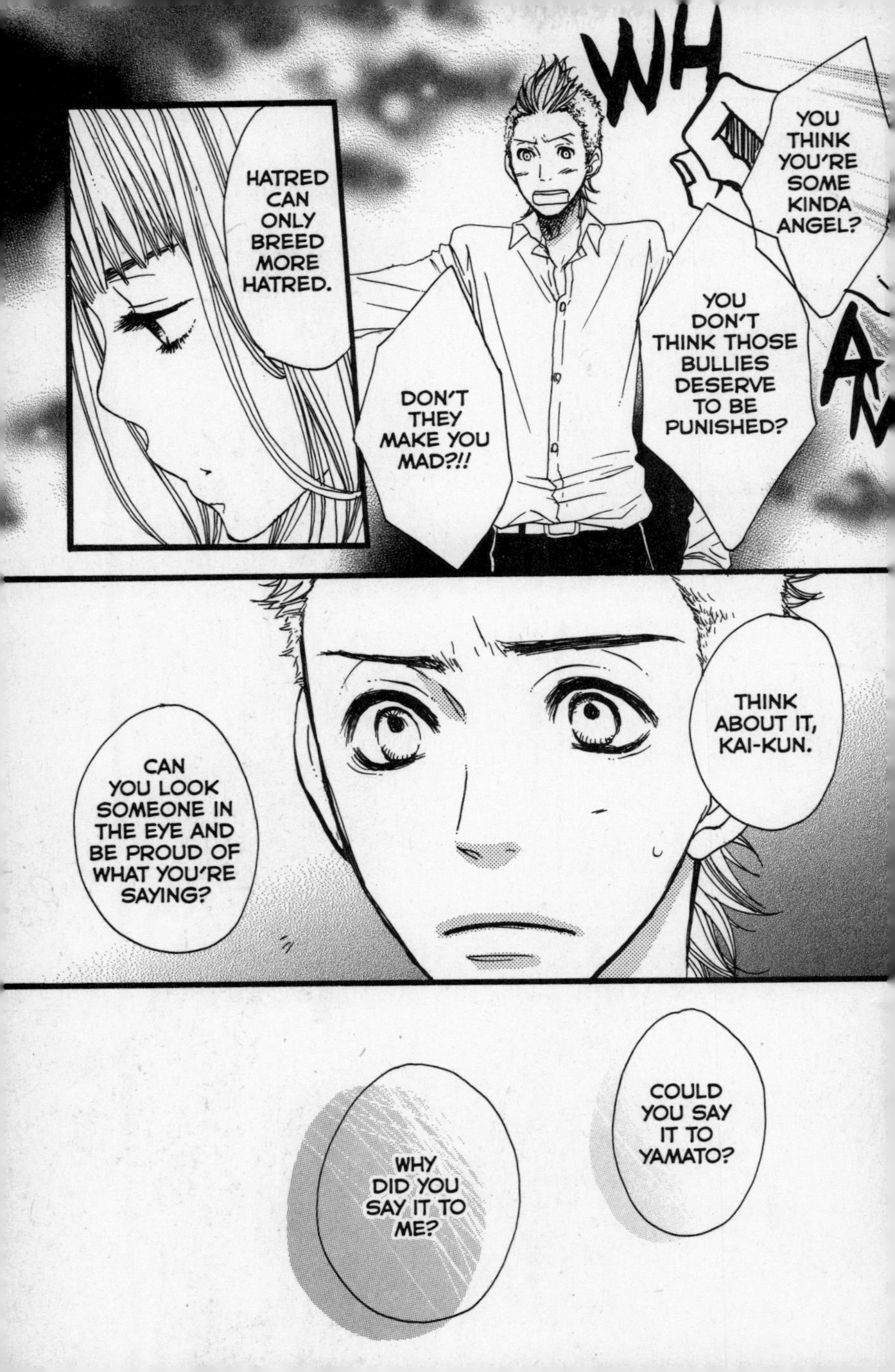
WHAM
YOU THINK YOU'RE SOME KINDA ANGEL?
YOU DON'T THINK THOSE BULLIES DESERVE TO BE PUNISHED?
DON'T THEY MAKE YOU MAD?!!
HATRED CAN ONLY BREED MORE HATRED.
THINK ABOUT IT, KAI-KUN.
CAN YOU LOOK SOMEONE IN THE EYE AND BE PROUD OF WHAT YOU'RE SAYING?
COULD YOU SAY IT TO YAMATO?
WHY DID YOU SAY IT TO ME?

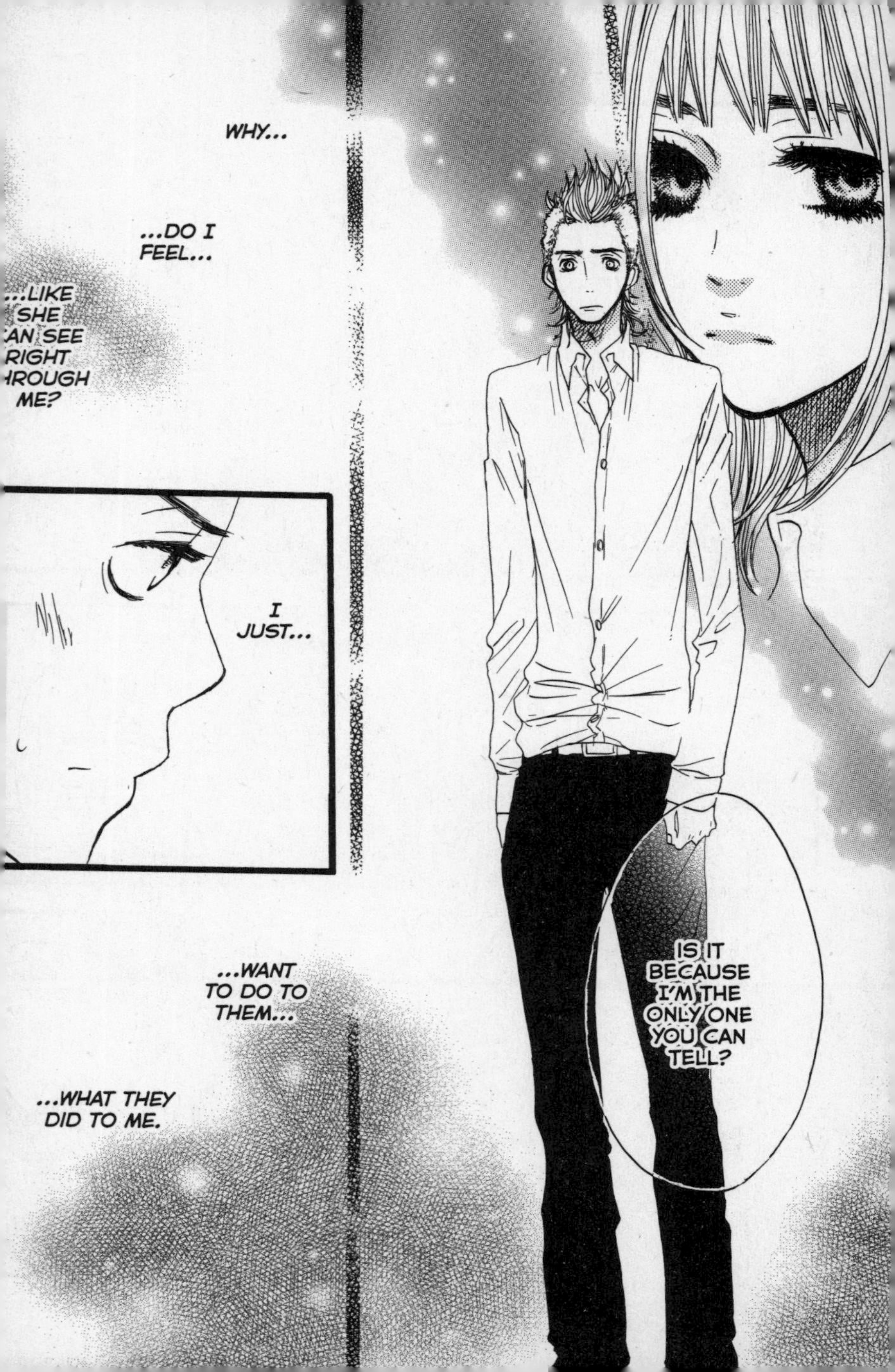
IS IT BECAUSE I'M THE ONLY ONE YOU CAN TELL?
WHY...
...DO I FEEL...
...LIKE SHE AN SEE RIGHT HROUGH ME?
I JUST...
...WANT TO DO TO THEM...
...WHAT THEY DID TO ME.

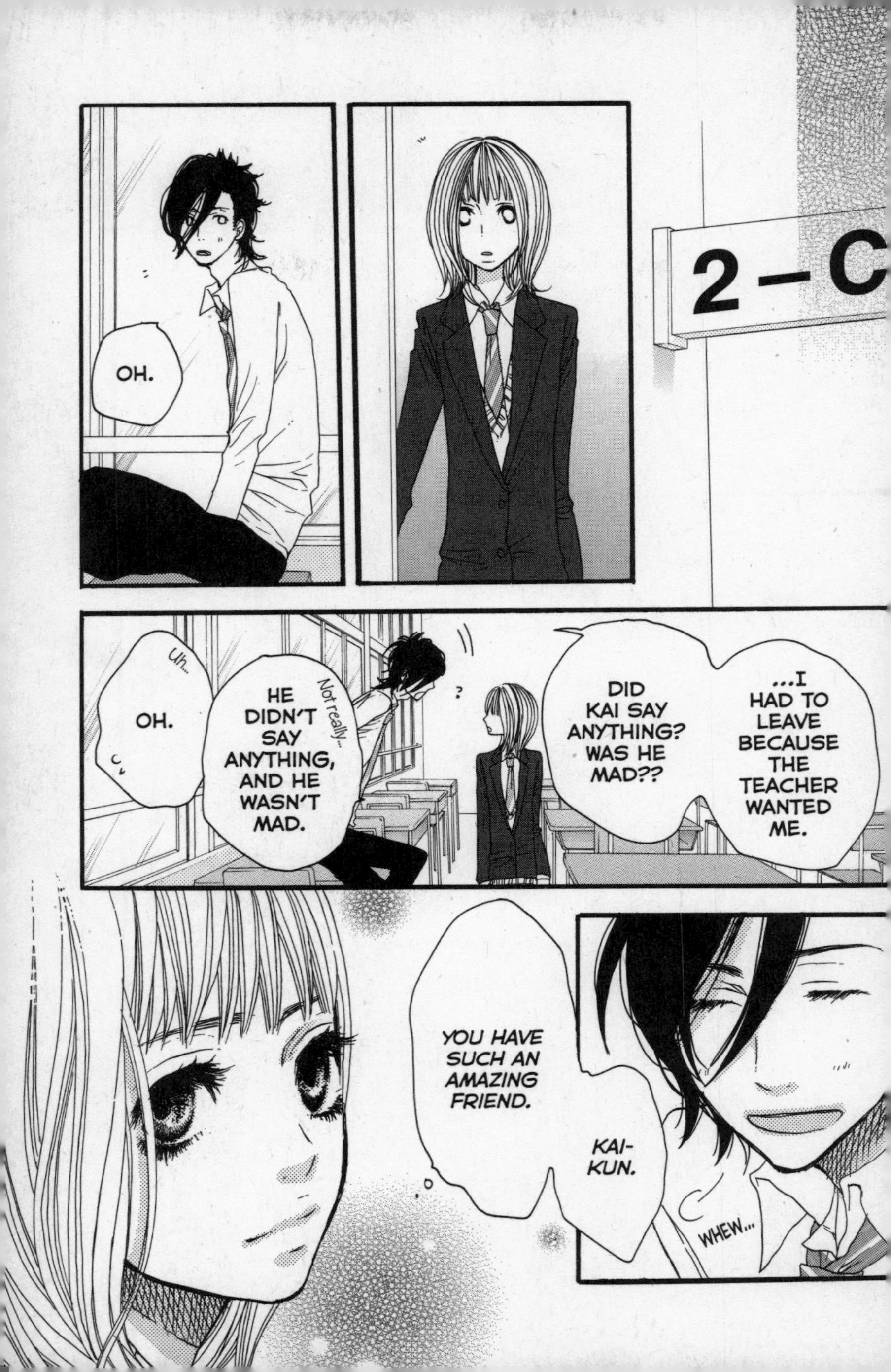
2-C
OH.
...I HAD TO LEAVE BECAUSE THE TEACHER WANTED ME.
DID KAI SAY ANYTHING? WAS HE MAD??
Not really...
HE DIDN'T SAY ANYTHING, AND HE WASN'T MAD.
Uh...
OH.
WHEW...
YOU HAVE SUCH AN AMAZING FRIEND.
KAI-KUN.

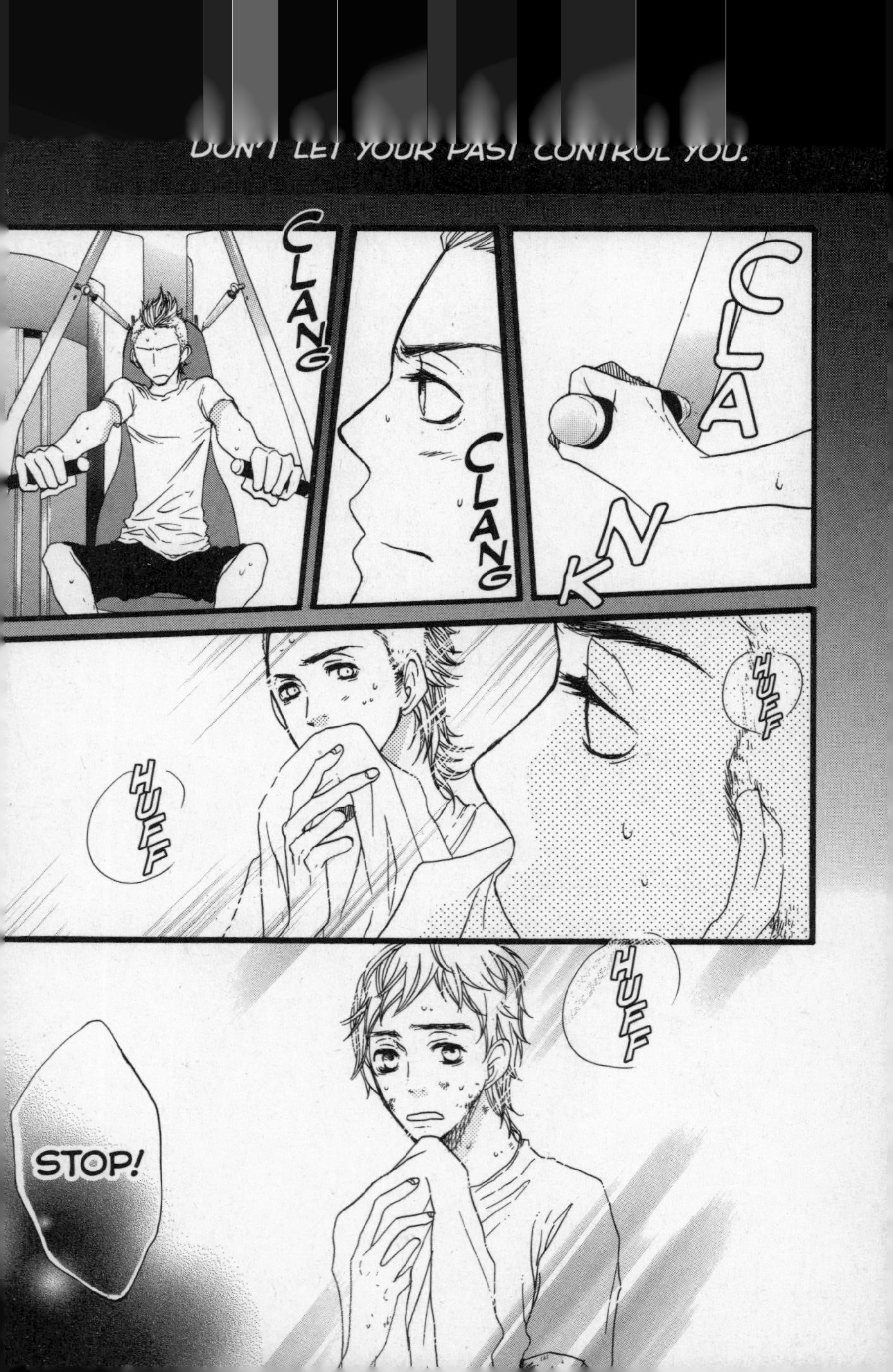
DON'T LET YOUR PAST CONTROL YOU.
CLANK
CLANG CLANG
CLANG
HUFF
HUFF
HUFF
STOP!

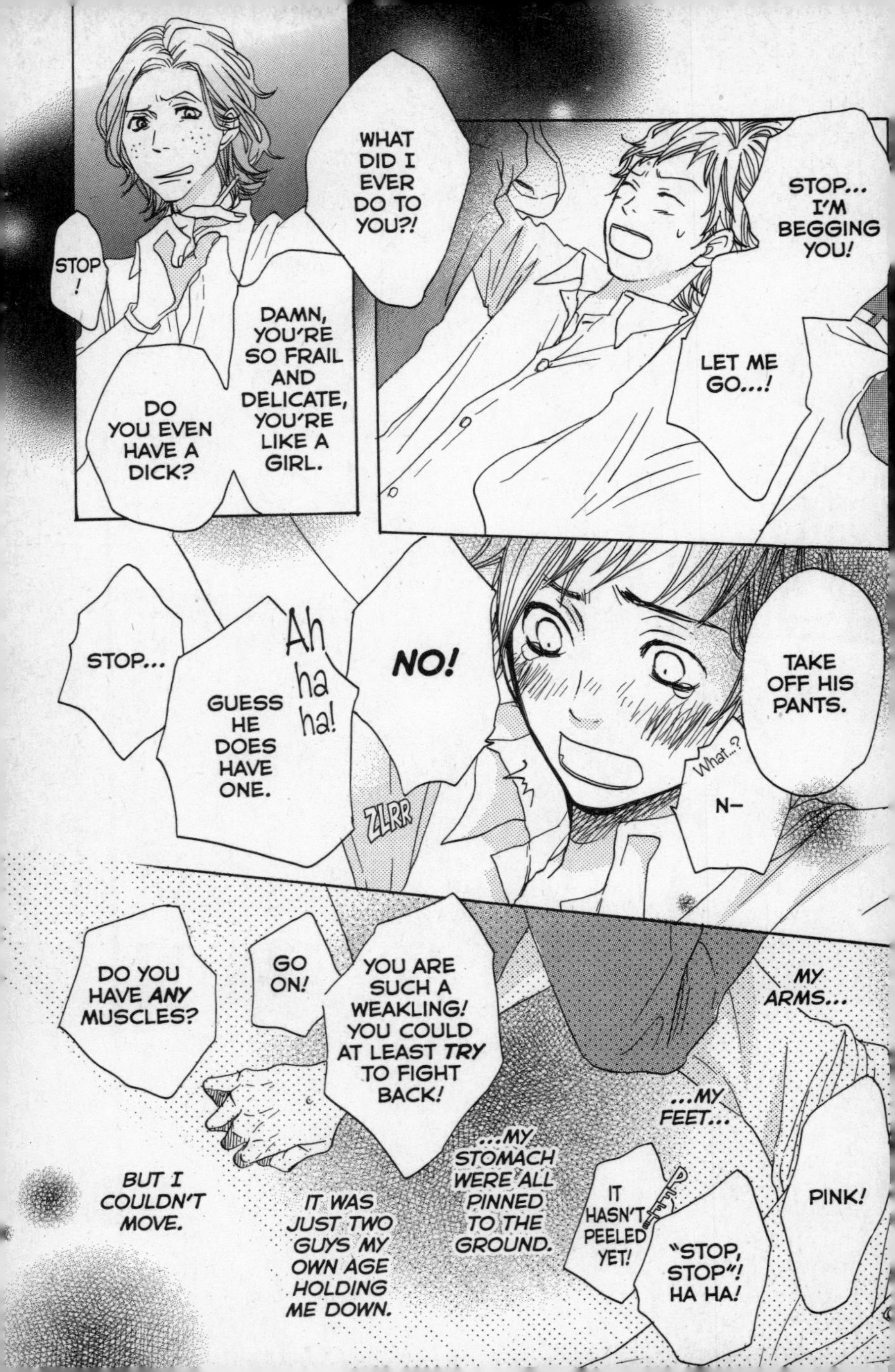
STOP... I'M BEGGING YOU!
LET ME GO...!
WHAT DID I EVER DO TO YOU?!
STOP!
DAMN, YOU'RE SO FRAIL AND DELICATE, YOU'RE LIKE A GIRL.
DO YOU EVEN HAVE A DICK?
TAKE OFF HIS PANTS.
What...?
N–
NO!
ZLRR
Ah ha ha!
GUESS HE DOES HAVE ONE.
STOP...
MY ARMS...
...MY FEET...
...MY STOMACH WERE ALL PINNED TO THE GROUND.
PINK!
"STOP, STOP"! HA HA!
IT HASN'T PEELED YET!
YOU ARE SUCH A WEAKLING! YOU COULD AT LEAST *TRY* TO FIGHT BACK!
GO ON!
DO YOU HAVE *ANY* MUSCLES?
IT WAS JUST TWO GUYS MY OWN AGE HOLDING ME DOWN.
BUT I COULDN'T MOVE.

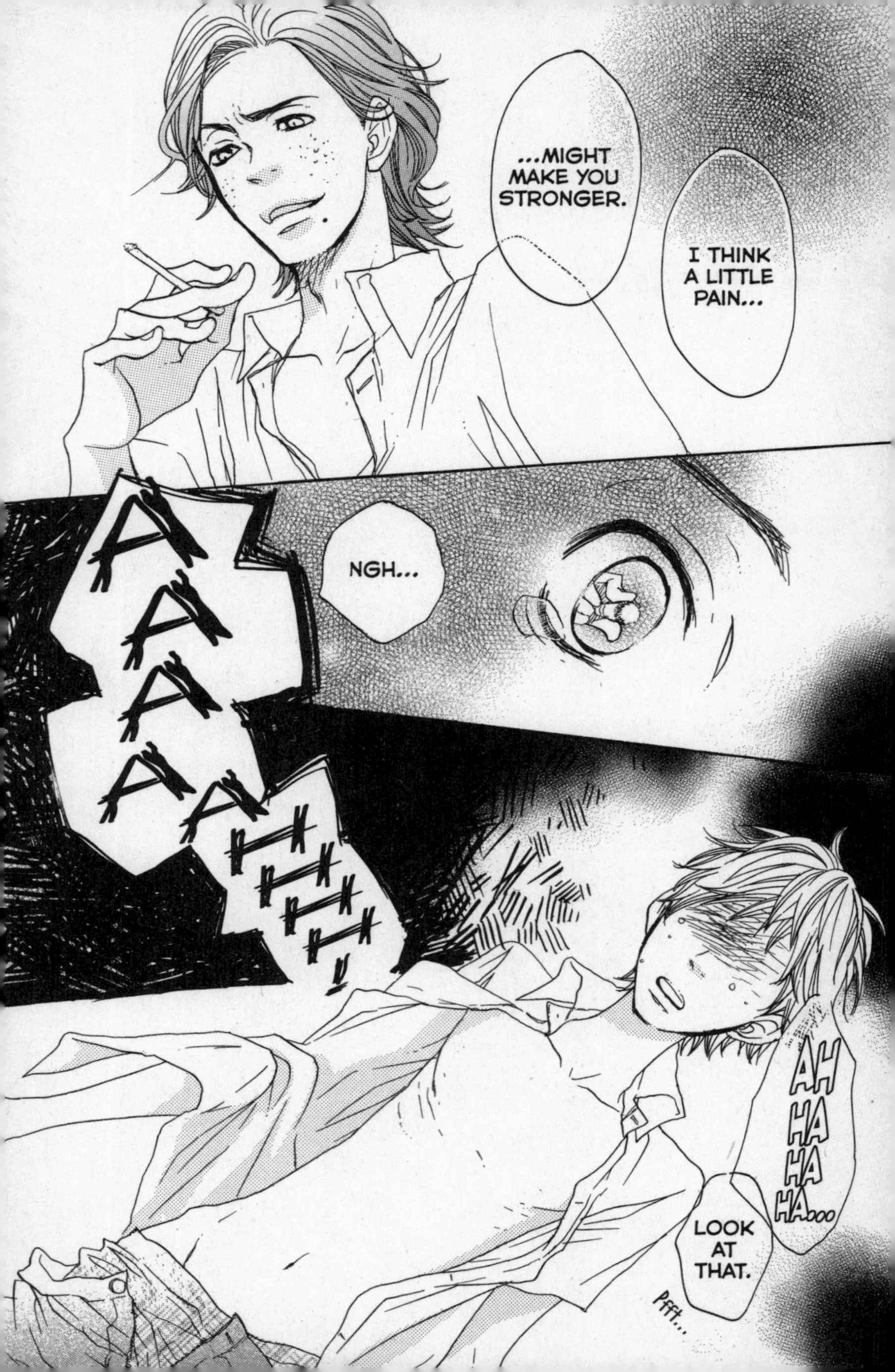
I THINK A LITTLE PAIN...
...MIGHT MAKE YOU STRONGER.
NGH...
AAAAAHHHH!!
AH HA HA HA HA...
LOOK AT THAT.
Pfft...

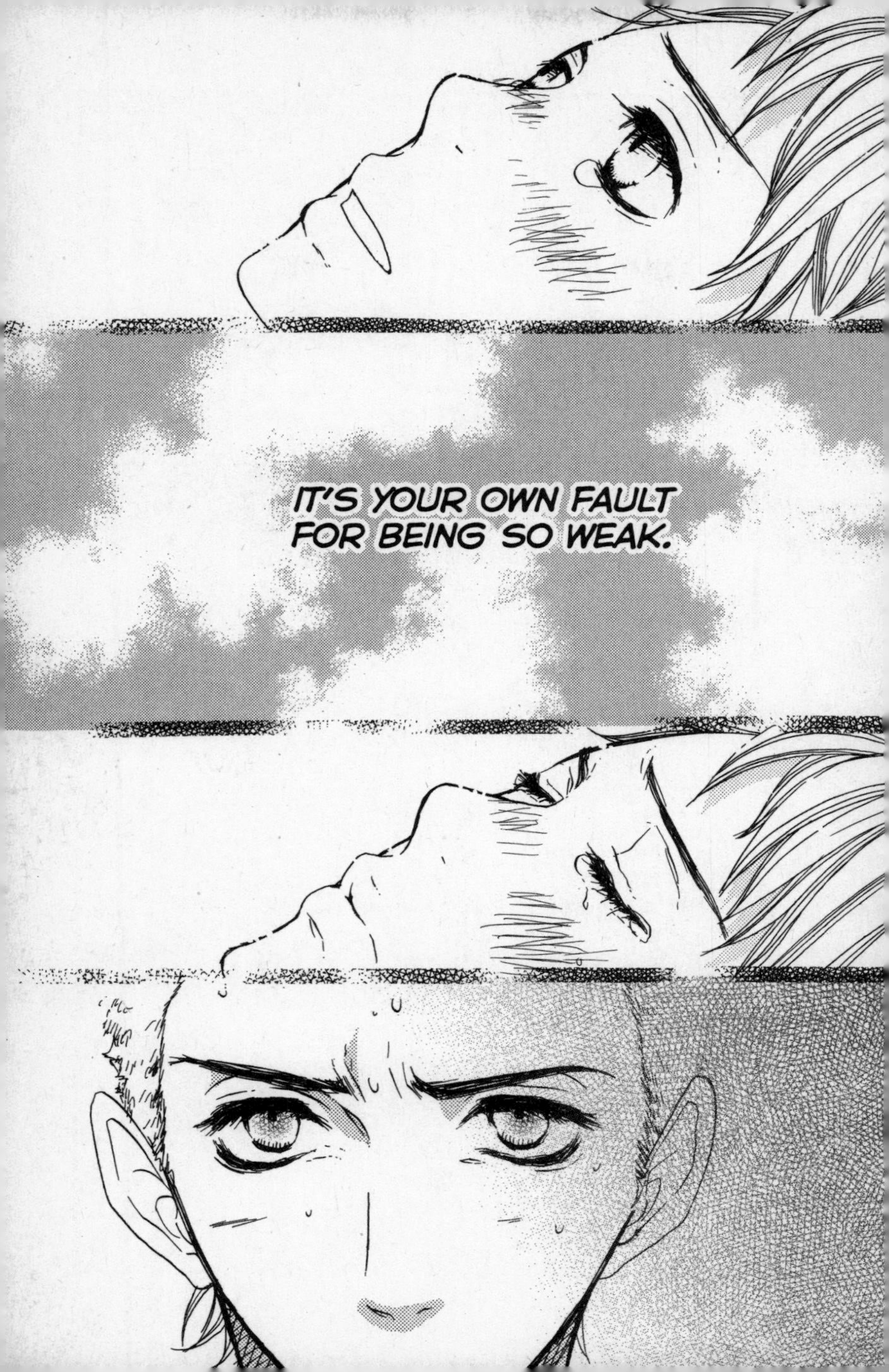
IT'S YOUR OWN FAULT FOR BEING SO WEAK.

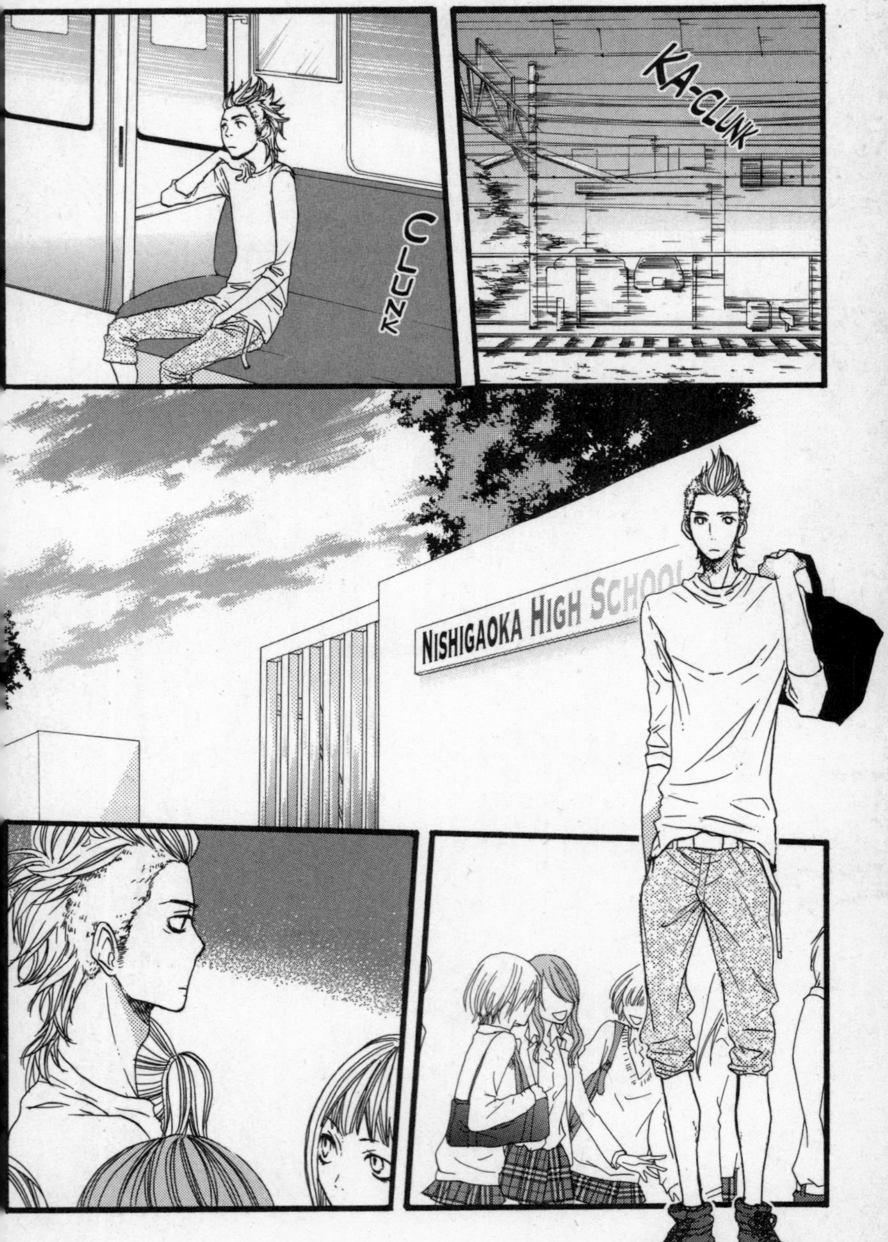
KA-CLUNK
CLUNK
NISHIGAOKA HIGH SCHOO

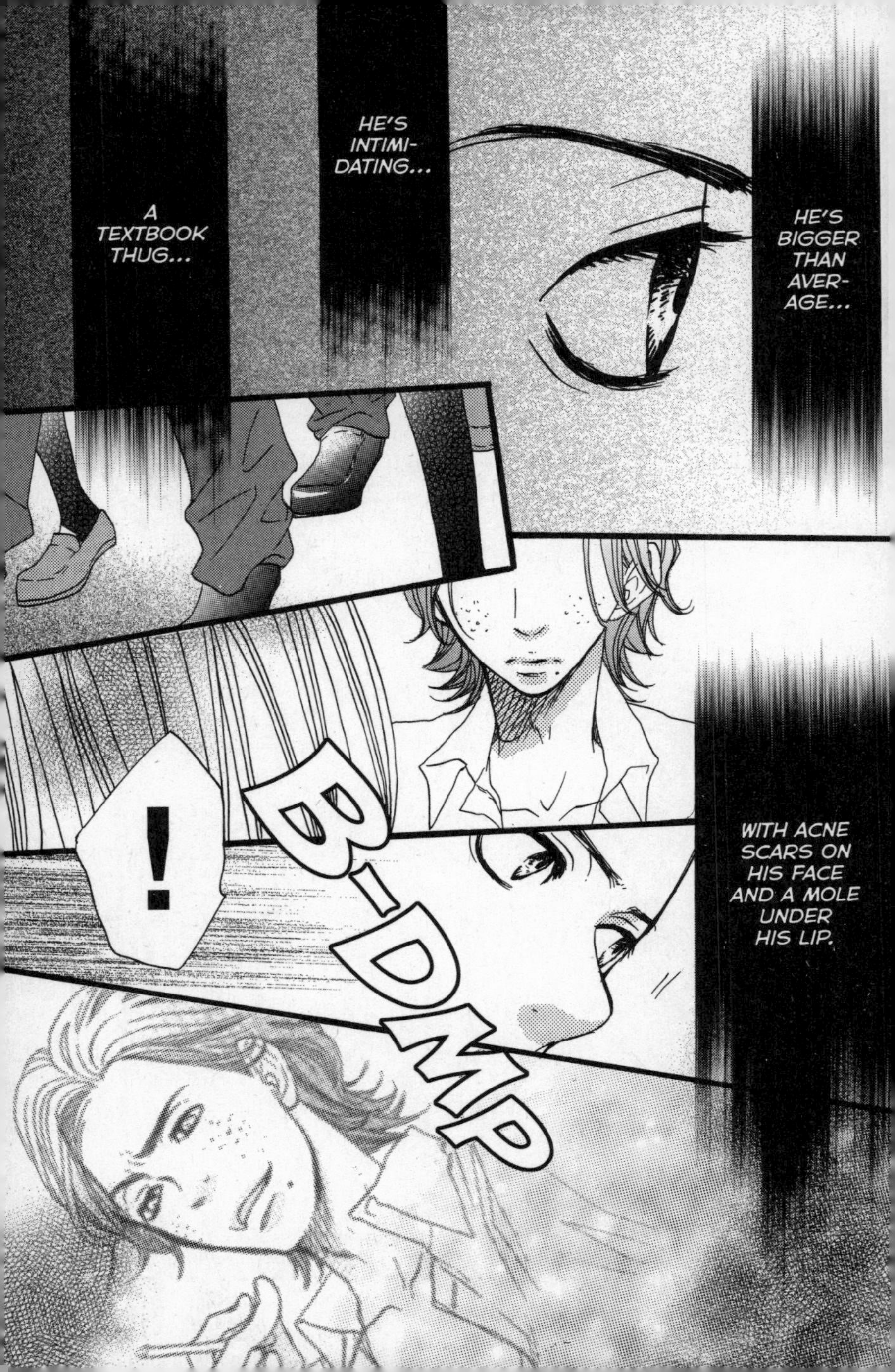
HE'S BIGGER THAN AVER-AGE...
HE'S INTIMI-DATING...
A TEXTBOOK THUG...
WITH ACNE SCARS ON HIS FACE AND A MOLE UNDER HIS LIP.
!
B-DMP

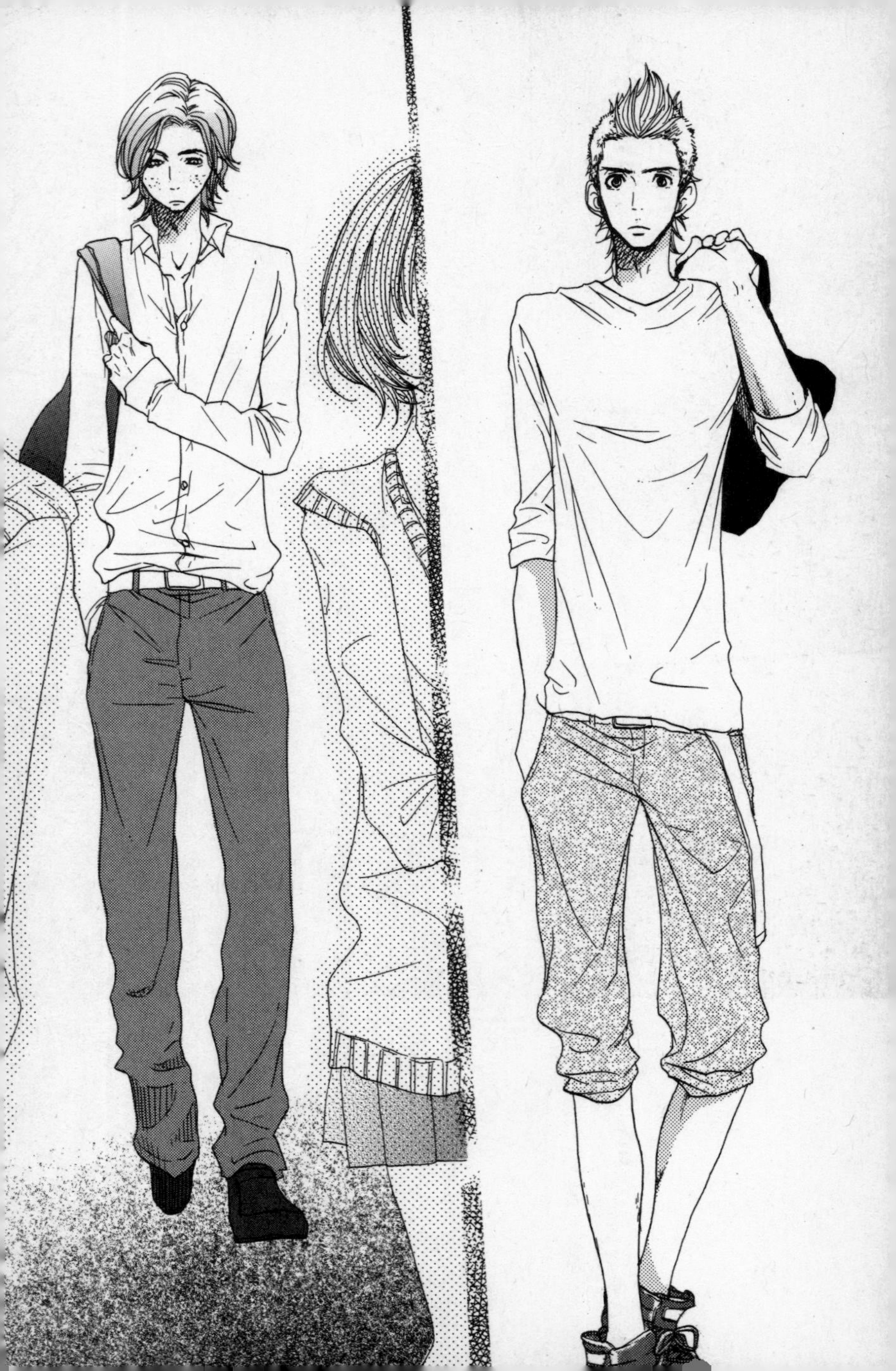

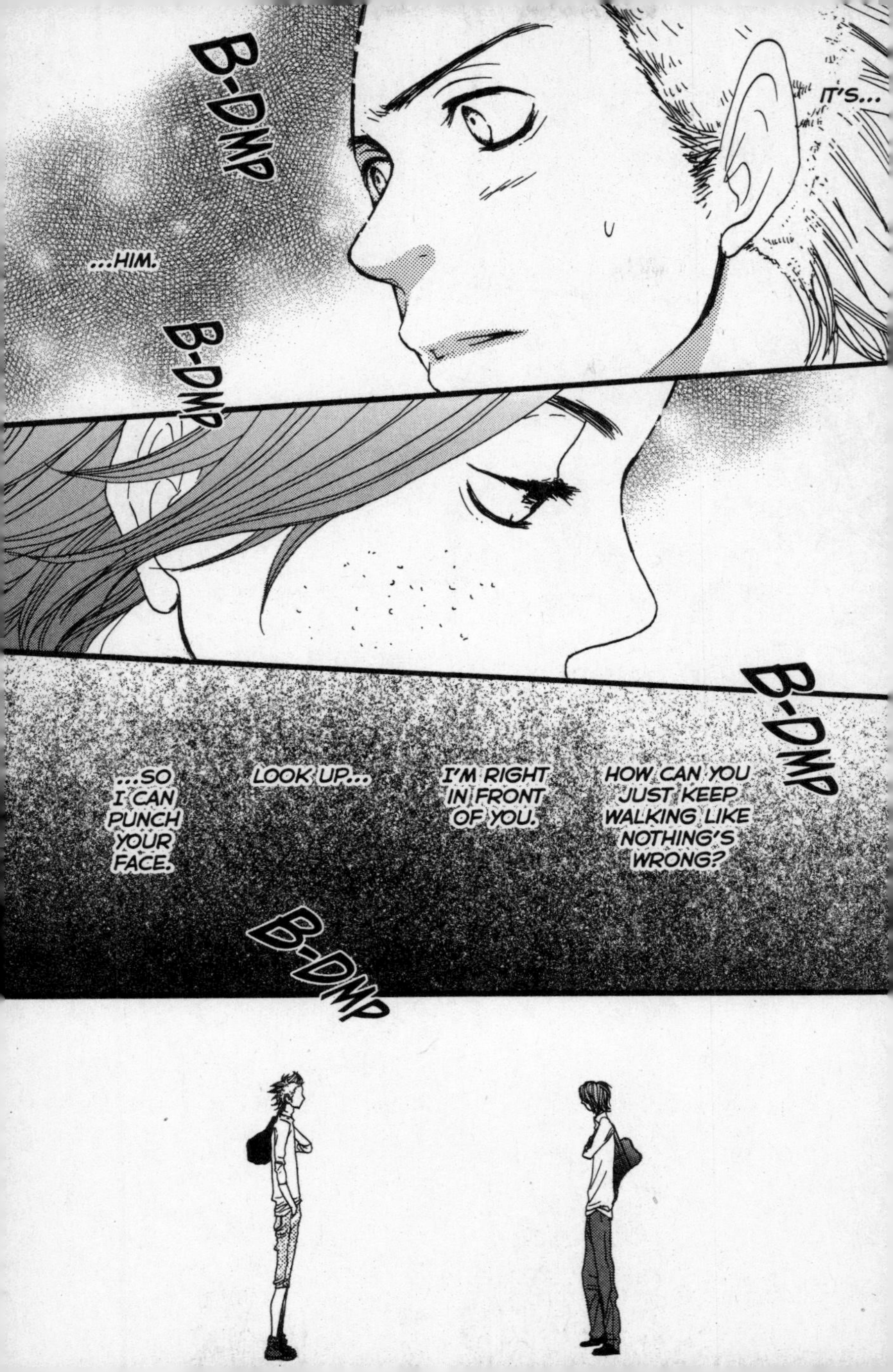
IT'S...
B-DMP
...HIM.
B-DMP
B-DMP
HOW CAN YOU JUST KEEP WALKING LIKE NOTHING'S WRONG?
I'M RIGHT IN FRONT OF YOU.
LOOK UP...
...SO I CAN PUNCH YOUR FACE.
B-DMP

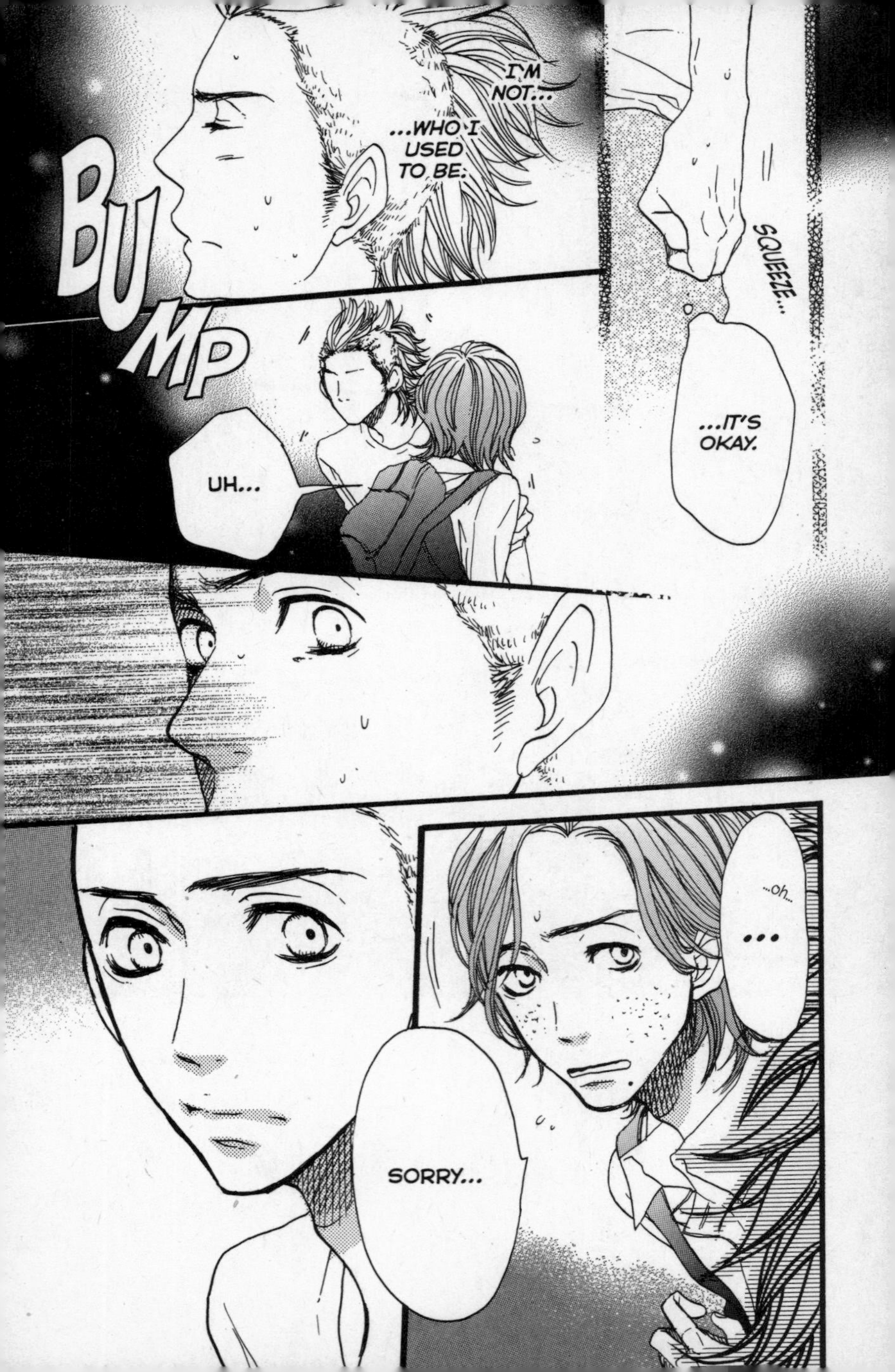
SQUEEZE...
...IT'S OKAY.
I'M NOT...
...WHO I USED TO BE.
BUMP
UH...
...oh...
...
SORRY...

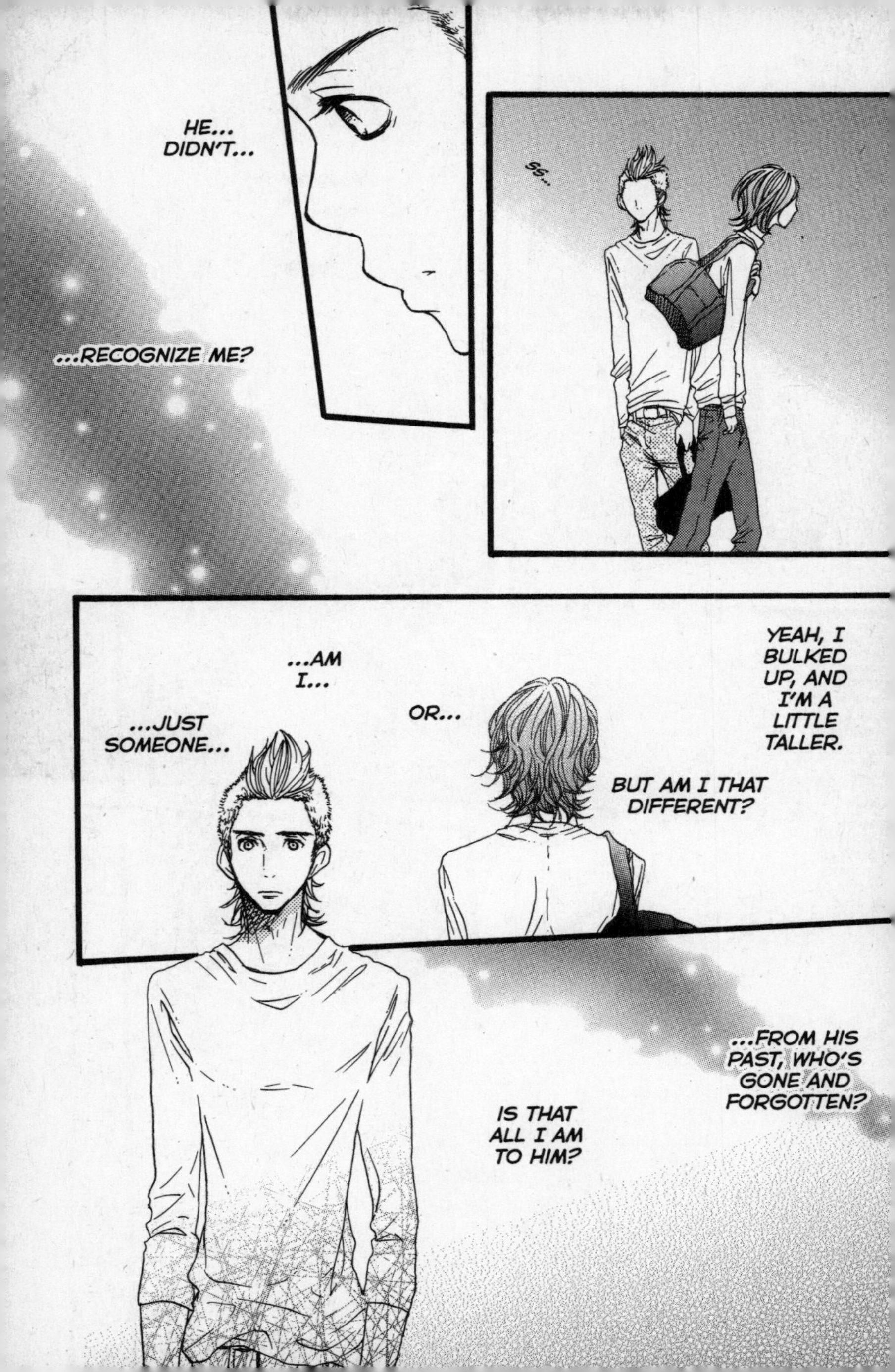
SS...
HE... DIDN'T...
...RECOGNIZE ME?
YEAH, I BULKED UP, AND I'M A LITTLE TALLER.
BUT AM I THAT DIFFERENT?
OR...
...AM I...
...JUST SOMEONE...
...FROM HIS PAST, WHO'S GONE AND FORGOTTEN?
IS THAT ALL I AM TO HIM?

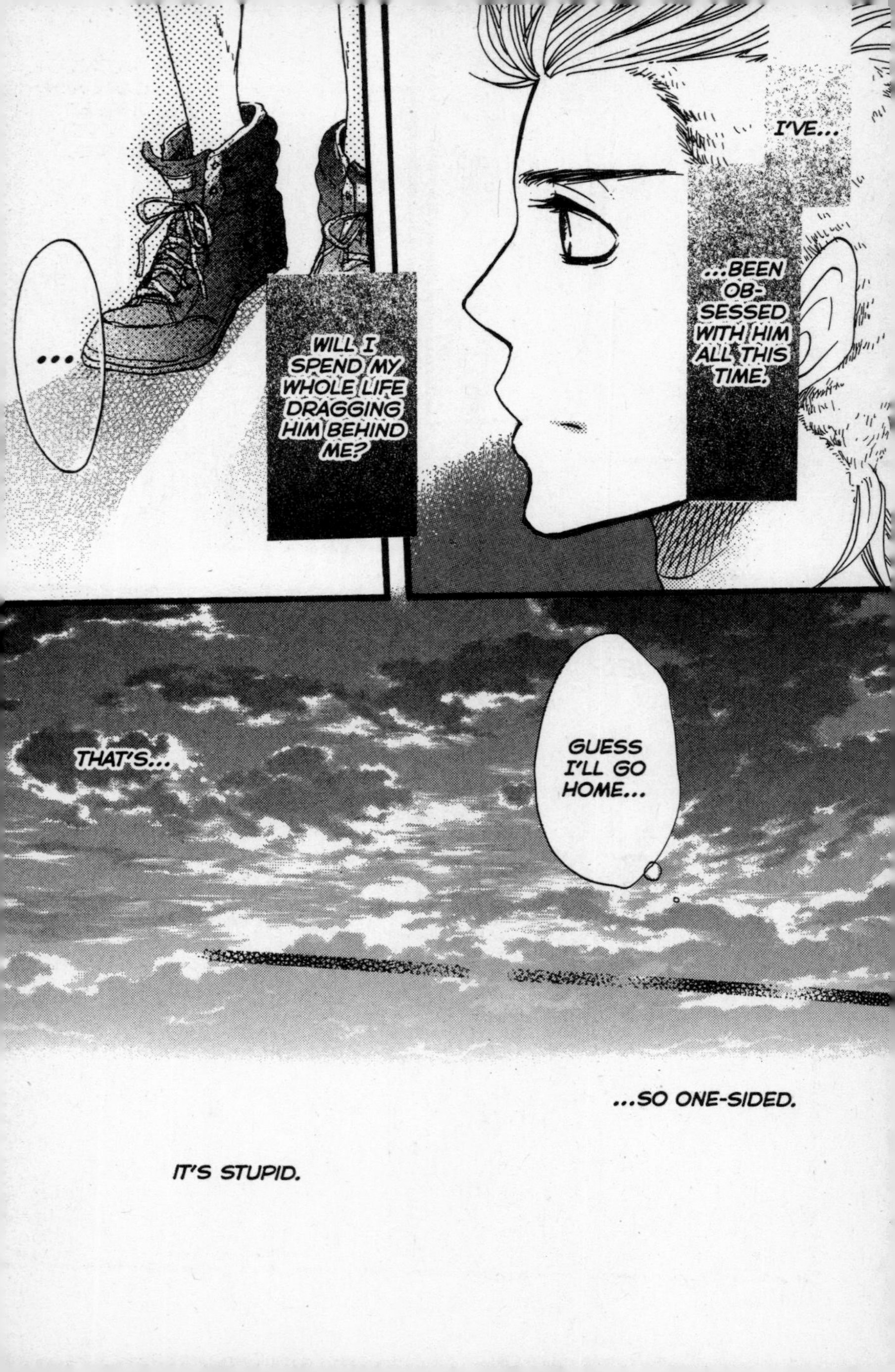
I'VE...
...BEEN OB-SESSED WITH HIM ALL THIS TIME.
WILL I SPEND MY WHOLE LIFE DRAGGING HIM BEHIND ME?
...
GUESS I'LL GO HOME...
THAT'S...
...SO ONE-SIDED.
IT'S STUPID.

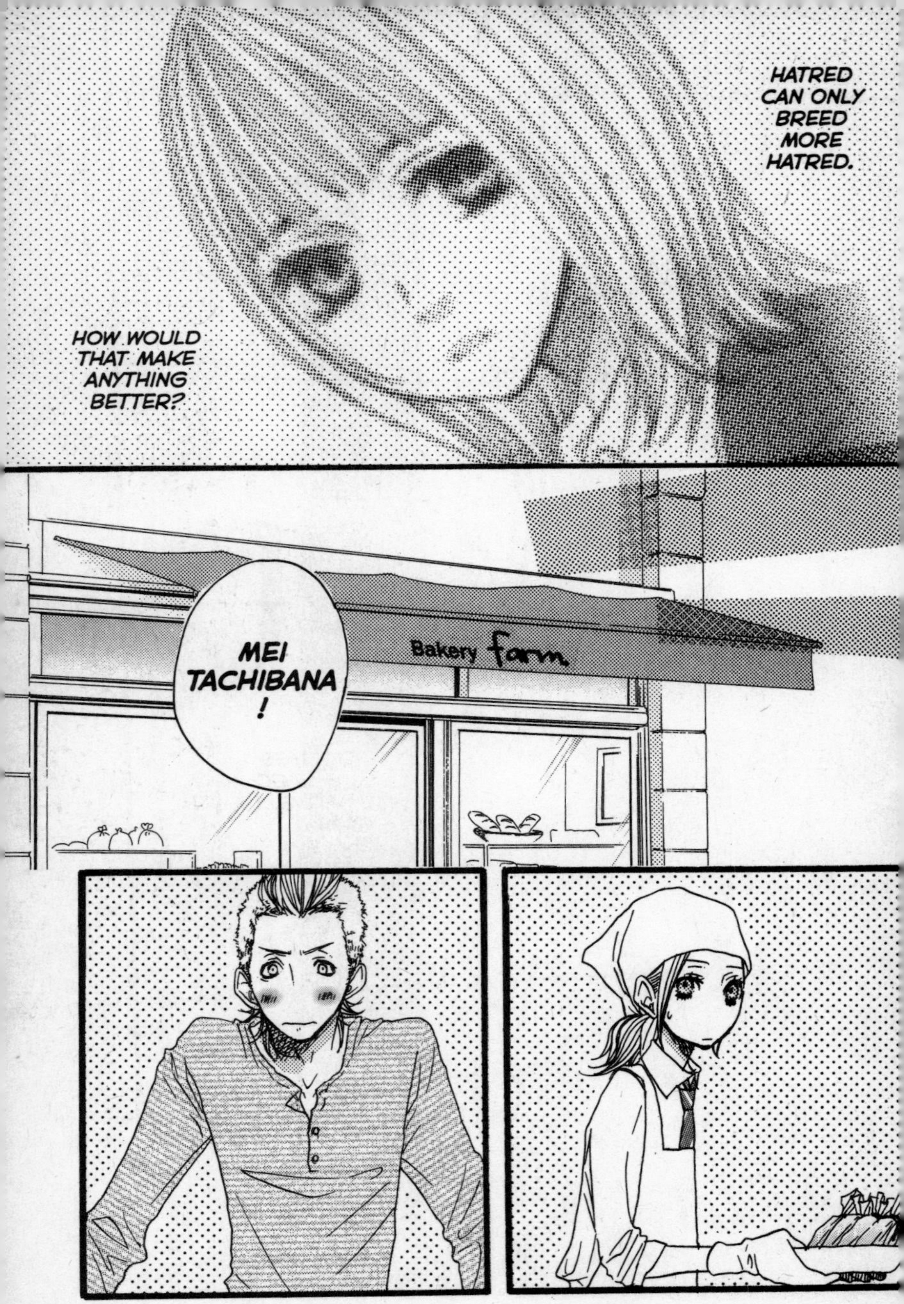
HATRED CAN ONLY BREED MORE HATRED.
HOW WOULD THAT MAKE ANYTHING BETTER?
Bakery farm
MEI TACHIBANA!

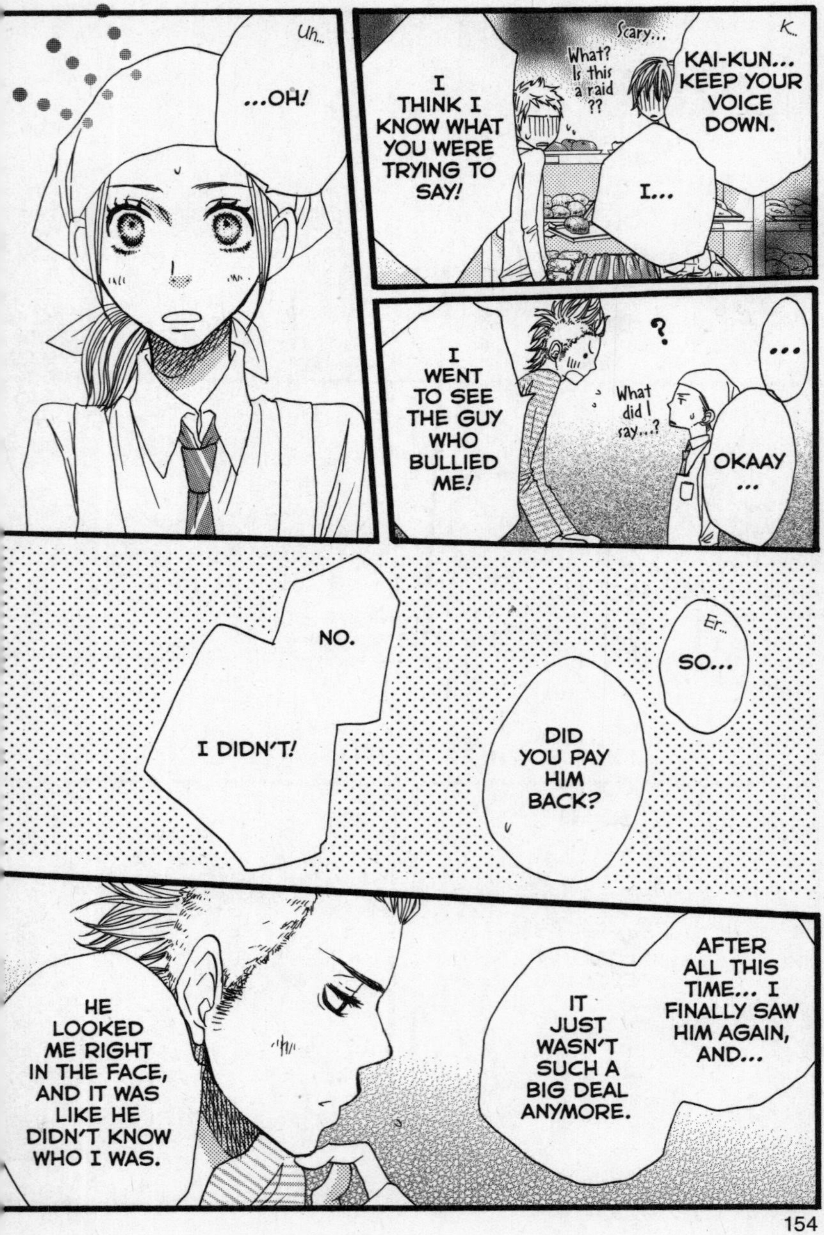
K...
KAI-KUN... KEEP YOUR VOICE DOWN.
Scary...
What? Is this a raid ??
I...
I THINK I KNOW WHAT YOU WERE TRYING TO SAY!
...
OKAAY ...
?
What did I say...?
I WENT TO SEE THE GUY WHO BULLIED ME!
Uh...
...OH!
Er...
SO...
DID YOU PAY HIM BACK?
NO.
I DIDN'T!
AFTER ALL THIS TIME... I FINALLY SAW HIM AGAIN, AND...
IT JUST WASN'T SUCH A BIG DEAL ANYMORE.
HE LOOKED ME RIGHT IN THE FACE, AND IT WAS LIKE HE DIDN'T KNOW WHO I WAS.

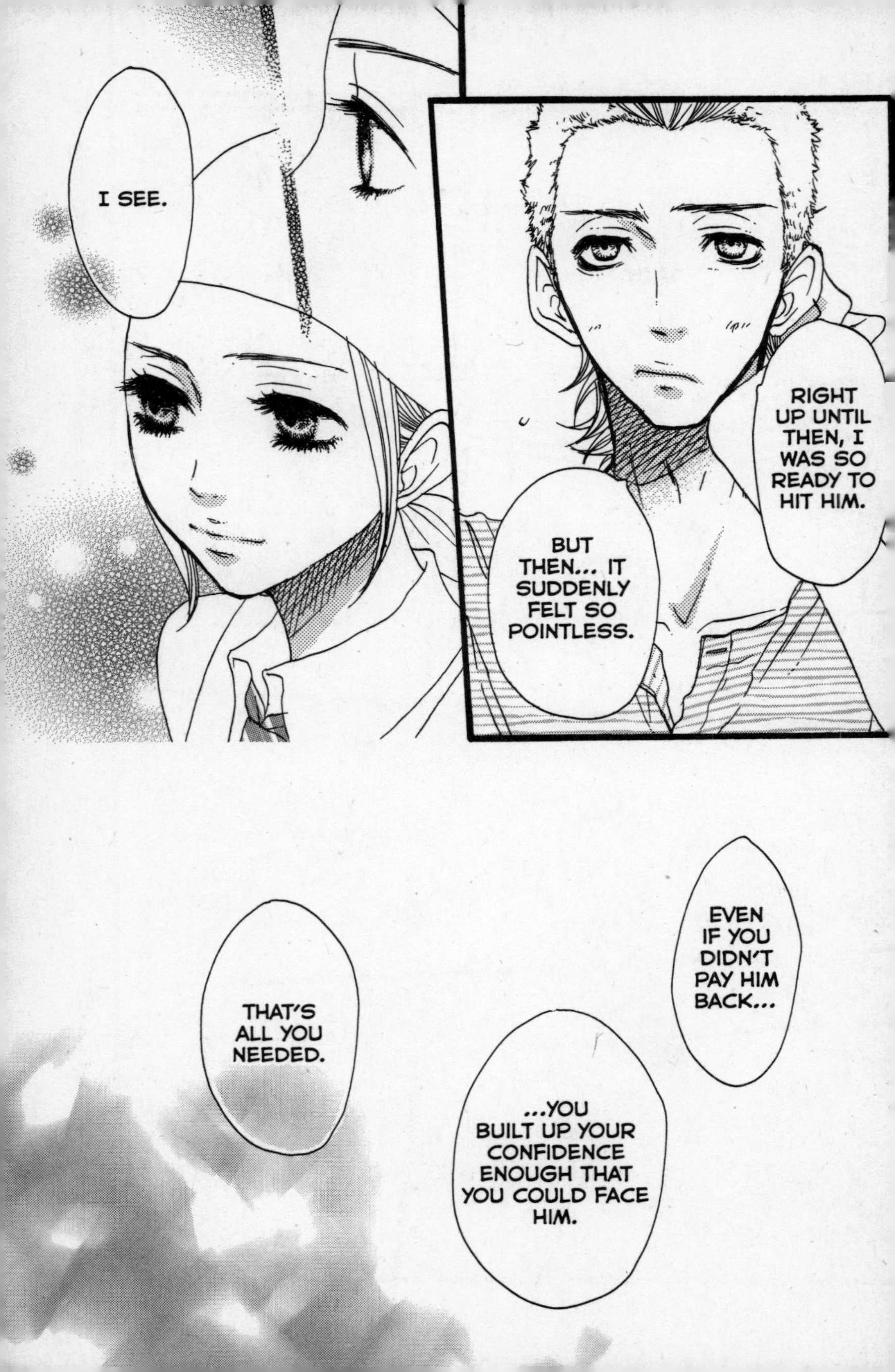
RIGHT UP UNTIL THEN, I WAS SO READY TO HIT HIM.
BUT THEN... IT SUDDENLY FELT SO POINTLESS.
I SEE.
EVEN IF YOU DIDN'T PAY HIM BACK...
...YOU BUILT UP YOUR CONFIDENCE ENOUGH THAT YOU COULD FACE HIM.
THAT'S ALL YOU NEEDED.

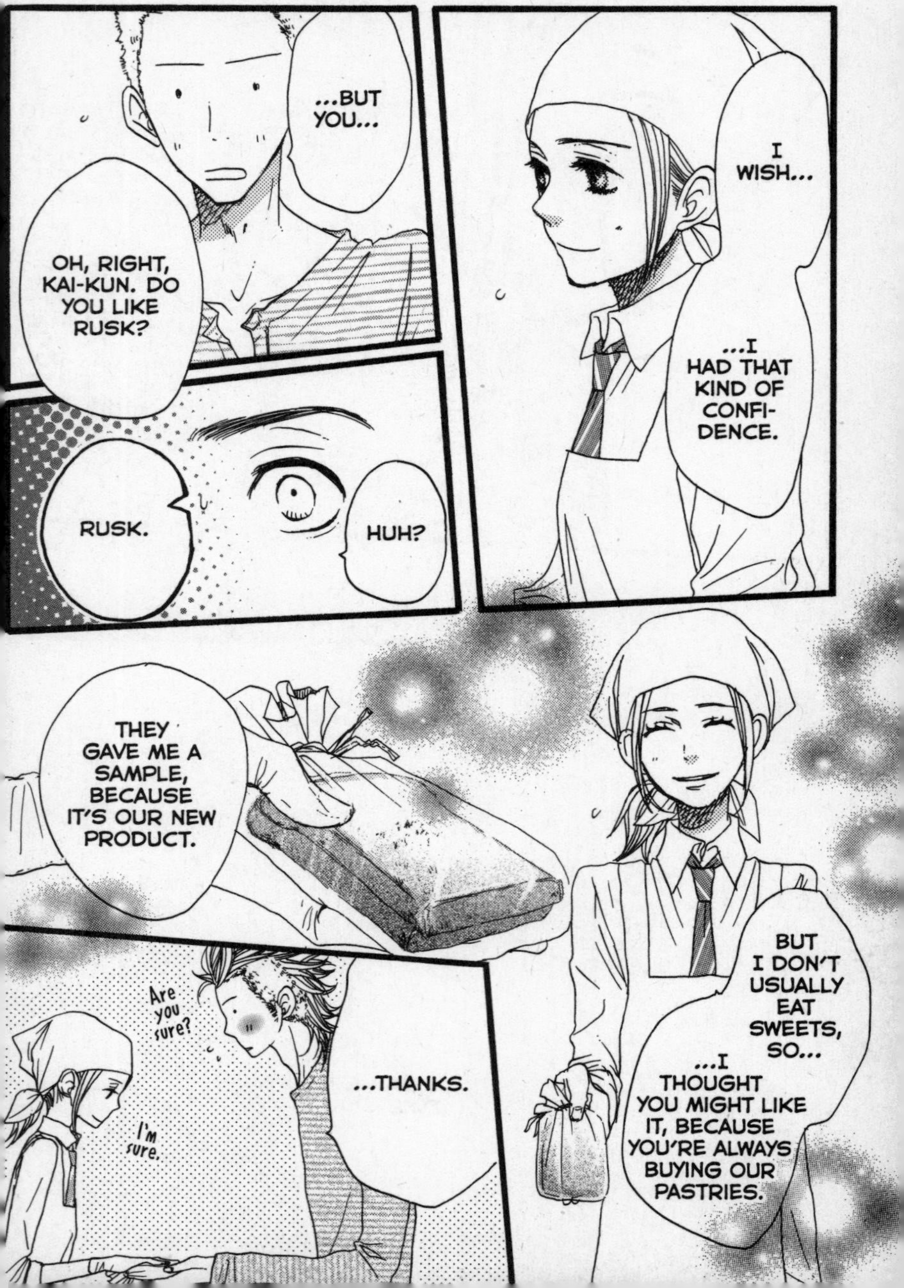
I WISH...
...I HAD THAT KIND OF CONFIDENCE.
...BUT YOU...
OH, RIGHT, KAI-KUN. DO YOU LIKE RUSK?
HUH?
RUSK.
THEY GAVE ME A SAMPLE, BECAUSE IT'S OUR NEW PRODUCT.
BUT I DON'T USUALLY EAT SWEETS, SO...
...I THOUGHT YOU MIGHT LIKE IT, BECAUSE YOU'RE ALWAYS BUYING OUR PASTRIES.
...THANKS.
Are you sure?
I'm sure.

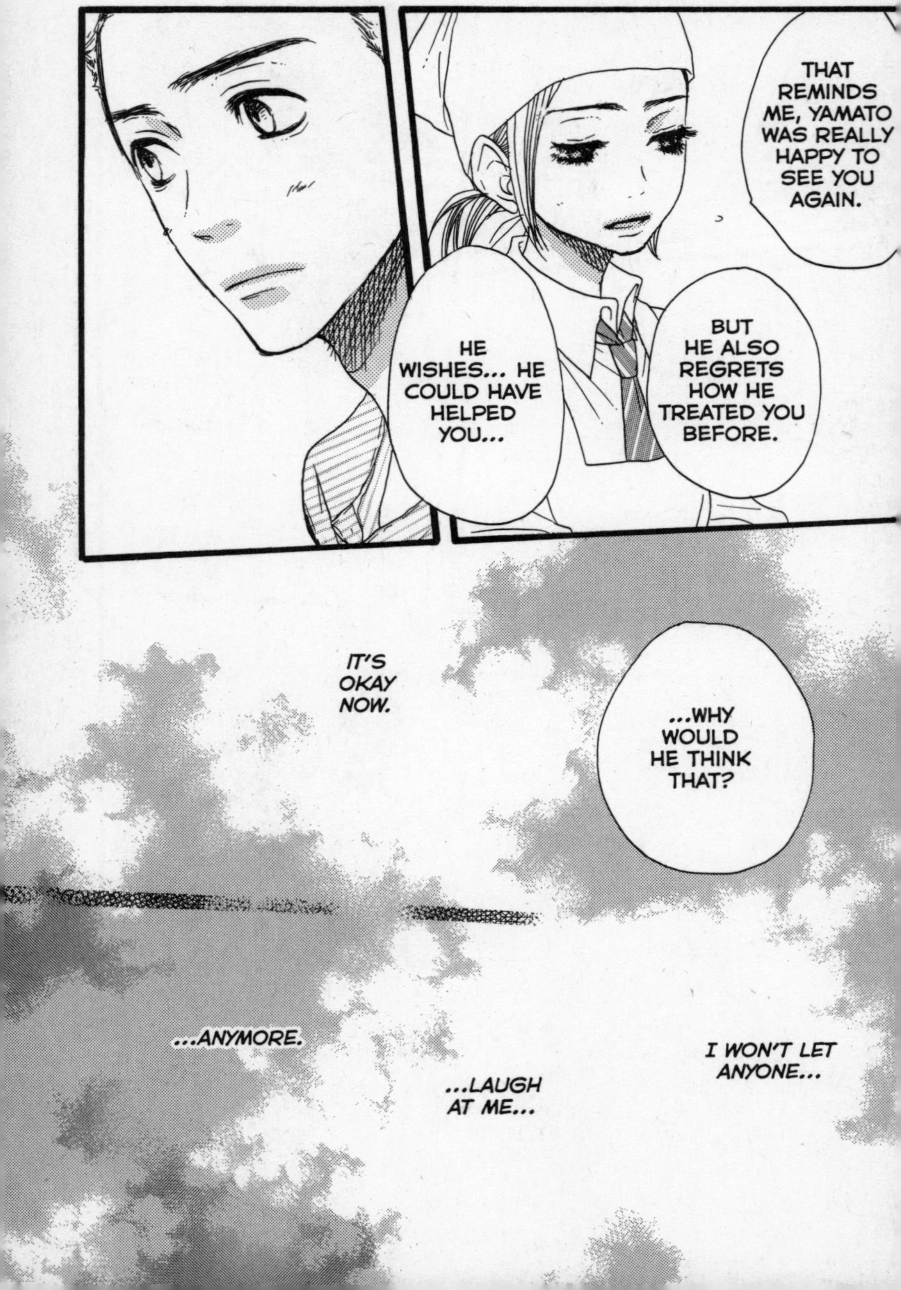
THAT REMINDS ME, YAMATO WAS REALLY HAPPY TO SEE YOU AGAIN.
BUT HE ALSO REGRETS HOW HE TREATED YOU BEFORE.
HE WISHES... HE COULD HAVE HELPED YOU...
...WHY WOULD HE THINK THAT?
IT'S OKAY NOW.
I WON'T LET ANYONE...
...LAUGH AT ME...
...ANYMORE.

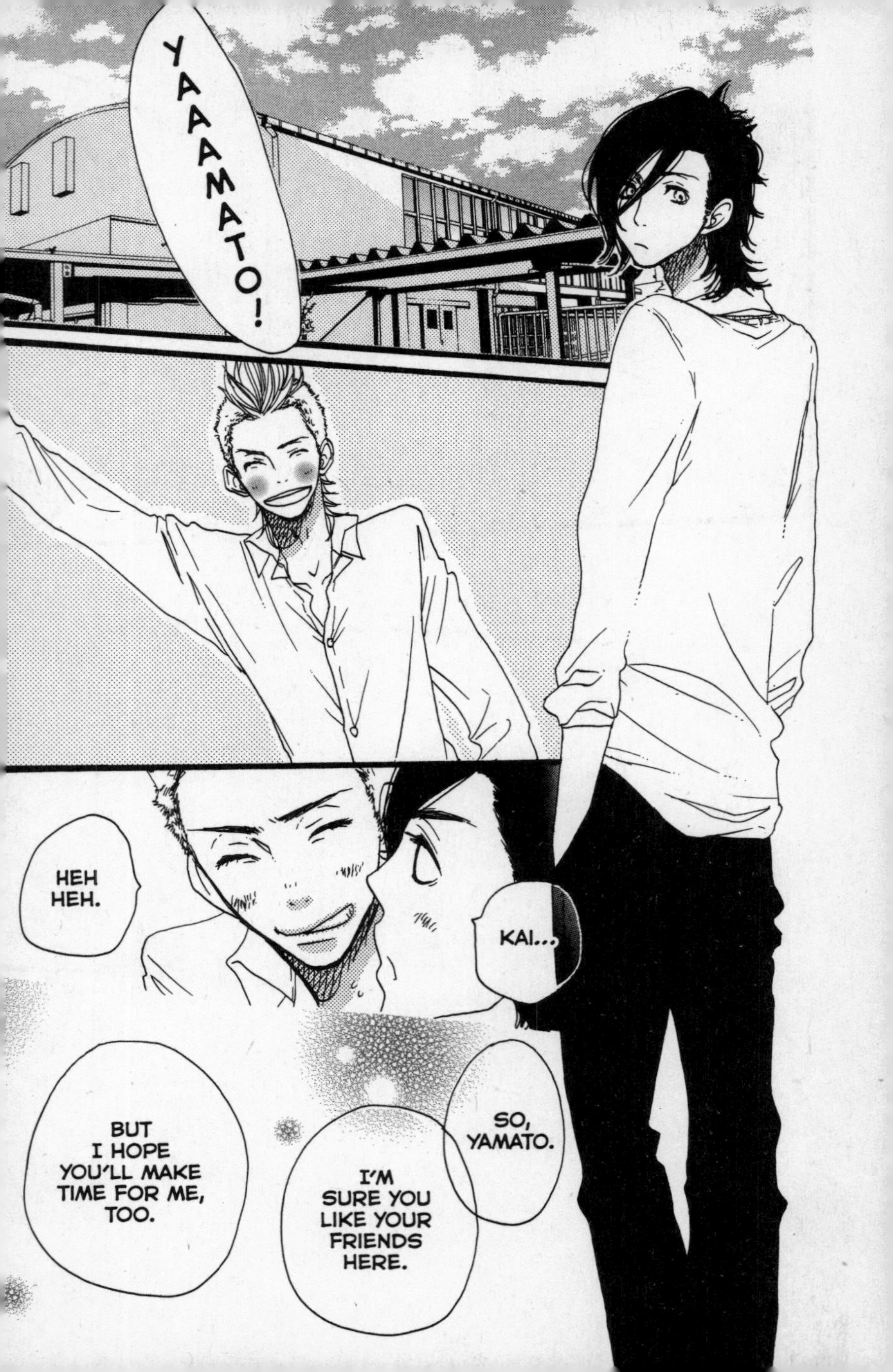
YAAAMATO!
KAI...
HEH HEH.
SO, YAMATO.
I'M SURE YOU LIKE YOUR FRIENDS HERE.
BUT I HOPE YOU'LL MAKE TIME FOR ME, TOO.

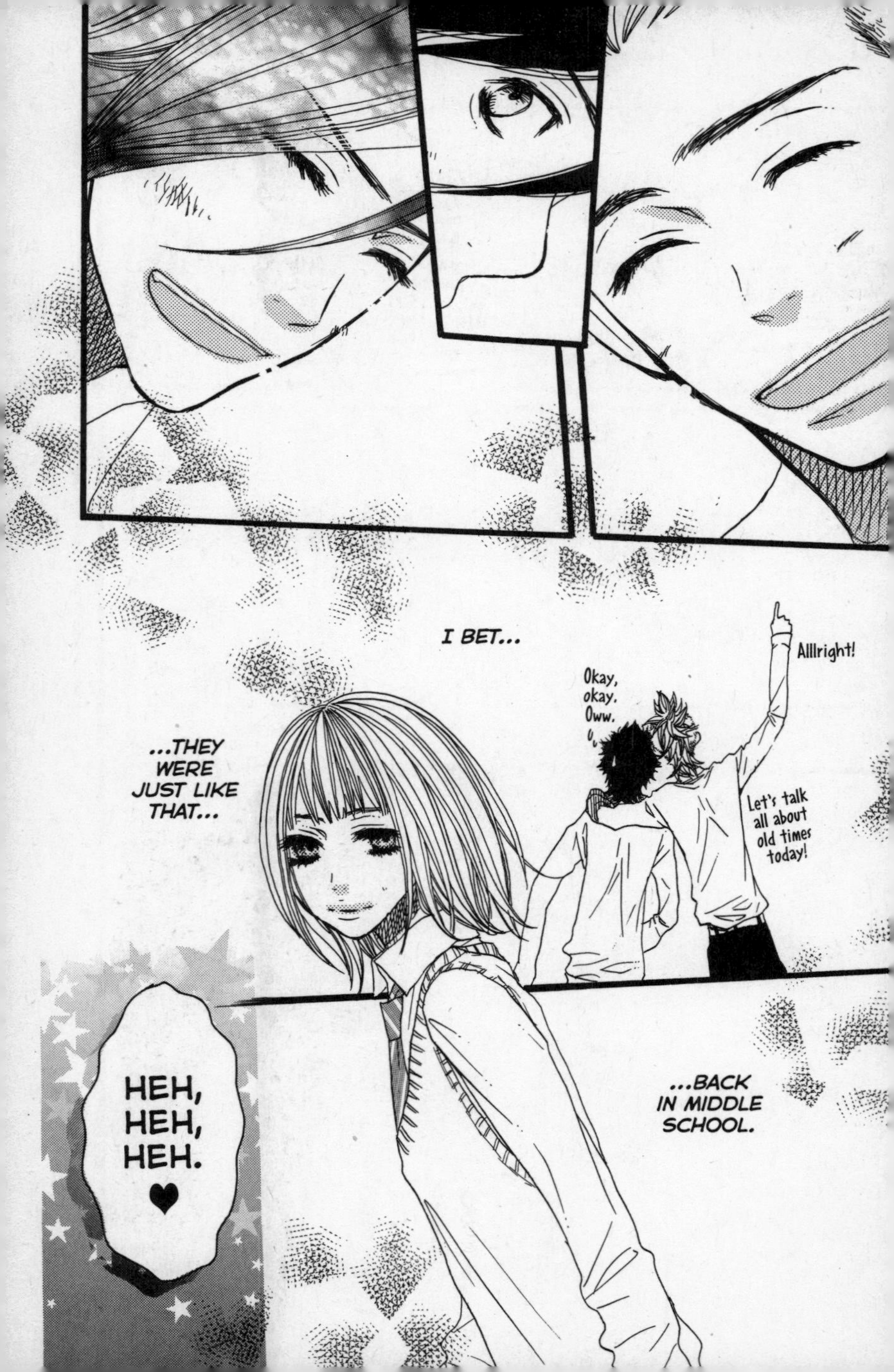
Alllright!
I BET...
Okay, okay. Oww.
Let's talk all about old times today!
...THEY WERE JUST LIKE THAT...
...BACK IN MIDDLE SCHOOL.
HEH, HEH, HEH. ♥

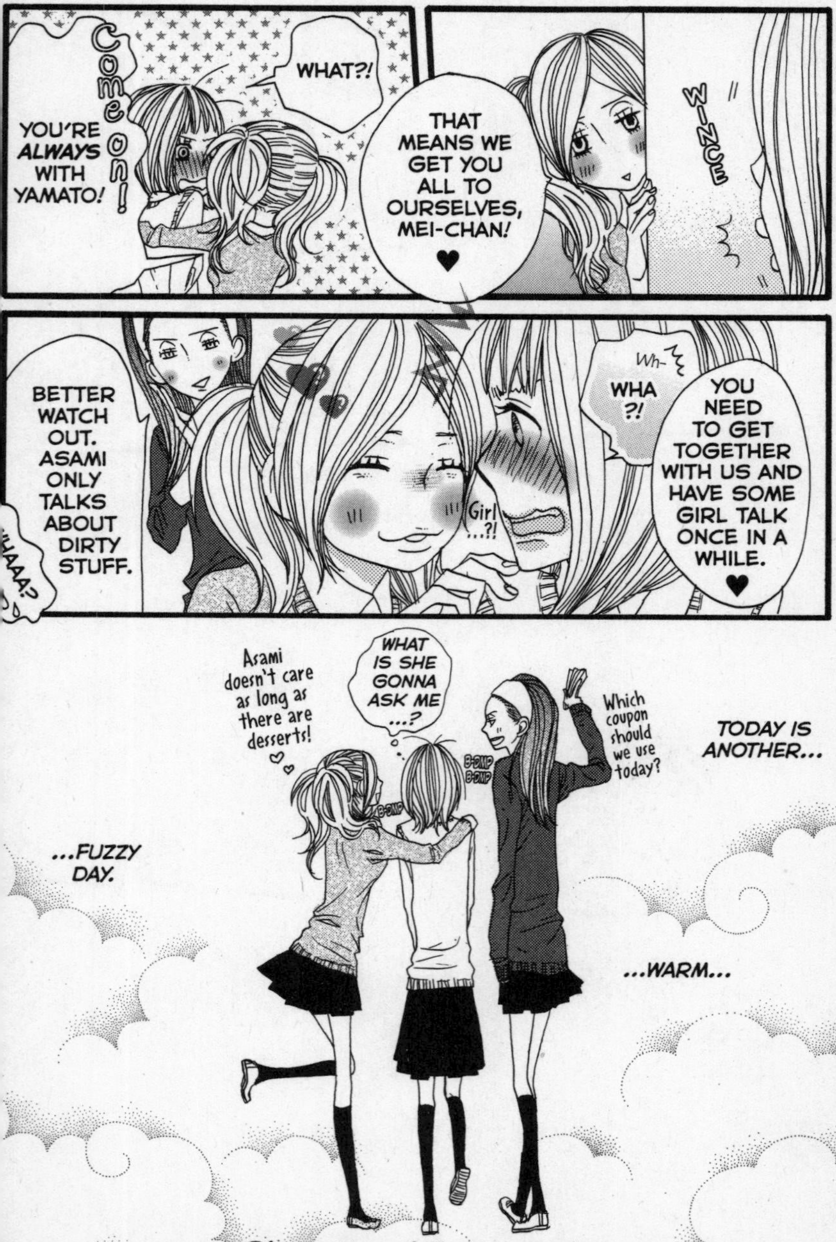
WINCE
THAT MEANS WE GET YOU ALL TO OURSELVES, MEI-CHAN! ♥
WHAT?!
Come on!
YOU'RE *ALWAYS* WITH YAMATO!
YOU NEED TO GET TOGETHER WITH US AND HAVE SOME GIRL TALK ONCE IN A WHILE. ♥
WHA ?!
Wh-
Girl ...?!
BETTER WATCH OUT. ASAMI ONLY TALKS ABOUT DIRTY STUFF.
HAAA?
TODAY IS ANOTHER...
Which coupon should we use today?
B-DMP B-DMP
WHAT IS SHE GONNA ASK ME ...?
Asami doesn't care as long as there are desserts!
B-DMP
...WARM...
...FUZZY DAY.

Chapter 16 — end

Would you like...

...to see the
afterword?

A BIT OF AN AFTERWORD

Hello, Kanae Hazuki here, and this is Vol. 4. It's a new personal record for volumes in a series. Even I can't believe the series has gone on this long—it all went by so fast.

This time, I drew a character named Megumi and a character named Kai, and they're both very important characters to me... Megumi's not just cute—there was a story about how she got to be cute, and Kai is Kai—he's honest and straightforward, but he is twisted in some ways. They both have stories that lead up to where they are now...

But well, there will be more about that later... ☺ Heh heh.

In this volume, we saw Kai for the first time, and like Mei, he was bullied in the past, but his way of thinking is different from Mei's... It's just... y'know... I think Mei is a little unique. I think most people who have been bullied do feel the way Kai does once in their life. Like, "One day they'll pay," "I'll get you back for this." I felt that way, too.

I wrote this in Vol. 1, but bullying only happens in groups. When I was in school, there was a group that said vicious things about my body. One day, I passed by their leader in the hall. She was all alone, and she didn't say anything to me like she always would. I said, "You're not saying anything. Can't you say anything without your friends around?" And she ran away.

When I said it, my chest hurt I was so scared, but after she reacted like that, it was like the biggest letdown. I started to think that people like her really weren't as big a deal as they seemed. I thought I must be a lot stronger than she was. Physically, I might not have been, though. But when you have more experience, then you do get stronger mentally. If anyone reading this now has been bullied or is being bullied now, don't ever think that you're weak. If you start thinking that, then it's all over. Whether you use that as fuel to make yourself stronger, or don't do anything, it all depends on you.

I think that manga isn't just for showing the nice side of things. Oh, but that doesn't mean I'm denying the value of the nice things. This is strictly a personal opinion. Humans have nice sides, but they also have filthy sides. They lie and cheat, but they're just human. Some people will criticize that filthy side, but if they trace the source of it, I think they'll find that sometimes people develop those traits as a means of protecting themselves. That doesn't make them bad people. It's a type of shell, their particular self-defense strategy.

No one is born strong, so they try in their own way to get stronger, to appear stronger, and that's how they become the people that they are now. That's my opinion. But if you keep showing that filthy side to the people close to you, then your relationships are not going to go well. Unless you notice your own filthy traits and clean them up, you can't hope for you or the other person to build a good relationship out of that. But still, you want them to see the good parts of you. Everyone feels that way. It's okay.

That's the kind of thing that your friends will know, whether you actively do something to show them or not (ha ha). That's exactly why those people are still with you, despite your flaws. I feel like we'd all be surprised to see how much better other people know us than we know ourselves. When I look at it that way, whether it's a big group or a small group, I think it's such a blessing to have people close to me. Oh, man, I'm sorry. I think I've gotten off track again... ☺

Anyway, I want to keep drawing all kinds of characters. Characters that you will love all of—the nice sides and the filthy sides. I hope you'll continue to watch them.

Kanae Hazuki
November 2009

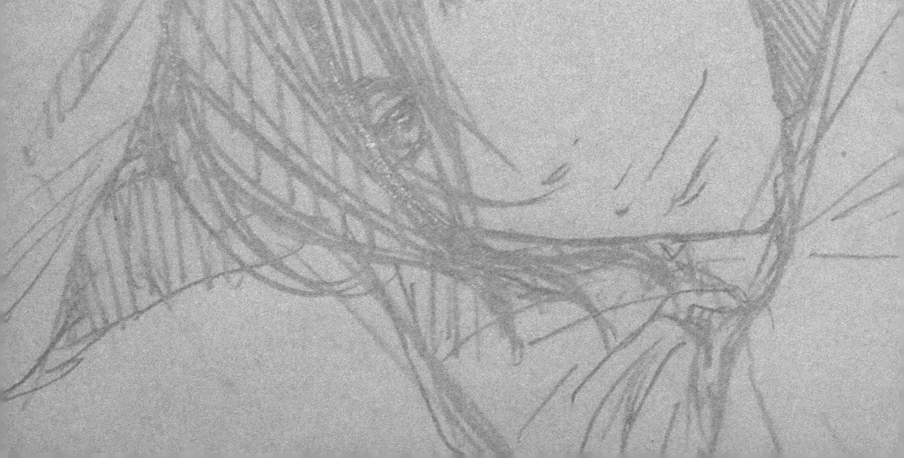

TRANSLATION NOTES

Page 25: Amateur model

Specifically, Megumi classifies herself as a *dokumo*, short for *dokusha* model or "reader model." This is a term used for models that don't model full-time—they haven't quit their day jobs, so to speak. They are called "reader models" because originally they were models chosen from a fashion magazine's readership.

Page 51: Her face is so small

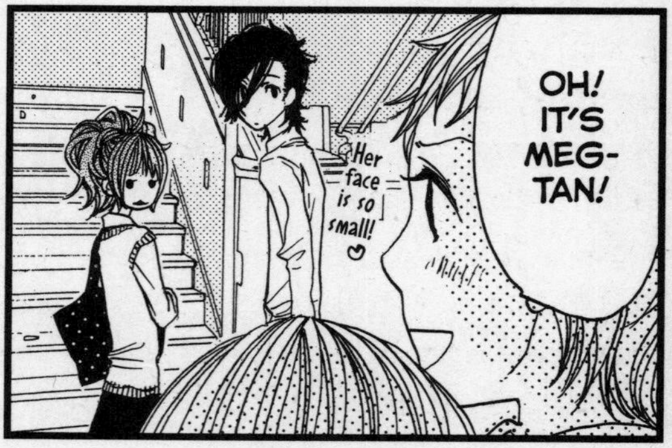
OH! IT'S MEG-TAN!
Her face is so small!

This is commonly said in Japan of people with beautiful faces, but it doesn't necessarily have to do with the actual size of the face. Often it has more to do with proportions—either of the face itself, or of the face in relation to the body. It can also refer to having a cute, childlike face. Basically, this girl is calling Megumi adorable.

Page 56: Land

In Japan, Land is slang for a certain famous theme park. The one in Tokyo has carnival games that offer collectible prizes for high scorers. Because the key Asami gives Mei has cat ears, and not the mouse ears you might expect from the famous "Land" near Tokyo, it's a safe bet that the Land in this universe is short for a place with a different name, but a very similar atmosphere.

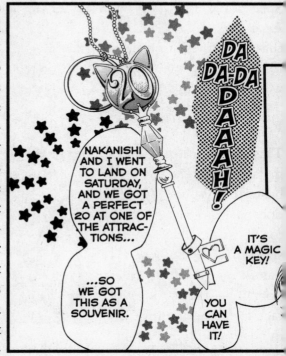

NAKANISHI AND I WENT TO LAND ON SATURDAY, AND WE GOT A PERFECT 20 AT ONE OF THE ATTRACTIONS...

DA DA DA DAAAH!

...SO WE GOT THIS AS A SOUVENIR.

IT'S A MAGIC KEY!

YOU CAN HAVE IT!

PRAISE FOR THE ANIME!

"This series never fails to
ut a smile on my face."
-Dramatic Reviews

"A very funny look at what happens when
two strange and strangely well-suited people
try to navigate the thorny path to true love
together."

-Anime News Network

My Little Monster

PPOSITES ATTRACT...MAYBE?

aru Yoshida is feared as an unstable and violent "monster."
zutani Shizuku is a grade-obsessed student with no friends.
te brings these two together to form the most unlikely pair. Haru
mly believes he's in love with Mizutani and she firmly believes
's insane.

KC
KODANSHA
COMICS

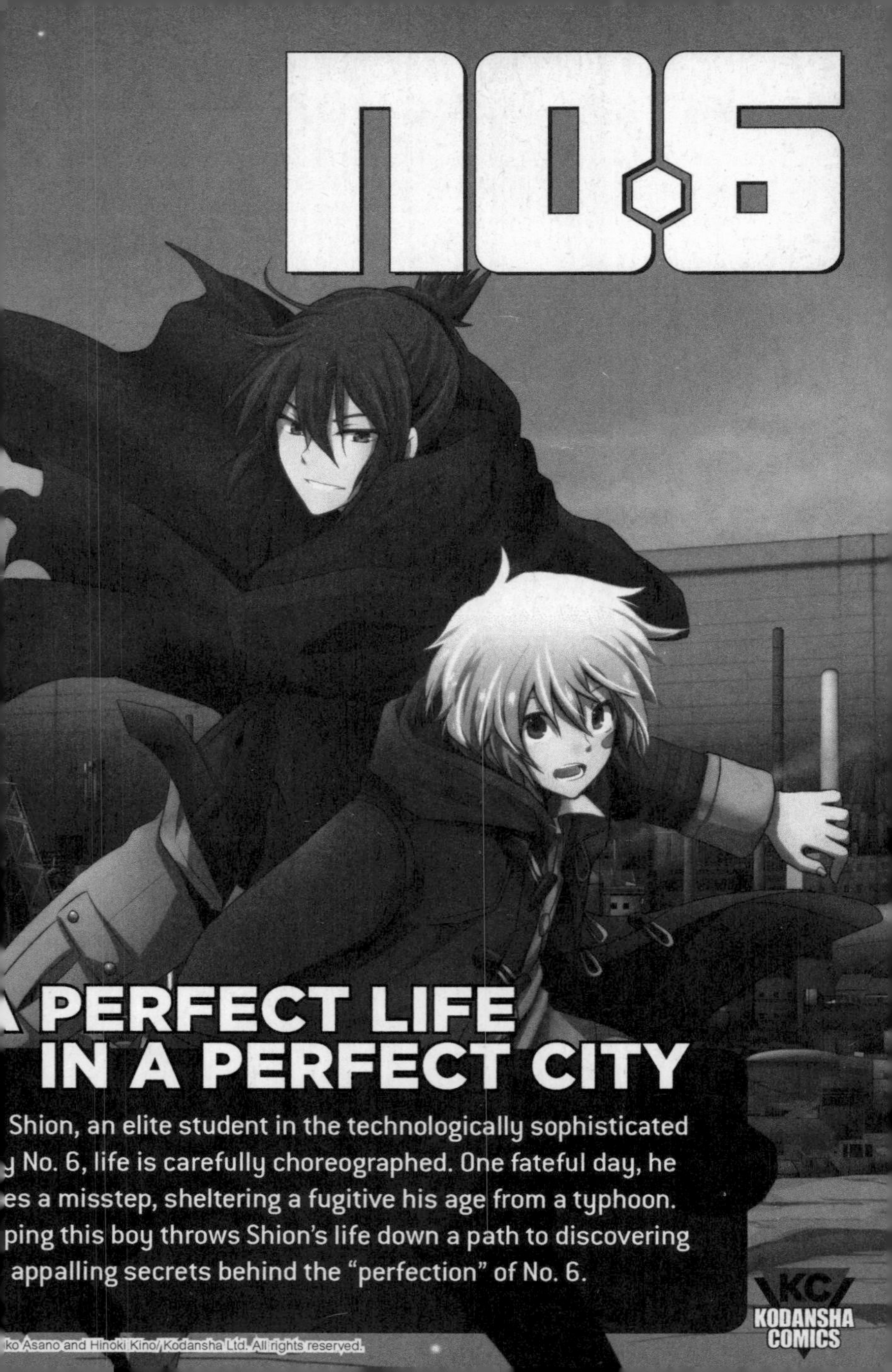
NO.6
PERFECT LIFE
IN A PERFECT CITY
Shion, an elite student in the technologically sophisticated
y No. 6, life is carefully choreographed. One fateful day, he
es a misstep, sheltering a fugitive his age from a typhoon.
ping this boy throws Shion's life down a path to discovering
appalling secrets behind the "perfection" of No. 6.
KC
KODANSHA COMICS
ko Asano and Hinoki Kino/ Kodansha Ltd. All rights reserved.

SANKAREA
undying love

"I ONLY LIKE ZOMBIE GIRLS."

Chihiro has an unusual connection to zombie movies. He doesn't feel bad for the survivors – he wants to comfort the undead girls they slaughter! When his pet passes away, he brews a resurrection potion. He's discovered by local heiress Sanka Rea, and she serves as his first test subject!

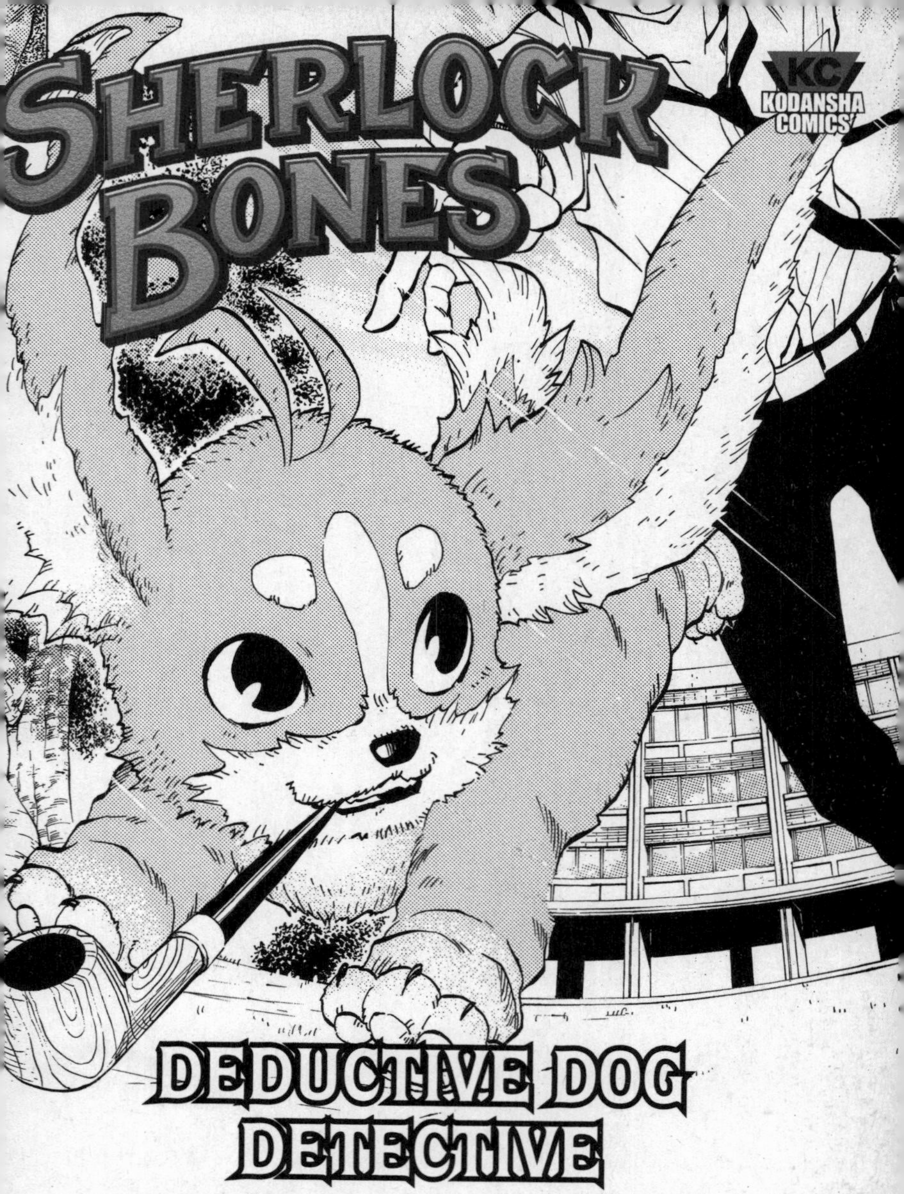
SHERLOCK BONES
KC KODANSHA COMICS

DEDUCTIVE DOG DETECTIVE

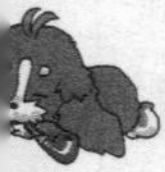

When Takeru adopts a new pet, he's in for a surprise—the dog is none other than the reincarnation of Sherlock Holmes. With no one else able to communicate with Holmes, Takeru is roped into becoming Sherdog's assistant, John Watson. Using his sleuthing skills, Holmes uncovers clues to solve the trickiest crimes.

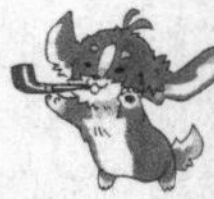

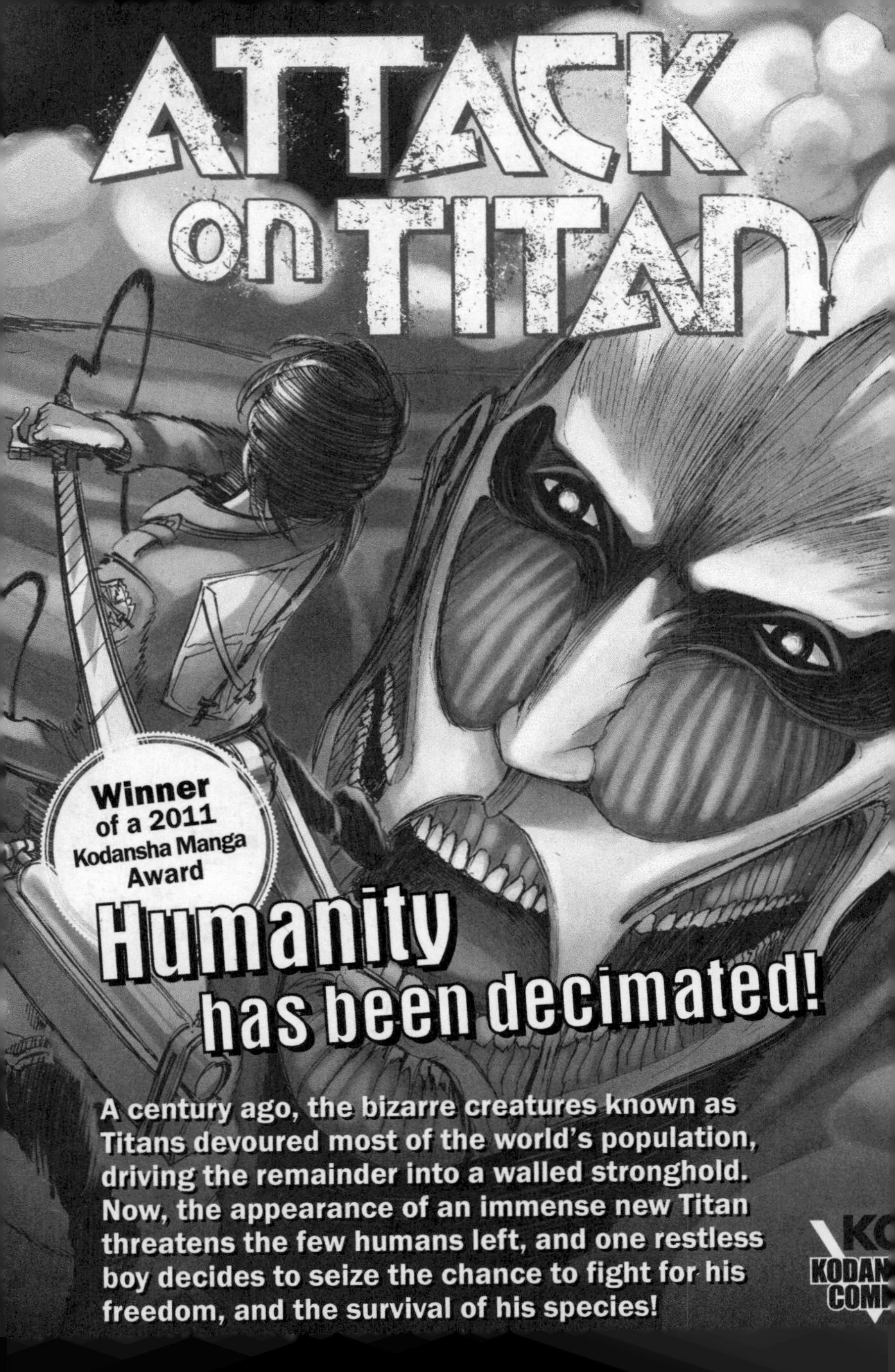
ATTACK on TITAN
Winner of a 2011 Kodansha Manga Award
Humanity has been decimated!
A century ago, the bizarre creatures known as Titans devoured most of the world's population, driving the remainder into a walled stronghold. Now, the appearance of an immense new Titan threatens the few humans left, and one restless boy decides to seize the chance to fight for his freedom, and the survival of his species!
KODAN
COMI

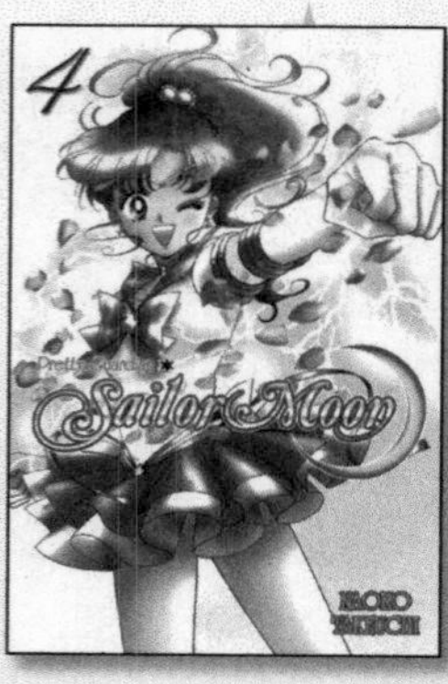
4
Pretty Guardian
Sailor Moon
NAOKO TAKEUCHI

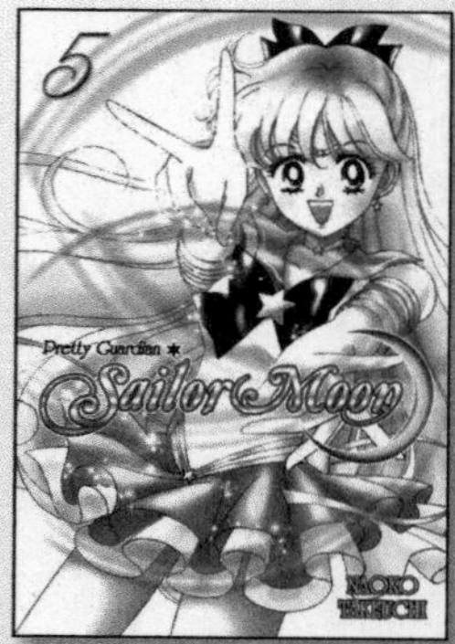
5
Pretty Guardian
Sailor Moon
NAOKO TAKEUCHI

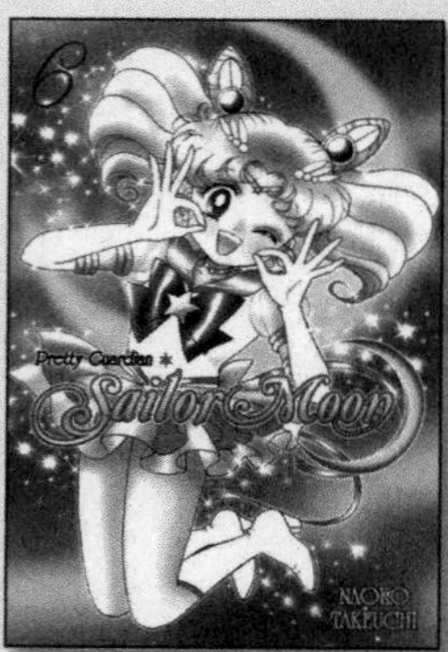
6
Pretty Guardian
Sailor Moon
NAOKO TAKEUCHI

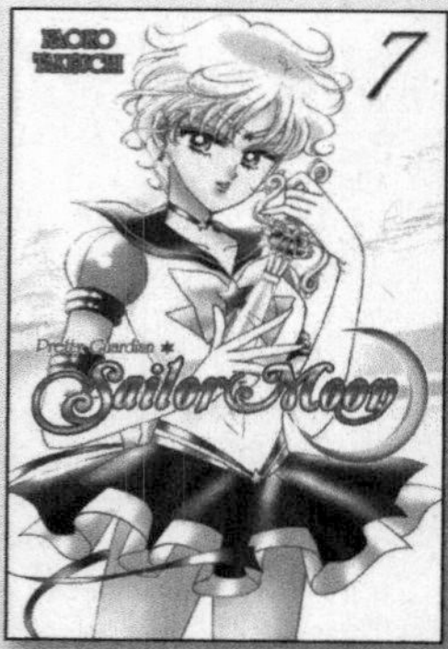
NAOKO TAKEUCHI
7
Pretty Guardian
Sailor Moon

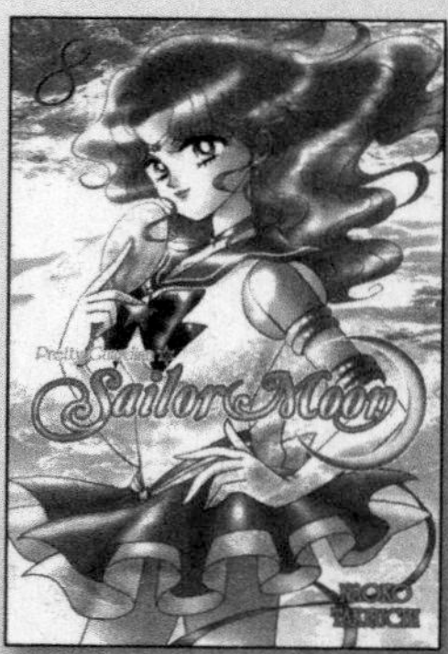
8
Sailor Moon
NAOKO TAKEUCHI

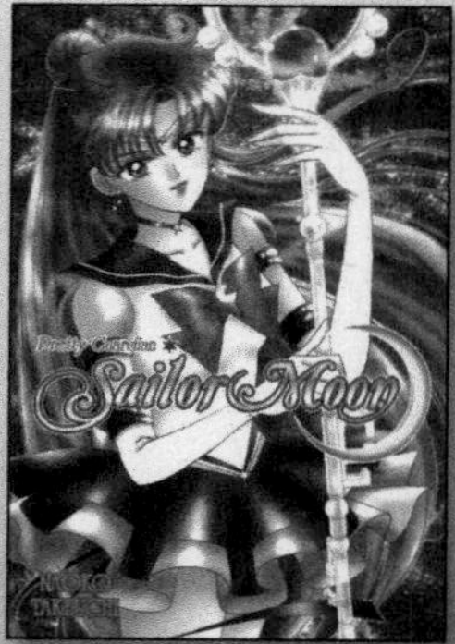
Sailor Moon

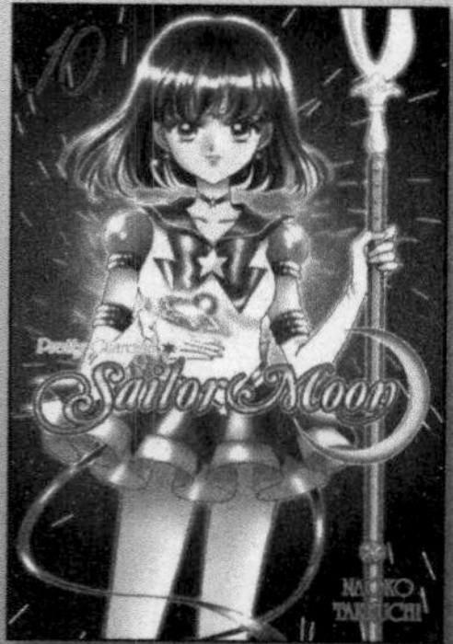
10
Sailor Moon
NAOKO TAKEUCHI

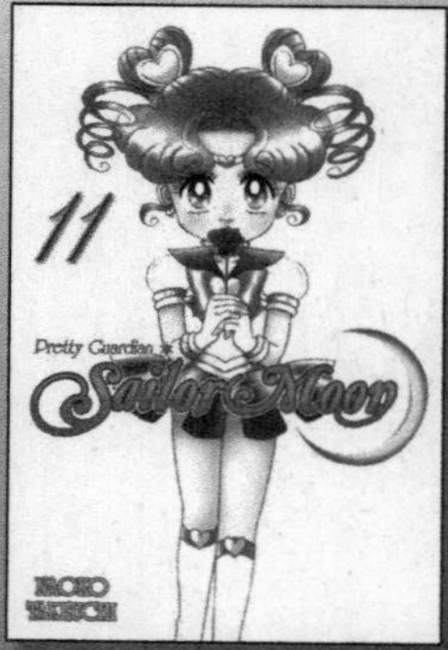
11
Pretty Guardian
Sailor Moon
NAOKO TAKEUCHI

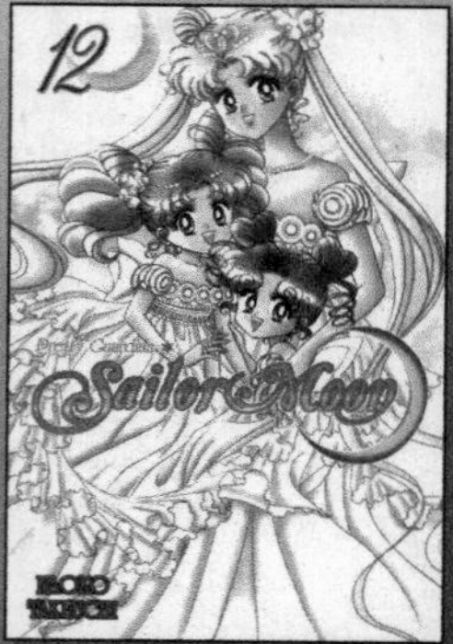
12
Sailor Moon
NAOKO TAKEUCHI

KC
KODANSHA COMICS

The Pretty Guardians are back!

Kodansha Comics is proud to present *Sailor Moon* with all new translations.

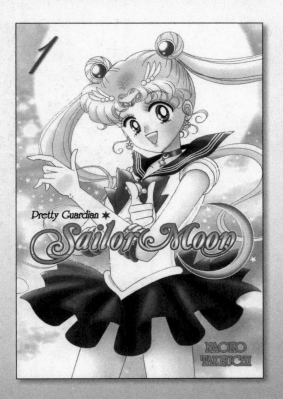

For more information, go to **www.kodanshacomics.com**

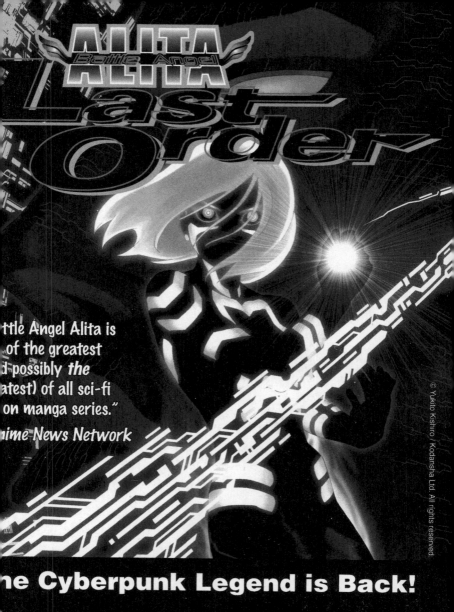

Say I Love You. volume 4 is a work of fiction. Names, characters, places, and incidents are the products of the author's imagination or are used fictitiously. Any resemblance to actual events, locales, or persons, living or dead, is entirely coincidental.

A Kodansha Comics Trade Paperback Original

Published in the United States by Kodansha Comics, an imprint of Kodansha USA Publishing, LLC, New York.

Publication rights for this English edition arranged through Kodansha Ltd, Tokyo.

First published in Japan in 2010 by Kodansha Ltd., Tokyo as *Sukitte iinayo.* volume 4.

ISBN 978-1-61262-605-5

Printed in the United States of America.

www.kodanshacomics.com

9 8 7 6 5 4 3 2 1
Translation: Alethea and Athena Nibley
Lettering: John Clark
Editing: Ben Applegate
Kodansha Comics edition cover design by Phil Balsman

TOMARE!

[STOP!]

You're going the wrong way!

Manga is a completely different type of reading experience.

To start at the *beginning,* go to the *end!*

That's right! Authentic manga is read the traditional Japanese way—from right to left, exactly the *opposite* of how American books are read. It's easy to follow: Just go to the other end of the book and read each page—and each panel—from right side to left side, starting at the top right. Now you're experiencing manga as it was meant to be!